ANIMAL

Bloomsbury Visual Arts

An imprint of Bloomsbury Publishing Plc

50 Bedford Square
London
WC1B 3DP
UK

1385 Broadway
New York
NY 10018
USA

www.bloomsbury.com

BLOOMSBURY and the Diana logo are trademarks of Bloomsbury Publishing Plc

First published in France under the title Animal © 2014, Bibliothèque nationale de France

English language translation © 2017, Bloomsbury Publishing Plc

British Library Cataloguing-in-Publication Data

A catalogue record for this book is available from the British Library.

ISBN: HB: 978-1-4742-7494-4
ePDF: 978-1-4742-7497-5
ePub: 978-1-4742-7498-2

Library of Congress Cataloging-in-Publication Data

Names: Bibliothèque nationale de France. Département des estampes et de la photographie, author. | Sueur-Hermel, Valérie, editor. | Mathis, Rémi, 1982- editor. | Pastoureau, Michel, 1947- writer of preface. | Dörr, Augusta, translator.
Title: Animal : a beastly compendium : treasures from the Prints and Photographs Department at the Bibliothèque Nationale de France / edited by Rémi Mathis and Valérie Sueur-Hermel ; preface by Michel Pastoureau ; translated from the French by Augusta Dörr.
Other titles: Animal. English
Description: New York : Bloomsbury Visual Arts, 2017. | "First published in France under the title Animal "2014, Bibliothèque nationale de France."
Identifiers: LCCN 2016056301| ISBN 9781474274944 (hardback) | ISBN 9781474274975 (epdf)
Subjects: LCSH: Animals in art—Catalogs. | Prints, French—Catalogs. | Prints, European—Catalogs. | Prints, American—Catalogs. | Prints—France—Paris—Catalogs. | Bibliothèque nationale de France. Département des estampes et de la photographie—Catalogs. | BISAC: ART / General. | ART / Subjects & Themes / Plants & Animals. | ART / History / General.
Classification: LCC N7660 .B49613 2017 | DDC 704.9/432—dc23 LC record available at https://lccn.loc.gov/2016056301

Photo-engraving: Les Artisans du Regard, Paris

Legal deposit: September 2014

Typeset by Lachina

Printed and bound in China

To find out more about our authors and books visit www.bloomsbury.com. Here you will find extracts, author interviews, details of forthcoming events and the option to sign up for our newsletters.

Bibliothèque nationale de France

President
Bruno Racine

General Director
Sylviane Tarsot-Gillery

Head of Collections
Denis Bruckmann

Director of the Prints and Photographs Department
Sylvie Aubenas

Director of Cultural Affairs
Thierry Grillet

Head of Publications
Benjamin Arranger

Head of Communications
Marc Rassat

Head of Media Services
Claudine Hermabessière

Director of Development
Kara Lennon Casanova

Publication

Editorial Directors
Benjamin Arranger, Marie-Caroline Dufayet

Editorial Manager and Head of Editorial Office
Jacqueline Michelet

Management and coordination of iconographic material
Laurianne Bossis, Caterina D'Agostino

Graphics and Page Layout
Wijntje van Rooijen, Pierre Péronnet

Cover Illustrations

Front: François Ertinger, after John Dunstall and Wenceslas Hollar, *Lion and Flowers*, ca. 1665 (see no. 23)

Back: Pieter Soutman after Pieter Paul Rubens, *The Hunting of the Crocodile and Hippopotamus* (detail) between 1642 and 1657 (see no. 35)

ANIMAL

Bloomsbury Visual Arts

An imprint of Bloomsbury Publishing Plc

50 Bedford Square
London
WC1B 3DP
UK

1385 Broadway
New York
NY 10018
USA

www.bloomsbury.com

BLOOMSBURY and the Diana logo are trademarks of Bloomsbury Publishing Plc

First published in France under the title Animal © 2014, Bibliothèque nationale de France

British Library Cataloguing-in-Publication Data

A catalogue record for this book is available from the British Library.

ISBN: HB: 978-1-4742-7494-4
ePDF: 978-1-4742-7497-5
ePub: 978-1-4742-7498-2

Library of Congress Cataloging-in-Publication Data

Names: Bibliothèque nationale de France. Département des estampes et de la photographie, author. | Sueur-Hermel, Valérie, editor. | Mathis, Rémi, 1982- editor. | Pastoureau, Michel, 1947- writer of preface. | Dörr, Augusta, translator.
Title: Animal : a beastly compendium : treasures from the Prints and Photographs Department at the Bibliothèque Nationale de France / edited by Rémi Mathis and Valérie Sueur-Hermel ; preface by Michel Pastoureau ; translated from the French by Augusta Dörr.
Other titles: Animal. English
Description: New York : Bloomsbury Visual Arts, 2017. | "First published in France under the title Animal "2014, Bibliothèque nationale de France."
Identifiers: LCCN 2016056301| ISBN 9781474274944 (hardback) | ISBN 9781474274975 (epdf)
Subjects: LCSH: Animals in art—Catalogs. | Prints, French—Catalogs. | Prints, European—Catalogs. | Prints, American—Catalogs. | Prints—France—Paris—Catalogs. | Bibliothèque nationale de France. Département des estampes et de la photographie—Catalogs. | BISAC: ART / General. | ART / Subjects & Themes / Plants & Animals. | ART / History / General.
Classification: LCC N7660 .B49613 2017 | DDC 704.9/432—dc23 LC record available at https://lccn.loc.gov/2016056301

Photo-engraving: Les Artisans du Regard, Paris

Legal deposit: September 2014

Typeset by Lachina

Printed and bound in China

Publication

Editorial Directors
Benjamin Arranger, Marie-Caroline Dufayet

Editorial Manager and Head of Editorial Office
Jacqueline Michelet

Management and coordination of iconographic material
Laurianne Bossis, Caterina D'Agostino

Graphics and Page Layout
Wijntje van Rooijen, Pierre Péronnet

Cover Illustrations

Front: François Ertinger, after John Dunstall and Wenceslas Hollar, *Lion and Flowers*, ca. 1665 (see no. 23)

Back: Pieter Soutman after Pieter Paul Rubens, *The Hunting of the Crocodile and Hippopotamus* (detail) between 1642 and 1657 (see no. 35)

ANIMAL

A BEASTLY COMPENDIUM

TREASURES FROM THE PRINTS AND PHOTOGRAPHS DEPARTMENT
AT THE BIBLIOTHÈQUE NATIONALE DE FRANCE

EDITED BY RÉMI MATHIS AND VALÉRIE SUEUR-HERMEL
PREFACE BY MICHEL PASTOUREAU

TRANSLATED FROM THE FRENCH BY AUGUSTA DÖRR

BLOOMSBURY VISUAL ARTS
AN IMPRINT OF BLOOMSBURY PUBLISHING PLC

B L O O M S B U R Y
LONDON • OXFORD • NEW YORK • NEW DELHI • SYDNEY

ABOUT THE AUTHORS

This publication comprises a selection of works from the collections held in the Prints and Photographs Department at the Bibliothèque nationale de France, whose Director is Chief Curator Sylvie Aubenas. It would not have been possible to create this book without the collaborative work of all the Department staff, in particular those responsible for the collections. The publication is edited by Rémi Mathis and Valérie Sueur-Hermel. Each description is signed with the initials of its author.

CÉLINE CHICHA-CASTEX (C.C.-C.)
A curator at the Prints and Photographs Department, Céline Chicha-Castex is in charge of the collection of 20th century prints. She has curated several exhibitions devoted to this subject, including *Les impressions de Pierre Alechinsky* (*The Prints of Pierre Alechinsky*) (with Marie-Françoise Quignard, BNF, 2005); *Zao Wou-Ki. Estampes et livres illustrés* (*Zao Wou-Ki: Prints and Illustrated Books*) (with Marie Minssieux, BNF, 2008); *Jean-Michel Alberola. L'œuvre imprimé* (*Jean-Michel Alberola: The Printed Artwork*) (with Marie-Cécile Miessner, BNF/Ereme, 2009); *Hans Hartung, estampes* (*Hans Hartung: Prints*) (with Christian Rümelin and Andreas Schalhorn, BNF, 2010); *Matisse: Drawing Life* (with Emilie Ovaere, Brisbane, Queensland Art Gallery, 2011); *Erik Desmazières. Voyage au centre de la Bibliothèque* (*Erik Desmazières: Journey to the Center of the Library*) (BNF/Hazan, 2012); *Matthew Barney. La Chambre de sublimation* (*Matthew Barney: The Sublimation Chamber*) (with Marie Minssieux, BNF, 2013); *De Picasso à Jasper Johns: l'atelier d'Aldo Crommelynck* (*From Picasso to Jasper Johns: Aldo Crommelynck's Workshop*) (with Cécile Pocheau-Leseteven and Marie-Cécile Miessner, BNF, 2014). She also works at the École du Louvre, specializing in the History of Prints.

LISE FAUCHERAU (L.F.)
A librarian at the Prints and Photographs Department, Lise Faucherau manages the collection of contemporary prints, and in particular the 'graphzines' held at the BNF, which is the only public national institution to contain a collection of this type. In daily contact with artists and their works, she has written articles on every type of movement relating to the contemporary graphic arts, and has had a number of interviews with contemporary artists published in the journal Nouvelles de l'estampe, including Fabrice Gygi, Rémy Jacquier, Frédérique Lucien and Barthélemy Toguo.

RÉMI GAILLARD (R.G.)
Rémi Gaillard is an archivist-paleographer and a librarian. A former student at the École des chartes, he wrote his thesis on the disposal of the royal furniture during the French Revolution and on the general administrative procedures applied in confiscations of furnishings. He is currently in charge of library policy and collection development at the Bibliothèque universitaire Pierre-et-Marie-Curie (BUPMC).

CORINNE LE BITOUZÉ (C.L.B.)
An archivist-paleographer, Corinne Le Bitouzé is the curator in charge of 18th century prints and is also Deputy Director of the Prints and Photographs Department. She participated in the compilation of the *Dictionnaire des éditeurs d'estampes à Paris sous l'Ancien Régime* (*A Dictionary of Parisian Print-Publishers under the Ancien Régime*) (1987) and is the author of several articles on the conservation and restoration of iconographic documents. She curated the exhibition *Casanova: la passion de la liberté* (*Casanova: The Passion for Freedom*) (BNF, 2011).

SÉVERINE LEPAPE (S.L.)
Séverine Lepape is an archivist-paleographer, a curator of 15th and 16th century prints, Head of the Ancient Prints Department and of the Reserve Collections at the Prints and Photographs Department. She also lectures in the history and techniques of printing at the École des chartes. A Doctor in Medieval History, she wrote her thesis on the iconography of the Tree of Jesse in France and England from the 13th to the 17th centuries. She is a specialist in the origins of wood engraving and its applications in the 15th and 16th centuries, the Northern Schools of engraving, medieval devotion and the iconography of the Virgin Mary.

RÉMI MATHIS (R.M.)
An archivist-paleographer, Rémi Mathis is a curator of 17th century prints at the Prints and Photographs Department in the Bibliothèque nationale de France. He studied at the École des chartes, where he completed his thesis on Simon Arnauld de Pomponne, Secretary of State for Foreign Affairs under Louis XIV, and went on to write several academic articles on the history of the book and the print, diplomacy and Jansenism. He is also Editor-in-Chief of *Nouvelles de l'Estampe*, the French specialist journal devoted to prints and engravings, and a lecturer on ancient prints at the École des chartes. He is committed to disseminating knowledge, and was President of Wikimédia France from 2011 to 2014.

MONIQUE MOULÈNE (M.M.)
A librarian, Monique Moulène manages the collection of 19th century prints in the Prints and Photographs Department.

CÉCILE POCHEAU-LESTEVEN (C.P.-L.)
Cécile Pocheau-Lesteven is a Head Curator of the Prints and Photographs Department, where she is in charge of the collections of contemporary prints and artists' books. She curated the exhibition *De Picasso à Jasper Johns, l'atelier d'Aldo Crommelynck* (*From Picasso to Jasper Johns: Aldo Crommelynck's Workshop*) (BNF, 2014).

ANNE-MARIE SAUVAGE (A.-M.S.)
A general curator at the Prints and Photographs Department, Anne-Marie Sauvage is in charge of the poster collection. She has been involved in several exhibitions, including *Les Lautrec de Lautrec* (*The Lautrecs by Lautrec*) (BNF, 1992) and *Paul Colin et les Spectacles* (*Paul Colin and the Spectacles*) (Nancy, 1994), as well as curating the following exhibitions held at the BNF: *Graphisme(s) 200 créateurs, 1997–2001* (*Graphic Design(s): 200 Artists, 1997–2001*) (BNF, 2001); *A.M. Cassandre. Œuvres graphiques modernes, 1923–1939* (*A.M. Cassandre: Modern Graphic Artwork, 1923–1939*), for which she edited the accompanying catalogue (BNF, 2005), and *Graphisme et création contemporaine* (*Graphic Design and Contemporary Creative Work*) (BNF, 2011).

VANESSA SELBACH (V.S.)
An archivist-paleographer, Vanessa Selbach is a curator of 17th century prints at the Prints and Photographs Department and also lectures on prints at the École du Louvre. She studied at the École des chartes, where the subject of her thesis was the iconography of illustrated French Catholic Bibles (1996). Formerly a librarian in the legal deposit department at the BNF (1997–1998), she later became a university lecturer and researcher in the history of books and prints at the École nationale supérieure des sciences de l'information et des bibliothèques (ENSSIB) in Villeurbanne (1999–2007). She specializes in the use of religious prints (16th to 17th centuries), the history of print collecting (16th to 17th centuries) and the history of woodcuts in 16th century Lyon.

VALÉRIE SUEUR-HERMEL (V.S.-H.)
Valérie Sueur-Hermel is a Head Curator of the Prints and Photographs Department, where she is in charge of the 19th century collections. She also lectures at the École du Louvre, her specialist subject being the History of the Print. She has curated several exhibitions devoted to this subject, including *Daumier, l'écriture du lithographe* (*Daumier: The Lithographer's Script*) (BNF, 2008); *Henri Rivière. Entre impressionnisme et japonisme* (*Henri Rivière: Between Impressionism and Japonisme*) (BNF, 2009); *L'Estampe impressionniste. Trésors de la Bibliothèque nationale de France* (*The Impressionist Print: Treasures of the Bibliothèque nationale de France*) (Musée des beaux-arts de Caen, 2010) and *Odilon Redon: prince du rêve, 1840–1916* (*Odilon Redon: Prince of Dreams, 1840–1916*) (Grand-Palais, 2011). She was research director for the virtual exhibition *Gustave Doré: L'imaginaire au pouvoir* (*Gustave Doré: The Reign of Imagination*) (BNF, 2014).

JUDE TALBOT (J.T.)
Jude Talbot, a librarian, is in charge of digitization at the Prints and Photographs Department.

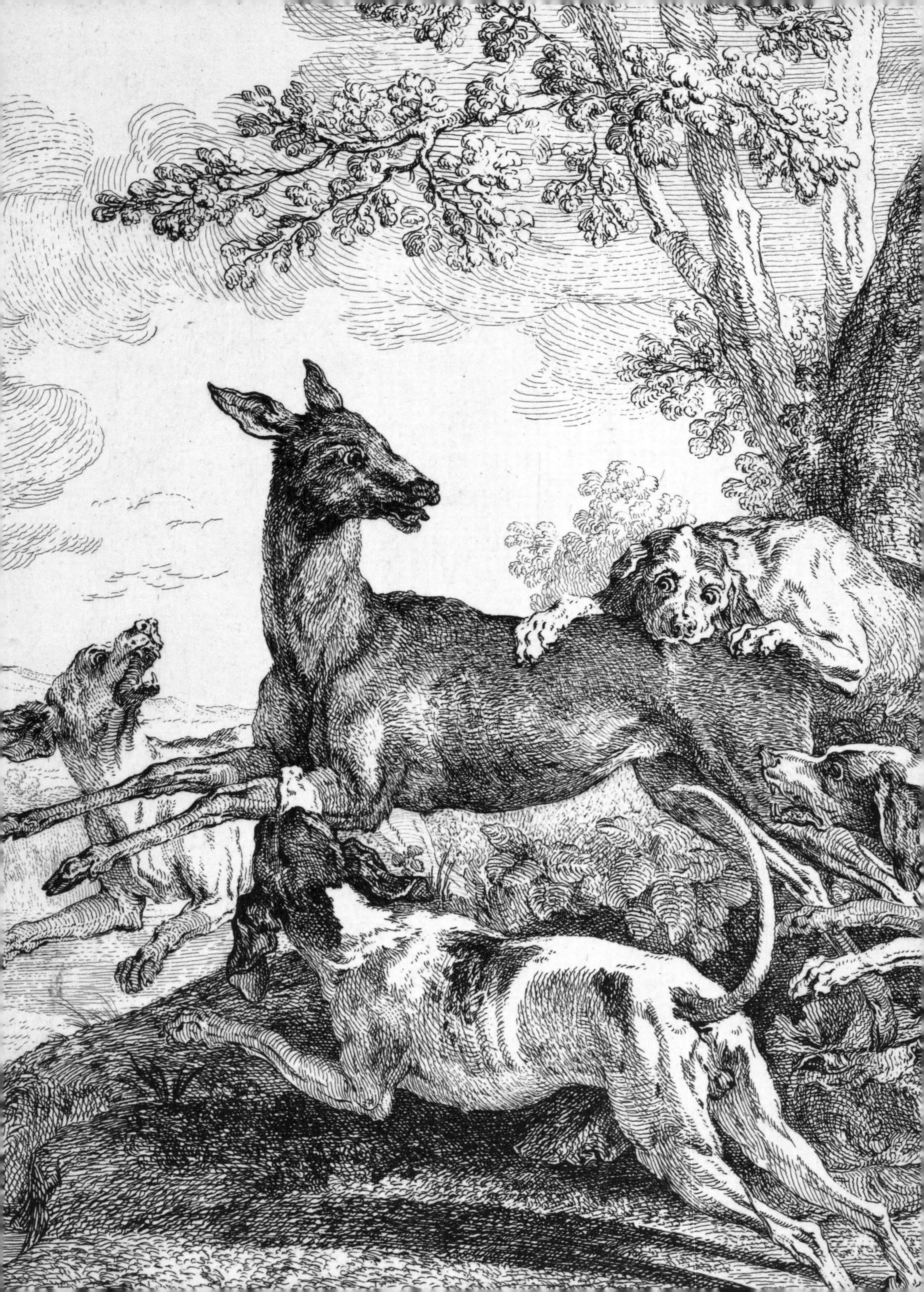

Ass 27 46 Bear 1 10 44 46 66 “Beast of Gévaudan” 45 Beaver 37 Bee 24 Bird 33 “Bird-Woman” 96 Bull 44 94 Butterfly 39 47 Camel 71 99 Carp 33 79 Cat 2 21 22 49 80 84 Chimera 43 Cow 27 75 93 Crocodile 35 46 Deer 57 Dinosaur 73 Dog 7 17 18 20 27 35 48 49 57 58 68 83 90 95 Dolphin 69 Dromedary 46 Duck 27 77 Elephant 11 28 52 55 61 71 101 Fish 12 34 40 74 Fox 46 Frog 41 Giant Squid 32 Giraffe 70 Goat 46 Goose 51 Grasshopper 66 Hippopotamus 35 Horse 6 7 8 27 35 58 59 60 97 98 Jaguar 58 Lion 1 9 23 46 59 62 Mole 30 Monkey 9 33 48 49 68 69 100 Mouse 21 31 33 Ostrich 88 Owl 25 Ox 26 50 65 93 Panther 9 33 Parrot 53 Peacock 9 15 67 85 Pelican 38 Pig 4 29 Porcupine 14 Rabbit 13 33 82 Ram 64 Rhinoceros 5 56 Salamander 41 Shrimp 78 Snake 86 91 Snowy Owl 63 Sperm Whale 36 Spider 76 81 Spiny Lobster 78 Stag 7 9 46 66 92 Swan 89 Tiger 62 87 Turtle Dove 42 Unicorn 3 9 46 Water Spaniel 16 Wild Boar 9 Wolf 27 46 54 Zebra 19

Numbers refer to image figures

Jean-Baptise Oudry, *Deer Attacked by Dogs* (detail), 1736 → description on p. 96

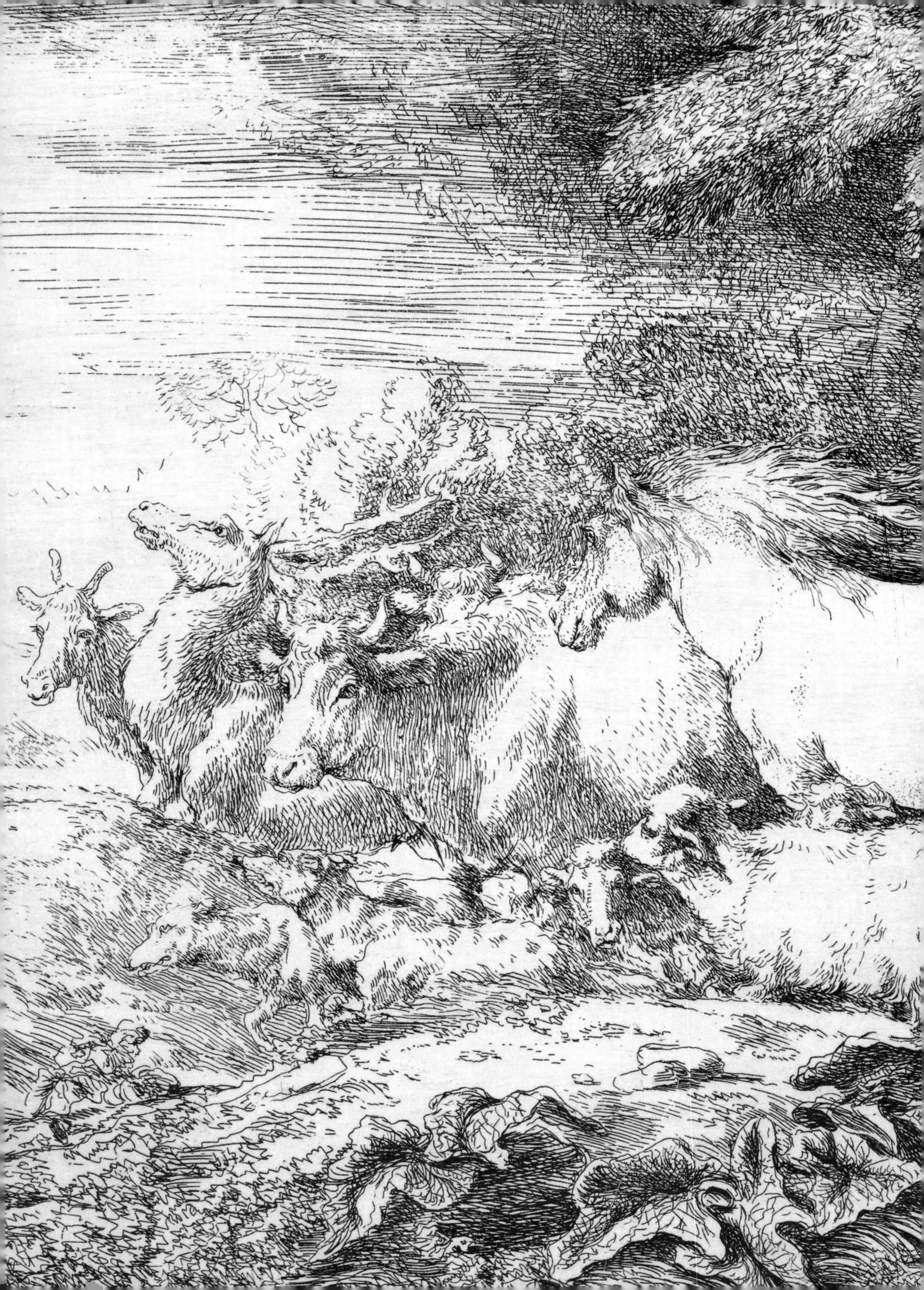

Preface
Michel Pastoureau

For a considerable period of time, historians and art historians showed little interest in animals. They treated the subject merely as a 'footnote', as they did with every theme that they regarded as marginal, or of purely anecdotal value. Fortunately, however, this situation has changed in the course of the last two or three decades. Thanks to certain pioneering studies and to the increasingly frequent collaborations between researchers from other domains (zoologists, naturalists, ethnologists, anthropologists and linguists), animals have become a subject for historical study in their own right. The theme has even found itself at the cutting edge of research and at the intersection of several disciplines. Indeed, by its very nature it is bound to be trans-disciplinary and trans-informational in character. These two adjectives have become somewhat clichéd nowadays due to misuse, yet it is precisely this type of research that should be conducted by any historian interested in animals.

Images occupy a central place in the documentation that such historians need to study, as this publication so elegantly and aptly demonstrates. I am delighted to see that the Prints and Photographs Department at the Bibliothèque nationale de France is able to display the wealth and diversity of its collections of animal iconography to the general public. An initiative of this nature would have been impossible to achieve forty years ago. I have unhappy memories of the occasion when, as a young curator in the Coin Room, I was asked by the General Administrator to present a suggestion for an interdisciplinary exhibition to the heads of department. The theme I proposed, the natural and cultural history of the elephant, was described as 'ridiculous'.

Giovanni Benedetto Castiglione, *Noah and the Animals Entering the Ark* (detail), ca. 1650-1655, → description on p. 56

Viewed in relation to their connections with human beings, animals are involved in every aspect of social, material, intellectual, religious, artistic and symbolic history. They are ubiquitous; in evidence throughout history and in every circumstance, they present historians, sociologists, ethnologists and philosophers alike with a multitude of complex questions. It is not through coincidence or passing fad that over the last two years in France, the main subject presented at the *Agrégation* in Philosophy was that of man's relationship with animals.

Over the centuries, the European Christian conception of animals has undergone considerable variations. However, these may be reduced to two major currents of thought. According to the first perspective, it was imperative that man should be as clearly differentiated from animals as possible, the former having been created in the image of God, whereas the latter were abject, imperfect, and even impure. The second perspective, conversely, emphasizes a state of community between all living things, and a kinship between man and animals based on more than purely biological factors.

The first school of thought remained dominant for a long period, which explains why animals were so frequently used in references and images from the Middle Ages to the 17th century. Through this standard contrast between man and animals, whereby the latter were viewed as inferior creatures, serving to accentuate the prestige of the former, animals were constantly discussed and depicted. Introduced into every possible context, they provided a popular theme for metaphors and comparisons, and were a general focus for 'symbolic thinking'. This attitude likewise led to the stringent repression of any behaviour that might lead to confusion between the human and animal species. Hence the constantly reiterated injunctions issued by the Church forbidding people to dress up as animals, to imitate their behaviour or to extol or celebrate them in any way. Unsuitable relationships between humans and animals were seen as particularly culpable, and these ranged from excessive affection shown to pets or domestic animals, to the most infamous of crimes, such as those involving sorcery or bestiality.

Although the second perspective is less forceful in character, it is equally significant and clearly more modern. Its origins lie in Aristotelian thought, but it was disseminated within the very heart of the Christian religion through an attitude towards the animal kingdom that reflected similar principles, for a variety of reasons. The most famous example of this viewpoint is that of Saint Francis of Assisi, who preached to the birds; its origins may be found in a verse of Saint Paul's: 'Because the creature itself also shall be delivered from the bondage of corruption into the glorious liberty of the children of God' (Romans, 8:21, KJV). This phrase had a profound effect on the theologians who interpreted it. Some sought the possible meaning behind those words, wondering whether Christ had really come to save *all* creatures, and whether *all* animals were truly 'children of God'. The fact that Jesus was born in a stable was seen by certain authors as proof that Christ came to this earth for the redemption of animals *as well as* mankind. Other theologians, who strongly favoured the Scholastic method, asked themselves questions that were still being debated at the University of Paris in the mid-17th century. These included the theme of animals and the afterlife: Were they resurrected after death? Did they go to heaven? Did they have a specifically reserved area there? Was this the case for all animals, or for just one of each species? Other questions related to their life on earth: Could they work on Sundays? Should they be made to observe days of fasting? And, above all, should they be treated here on earth as morally responsible beings?

Many Christian authors in the Middle Ages, and some 18th and 19th century philosophers, believed that animals possessed a soul that was not simply vegetative, like that of plants, but also sensitive and intellectual/rational, like that of human beings. At least, this was thought to be the case for those animals deemed 'superior', in other words, quadrupeds, particularly if they were domesticated. In the same way, such animals were seen as responsible for their actions and capable of understanding the difference between Good and Evil; they were therefore to be judged if they committed crimes or misdemeanours. This explains their presence in courts of law and at trials from the 13th century until well into the 1700s.

Certain authors, such as Albert the Great, Michel de Montaigne, Georges-Louis Leclerc, comte de Buffon and Charles Darwin, noted that animals are able to dream, recognize, deduce, remember and acquire new habits. Nevertheless, the question remained as to whether the superior members of the animal kingdom also possessed a spiritual dimension, like man. Many denied this, asserting that, to animals, signs remain signals and never become symbols. This is an essential difference, and seems to establish an impenetrable boundary between humankind and animals, denying the latter access to the immaterial world and to the possibility of formulating abstract notions or religious ideas.

Many of these questions just described – is it lawful to make animals work on Sundays? Should they observe fasting days? Do they go to heaven or hell? – make us smile nowadays. We are wrong to do so, however; the greatest trap into which the historian can fall with regard to such matters is that of anachronism. We cannot and must not project our own contemporary knowledge, definitions, classification systems, sensibilities and morals onto the past. They cannot be applied to previous eras, nor will they be applicable to those of the future. Our current wisdom does not stand as absolute and definitive truth, but simply as a phase in the constantly advancing history of knowledge. If we fail to recognize this, we will lapse into reductionist scientism and a positivist perspective incompatible with historical research.

Let us take, for example, the notion of 'mammals', unknown before the 18th century, and the particular case of the dolphin. If we approach the study of animals in texts and images by separating mammals from non-mammals, it would involve removing the dolphin from the category of 'fish' – where it had been placed in all zoological works up to the Age of Enlightenment – and classifying it with 'cetaceans, or marine mammals', a category that remained long unknown and is much too modern. This would also mean that the dolphin would lose his status as the 'king of fish', and the crown he wears in medieval miniatures and 16th and 17th century engravings would therefore lose all its significance.

A similar example of anachronistic irregularity is that of the claims, arising from investigations conducted with a positivist slant, that animal species which have now been named and meticulously classified may be identified in the hybrid or indefinable types presented in texts or images dating from the Middle Ages to the 19th century. Certain zoologists even believed that they had detected traces of prehistoric animals, extinct for tens of millennia, in various monstrous beasts represented in sculptures, paintings or prints. Others scrupulously endeavoured to distinguish the 'truths' from the 'errors' in the first printed zoology books, as well as in the textbooks subsequently published. Even Buffon, Lamarck, Geoffroy-Saint-Hilaire and Darwin were sometimes mistaken! Why do historians of the sciences, who generally manage to avoid judging the knowledge of the past from the perspective of the present, fall into this trap of anachronism in the case of animals?

A number of contrasting categories now used to define and classify the various species in the animal kingdom have hardly any relevance when applied to the past, and, in some instances, to the recent past. This is the case with three basic opposing pairs in contemporary zoological classifications: indigenous/exotic; domestic/wild; and real/fantastical. For example, although by the 17th century lions had long ceased to exist in a wild state in Europe, they were not exotic animals in the strict sense of the word. They were part of the everyday landscape and featured abundantly, in painted or sculpted form, in all the churches. They were regularly spoken of, depicted in countless images, represented as kings of bestiaries and served as the basis for emblems and symbols of every kind. In the same way, blackbirds, magpies, crows, mice, weasels and foxes – those frequent visitors to chicken coops – were still at that time seen as 'domestic' animals, as they lived around the house (or *domus* in Latin). It was not until the 18th, or even the 19th century, that the term 'domestic' was no longer used to describe animals that lived in close proximity to human beings, but those whose reproduction was controlled by man. As for the boundary separating real from fantastical animals, it has remained porous for some time. Although we have not believed in mermaids, or the phoenix, since the 13th century, dragons were included in zoological books until the 17th century, while it was not until the Age of Enlightenment that people finally ceased to believe in unicorns.

The engraved image has played a considerable role in this development of understanding and beliefs. Not only has it facilitated the circulation of an unprecedented amount of knowledge with regard to the seals and miniatures of the Middle Ages, it has also, and above all, inspired comparisons and reflections, stimulated the imagination, and taken artistic creation in a multitude of different directions. This publication provides precious evidence of that role, in relation to both modern and contemporary history. It displays the treasures of the Prints and Photographs Departments to magnificent advantage, vividly reflecting the fact that animals have always provided humankind with an immense repertoire of signs and dreams.

One Print: Many Prints
Rémi Mathis and Valérie Sueur-Hermel

Visitors to the International Print Fair, held in Paris in 2013, were attracted by the 'natural histories' theme. Captivated by the images of animals that we had selected from our collections, they asked us about the techniques that had been used; in comparison with painting, they seemed so effective for such economy of means. Of course, much time has elapsed since Baudelaire wrote of 'the child, entranced by maps and prints', and the term 'print' itself does not hold a great deal of meaning for most people in the early twenty-first century. We will therefore present a general outline of the history of prints and printmaking, followed by a brief description of the Prints Department at the Bibliothèque nationale de France.*

*See also the "Glossary of Printmaking Techniques" at the end of this publication.

First and foremost, a print is an image that has been printed. The techniques used in this process developed at the same time as those of book printing, and were initiated during the 15th century in goldsmiths' workshops, as a result of the idea of engraving an image onto a surface, or 'matrix' made of wood or metal, which was then covered with ink and transferred onto a sheet of paper. This process can be repeated a countless number of times, depending only on the engraved plate's resistance to wear and tear. This explains why, for over four centuries, prints were the only means of circulating large quantities of a particular image to fulfill a whole variety of functions. They were used for artistic, religious, journalistic or technical purposes, for documents, in the worlds of publishing and science and particularly in the domain that interests us here – zoology.

Over the first few decades of printmaking, the woodcut was the predominant technique; it generated some superb works produced by artists who mastered the processes very rapidly, such as Dürer. However, its importance declined with the dawning of the 17th century, a period of great innovation. Consequently, xylography was no longer used as a technique by leading artists, although it survived in the domain of publishing, notably in the form of decorative elements at the beginnings and endings of chapters, and in popular images. The intaglio method, on the other hand, enjoyed a significant rise in popularity. It essentially involved engraving with a burin, cutting directly into a copper plate. Then, in the reign of Louis XIII, a new technique known as etching emerged. This entailed covering the plate with a layer of varnish, which was easier to cut into than the plate itself and created compositions of greater finesse. When the plate was immersed into an acid bath, the areas left exposed by the tip of the etching tool were bitten away by the acid, while the areas protected by the varnish remained intact. This process had marked consequences, not only on the style of prints produced, but also on its practitioners. While the engraving tool, known as a burin, could only be used by professionals skilled in manipulating it, the etching process allowed artists and designers to create prints themselves. However, the technique was reserved for certain highly specific themes and luxury products, as it was only possible to produce a small number of prints in this manner.

The 18th century witnessed the appearance of further innovations, intended to correspond to the developing requirements and tastes of the public. Engravers, and, more broadly, all members of society who were interested in prints (inventors of designs, publishers, and so forth) sought new techniques that would resemble other artistic media as closely as possible; this led to the invention of new ways to imitate drawing, and to the production of coloured prints.

Lithography, which emerged in the 19th century, was a revolutionary technique as it enabled prints to be produced without the engraving process. The artist draws the image with a greasy lithographic crayon on a very finely grained limestone plate. The ink remains on the drawn sections, but disappears on the other areas of the plate, following the principle of the mutual repulsion of water and fats. Lithography became a major medium, not only in terms of art, but also because it was much easier to circulate large numbers of images in this manner, a significant development in the century that witnessed the Industrial Revolution. Lithography was frequently used, for example, in the newspapers of the day, which had print runs of several thousand. The same was true of a new method of engraving on wood, known as 'endgrain' wood engraving, whereby the wood is incised perpendicularly to the fibres, which produces much more finely detailed images than in the case of traditional xylography.

The numerous mechanical procedures that subsequently developed during the 20th century might have rendered the print obsolete, as it was now possible to reproduce and print millions of photographs on an offset printing press. However, far from being abandoned, the medium gradually became appropriated by the world of art. Due to its status as an original work, yet one from which multiple copies can be generated, the print was favoured by those who championed democracy in art, within the political and social context that characterized the mid-20th century. The greatest artists (such as Matisse, Picasso and Miró) took to printmaking, notably producing lithographs and silk-screen prints, which were easy to create without having highly advanced technical knowledge.

There is one particular location in France where the public has the opportunity to access this immense heritage of printed images dating from the 15th century to the present day: the Prints and Photographs Department at the Bibliothèque nationale de France. In the late 19th century, the Department was described by Henri Bouchot, who created the guidebook for the collections, as the 'National Museum of Prints'. It holds the largest collection of images in the world. This comprises fifteen million graphic items, which are highly varied in nature; as well as prints and photographs, there are drawings, posters, postcards, playing cards, labels and even samples of material.

The *Cabinet des Estampes*, or Print Room, was first established in 1667, when the collection brought together by the Abbé Michel de Marolles, which boasted eighty-four thousand prints, was acquired for the King's library. This magnificent series was added to the items acquired through legal deposit, which had been initially established for books in 1537 and subsequently extended to prints in 1632. The richness of the collection, and its admirably extensive reflection of national production, stems from this obligation on the part of publishers and printmakers to deposit two copies of every item they produced at the library. Since the 17th century, a number of valuable acquisitions and gifts – legacies and, more recently, donations – have been added to these regular deposits. Significantly, these items have extended the collection to works originating from countries other than France.

The Print Room, recommended to visitors by the tourist guides of the day, opened its doors to the public in the early 18th century. From 1840, with heating now installed in the reading rooms, the number of visitors increased. The department, located in the rue de Richelieu on the historic library premises, was accessible to all for the consultation of original works, but also for informative publications on the collections housed there.

The Print Room, which became the Department of Prints and Photographs in 1972, remains a museum of the history of prints and contains works by its greatest masters, from Dürer to Picasso, yet it also offers a priceless, encyclopedic repertoire of images. Indeed, in addition to artists' creations, which account for nine million items, the Department holds a collection of six million images categorized by subject, according to a system initially devised by Hugues-Adrien Joly, Custodian of the Print Room from 1750–1792. His classification scheme was developed and completed as it is today by Jean Duchesne in the very early 19th century. These informative series cater for iconographic research of every type, some of the richest and most widely consulted material being portraits and images relating to the topography and history of France, costumes and customs. The series devoted to natural history, which encompasses zoology, botany, anatomy and minerology, originates from the three hundred prints owned by the Abbé de Marolles and has been developed over the years. In order to create the compendium of animal images presented here, which range from the early days of printmaking to contemporary examples, this subdivision has been explored by various curators from the Prints Department. They each specialize in a particular century, and in the works of the engravers and printmakers in question. Some of these artists' creations are held in the Reserve Collection, which since 1850 has housed the rarest and most precious items in the department.

The one hundred and one prints shown here have either been selected for their emblematic status within the history of the medium, or simply on account of the anatomy of the animals presented. Depending on the era in which they were created, some are appealing, while others are disconcerting, reflecting the different aims governing the depiction of animals in the course of history. This eclectic bestiary also has the merit of illustrating the many and varied techniques used for printmaking, together with the different purposes that prints have served, not the least of which is their value as purely artistic creations.

ANIMAL

WILD AND EXOTIC CREATURES

Artists have long been fascinated by the exotic quality of animals from far-flung lands, their presence in Europe being very rare until the early 19th century. In the 16th century, knowledge of species from outside Europe could be acquired only via the accounts, of varying reliability, given by witnesses who described creatures that they had glimpsed and often imperfectly observed. When, in 1515, Dürer executed his famous woodcut of a rhinoceros (no. 5), he had been inspired by the story of one of these animals that had arrived in Lisbon during that same year and had died shortly afterwards, on the way to Rome. A century later, in 1643, the journey of an elephant from Ceylon across Europe provided the Italian engraver Stefano Della Bella with the opportunity to draw the animal from life (no. 28). Because they were not the result of this type of encounter between artist and model, images of certain species are sometimes so fanciful that they have all the charm of an imaginary bestiary. One such example is the image of the zebra resembling a horse that has been simply clad in a series of stripes which are a little too perfectly parallel (no. 19).

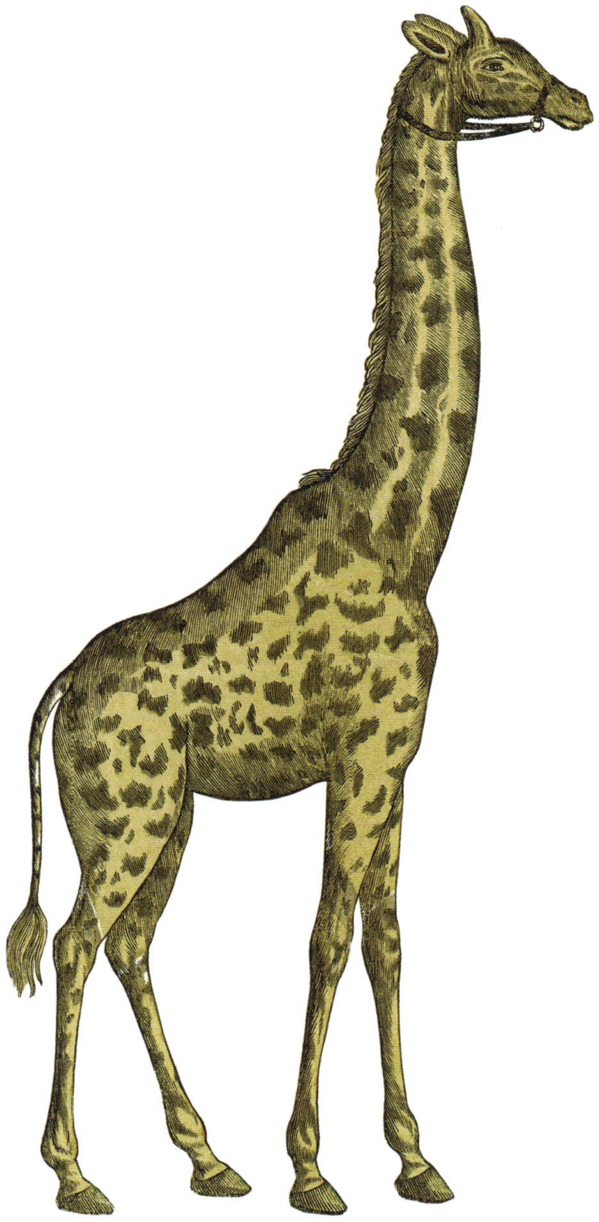

The print played its part in disseminating motifs by offering engravers the possibility of copying the anatomy of animals that they had never seen. In Paris, in around 1665, François Langlois published the image of a lion etched by François Ertinger (no. 23). The floral decoration surrounding the wild animal accentuates the artistic dimension of the work, which is the copy of an English print that had itself been executed from a drawing made in Prague! The approach to such works became more scientific in the mid-18th century, when a female rhinoceros named Clara, who had been captured in Bengal, was brought to Europe. She was subsequently moved from fair to fair, affording artists the opportunity to draw her with the attention to accuracy typically required at that time. Her 'true portrait' was circulated by means of a print published in Paris, in the rue Saint Jacques (no. 56).

It was also a print, notably in the form of a woodcut published in Épinal, which in 1827 contributed to disseminating the image of the first giraffe to appear in France, a gift from Muhammad Ali to King Charles X (no. 70). She was kept in the ménagerie at the Museum of Natural History, which became a meeting place for animal artists. It was there that Delacroix drew the models for his *Royal Tiger* and *Lion of the Atlas*, which were depicted in lithographs in 1829 (no. 62). Much in evidence in circuses, the elephant provided Goya with a model for his etching *Animal Folly* (no. 61). During the 1850s, elephants took centre stage when they appeared with other animals in a spectacle presented at the Hippodrome in the Porte Dauphine (no. 71).

At the end of the 19th century, the requirement for naturalistic depiction gave way to the vogue for stylized images. Paul Ranson, an artist from the Nabis group who was influenced by Japanese prints, played with curves and undulating lines in *Tiger in the Jungle*, a lithograph he created for *L'Estampe originale* (no. 87). Raoul Dufy seems to have been engaged in similar artistic explorations when he executed his woodcut of a snake in the midst of stylized vegetation for Apollinaire's *Bestiaire* (no. 86). Oscillating between realism (nos. 99 and 100) and fantasy (no. 101), contemporary printmaking artists continue to find the theme of wild animals a stimulating source of creativity. V.S.-H.

DOMESTIC ANIMALS

Although they do not share the same affectionate relationship with humans as dogs and cats, who have a separate status in this respect (see 'Man's Best Friends', p. 21), domestic animals nonetheless live in close proximity with humankind. Through this contact they became a popular subject for artists, being naturally more cooperative as models than wild animals (see above, 'Wild and Exotic Creatures'). The principal subject among the domestic animals featuring in prints is the horse, majestically depicted in German Renaissance woodcuts by Albrecht Dürer and Hans Baldung Grien. The imposing musculature of Dürer's *The Large Horse* is indicative of the animal's power, yet the presence of the bridle and the man at his side is a reminder of its domesticated state (no. 6). In the woodcuts of stallions created by Baldung Grien, however, there is no trace of the horse's submission to man; the only characteristic emphasized by the artist in this case is the animal's wild and fiery nature (no. 8). The fundamental duality of the horse, both a paragon of servitude to humankind and at the same time an emblematic symbol of liberty, is strikingly conveyed through these printed images. Thoroughbreds

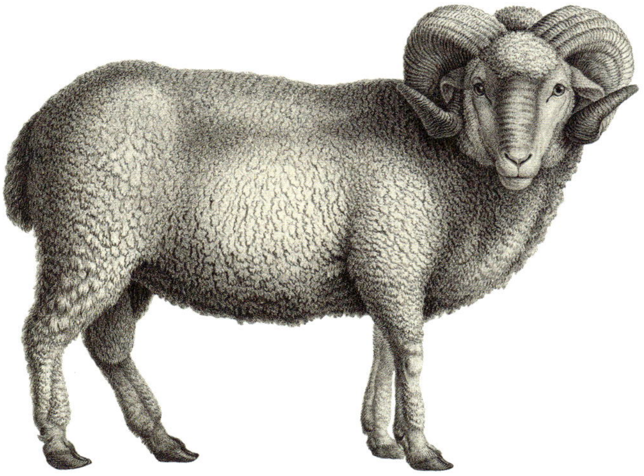

have been much admired by artists on account of the beauty of their anatomy. A horseman captivated by the breed, Carle Vernet frequently sketched these animals, and engravers such as Gilles-Antoine Demarteau subsequently depicted them in numerous portraits (no. 60). At a much more recent date, the sculptor Barry Flanagan created a linocut of an Irish thoroughbred, its expression both wary and vulnerable (no. 98).

Bovine livestock also has its place among the ranks of farm animals. Rosa Bonheur established herself as a specialist in this domain; her hefty Durham-Charolais ox, portrayed with exemplary realism, would catch many a butcher's eye (no. 65). A cow is an equally effective selling point, as demonstrated by the remarkable longevity of the laughing animal conceived by Benjamin Rabier in the early 20th century and still inseparably associated with the famous spreadable cheese created by Léon Bel (no. 75). At the end of the same century, Roy Lichtenstein's artistic explorations based on the profile of a bull developed the motif from figurative portrayal to abstract image (no. 94). At the same time, Marcel Broodthaers created an educational poster with an original twist, featuring illustrated examples of the bovine race, their names replaced by those of cars (no. 93).

Pigs are among the rarer types of farm animal to be portrayed in prints, yet when etched by Rembrandt they have a unique presence. His recumbent sow, depicted shortly before her slaughter, brings to mind the old saying: 'every part of a pig is the best part'. V.S.-H.

ANTHROPOMORPHISM

Animals have been presented in a humanized manner from ancient times, following an enduring literary tradition in both Western and Eastern cultures. In Phaedrus's fables, which were based on those of Aesop, animals were used to exemplify particular human traits. These were reprised by La Fontaine, whose work, still widely read today, has inspired the greatest illustrators, including Marc Chagall (no. 90). Artists have even depicted animals wearing clothes, striking human poses and engaged in human occupations. The negative connotations associated with certain types of animals provided an excellent means of denouncing the ridiculous habits of one's contemporaries from a moral, religious or satirical perspective.

For example, the Governors of the Low Countries, Isabella and Albert of Austria, were satirized by their alienated subjects in the United Provinces as a pair of dour-looking owls (no. 25). This type of representation sometimes creates an impact that extends well beyond the context from which it originated. Oblivious to the fact that this was a contemptuous portrayal of the Governors of the Low Countries as seen by their rebellious subjects, Parisians bought the print, copies of which were made and sold by the publisher Jacques Lagniet. To them, it was no more than an amusing image, at most a satire on worldly entertainments.

European art continued these games of mockery through metamorphosis and costume. The 18th century, when monkeys were a popular means of parodying human behavior (no. 48), led to a period of revolution that followed the same codes, with images portraying an 'Incroyable' as a goose and a 'Merveilleuse' as an ox (nos. 50 and 51). This genre even became a speciality in the 19th century, with its depictions of coquettes and demi-mondaines as peacocks (no. 67). Furthermore, while his *Metamorphoses of the Day* (no. 66) earned Jean-Jacques Grandville the nickname 'the Buffon of satire', the illustrations he produced for the best writers of the day were published in the *Scènes de la Vie Privée et Publique des Animaux* (no. 68).

Aside from the domain of satire, comparisons between man and animals provided material for reflection. The 17th and 18th centuries witnessed attempts to classify human types in a scientific manner, the aim being to associate appearance with behaviour (no. 26). There are indeed men whose physiognomy brings to mind that of an ox, a bear or a goat, and that physical resemblance might even shed light on certain personalities. This idea pleased adherents to the principles of physiognomy in the following century. It is certainly true that, in the history of European iconography from the Renaissance to the present day, the image of the animal remains a very useful substitute for that of man! R.M.

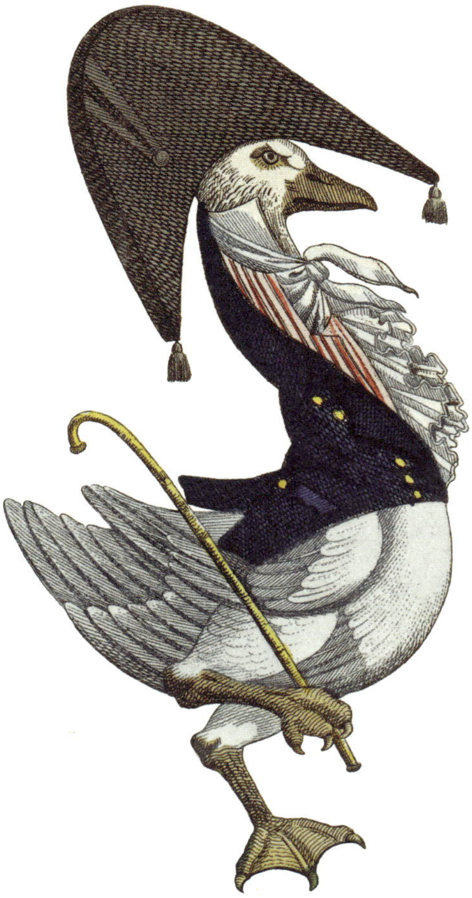

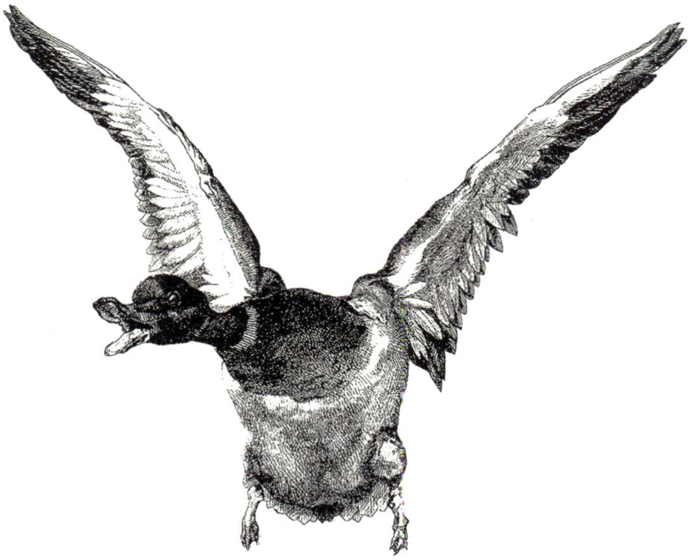

ALLEGORIES AND SYMBOLS

Whether real or fictitious, animals occupy an important place in symbolic and allegorical iconography, a fact abundantly reflected in historical prints. A legendary creature, whose existence was readily accepted during the Middle Ages and even beyond that era, the unicorn is endowed with strongly symbolic qualities. Due to the purifying powers attributed to the animal according to medieval tradition, it was frequently depicted dipping its horn into various springs, fountains or rivers, in order to cleanse the water (nos. 3 and 9). The elephant, a symbol of strength, was even used as an allegorical representation of King François I of France, in a fresco in the gallery of the Château de Fontainebleau that was painted by Rosso Fiorentino and etched by Antonio Fantuzzi (no. 11).

In the 16th century, birds were frequently associated with a particular virtue or a vice; the peacock features as a tyrant who cares little for the affection of his subjects (no. 15), unlike the cockerel, who symbolizes good government.

In certain cases, an entire scene lends the animal symbol its expressive power: the engraving by Peter Van der Heyden after Pieter Bruegel the Elder depicting a large fish, full of smaller fish, which has collapsed on the riverbank, is an original way of illustrating an old adage concerning the relationships between the weak and the strong (no. 12).

The conflicts between France and Spain that arose in the first half of the 17th century generated an abundance of prints deriding the Spanish side. In one satirical engraving, the taking of Arras, a Spanish stronghold, by the French in 1640 is represented with the image of a cat attacked by rats, an allusion to a local proverb. Later, in the 19th century, animals continued to offer their iconographic potential to artists who sought to condemn certain aspects of the social order. In this way, the etcher Félix Bracquemond adopted the image of the bird as a way of caricaturing human society. For instance, playing on the two meanings of the word 'canard', which in French refers to a duck and is also a slang term for newspaper, he uses that bird to criticize popular papers that circulated misleading information (no. 77). In an allegorical lithograph dating from 1850, Charles Rambert takes the image of the spider, a skillful predator which ensnares its victims in a web and destroys them mercilessly, in order to denounce the cruelty of the unscrupulous moneylender who feeds on the destitute (no. 76). V.S.-H.

MAN'S BEST FRIENDS

Dogs and cats occupy a special place in the domain of prints, just as they do in our lives; unlike other animals, therefore, they are essentially represented in terms of their connections with their owners, in a human context. They are shown in this way in images, as friends and members of the household, sometimes on an equal footing with the human being also depicted (no. 18). They likewise appear as beloved pets in individual portraits, where they are treated as human subjects (no. 83).

In more light-hearted images, they take the leading role: already, in the 17th century, a popular way of presenting the animals seen on a daily basis involved placing them in droll and whimsical situations. In this way, an image aimed at the general public shows a 'singing-master' who has established a full orchestra composed of cats (no. 22), with mandolin and viola players, and singers capable of reading a music score composed of 'miaows!' Likewise, in a singularly capricious gesture, a legendary sovereign once appointed his canine companion Viceroy of the land he had invaded, thus humiliating its inhabitants (no. 17) and creating an amusing yet unnerving story.

People were so fond of observing the activities of their four-legged friends (no. 80) that a society without dogs and cats was inconceivable, even in works intended to convey exoticism. They were therefore systematically included in 17th century bestiaries: although the Indian dog has a distinctive appearance, striking on account of his size and his morphological characteristics, he represents a definite canine presence (no. 20).

These images are integrated and given meaning through culture. Cats are used to symbolize lust, or quite simply as a euphemistic representation of the female sex (no. 2). Dogs are likewise endowed with strong symbolic significance, following an age-old tradition that presents them not only as helping their masters at work, but also as the embodiment of loyalty (no. 18). This is expressed in the verses accompanying a popular print (no. 16): 'And while his master sleeps / The trusty household dog keeps watch'. R.M.

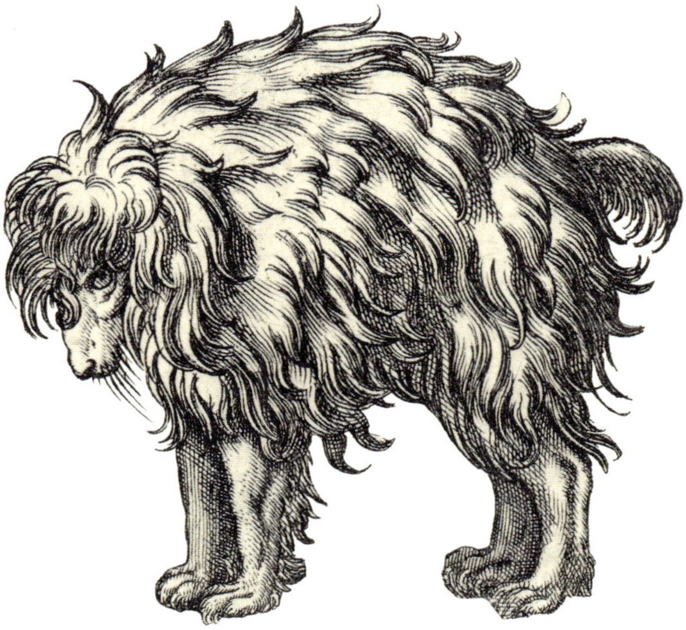

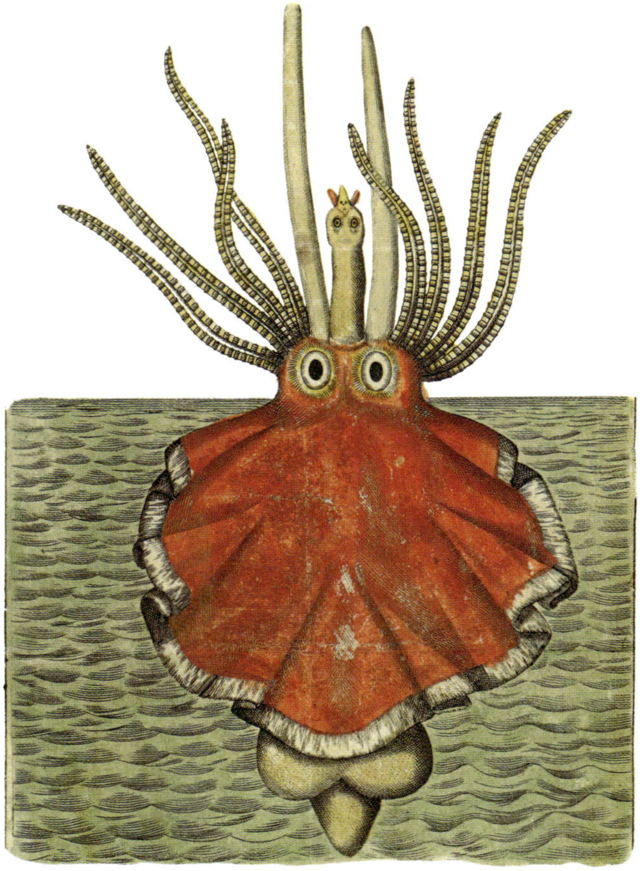

MONSTERS AND CHIMERAS

The figure of the monster acquires all its meaning through its contrast to ordinary animals. In the Renaissance, monsters were thought to reflect a state of disorder in the world, and were seen as a sign of God's anger; extraordinary occurrences were viewed with fascination and registered exclusively in terms of human events. Following the birth of a pig with an additional body and eight legs, the population was urged to redouble its religious fervour, this 'freak of nature' being seen as having certain connections with the Turkish Peril and the arrival of the Antichrist (no. 4). The same mindset prevailed a century and a half later, with the appearance of a beached sperm whale on the Dutch coast; the event was strongly associated with the war of independence conducted by the Protestants against their Spanish Catholic masters, and with the eclipse that occurred at the same time.

Although strange phenomena still attracted interest, as the centuries passed monsters were increasingly seen as unusual news items and treated as such in broadsheets (no. 31). In certain cases, curiosity even led to an approach akin to zoological investigation, the aim being to produce a precise description of unexplained phenomena and to enlighten the general public, always eager to hear of unfamiliar occurrences (no. 32).

This approach developed over the years, public interest and general context being equally relevant factors. The writings of the Ancients were still called upon in the mid-18th century, during the grisly and mysterious events relating to the *Beast of Gévaudan* (no. 45), on account of the cursory information they imparted regarding the hyena; this was thought to be the animal in question. In this way, the legend of the 'beast' was fuelled, while certain intellectuals railed against such 'childish nonsense', which, beneath its anodyne exterior, ran counter to the scientific perspective.

Later, when scientific studies began to encompass the whole living world, and fear of the unknown gave way to a reassuring system of classification, entirely new monsters were conceived by artists, who combined knowledge of the works of Antiquity with an inventive ability that was already Preromantic in character (no. 43). Sometimes, indeed, science itself satisfied this penchant for novelty with its discoveries of microscopic creatures (no. 72) and the first living beings (no. 73). R.M.

AN ORNAMENTAL BESTIARY

Animals, in natural or symbolic form, are part of European culture. In this way, they are everywhere to be seen, enriching art with their presence. Throughout the centuries, they have featured as an extremely popular decorative element, in distant civilizations as well as our own (no. 79). Animals may be seen on objects with which we are all familiar, from the commonplace (no. 13) to the most exclusive and prestigious (no. 34).

Under the Ancien Régime, every available surface testified to this ubiquitous animal presence. During the Renaissance, for example, very large prints served as decorative wallpaper; the animal motifs chosen corresponded to the moral and political discourse associated with each species (no. 15). Their aesthetic quality was also noted, however, as demonstrated by this exotic parrot selected two centuries later (no. 53).

Artists and artisans also obtained their models from the prints that were published expressly for that purpose (no. 33). It was an easy matter for a carpenter, a goldsmith or an engraver to glean ideas from these, adapting them to their own work, even if certain models originated from purely imaginative speculation and were the results of research and experimentation rather than the desire to see their projects carried out (no. 14).

The stylized approach became more pronounced over time, with Art Nouveau artists finding rich material in a variety of animal motifs, in particular the very elegant peacocks (no. 85). R.M.

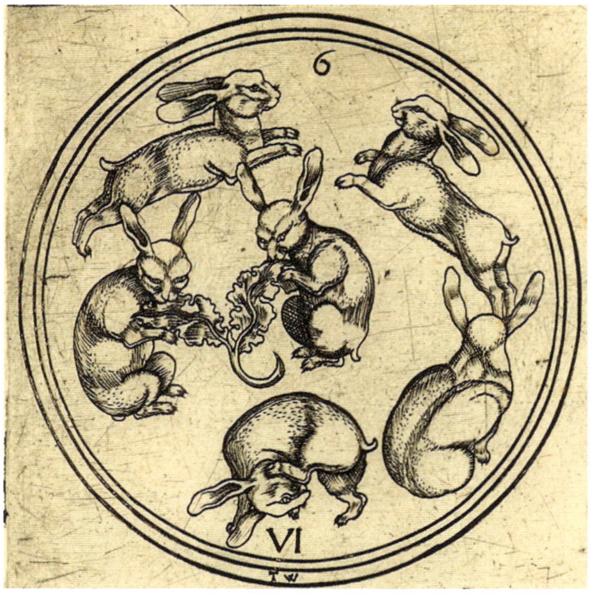

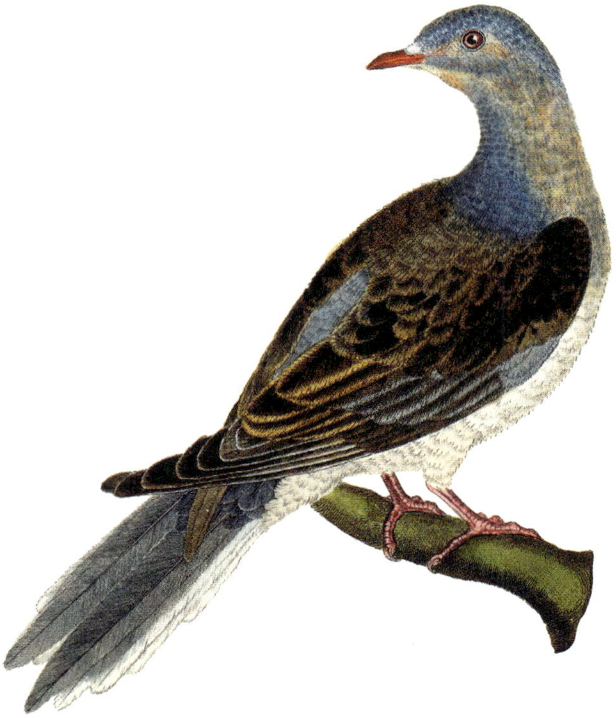

HUNTING SCENES

Man's fascination with animals did not only result from observations made at a distance, but also from encounters that took place at a much deeper level. This becomes clear from the fact that, long after it ceased to be a vital occupation for man's survival, hunting remained extremely important from a cultural standpoint, as reflected in a wealth of images. When Albrecht Dürer created his engraving of Saint Eustace (no. 7), the beauty of the saint and the stag, surrounded by the pack of hounds and set in a forest landscape, clearly prevailed over the religious symbolism. The interest accorded to the hunt was based on the strength and prestige of the animal hunted, and therefore on the risks undertaken. In this way, the bear, regarded as the king of beasts in traditional European societies, is a choice example of prey (no. 10), as are big cats and other powerfully built exotic species. The Prince of Nassau won huge renown for killing a jaguar (no. 58), while Rubens depicted a scene of direct combat between a crocodile and a hippopotamus in an image displaying the beauty of the baroque (no. 35). It has long been a tradition to decorate castles and country estates with hunting trophies and other slain beasts; in Jean Arp's stylized image of a stag, however, only the head and the antlers remain (no. 92). R.M.

NATURAL HISTORY

During the 17th century, traditional bestiaries – which originated directly from medieval science – gave way to new knowledge, as representations were more likely to result from first-hand, individual observation (no. 30). In France, this tendency was supported by the monarchy itself. The Académie des Sciences was founded in 1666, while the ménagerie at the Palace of Versailles was already receiving exotic animals (no. 38). These were used for dissections, the results of which were published by the royal printers and intended for academics and the curious public (no. 37).

With the Age of Enlightenment came the endeavour to produce an inventory of all living creatures, with a classification system reinforced by an increasingly methodical and accurate series of images, such as those that accompanied the works of Buffon, one of the leading naturalists of the day (no. 42). Interest was not confined to the more spectacular animals, and all living beings were included (no. 41). This even involved the adoption of new and costly techniques, such as the pastel manner used for colour printing, which reproduced all the fine hues of a butterfly's wing (no. 39). The penchant for depicting the extraordinary, the exotic and the unfamiliar did not disappear entirely, however (no. 40). This trend, which responded to the demands of science for precise observation, culminated in genuine artistic masterpieces, which made their mark on the history of printmaking and zoology alike. John James Audubon's *Birds of America* (no. 63), one of the most famous ornithology books in the world, commands extremely high prices at auctions on account of its beauty. It is equally precious as the publication that produced the first images of many species in their natural environment, all executed with meticulous care. R.M.

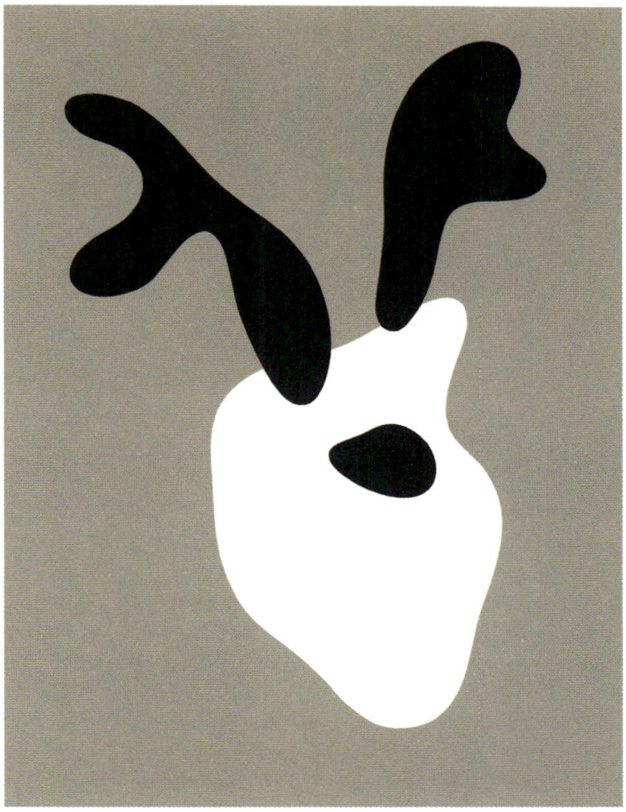

1 The Master of the Playing Cards, *Cards with Bear and Lion Suit Symbols*, Upper Rhine Valley, 1435–1445

These playing cards, which were printed from copper plates, are the first examples of engraving on metal to appear in Europe. They are the work of an anonymous artist based in the Upper Rhine Valley, who was familiar with the works of Konrad Witz and the paintings of the Rhineland.

The cards created by the Master, with their images of bears, lions, birds, stags and deer, were intended for aristocratic clients, who liked to see another of their favorite pastimes – the hunt – depicted on their playing cards. However, although the bears evoke a type of hunting practised during the Middle Ages (as documented by Gaston Phébus), the lions reflect a remote, imaginary realm. These types of figures were developed in a number of very richly ornamented decks of cards dating from this period, perhaps created on the orders of kings or princes. The pack known as the 'Stuttgart' playing cards was hand-painted in Southern Germany, possibly in Swabia, in about 1430. It depicts ducks, falcons, dogs and harts painted in gouache on a gold background. Our more modest engraved pieces certainly served as more than playing cards; they were also used as models, as the various animals shown there may also be found, reproduced with extreme exactitude, in manuscripts produced throughout Europe during the latter half of the 15th century. S.L.

Burin engraving | 14 x 9.5 cm (each card)

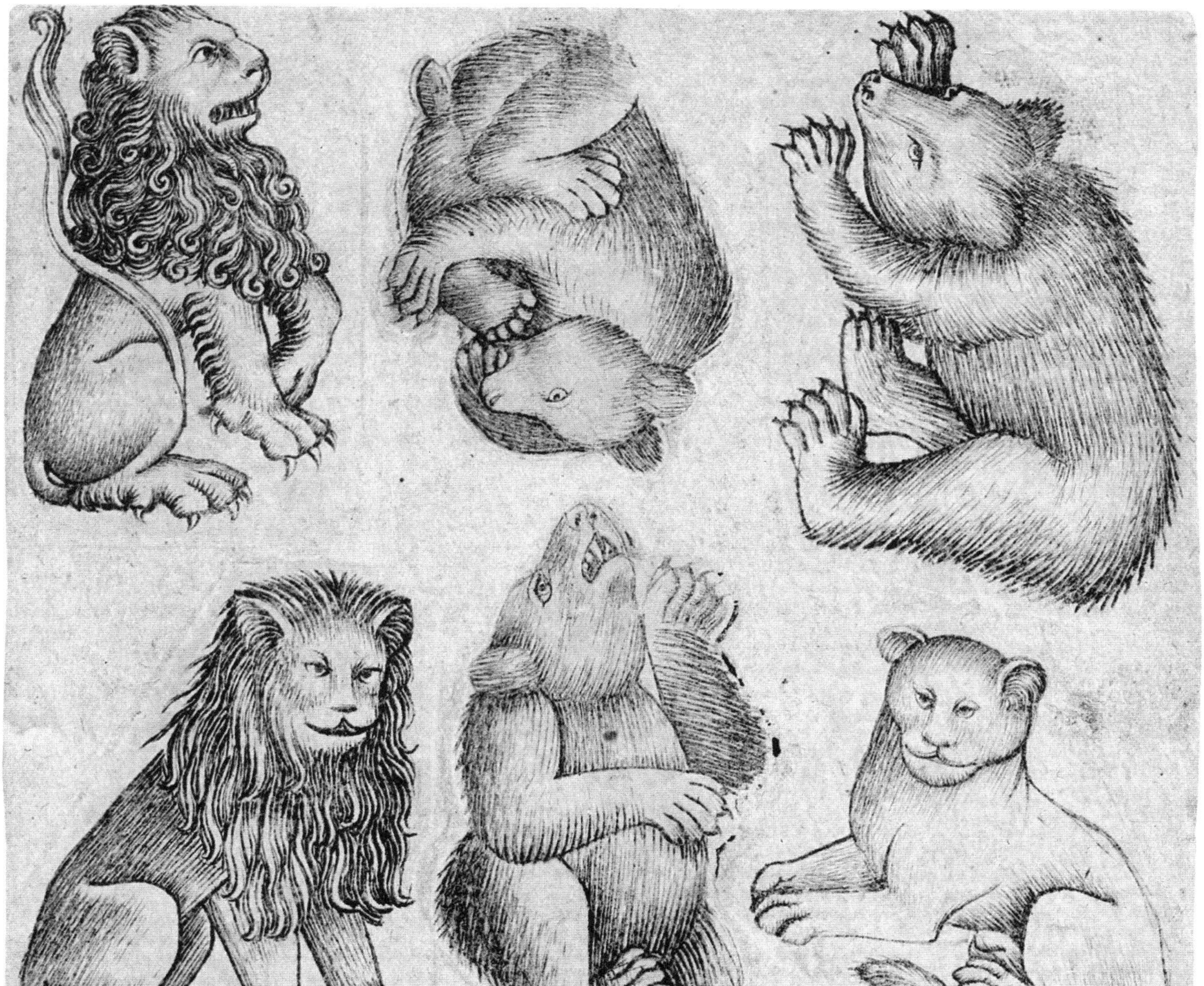

1

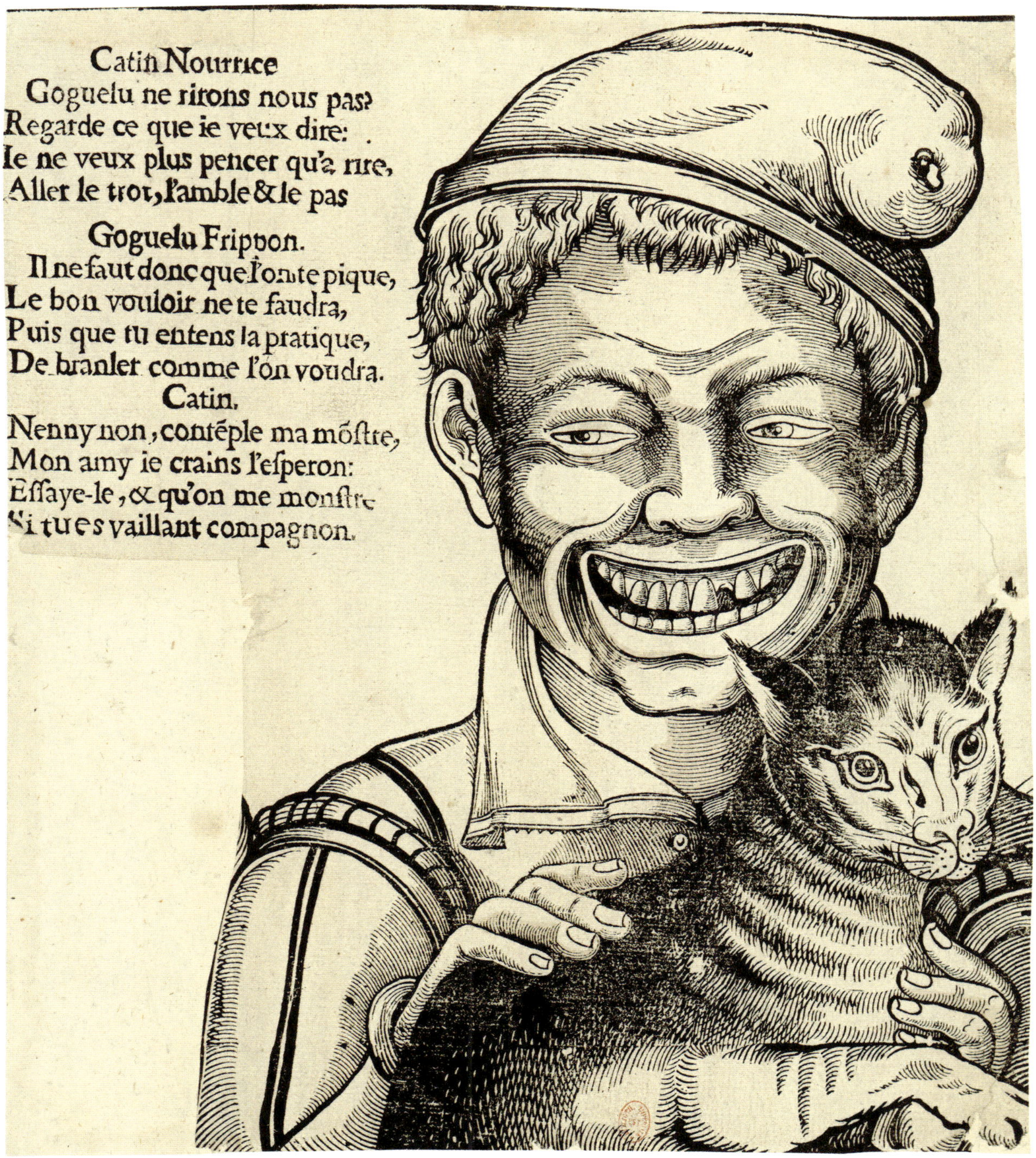

2

2 Anonymous, *Gogelu and His Cat*, latter half of the 16th century

This print is typical of the 16th century 'drolleries', which referred to characters from popular literature or farce. We are no longer familiar with the exact significance of the story of Gogelu (a word meaning cheerful or merry in 16th century French), and of the unseen 'Catin Nourrice' (a wet-nurse and bawd) with whom he is conducting a conversation seen in the accompanying text.

Gogelu is shown grinning from ear to ear, which probably indicates his dissolute life, as is corroborated by the description '*fripon*' (rascal) seen in the text. He is holding a cat, certainly intended as a symbol of lust, and his headgear, a type of jester's cap, has a phallic appearance. His interlocutor is eager to dance and laugh, but fears the 'spur', a further sexual reference in this exchange based on laughter and innuendo. The 'Catin Nourrice' character has been thought to refer to a young woman of loose morals mentioned by Ronsard in his *Livret de Folastries*, where she is described as 'so naïve in her simplicity' that she will happily oblige rich and poor alike for no recompense, provided they are well-endowed. A print of this nature should be viewed in the light of similar types of literary works. S.L.

Woodcut | 35 x 32.4 cm (boundary line)

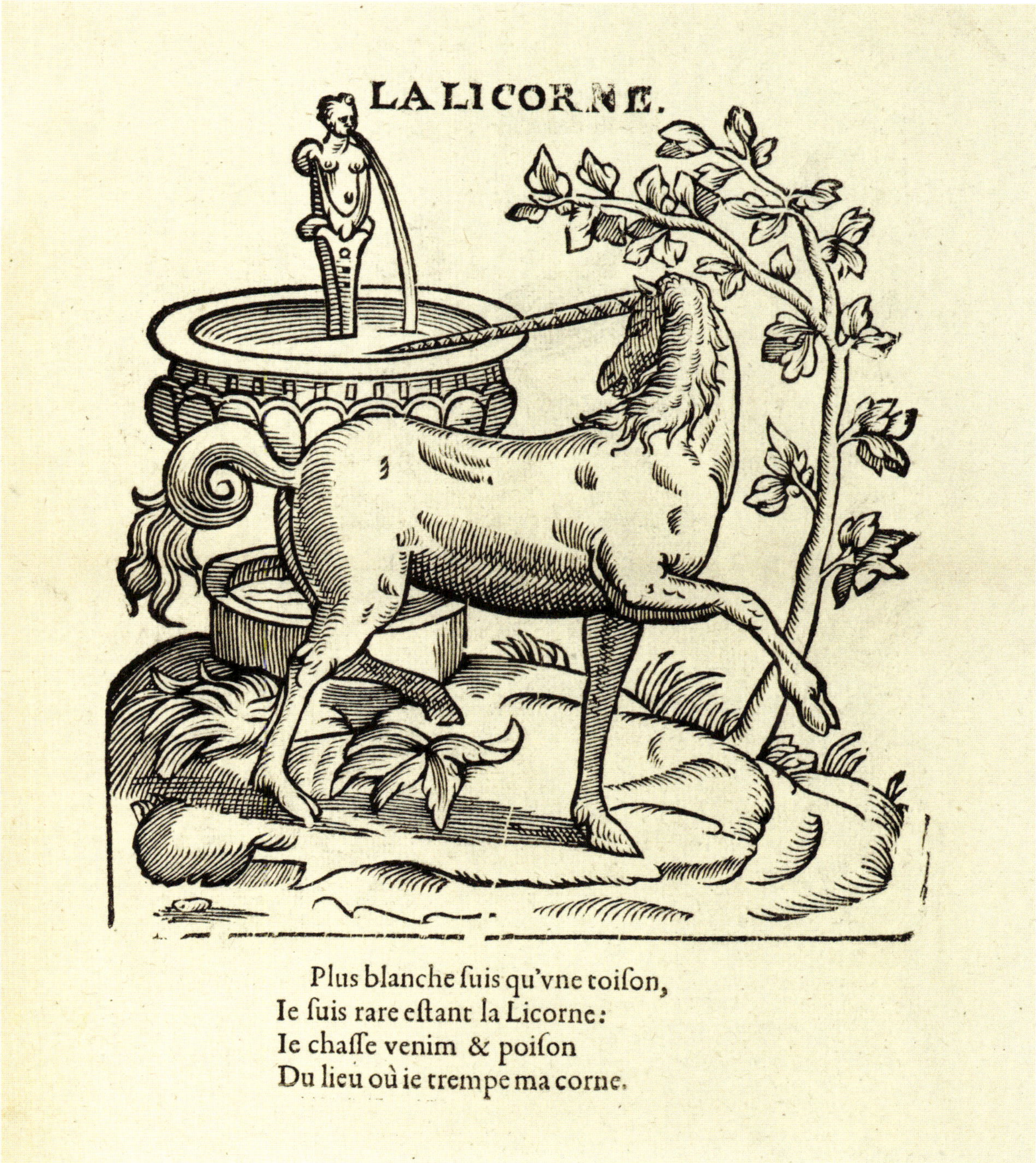

3

3 Anonymous, *Unicorn Purifying a Fountain*, ca. 1580

The twelve images of animals published by Philippe Pelletier, a print-seller established at the rue Saint-Jean-de-Latran in Paris in the late 16th century, form a curious series. Besides 'ordinary' domesticated animals, or those associated with hunting, such as the horse, the dog and the rabbit, they include illustrations of more exotic species – the rhinoceros, the elephant, the female and male monkey – and even purely mythical creatures.

This unicorn is a case in point. It is shown dipping its horn into a fountain, illustrating a medieval legend according to which it was able to purify unclean water in this way. 'Unicorn's horn' (which actually came from a rhinoceros or narwhal) was sold at a very high price as protection against poison or as decoration for purifying objects such as goblets or rings. This apotropaic practice, together with accounts of travels mentioning the existence of unicorns and their depiction with other creatures in a series of popular 16th century woodcuts, all testify to the fact that they were considered to be real, exotic animals until the 19th century. S.L.

From a series of 12 animal prints, Paris, Philippe Pelletier, ca. 1580 | Woodcut | 19.5 x 14.5 cm (boundary line)

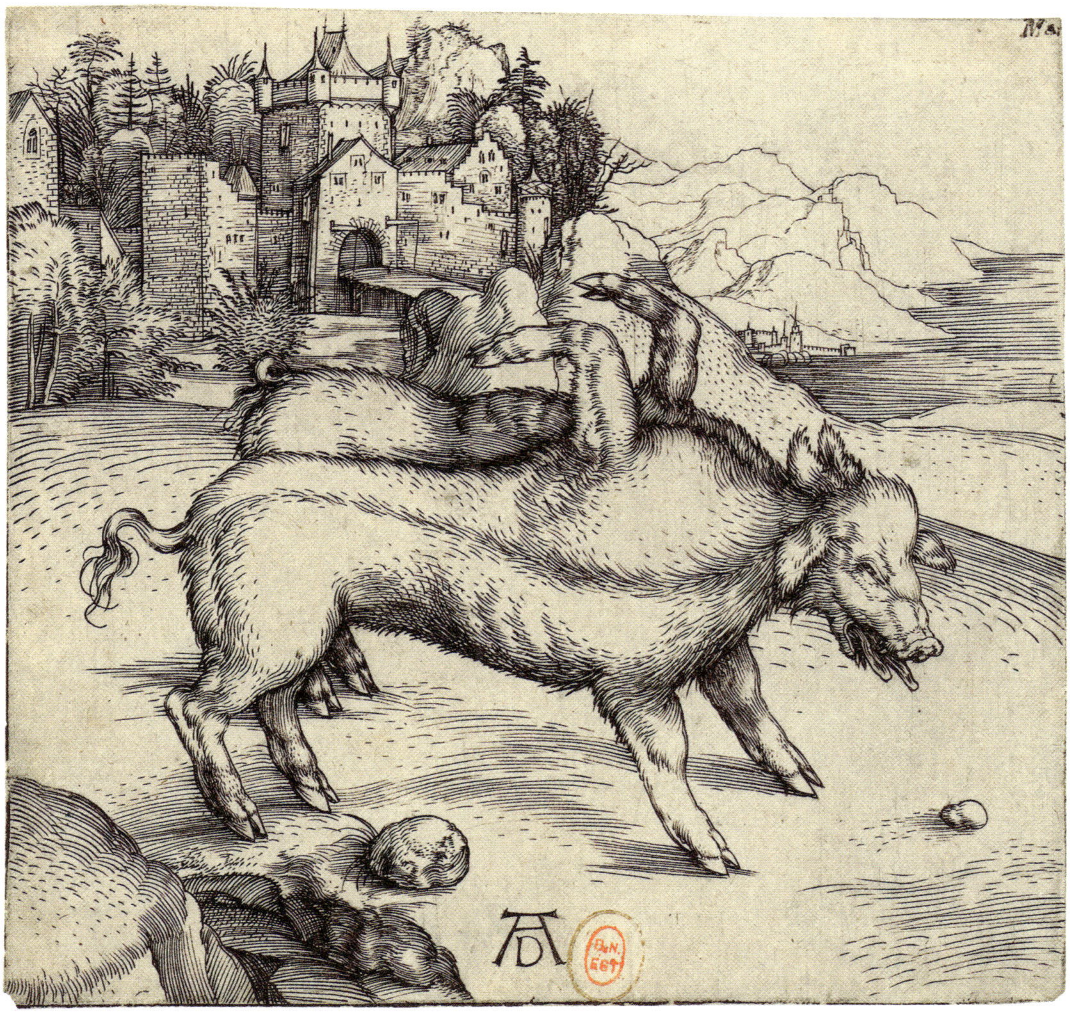

4

4 Albrecht Dürer, *The Monstrous Pig of Landser,* 1496

In 1496, an illustrated broadside bearing a text by Sebastian Brant, a famous humanist from Strasbourg, described the birth of a deformed pig with two torsos, eight legs, four ears and two tongues, which had occurred on 1 March in the village of Landser. These large sheets with woodcuts announcing the arrival of catastrophic events (such as meteorites, epidemics and the birth of conjoined twins) were used in Europe, with marked success, by the Church authorities and the professional writers of the day, who presented them as examples of divine retribution in order to compel the population to repent. According to Brant, the birth of the monstrous pig at Landser was an evil omen, indicative of the threat posed by Turkey to the Holy Roman Empire and of the arrival of the Antichrist. However, the author added that the animal's rapid demise was a sign of great hope for the reign of the new Emperor, Maximilian I. Dürer certainly used the broadside as inspiration for his small, succinct woodcut, while completely reinterpreting the animal's anatomy in order to heighten the effect of realism. In this way, he represented a porcine example of cephalothoracopagus, a condition known to the medical world of the day and defined as characterizing two individual twins with one head and conjoined torsos, while other body parts remained separate. Dürer's engraving would appear to reflect the artist's interest in these types of popular tales of monsters and unusual occurrences, but also his taste for the exact representation of the natural world; this approach demands a more precise, and consequently more rational observation of these cases of deformation.

S. L.

Burin engraving | 12 x 12.7 cm (boundary line)

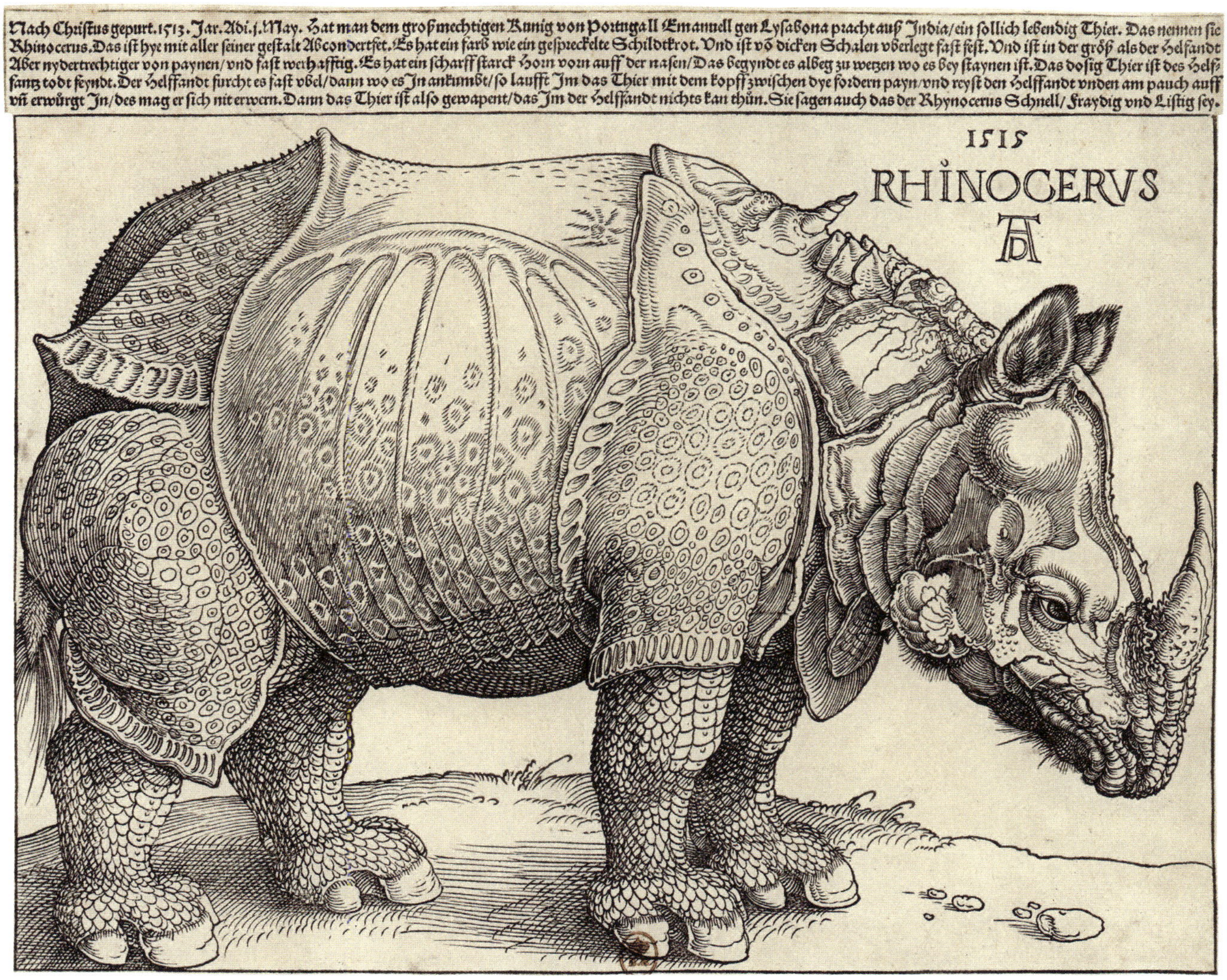

5

5 Albrecht Dürer, *The Rhinoceros*, 1515

On 20 May 1515 a rhinoceros disembarked in Lisbon, having travelled there in a Portuguese ship as a diplomatic gift from the Sultan of Cambay, Muzaffar II, to King Manuel I of Portugal. The species had not been seen in Europe since the days of Antiquity, and the rhinoceros caused a sensation. His subsequent tragic end endowed the animal with a heroic character; chained in the hold of the ship that was taking him as a present to Pope Leo II, he drowned in a shipwreck.

The news spread as far as Germany, perhaps due to Valentin Ferdinand, a printer established in Lisbon. Not having seen the rhinoceros, Dürer drew much of his inspiration from this account in order to create his composition, which he first drew, then printed. He accompanied the print with a letterpress text summarizing the known facts relating to the animal. Although largely unrealistic, Dürer's rhinoceros has a very powerful presence; a skillful and complex use of hatching gives his body a scaly yet solid quality. There are at least nine different editions of this woodcut. In the first quarter of the 17th century, the block came into the possession of Willem Janssen, a publisher in Amsterdam. He decided to re-issue it, adding a new tone block printed in different colours, thereby giving greater emphasis to the animal's power. The work was still used in zoological publications in the mid-18th century. S.L.

Woodcut | 21.2 x 30 cm (boundary line)

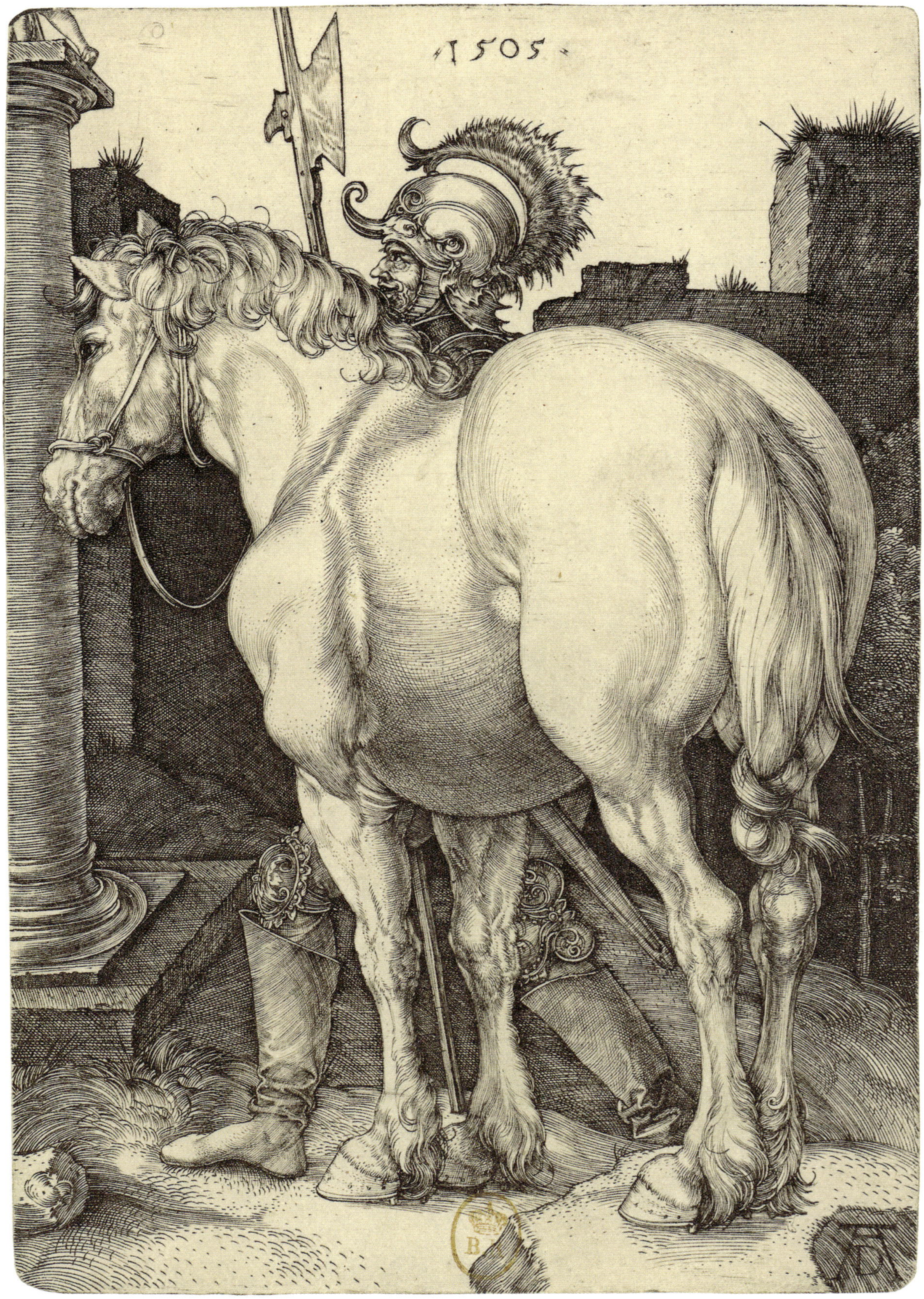

6

6 Albrecht Dürer, *The Large Horse* 1505

→ description on p. 32

7 Albrecht Dürer, *Saint Eustace*, ca. 1501

→ description on p. 32

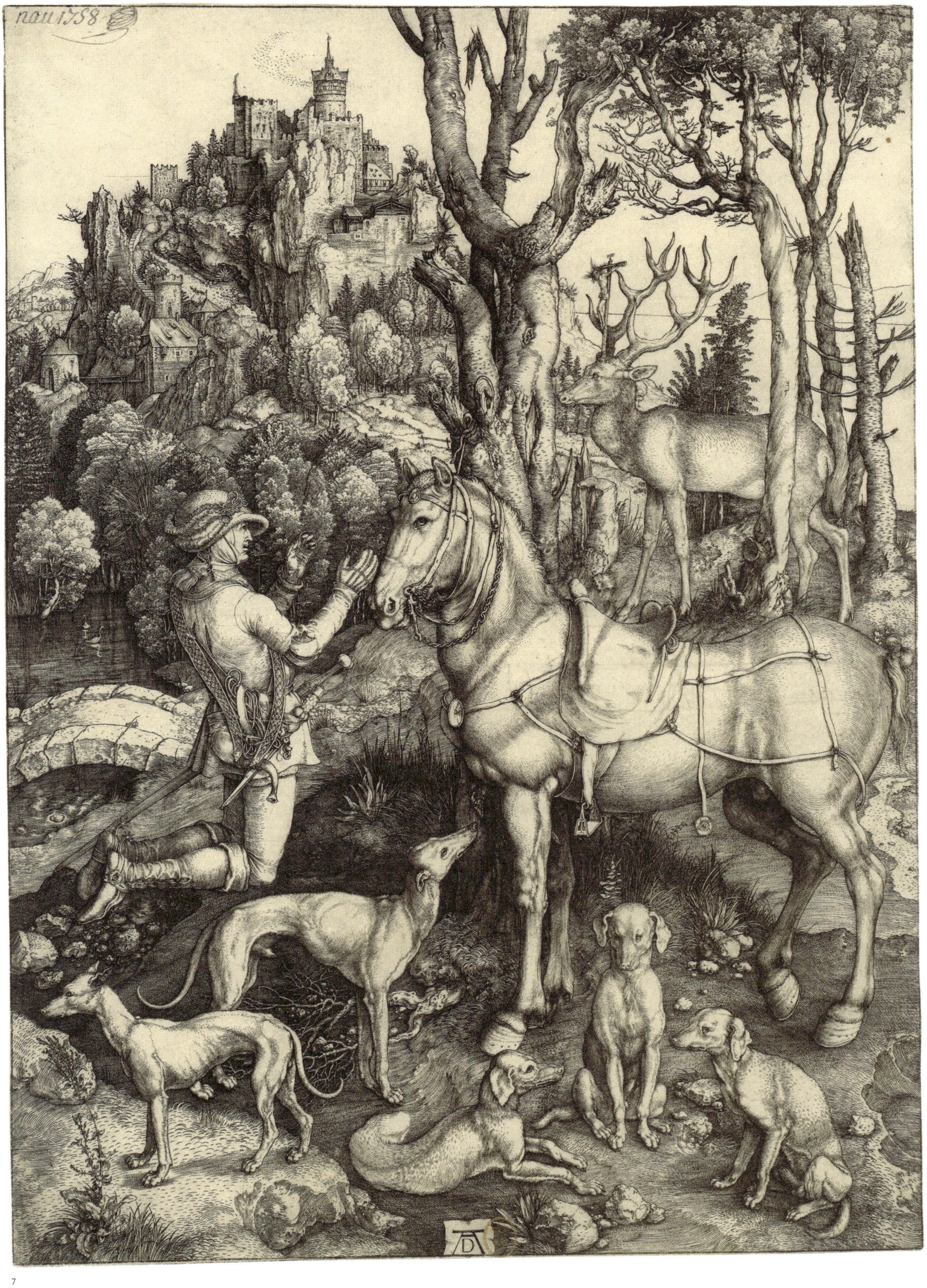

7

6 Albrecht Dürer, *The Large Horse*, 1505

→ Image on p. 30

Horses are a recurrent theme in Dürer's images. *The Large Horse*, which is the companion piece to *The Small Horse*, engraved in the same year, is a perfect example of this. Dürer chose a very specific angle, a three-quarter profile, the animal's rump being turned towards the spectator and slightly raised. He accentuated its musculature with a series of curved incisions, which he cross-hatched to give an impression of greater volume, thereby demonstrating his extreme proficiency with the burin. The horse's powerful body exudes a disconcerting impression of strength, reinforced by the confined space of the composition. This is closed off by the animal, all but concealing its master, a halberdier dressed in the style of the time. The print has been interpreted in a variety of ways. According to an allegorical reading, always possible with Dürer's work, *The Large Horse* represents sensuality held in check by the intellect, which would be symbolized by the dolphin on the soldier's helmet. The presence of the column on the left-hand side, which might be serving as a support to a classical statue, has led some to identify the soldier as the hero Hercules, who has come to steal the mares of Diomedes. The print was highly successful, and was copied by Antonio da Brescia, Benedetto Montagne and Jan Wierix. It also influenced Caravaggio, who imitated the unusual position of the horse in *The Conversion on the Way to Damascus* (1601), which he painted for the church of Santa Maria del Popolo in Rome. S.L.

Burin engraving | 16.5 x 12 cm (boundary line)

7 Albrecht Dürer, *Saint Eustace*, ca. 1501

→ Image on p. 31

The Golden Legend is the principal narrative source pertaining to the Roman General Placidus's conversion to Christianity during the reign of the Emperor Trajan. As he was chasing a large stag while out hunting one day, Placidus was blinded by a piercing light, just as he thought he had caught the animal. An image of Christ on the cross then appeared between the stag's antlers and began to speak to him through its mouth: 'Eustace, why are you pursuing me? I am Jesus Christ [. . .] Your offerings have risen before me, and for this reason I have come, to hunt you through the stag that you yourself are hunting.' The general converted to Christianity and took the Greek first name of Eustace.

Although the print portrays the momentous event, with the divine apparition that instigated the conversion, the real emphasis is on the animals, who are the principal figures in the image. The horse and the five dogs occupy the foreground and centre of the composition, somewhat to the detriment of Placidus and the stag. As with the print *The Large Horse*, the drawing of the saint's mount required a great deal of effort in order to depict the animal's proportions in the best possible manner. The very large size of the sheet, which may well be one of Dürer's largest prints, and the rich detail in the burin work endow this portrayal of animals with an unprecedented air of grandeur. S.L.

Burin engraving | 35.6 x 26 cm (boundary line)

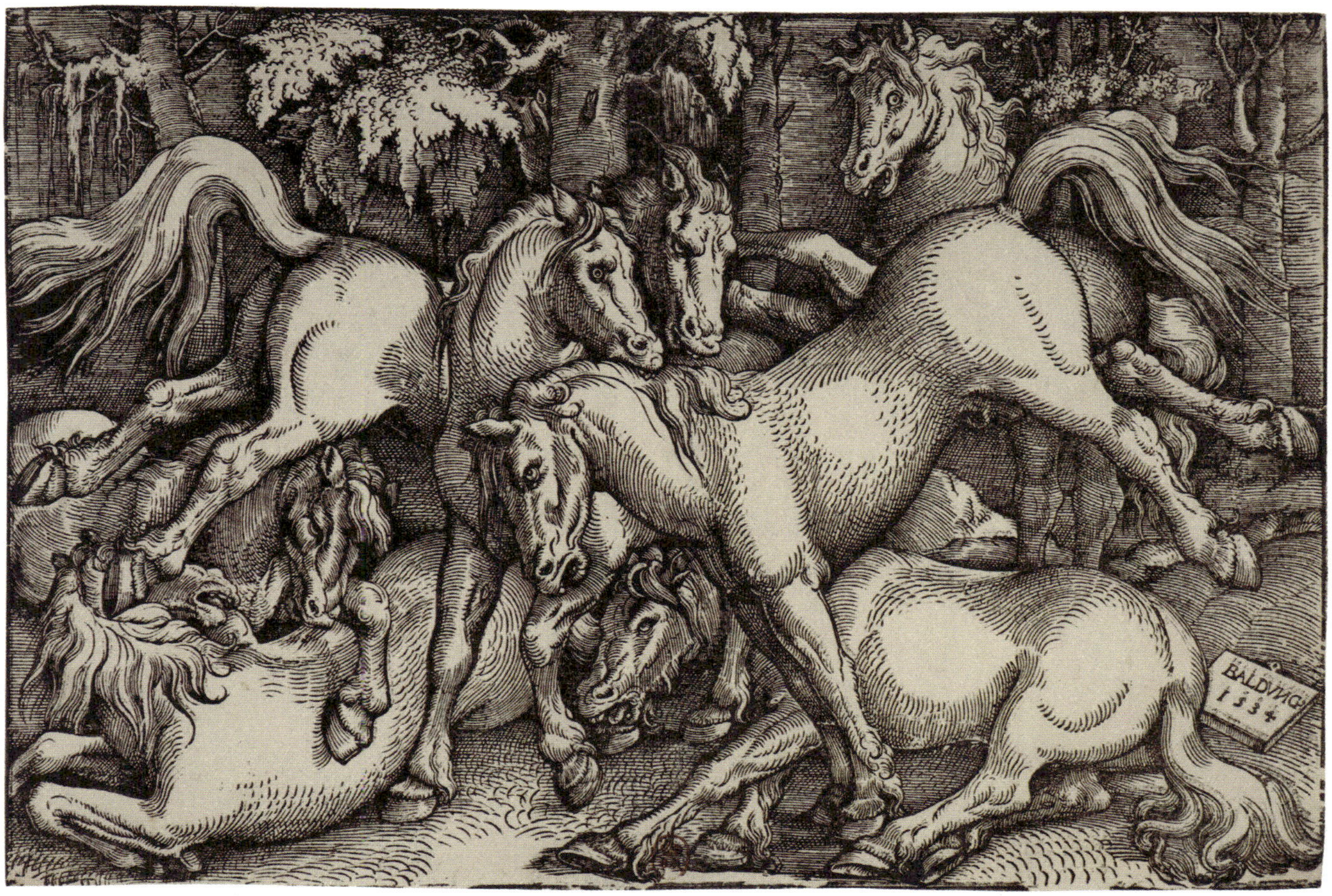

8

8 Hans Baldung Grien
Fighting Stallions, 1534

Hans Baldung was one of the leading artists of the Rhineland during the first half of the 16th century. By 1510 he had settled in Strasbourg, where he initially worked with the renowned Albrecht Dürer of Nuremberg, and appears to have managed the latter's studio while he was away on his second trip to Italy.

Unlike Dürer's *The Large Horse*, Baldung's image of stallions, a theme that inspired him with three woodcuts including this one, clearly expresses the violent, untamed sexuality of these fiery creatures. The horses, whose stormy countenances find their echo in Füssli's *The Nightmare*, are shown attacking one another with frenetic bucking movements, their eyes bulging. The artist has depicted them in a forest, a wild setting that was still seen during this period as a domain lying beyond that of man and the civilization he had created. S.L.

Woodcut | 22.50 x 33 cm (boundary line)

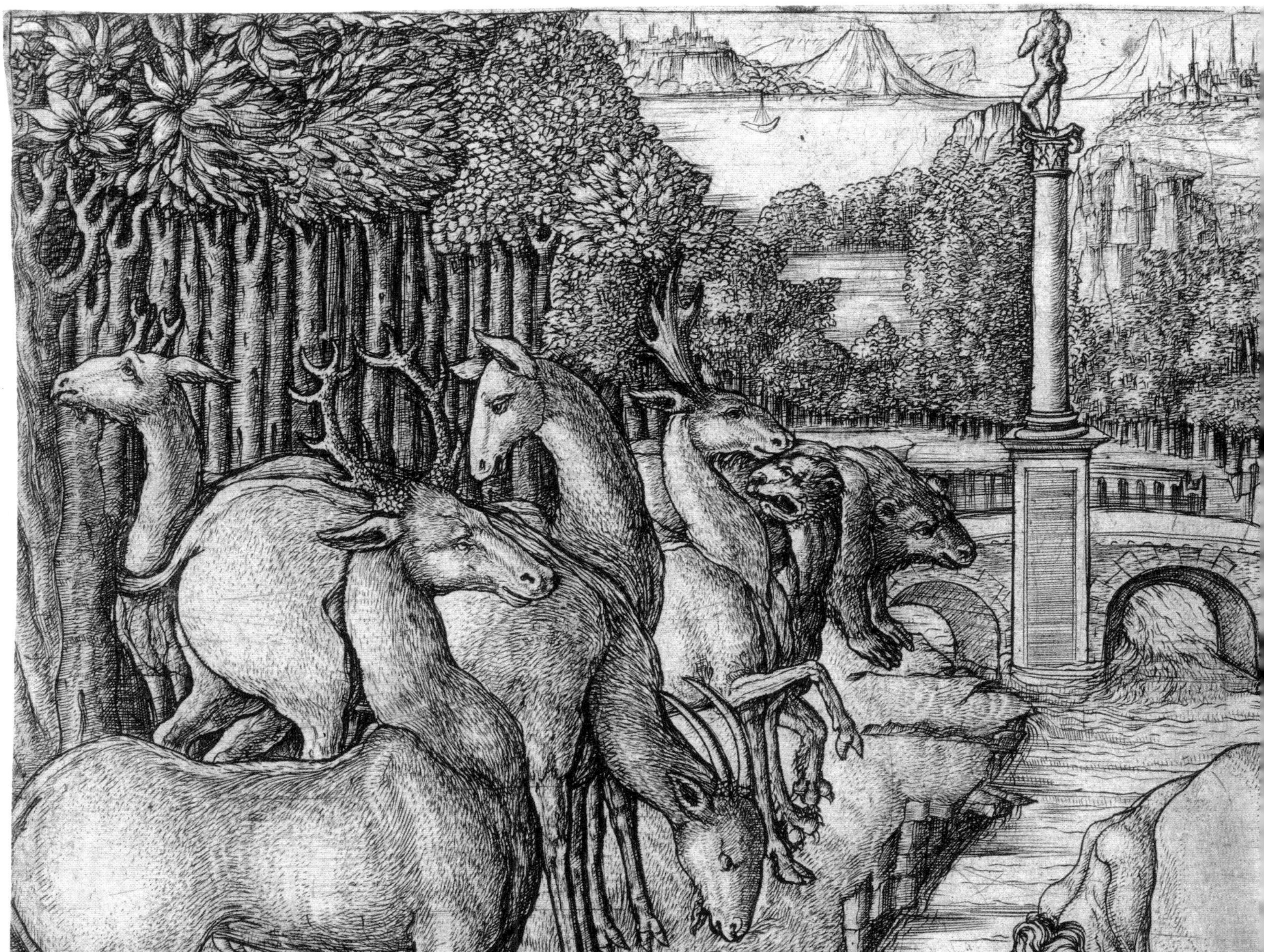

9

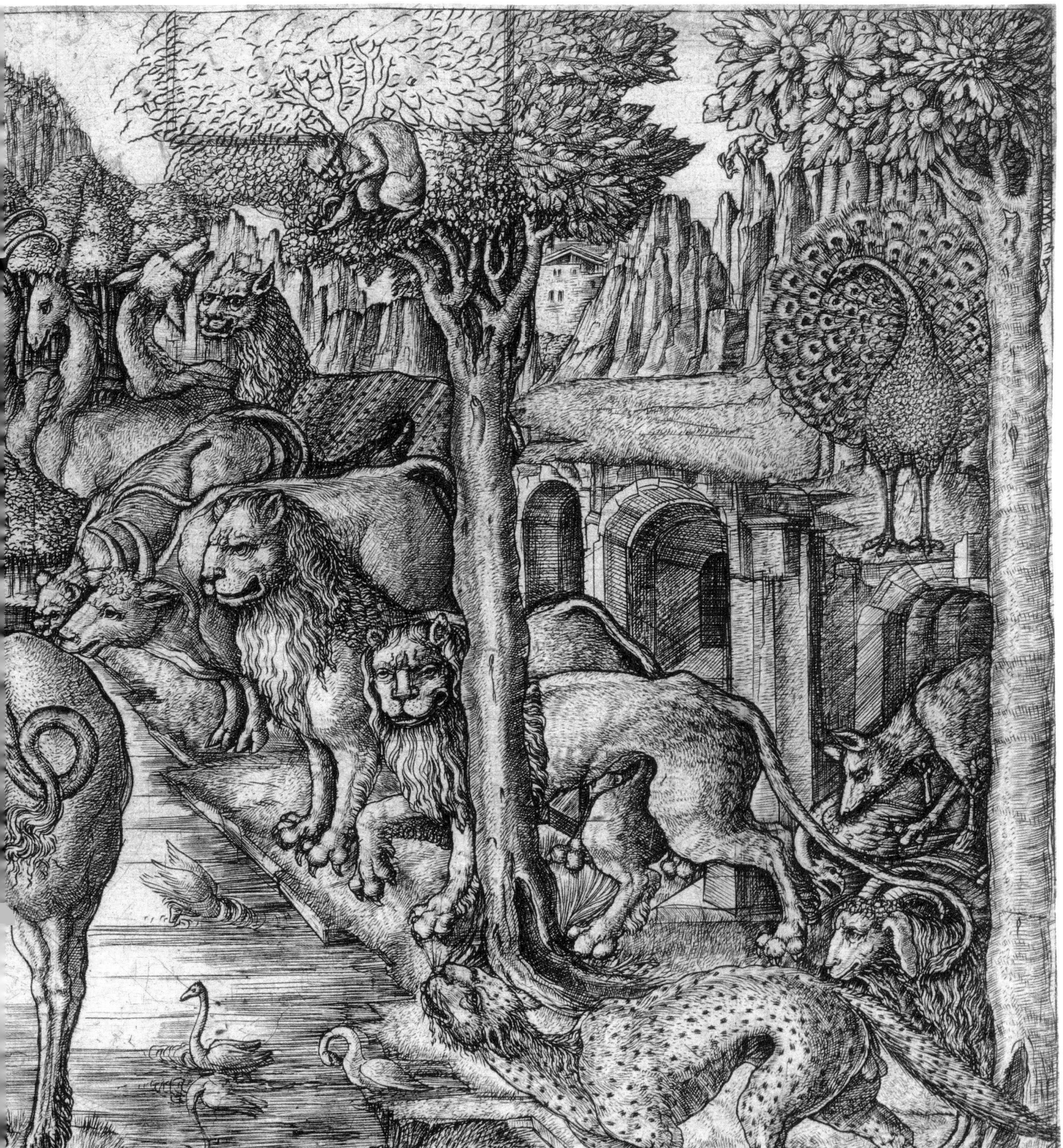

9 Jean Duvet, *The Unicorn Purifies the Water with its Horn*, ca. 1547–1550

→ description on p. 36

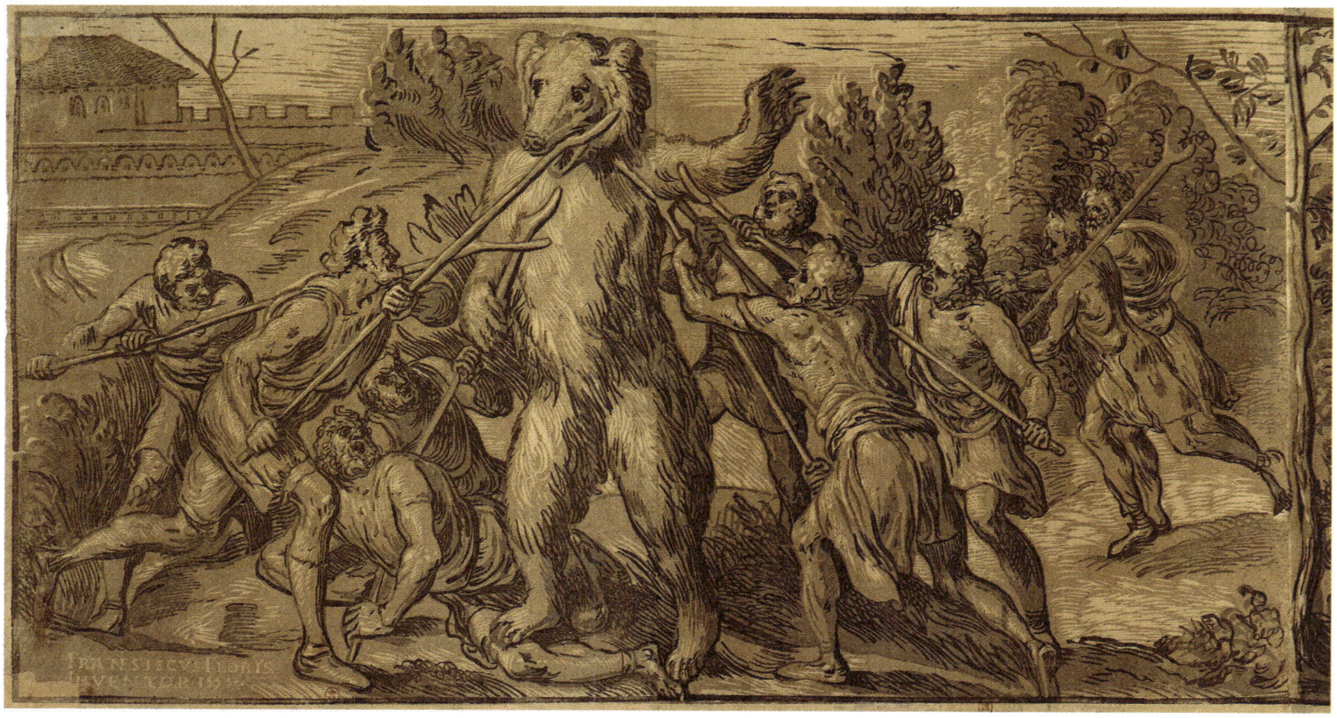

10

9 Jean Duvet, *The Unicorn Purifies the Water with its Horn*, ca. 1547–1550

→ Image on p. 34–35

This work belongs to a series of six prints devoted to the hunt of the unicorn, a very popular theme in the Middle Ages and depicted in miniatures, painted panels and wall hangings. Bestiaries dating from the 12th century onwards tended to generalize the portrayal of the unicorn as the incarnation of Christ. Its purity was so renowned that it could only be hunted down and killed if lured to the lap of a young maiden. It was also believed that the unicorn's horn was an effective remedy against poisons, as reflected by this scene taken from the *Physiologus* (an ancient Greek treatise popular in medieval times) showing thirsty animals waiting for the unicorn to purify the water, which has been poisoned by a serpent. In this case, too, the unicorn symbolizes Christ who, by His sacrifice, cleanses man's soul of sin.

Duvet's print is therefore established within the medieval tradition, yet the subsequent images in the series may be interpreted as a courtly allegory of the love between King Henri II and Diane de Poitiers. Indeed, certain authors have noted that the figures in the following print, *A King and Diana Receiving Hunters*, bear a physical resemblance to the King of France and his mistress. By introducing the figure of Diana, absent from medieval traditions associated with the unicorn, Duvet directs the series towards the world of the Renaissance, with its ubiquitous references to the gods and goddesses of Greek and Roman mythology. S.L.

Burin engraving | 22.6 x 39.5 (boundary line)

10 Joos Gietleughen after Frans Floris, *The Bear Hunt*, 1555

The genre of hunting scenes, depicted in prints dating from the early half of the 16th century, was much admired by the aristocrats of the day. Hunting was an important occupation for them, and symbolically portrayed their dominant status in the world. The vogue for Classical Antiquity led to a renewed interest in hunting scenes, a theme frequently portrayed in Roman mosaics. The two drawings depicting a bear and a bull hunt made by Frans Floris in 1555 were conceived as a Classical-style frieze; the artist was particularly inspired by one of the figures on the Arch of Constantine in Rome, as reflected by the pose of the hunter in the foreground on the left, whose leg is being broken by the bear.

It was Floris who introduced the coloured, or chiaroscuro, woodcut technique to the Low Countries. This invention originated in Germany and was developed in Italy; it involved the use of several woodcut matrices, each one having been coloured differently. These were then imprinted onto the sheet in succession. The works of this type that Floris entrusted to Joos Gietleughen, a Flemish publisher and engraver who specialized in the process, probably includes this large composition on paper that resembles a small tapestry, or even a fresco mural painting. S.L.

Coloured woodcut, 3 blocks | 43.1 x 262.5 cm (boundary line)

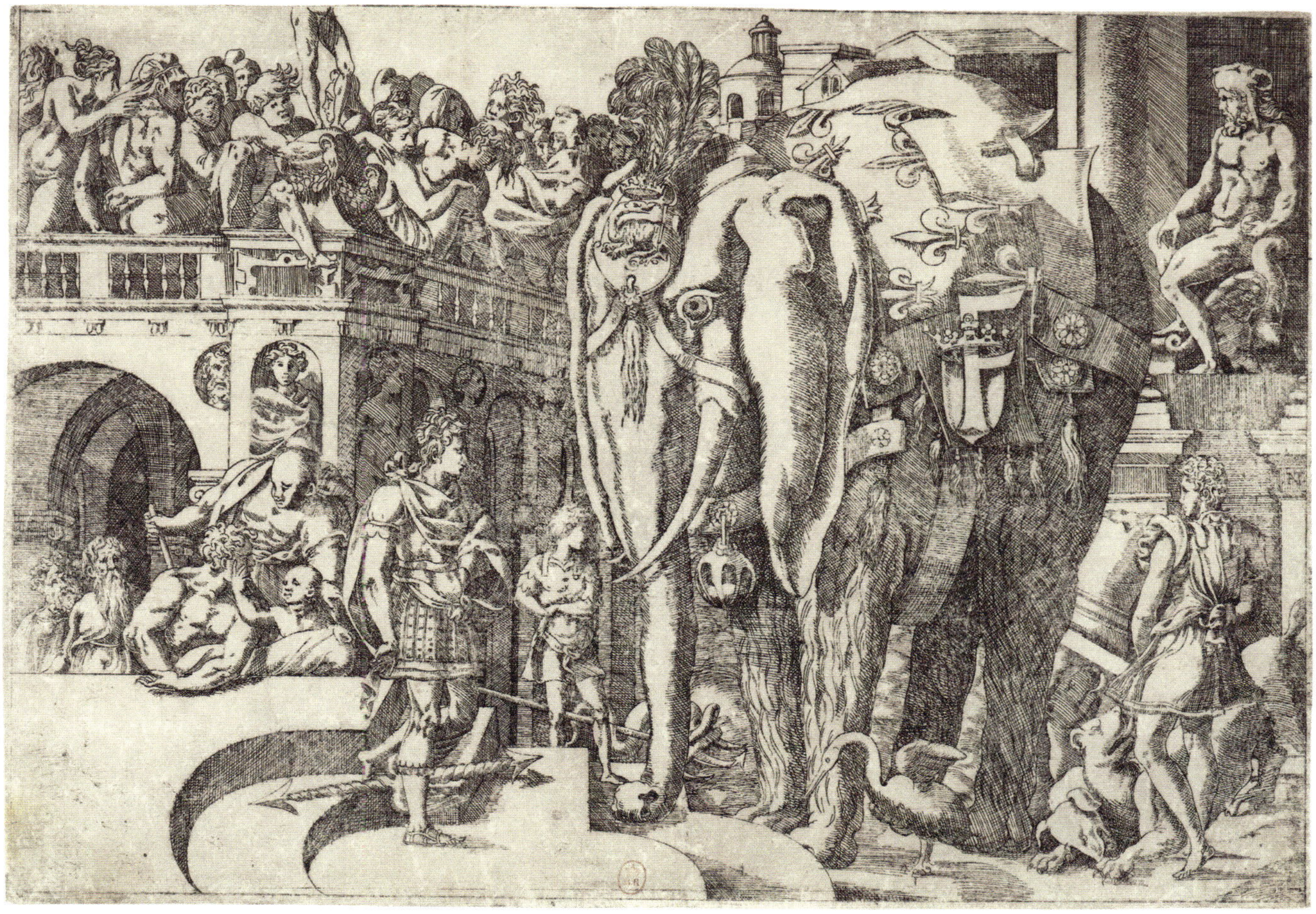

11

11 Antonio Fantuzzi, after Rosso Fiorentino,
The Elephant Adorned with Fleur-de-Lys,
ca. 1542–1543

This print is adapted from the fresco painted for François I by Rosso Fiorentino in the eponymous gallery in his château at Fontainebleau. The work as a whole displays complex iconography, but one of its functions was certainly to emphasize the power of the king. The elephant therefore represents sovereign majesty. Its headstall and caparison are adorned with the emblems of François I – the imposing letter *F*, the fleurs-de-lys and the salamander – while the animal itself dominates the whole composition, its impressive bulk overshadowing the Olympian gods and heroes. Among these we recognize Jupiter, who stands facing the animal with his thunderbolt in his hand; Neptune, depicted in the background with his trident; Pluto, accompanied by Cerberus; and finally Hercules, perched atop a pedestal. This last figure is particularly appropriate, given that the elephant traditionally symbolizes strength. All the gods of Antiquity, together with a motley crowd standing on the balcony, have been called upon to admire the majestic animal and to acknowledge, as should princes and commoners alike, the legitimate and natural character of King François I's power. S.L.

Etching | 29 x 43 cm (boundary line)

12 Pieter Van der Heyden after Pieter Bruegel the Elder *The Big Fish Eat the Little Fish*, 1557

The belly and mouth of a large dead fish are shown overflowing with small fish, while others, still alive in the water, are devouring yet smaller fish in their turn. The fishermen represent a type of culmination to this food chain. This is an original portrayal of an old proverb, reproduced in the text accompanying the engraving, which analyses the relationship between the weak and the powerful in the form of an ancient stoic maxim.

This print was no doubt widely circulated, as its publisher, Hieronymus Cock, head of a flourishing business in Antwerp, disseminated his engravings throughout Europe. It was probably for commercial reasons that Cock preferred to inscribe the name of Bosch on the print as its creator, although it was Pieter Bruegel whom he had commissioned to carry out the preparatory drawing, which has been preserved to this day. It may have been the case that a print would sell better if it bore the name of Bosch as 'inventor' rather than that of the Netherlandish master. At all events, the presence of the texts in both Latin and Dutch would suggest that the print was intended for both less highbrow and intellectual circles, as the humanists had a very marked interest in proverbs. S.L.

Grandibus exigui sunt pisces piscibus esca | Burin engraving | 23 x 29.5 cm (boundary line)

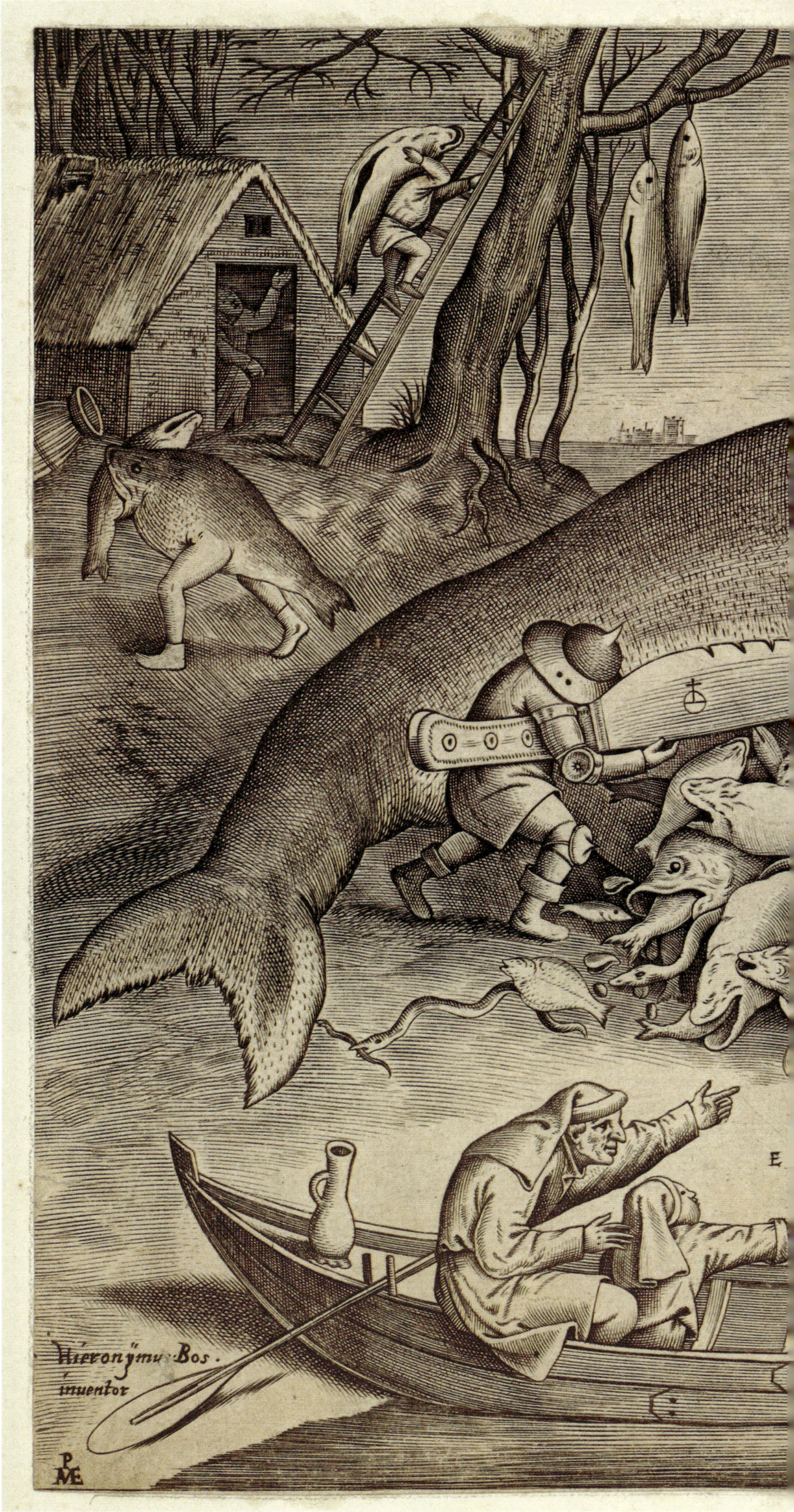

12

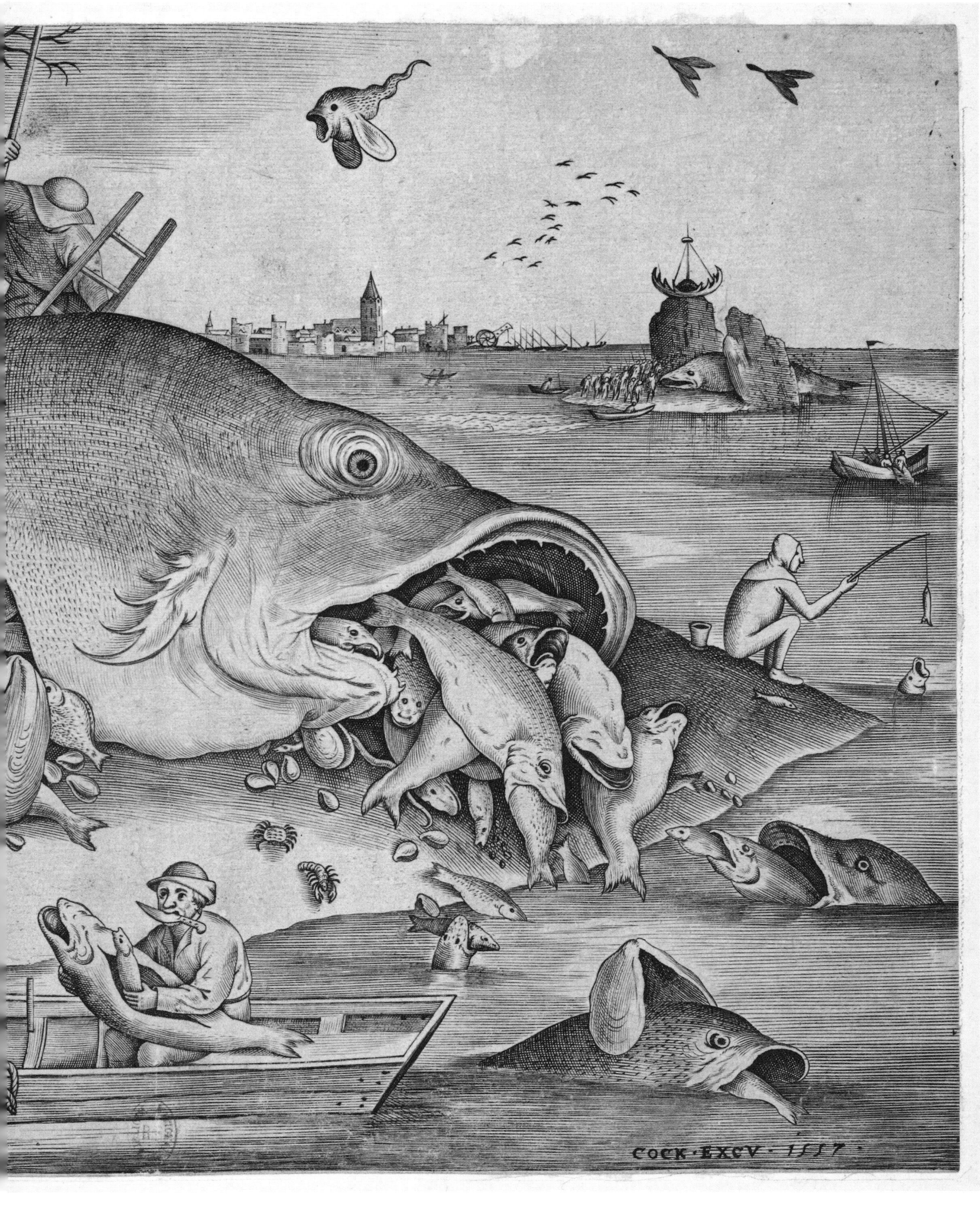
COCK·EXCV·1557·

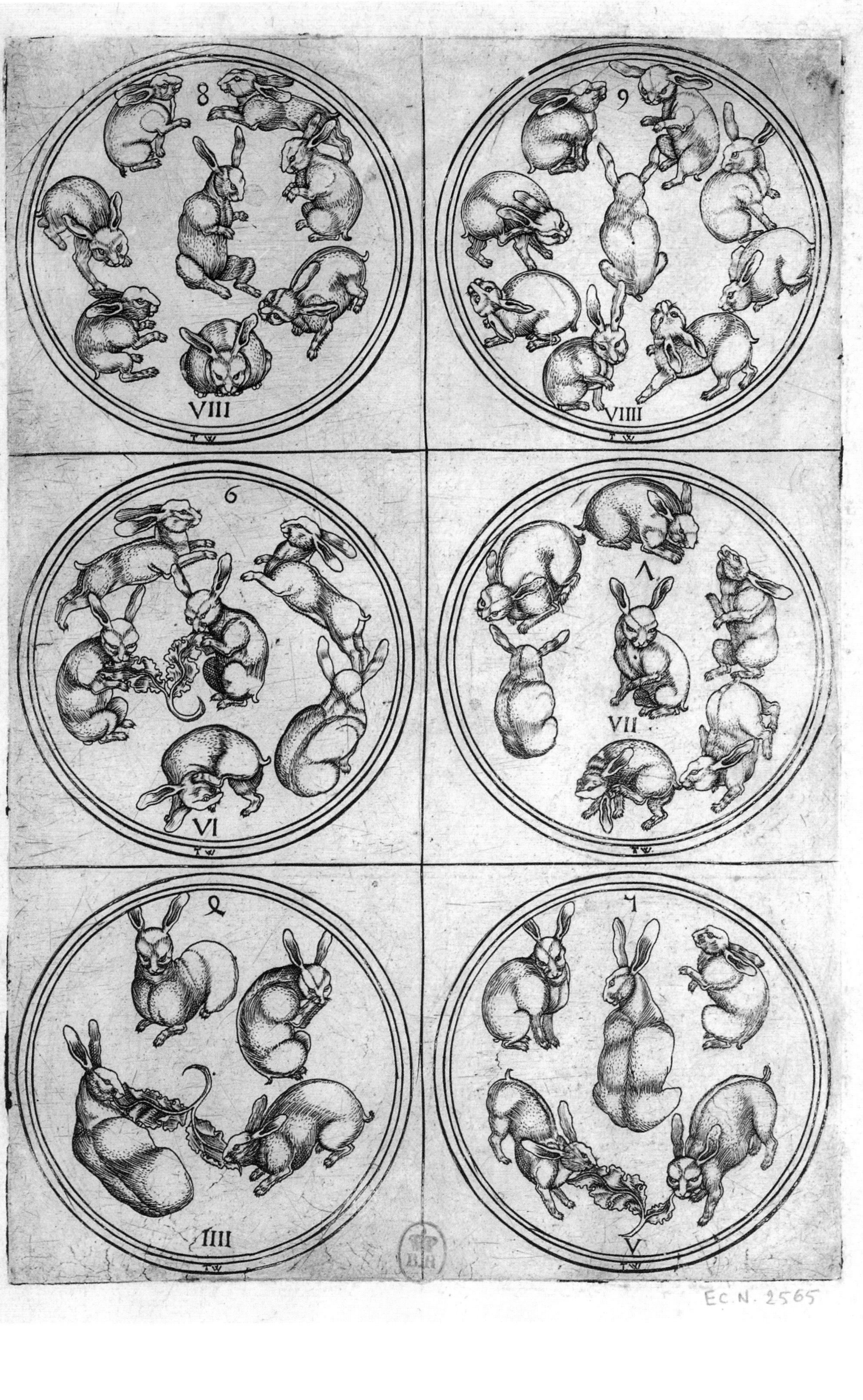

13

13 Telman de Wesel, *Playing Cards with Rabbit Suit Symbols*, Lower Rhine region (Wesel?), early 16th century

The practice of creating playing cards bearing animal suit symbols was developed by the 'Master of the Playing Cards' in Germany during the 1430s. Telman de Wesel, a little-documented goldsmith and engraver who mainly copied prints by Dürer, established himself within that tradition by engraving this circular deck of cards. It was actually copied from a pack created by the monogrammist PW, an artist who originated from Cologne and was likewise one of Dürer's contemporaries.

Here, Telman de Wesel combines images of flowers and birds, and has somewhat abandoned the domain of the hunt for that of decoration. Indeed, the images on these sheets lend themselves more readily to contemplation than to games. The fact that they have been left uncut on the sheet corroborates the theory that cards of this type were not necessarily used for entertainment, and may actually have served as models to various artists. S.L.

Burin engraving | 6.8 cm (diameter of each card)

14 Joseph Boillot, *Term Representing a Porcupine*, 1592

Breaking with a tradition that dates back to ancient times and which regained popularity during the Renaissance, Joseph Boillot's images offer examples from the animal kingdom as decorative elements for terms, rather than the human figure. Indeed, the artist seems to have believed that it degraded human beings to use them for ornamental purposes in this way. These plates provided Boillot with the opportunity to work with the theme of zoology, a subject of which he was fond. Authors such as Ambroise Paré had shown a lively interest in this domain, particularly in the natural sympathies and antipathies of living beings. This aim was shared by Boillot, who likewise depicted animals together with their enemies; in this way, the porcupine is shown with his 'antithesis', the dog, as he defends himself against them by bristling his spines to prevent them from approaching. Inspired by natural history texts, the whole work forms an original and entertaining fantasy, which was to feed the imagination of architects and specialists in the decorative arts. However, the porcupine is a good example of the limitations presented by this type of creative game, being so complex to portray that it is difficult to imagine how it could be reproduced in stone or wood. Indeed, it proved impossible to produce an actual creation comparable to the images in Boillot's *Pourtraits et figures*. S.L.

Taken from *Nouveaux Pourtraits et figures de termes pour user en architecture*, Langres, 1592 | Etching | 26 x 8.5 cm (boundary line)

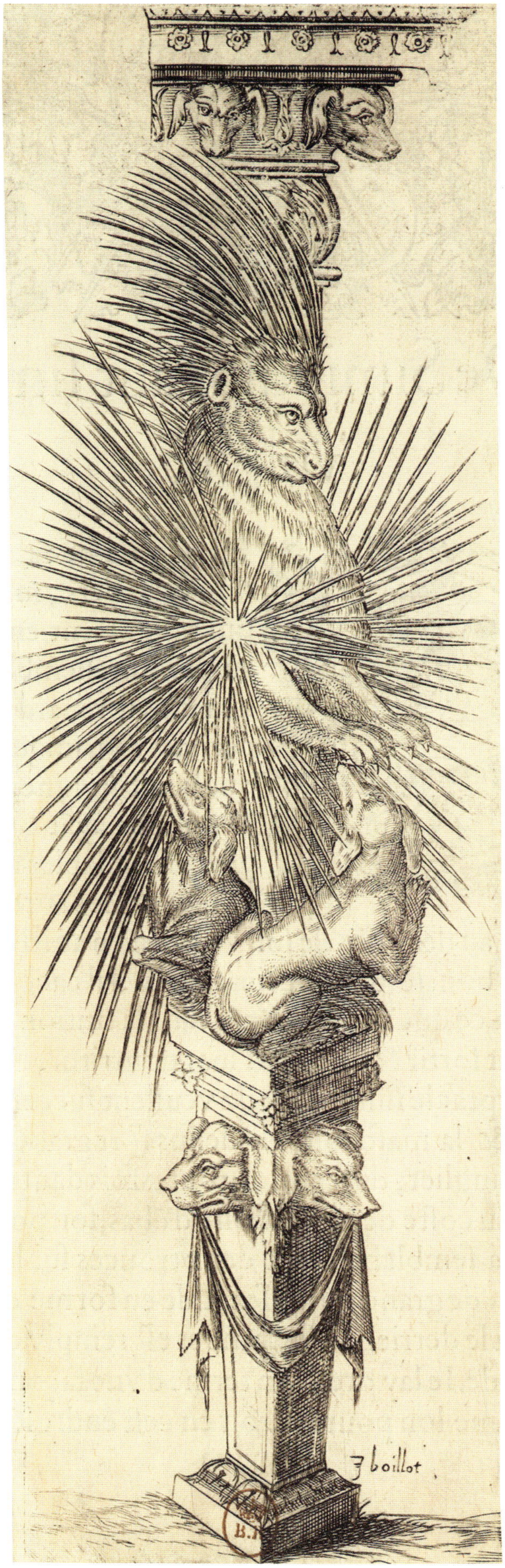

14

15 Anonymous, *The Peacock, Bad Counsel*, ca. 1535–1540

This large sheet depicting a peacock as a bad counsellor must be part of a more extensive collection based on the theme of wisdom and folly symbolized by birds. Indeed, the Prints Department holds two other large woodcuts with the same decorative borders, which feature a passerine bird advocating lust and a cockerel representing a good governor anxious to alleviate his subjects' hardship. The peacock, conversely, encourages the behaviour of a rich tyrant who has no desire to be loved.

In their composition and moralizing character these prints bear a resemblance to the emblems made fashionable by Alciato's *Emblematum Liber*, which appeared in France in 1534. Judging from their format, technique and ornamental quality, as well as the poor state of their reverse sides, they were likely to have been used as wallpaper. Although little is known about French woodcut artists of the first half of the 16th century, the printed inscription and certain terms also to be found in a xylograph by Jean Bézart could indicate that these works were created by this printmaker or publisher. There is no information about him, apart from the fact that from 1530 his family was known in Paris for running a bookshop and later for selling prints. S.L.

Woodcut, stencil-coloured | 40 x 29 cm (boundary line)

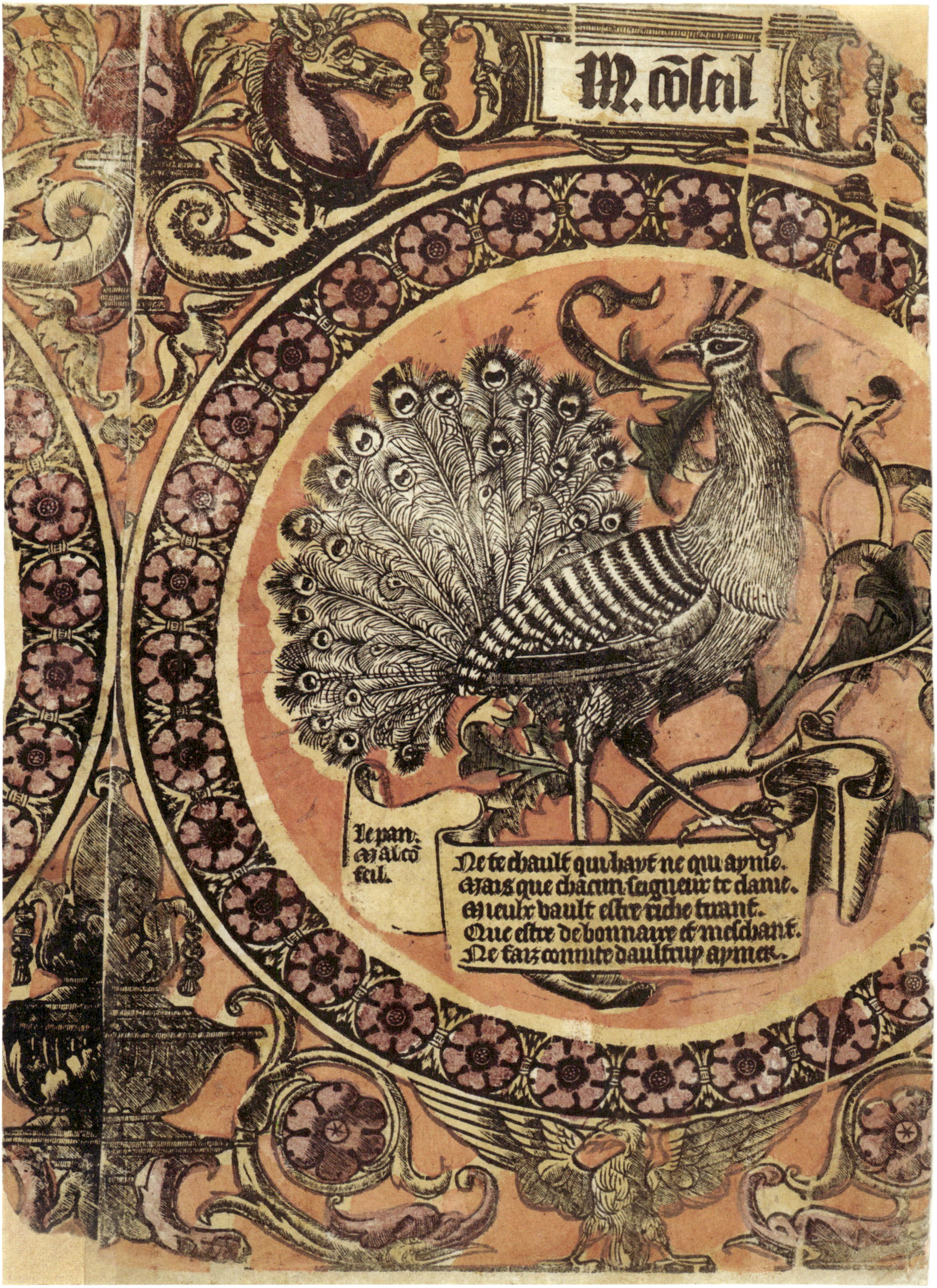
M. cõseil
Le pan. Ma alcõ seil.
Ne te chault qui hayt ne qui ayme.
Mais que chacun seigneur te dame.
Mieulx vault estre riche tirant.
Que estre debonnaire et meschant.
Ne faiz compte daultruy aymer.

15

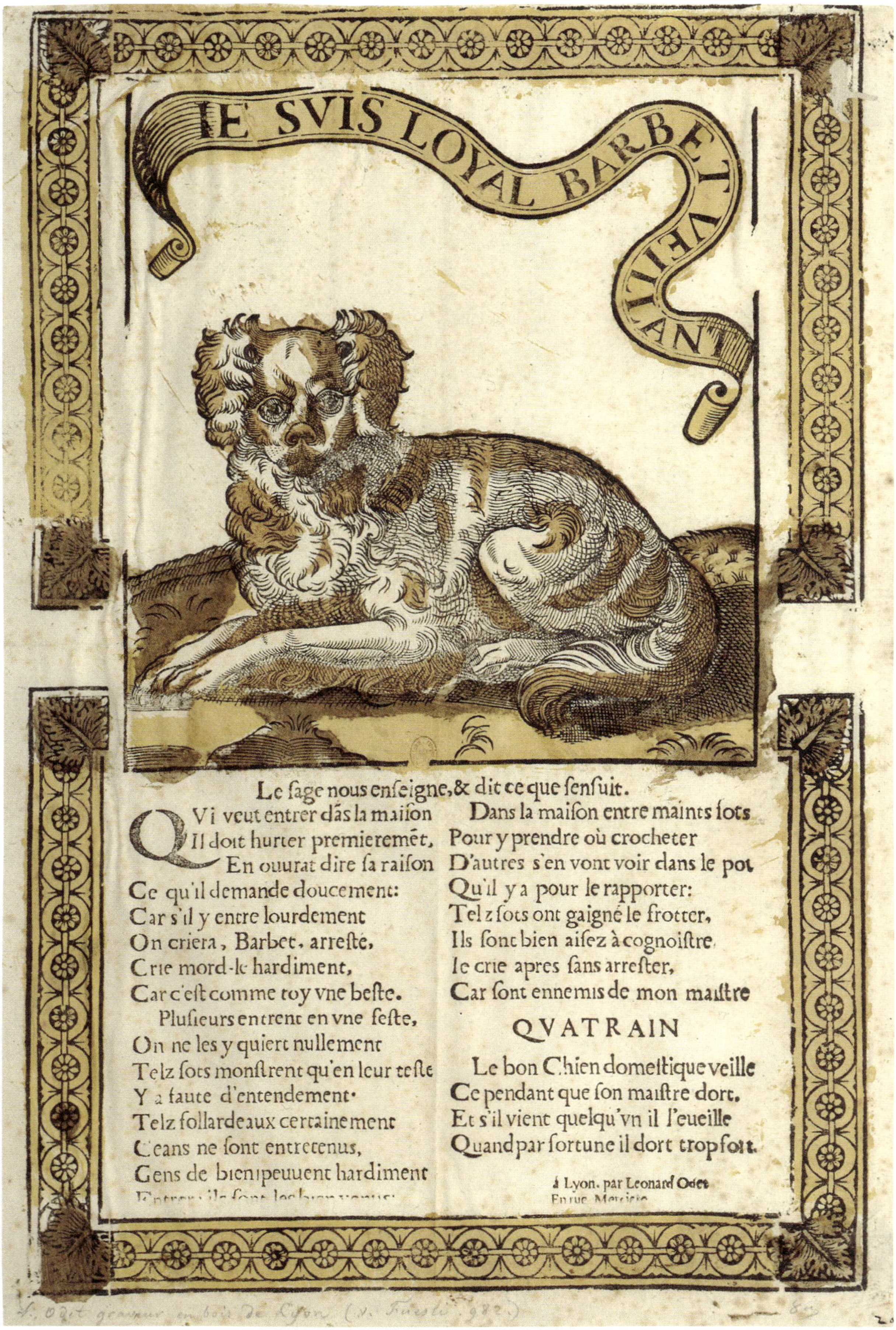

16

16 Léonard Odet, *I Am a Loyal and Watchful Barbet*, ca. 1600

→ description on p. 46

17 Anonymous, *The True Portrait of Gunnar's Dog*, ca. 1690–1700

→ description on p. 46

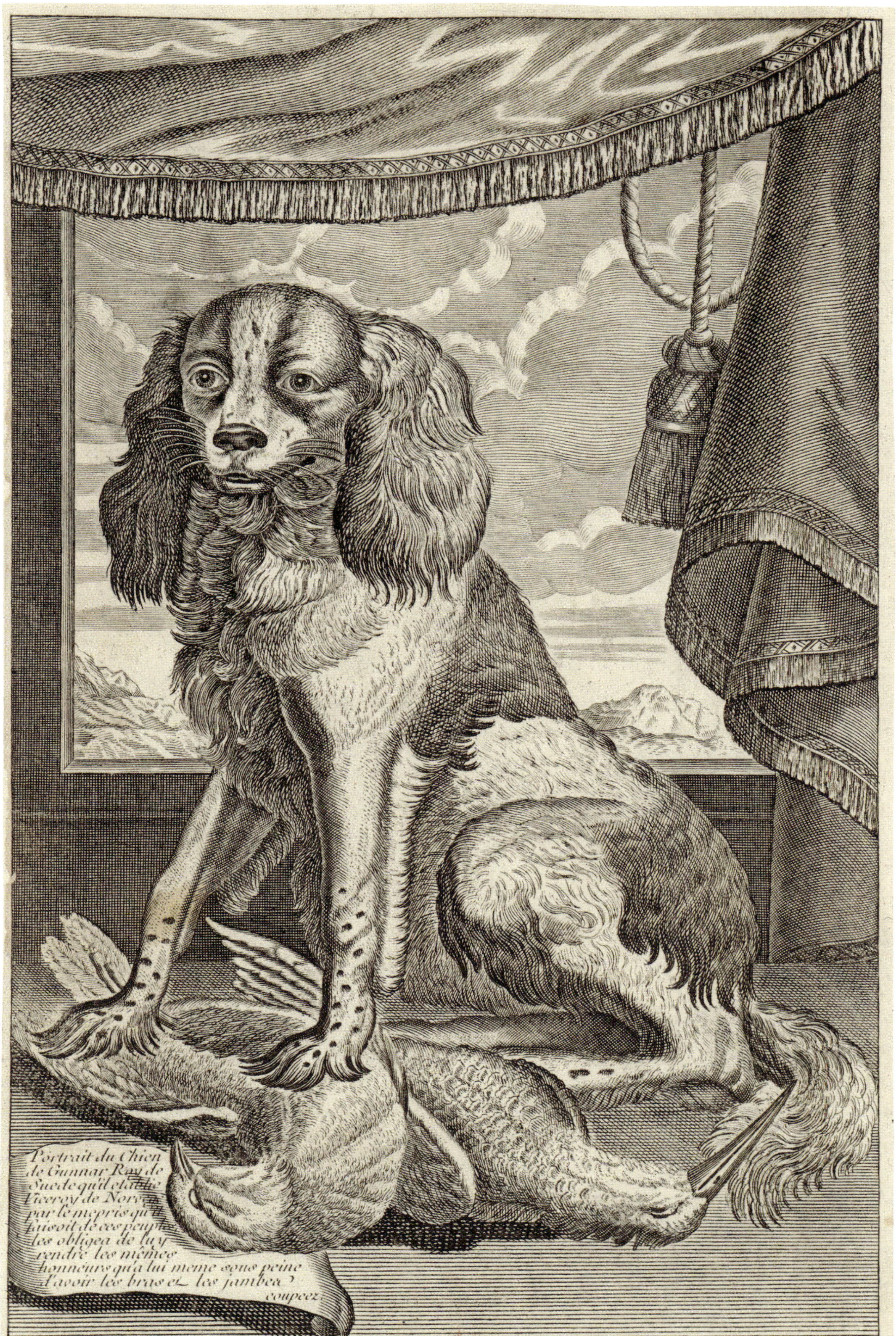
Portrait du Chien
de Gunnar Roy de
Suede qu'il etabli
Viceroy de Norv
par le mepris qu
faisoit de ces peup
les obligea de luy
rendre les mêmes
honneurs qu'a lui meme sous peine
d'avoir les bras et les jambes
coupez.
Non en termes pompeux ne crois pas que je fasse
L'Histoire de ce chien Prince des Norvegeois:
Tout ce que j'en dirai, c'est qu'il fut de sa race
Le premier, le dernier, le seul des Vicerois.
Ne le va pourtant pas tourner en raillerie:
Aprehende ses dents, redoute sa furie.

17

16 Léonard Odet, *I Am a Loyal and Watchful Barbet*, ca. 1600

→ Image on p. 44

The woodcut on this popular broadside presents a fairly accurate portrayal of a barbet, a curly-coated hunting dog used for retrieving water fowl, and renowned for its intelligence and loyalty. In the 16th century it was still a new breed, and was brought into fashion by the Chancellor René de Birague; a sculpture of a barbet – 'the most accurate likeness' – may be seen lying closely by the effigy of his wife, Valentine Balbiani, on the latter's tomb in the Louvre.

Léonard Odet was established in Lyon, on the rue Mercière in the booksellers' district, at least from 1578 to 1610. A woodcut printmaker and print seller, he also published booklets, such as embroidery patterns and satirical and moralizing literature. He seems to have specialized in these large broadsides illustrating the political events of the day, such as *Pourtaict de la Ligue infernalle*, ca. 1593. He also depicted popular traditional themes, frequently including animals, such as *La Grande et Merveilleuse Bataille d'entre les chats et les rats* (1610), or this *Loyal Barbet*, a symbol of genuine fidelity. This theme seems to have had some measure of success, as we know of another, similar version dating from the 17th century. Comprising an image and a French text engraved in wood, it is included in the collections held at the British Museum. V.S.

Woodcut | 49 x 33 cm (print area)

17 Anonymous, *The True Portrait of Gunnar's Dog*, ca. 1690–1700

→ Image on p. 45

Through living in the company of their masters, certain animals have come to play roles normally filled by human beings. This dog was placed on the throne of Norway by Gunnar, a legendary king of Sweden: '. . . after having made himself ruler of Norway and having established his garrisons in every quarter, as he was about to depart, and with a disdain more cruel than all the hostile acts he had committed, [Gunnar] left his dog there as Viceroy, with orders that he should be treated with as much honour as Gunnar himself, on pain of having one's arms and legs cut off. In this way, an entire kingdom found itself compelled to pay homage to this monstrous Viceroy, whose only responses to the tributes and respects paid to him were growls and barks.'

The text accompanying the print explains the origins of this idea, a rare practice. The print publisher François Guérard had in fact found this original and picturesque subject in the work *Parallèles historiques* (1680), where Incitatus, the horse appointed consul by Caligula, was compared to the canine Viceroy. As the print that was initially created was of average quality, its price was relatively modest. It was copied a few years later, but was still anonymous. R.M.

Burin engraving | 21.3 x 33.3 cm (boundary line)

18 Hendrick Goltzius, *Frederick de Vries*, 1597

An apprentice working for Goltzius, the young Frederick de Vries is seen here playing with the family dog, a Drentse partridge dog that Goltzius drew on several occasions. These were renowned hunting dogs, being excellent pointers and unfailingly dependable retrievers. What Goltzius is presenting here, as indicated in the written inscription, are the images of a faithful dog and a carefree child. However, certain elements invite us to interpret the work at a deeper level: the dove in Frederick's hand symbolizes innocence and some art theoreticians at that time saw the dog as a symbolic master figure, safeguarding souls against sin. Dedicated to the young boy's father, Dirck de Vries, a painter and a friend of the printmaker, this engraving may therefore be read at several levels as the emblematic portrayal of friendship: that of Goltzius and Dirck de Vries, the dog and the child, the master and the pupil. The very simple style was a departure from the elegant Mannerism characteristic of Goltzius's work and was perhaps intended to echo the simplicity advocated in the inscription, whilst paying homage to Dirck de Vries, a painter with strong Realist tendencies. S.L.

Burin engraving | 35.7 x 26.4 cm (boundary line)

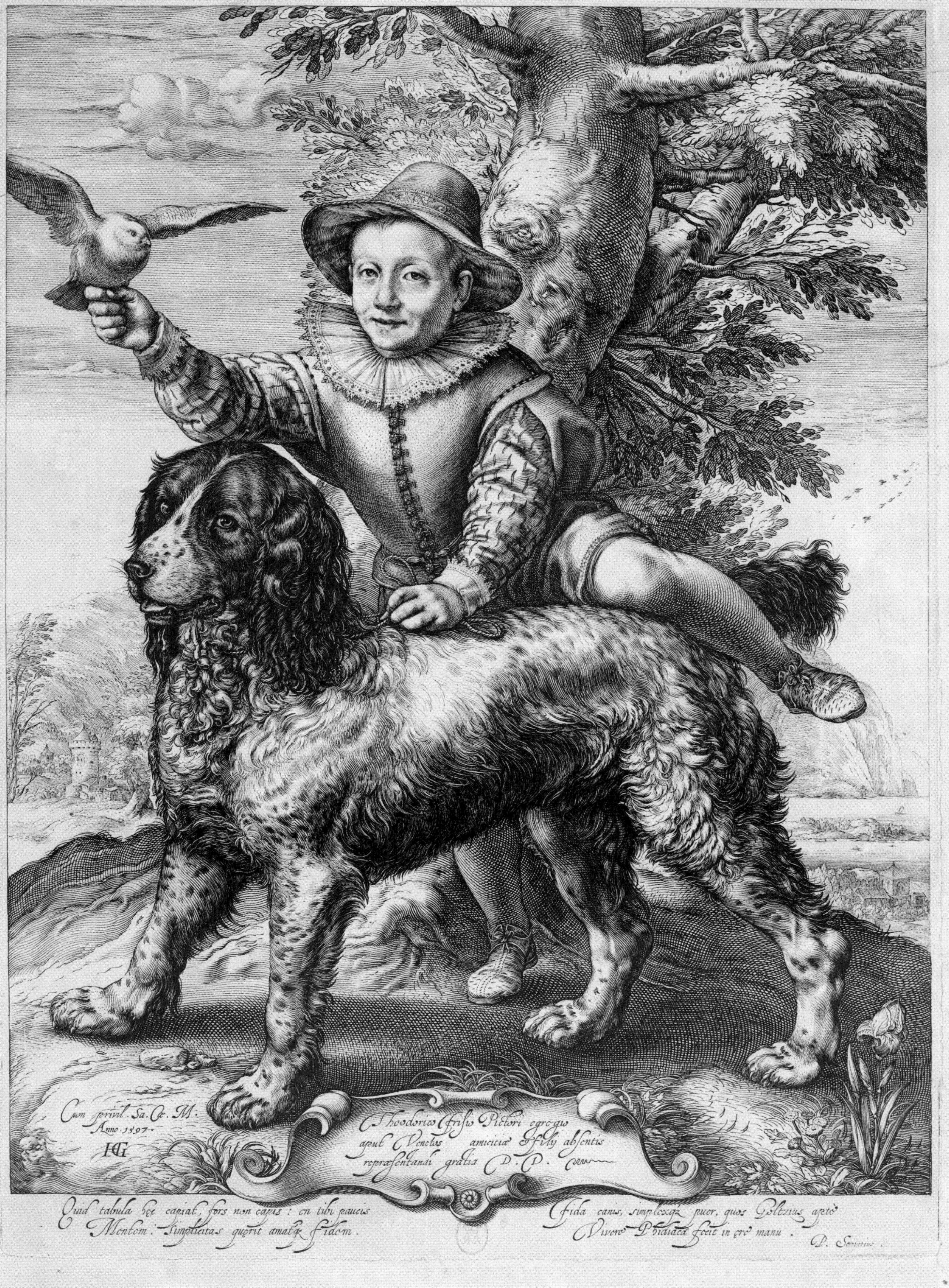
Cum privil. Sa. Cæ. M.
Anno 1597
HG
Theodorico Frisio Pictori egregio
apud Venetos amicitiæ et filij absentis
repræsentandi gratia D. D.
Quid tabula hæc capiat, fors non capis: en tibi paucis
Mentem: simplicitas quærit amatq; fidem.
Fida canis, simplexq; puer, quos Goltzius apto
Vivos Phidiaca fecit in ære manu.
P. Scriverius.

18

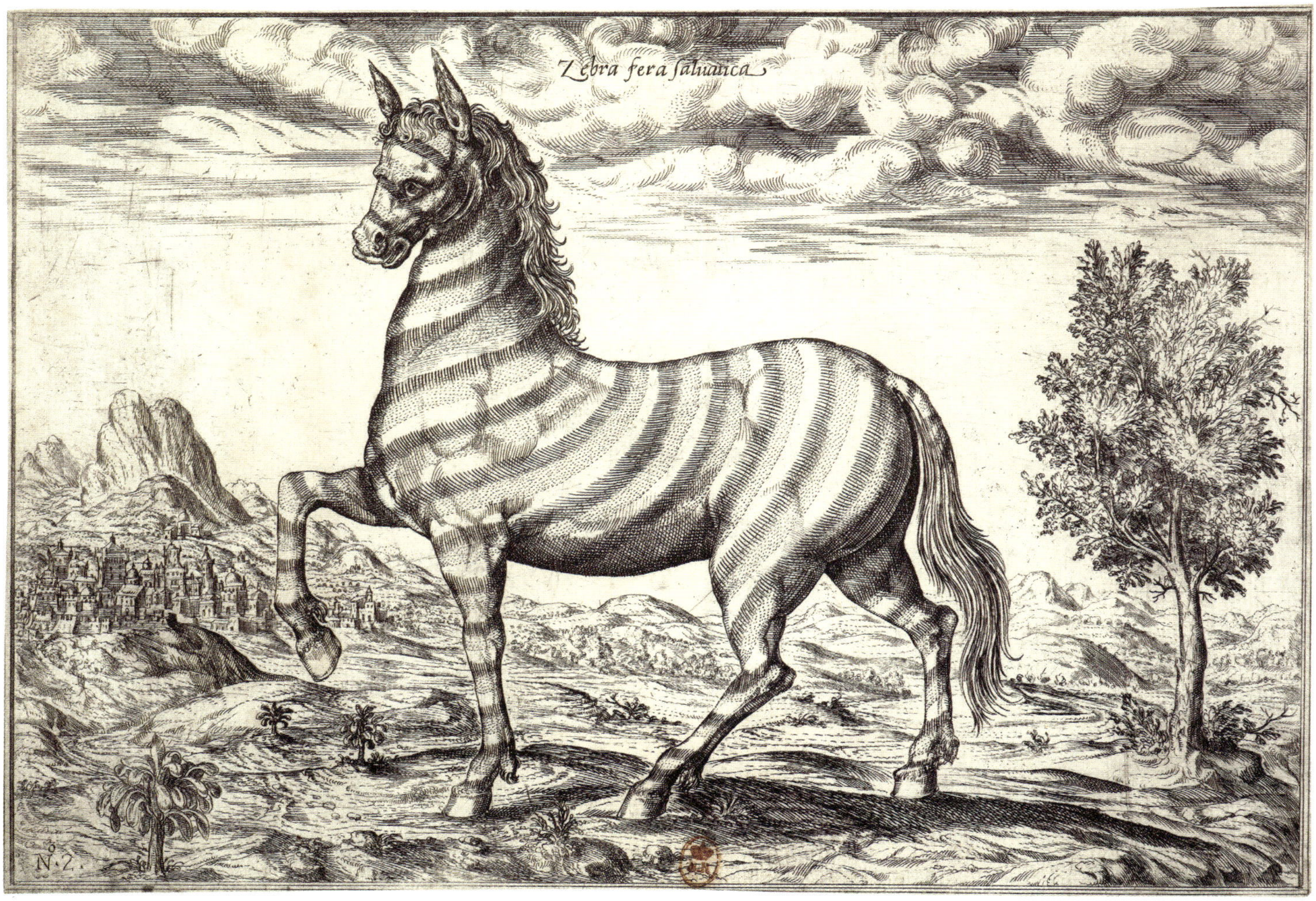

19

19 Anonymous, *Zebra fera salvatica*, early 17th century

The zebra is one of the most curious examples of the animals represented in bestiaries. It was shown in proximity to images of the unicorn, and there were still doubts regarding its actual existence. This very beautiful Italian etching presents the animal in a setting that reflects its exotic character: a desert landscape with a few unusual plants and above all a city standing in the distance, its architecture suggestive of the Orient. Prints also provide us with information concerning the resources available to practitioners when depicting species that they themselves had never seen. Curiously, this particular etching does not seem to have been inspired by an actual model, but instead to result from a request that simply involved portraying 'a striped horse'! R.M.

Etching | 20.2 x 29.7 cm (boundary line)

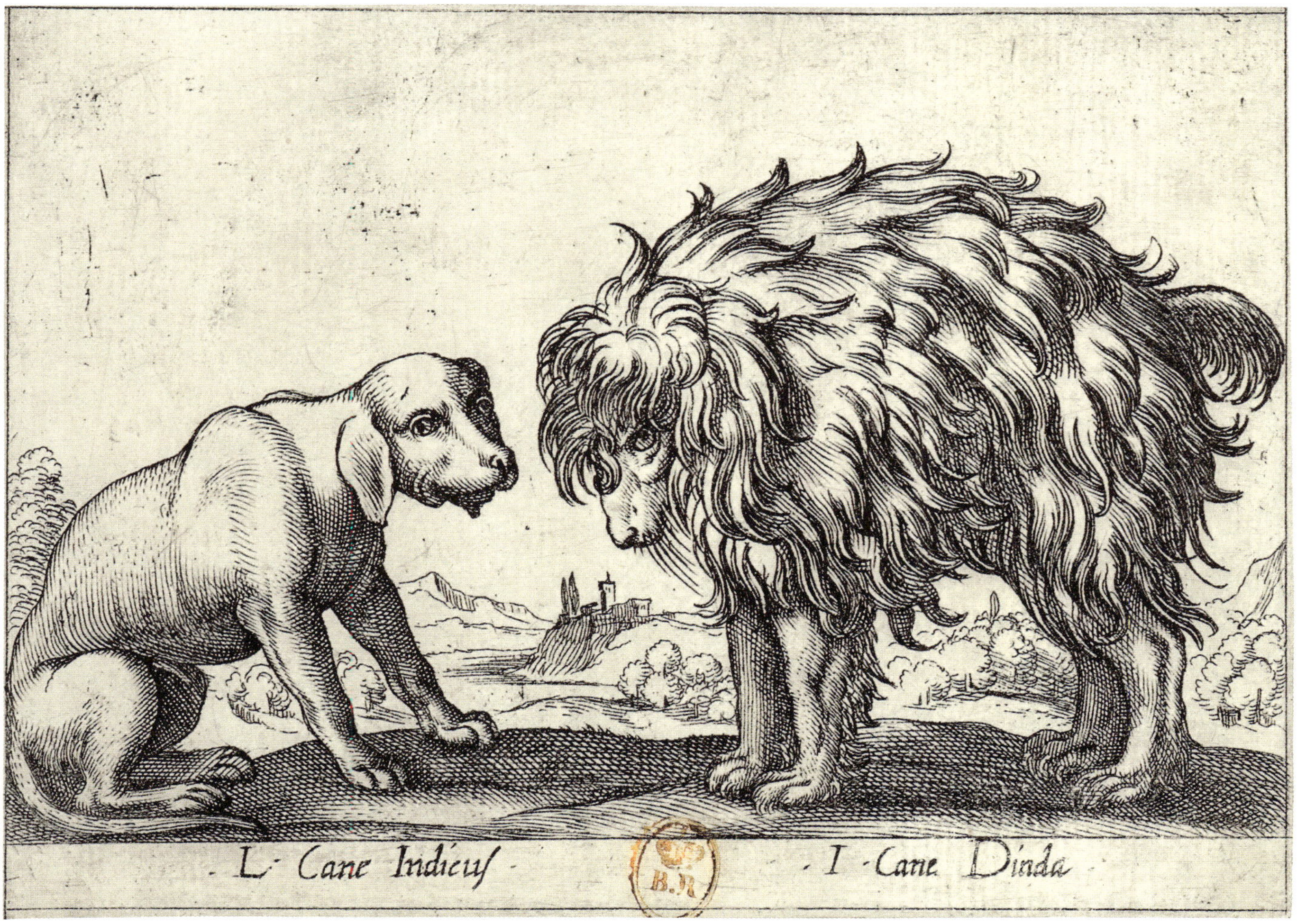

20

20 Anonymous (falsely attributed to Antonio Tempesta), *An Indian Dog*, 1636

Knowledge of zoology advanced slowly in the 16th and 17th centuries; science as understood in ancient times was still being used as a point of reference, and descriptions were copied from medieval and Renaissance sources. A series of animal prints reflecting this approach appeared in Rome in 1636. They portrayed over two hundred quadrupeds, some imaginary and some still far from being what we would recognize as genuine likenesses. The artist had never seen most of the animals he depicted and therefore based his work on previous models: Dürer's rhinoceros may be found among these items, together with images taken from the work of Jan Jonston of Poland. The notion of species was yet to be properly defined: this 'Indian dog', with its luxuriant coat and menacing stare is no different from the type of guard dog one might find in rural France. Nevertheless, these bestiaries fuelled the imagination of a society just discovering exoticism and Otherness.

At all events, the images achieved success, as a new edition appeared in 1651, with prints attributed to the famous Italian engraver Antonio Tempesta – a fraudulent act committed by the publisher in order to boost his sales! R.M.

Cane Indicus – Cane d'Inda | From the *Curiosa Raccolta di diversi animali quadrupedi*, Rome, Giacomo Marucci, 1636 | Burin engraving| 13.5 x 9.5 cm (boundary line)

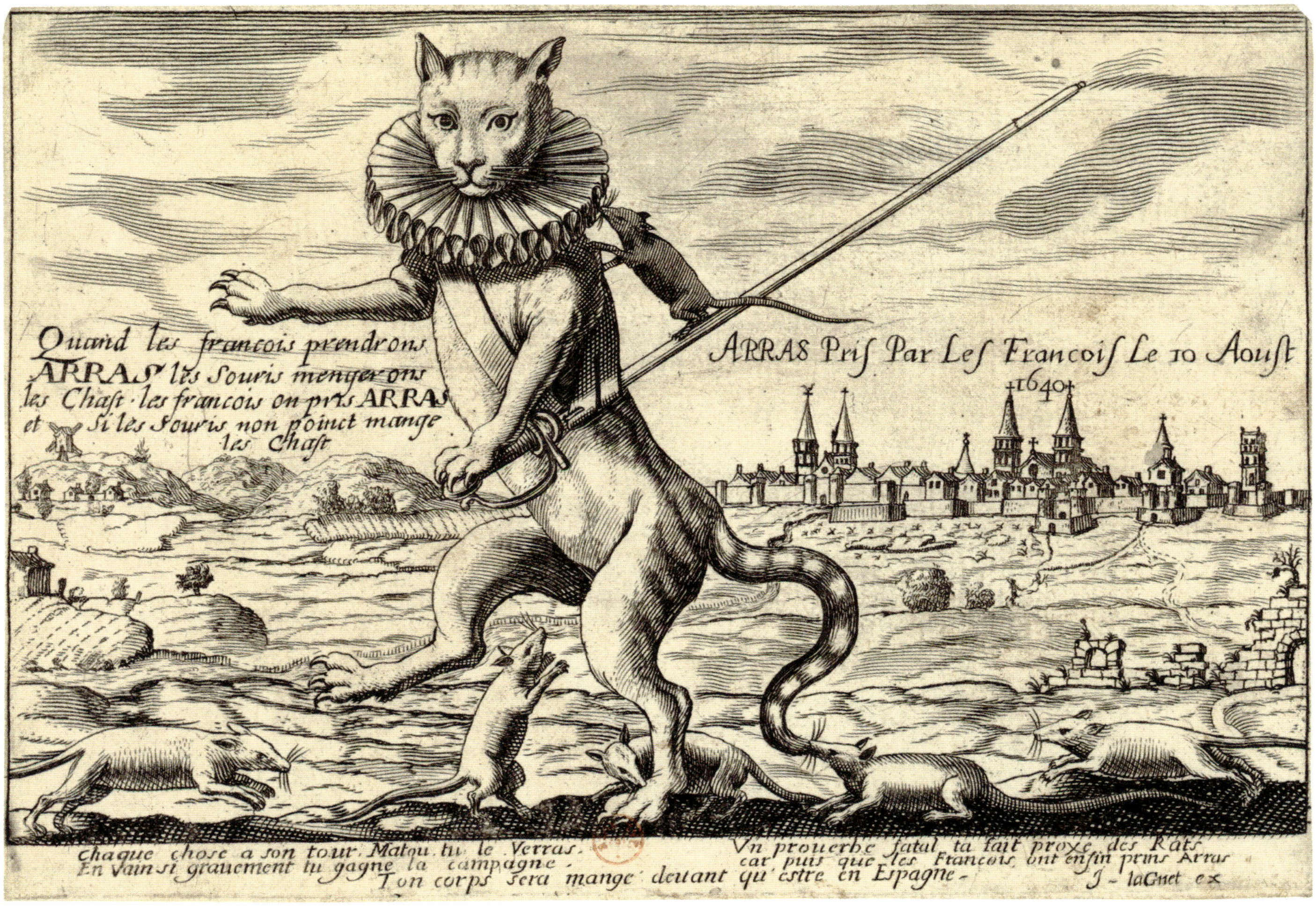

21

21 Anonymous, *Satirical Print Showing the Storming of Arras*, ca. 1640

The first half of the 17th century was marked by the rivalry between France and Spain, which led to a series of major battles such as Rocroi (1643) and Lens (1648). The focus of the conflict, among other issues, was the establishment of France's north-eastern border with the Spanish Netherlands (now Belgium), particularly in Artois and Flanders. Arras, the capital of Artois, formed part of the most important Spanish strongholds and had long been coveted by France. A very large number of prints circulated in relation to these conflicts, mocking the enemy. Spain was often represented as a swaggering braggart, and the local proverb – 'When the French take Arras / The mice will eat the cats' – served as inspiration to print publishers, who vied with each other in their portrayals of the war between the French and the Spanish, depicted respectively in rodent and feline form, until the advent of the victorious siege that challenged the old saying. This print presents a contemporary view of that historical event, as perceived from a specific, partisan standpoint. R.M.

Burin engraving | 18 x 12.5 cm (boundary line)

22 Anonymous, *The Cats' Singing Master*, ca. 1640

This print stands on the borderlines between art, craft and commerce, as it was not unusual for a publisher to be in command of a bona fide printmaking studio, able to provide an eager Parisian market with a steady supply of images. Large teams of engravers were employed for this purpose; in some cases these were not even named on a regular basis. In this way, Pierre Bertrand engaged a number of engravers in order to sell popular or *demi-fine* prints. Here he takes up the theme of a cats' concert; certain contemporary sources testify to the fact that such events actually took place, despite the difficulties involved in training the animal in question. The print depicts a smiling man bearing cats on his head and shoulders. On the table, three others are preparing to sing the 'miaows' written on their music sheets, while yet more are playing the flute, mandolin and viola, creating a humorous parody of this popular spectacle. Another version of this scene exists in the form of a woodcut, reflecting the success of the image. R.M.

From the studio of Pierre Bertrand (ca. 1600–ca. 1678)
Burin engraving | 30 x 20.5 cm (boundary line)

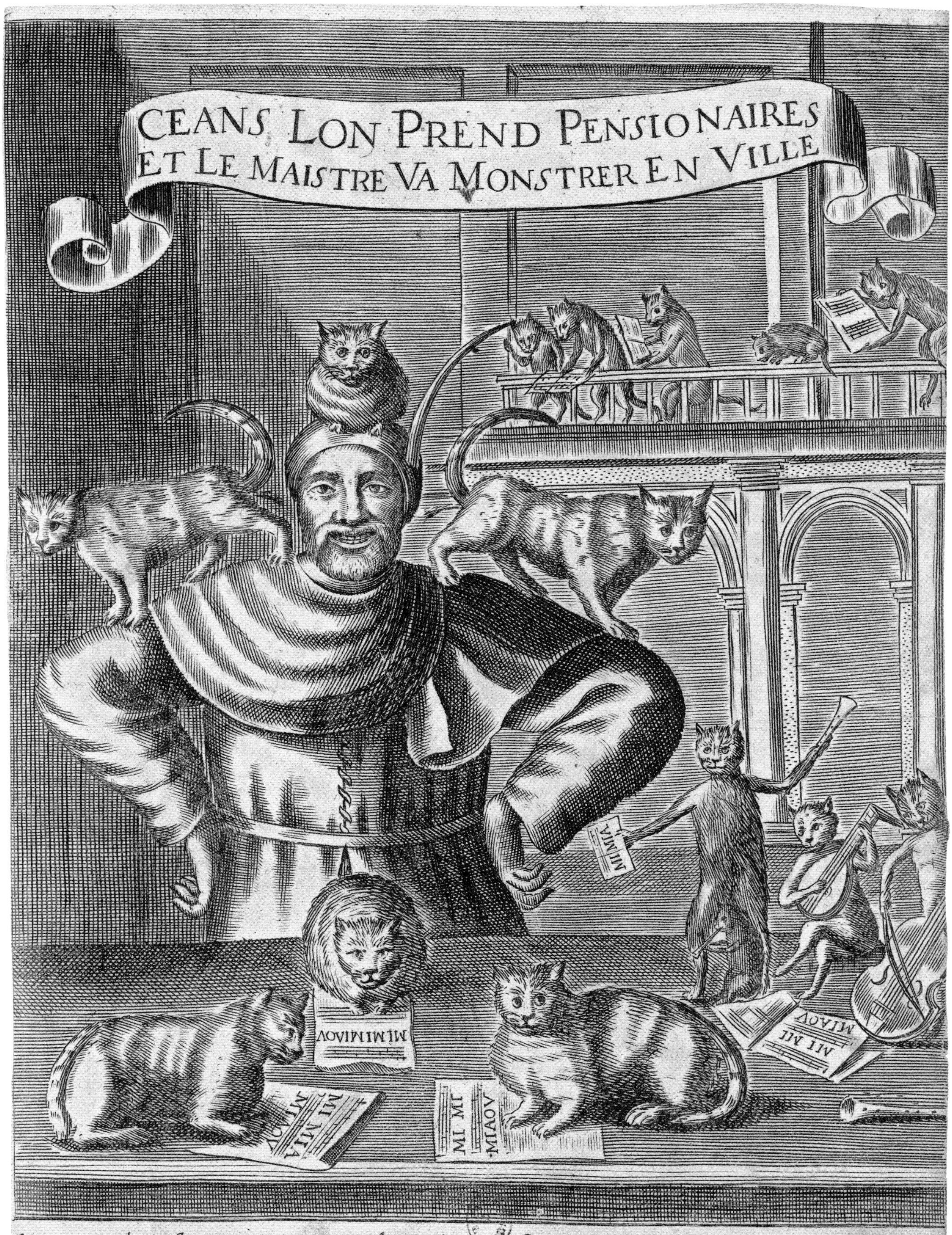
CEANS LON PREND PENSIONAIRES
ET LE MAISTRE VA MONSTRER EN VILLE
MI MIA
MI MI MIAOV
MI MI MIAOV
MI MI MIAOV
MI MI MIAOV
Vous qui ne sauez pasceque vaut la musique
Venez vous en ouir le concert manifique
et les airs rauissans que iaprens aux Matous
Puisque ma belle voix ren ces bestes docill
Ie ne scaurois manquer de vous instruire to
Ni de vous esclairsir les nottes Difficille
P. Bertrand excudit

22

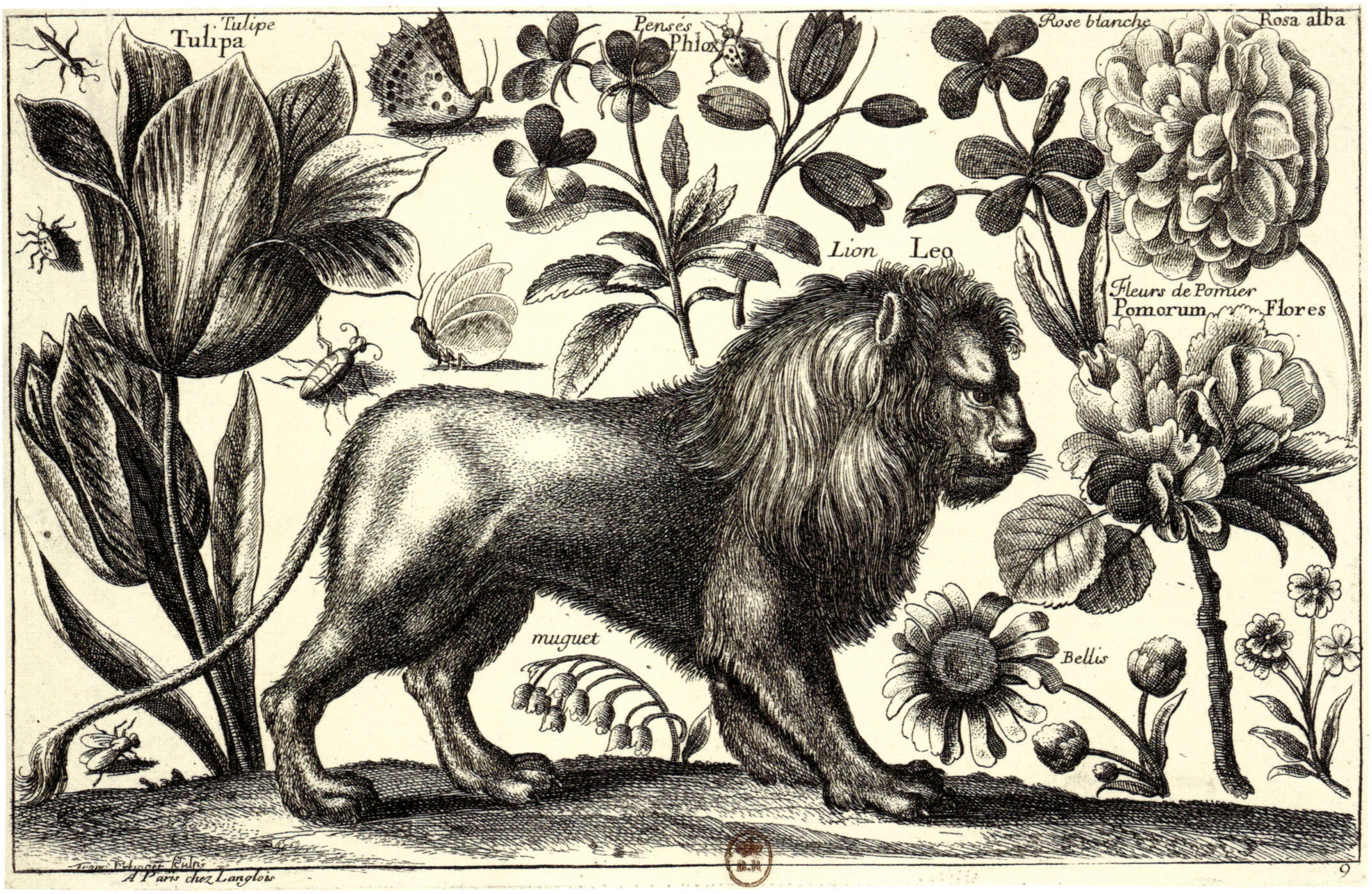

23

23 François Ertinger, after John Dunstall and Wenceslas Hollar, *Lion and Flowers*, ca. 1665

As knowledge of animals developed, it was disseminated through collections of images that circulated in one country after another. In 1663, Peter Stent published a series of prints in London depicting various quadrupeds, including exotic creatures, in their natural state, together with plants, insects and arthropods. There was even a dragon! Their names were given in both English and Latin.

François Langlois, one of the leading Parisian publishers, promptly had these copied by François Ertinger; as the engraver began with a paper proof that he transferred onto his printing plate, the result was a mirror image. The names were translated from English into French and the information provided was enhanced as certain plants (such as lily of the valley) were also identified and named during this process. The plates are of good quality in the artistic sense, a principle that prevailed over the strictly scientific approach. Although the animals were etched with the utmost precision – as emphasized by the text on the title page – they are depicted together with plants and insects following purely aesthetic, rather than scholarly criteria. R.M.

Etching | 27.5 x 17.5 cm (boundary line)

24 Matthäus Greuter, *Melissographia*, 1625

The Italian scientists working at the Accademia dei Lincei, the first scientific academy in the world, developed the practice of using a microscope for their observations, which resulted in a number of drawings. Its founder, Federico Cesi, hastened to publish his treatise on bees, *Apiarium*, for the jubilee of 1625, dedicating it to the new Pope, Urban VIII (Maffeo Barberini). This was intended as a gesture of reconciliation with the pontifical authority, and to suppress both anti-Copernican polemic and anti-Galilean censure. As bees were included in the Barberini family crest, it was a fitting tribute. Cesi had this exceptional plate, the *Melissographia*, engraved by Matthäus Greuter of Germany, who created the first entomological illustration produced as a result of microscopic observation. V.S.

Taken from *Apiarium*, by Federico Cesi, Rome, 1625 | Burin engraving | 37 x 26.5 cm (print area)

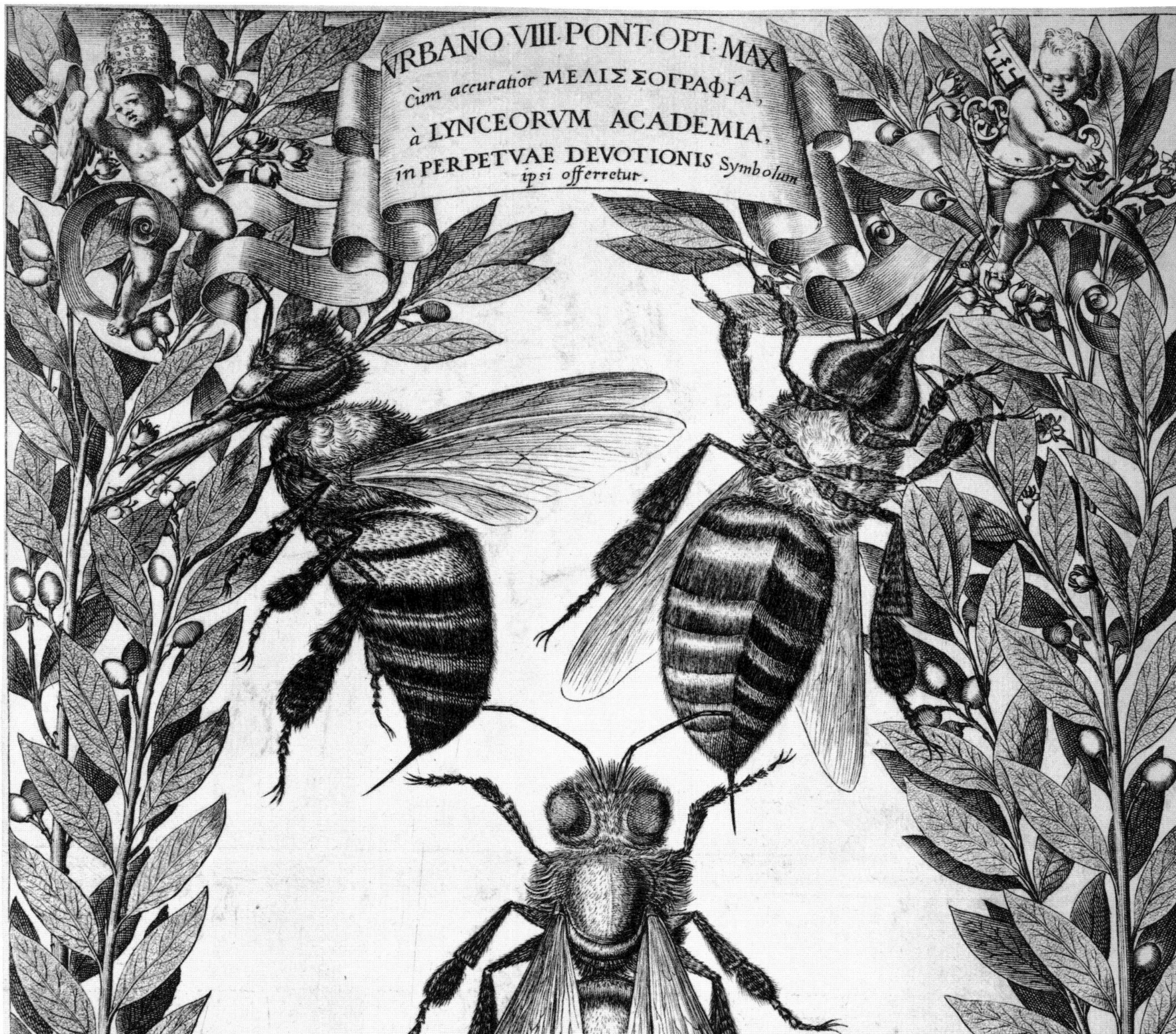
VRBANO VIII PONT OPT MAX
Cùm accuratior ΜΕΛΙΣΣΟΓΡΑΦΊΑ,
à LYNCEORVM ACADEMIA,
in PERPETVAE DEVOTIONIS Symbolum
ipsi offerretur.
Magne Parens rerum, cui se Natura volentem
Subijcit, et dominos collocat ante pedes,
Respice, Naturâ quâ nil præstantiꝰ omni,
E BARBERINAE stemate Gentis APEM:
Hâc vti Lynceidum, ꝑpiori lumine lustrans,
Disposuit Tabulis, explicuitq; labor.
Cæsiadę Genio sacrum stimulante laborem,
Palladis et promptos arte iuuante viros,
Maxima dum tereti surgunt miracula vitro,
Maioremq; oculus discit habere fidem.
Quis nôrat quinas Hybleo in corpore linguas
Atque leoninæ proxima colla iubæ,
Hirsutosq; oculos, binasque labris vaginas?
Ni facerent artis dia reperta nouæ.
Sic decet, vt dum te miradū suspicit Orbis,
Et magè mirandā se Tua præstet APIS.
Ponebat IVSTVS RIQVIVS LYNCEVS BELGA DEDIC. S.E.
ROMAE Superior permissu 1625
FRANCISCVS STELLVTVS LYNCEVS FABR.IS MICROSCOPIO obseruabat
M. Greuter delineab. incid.

24

25 Anonymous, *A Pair of Skating Owls*, 1663

This French print is a copy of an engraving by Adriaen Matham of Holland, after a work by Adriaen Van de Venne, a painter from The Hague who created five images of animals disguised as humans. These feature a cat and a dog dancing, frogs clad in armour and gowns, two pigs dressed as peasants, two monkeys dancing to music and this pair of skating owls. Van de Venne's image was a covert political satire, as the birds represent the Archdukes Isabella and Albert of Austria, Governors of the Low Countries. However, the print sold by Jacques Lagniet, a Parisian publisher who specialized in caricatural works and illustrations of proverbs, simply suggests a moralizing comment on the vanity and the folly of mankind. V.S.

In *Les Plus Illustres Proverbes*, Paris, Jacques Lagniet, 1663 | Burin engraving | 20 x 14 cm (print area)

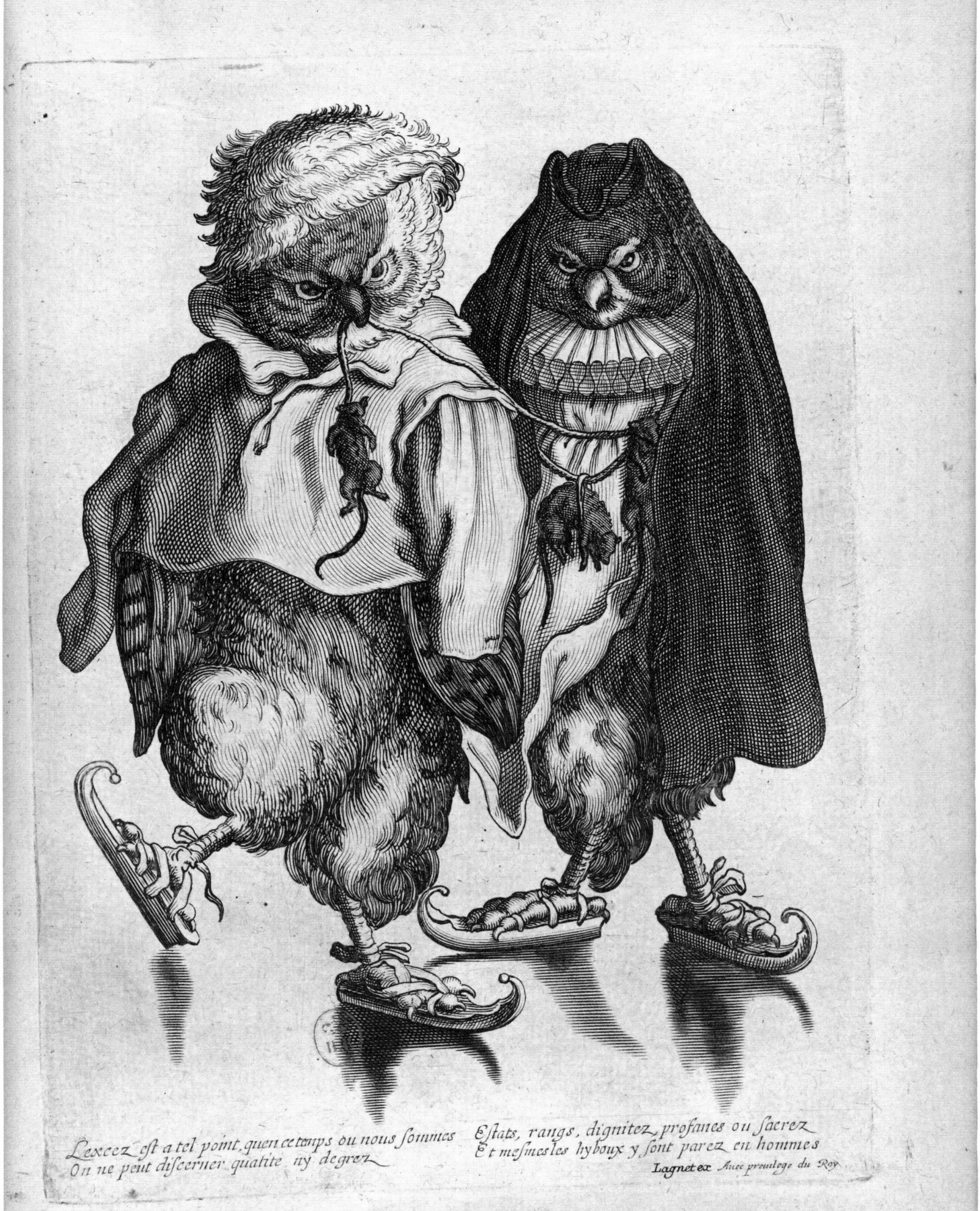
Lexcez est a tel point, quen ce temps ou nous sommes
On ne peut discerner quatite ny degrez
Estats, rangs, dignitez, profanes ou sacrez
Et mesmes les hyboux y sont parez en hommes
Lagnet ex Auec preuilege du Roy

25

26 Louis Simonneau, after Charles Le Brun, *Similarities Between the Head of an Ox and a Man*, ca. 1683

The question of the passions and their influence over the human physique was central to the reflections conducted during the 17th century, not only in the domain of art but also in the works of writers and philosophers such as Descartes and La Bruyère. Charles Le Brun, painter to the King at Versailles, contributed to these studies with his portrait drawings comparing certain animals to human 'types', in a physiognomic approach that included goats, bears, camels, monkeys and parrots.

Some of these works were circulated from the mid-1680s in the form of burin engravings executed by Louis Simonneau; they then served as amusing and educational models to copy as drawings. Most of them, however, remained unpublished until 1806, when the originals held in the Louvre were systematically interpreted by André Legrand, while physiognomy gained considerable popularity thanks to Lavater's theories. R.M.

From *Livre de portraiture pour ceux qui commencent à dessiner*, Paris, Chéreau, after 1718 | Burin engraving | 23 x 31.5 cm (boundary line)

27 Giovanni Benedetto Castiglione, *Noah and the Animals Entering the Ark*, ca. 1650–1655

→ Image on p. 58

Castiglione, a baroque painter and engraver from the Genoese school who lived in the first half of the 17th century, is principally known for his rural scenes and his historical and biblical subjects. These works served as a pretext for his minutely detailed paintings of farm animals and landscapes. In his depiction of this episode from the Book of Genesis, for example, Noah's family and the Ark are relegated to a vaguely-sketched background on the left, while the foreground is entirely devoted to the procession of very realistic animals, even including a urinating goat! The whole image is etched with a very fine point, showing variations in light and shade in a style influenced by Rembrandt. Castiglione portrayed this subject several times in his paintings and prints, and even in a monotype, a technique he invented that involves making a single impression of an image drawn in ink on a copper plate. V.S.

Etching | 20.6 x 40.3 cm (boundary line)

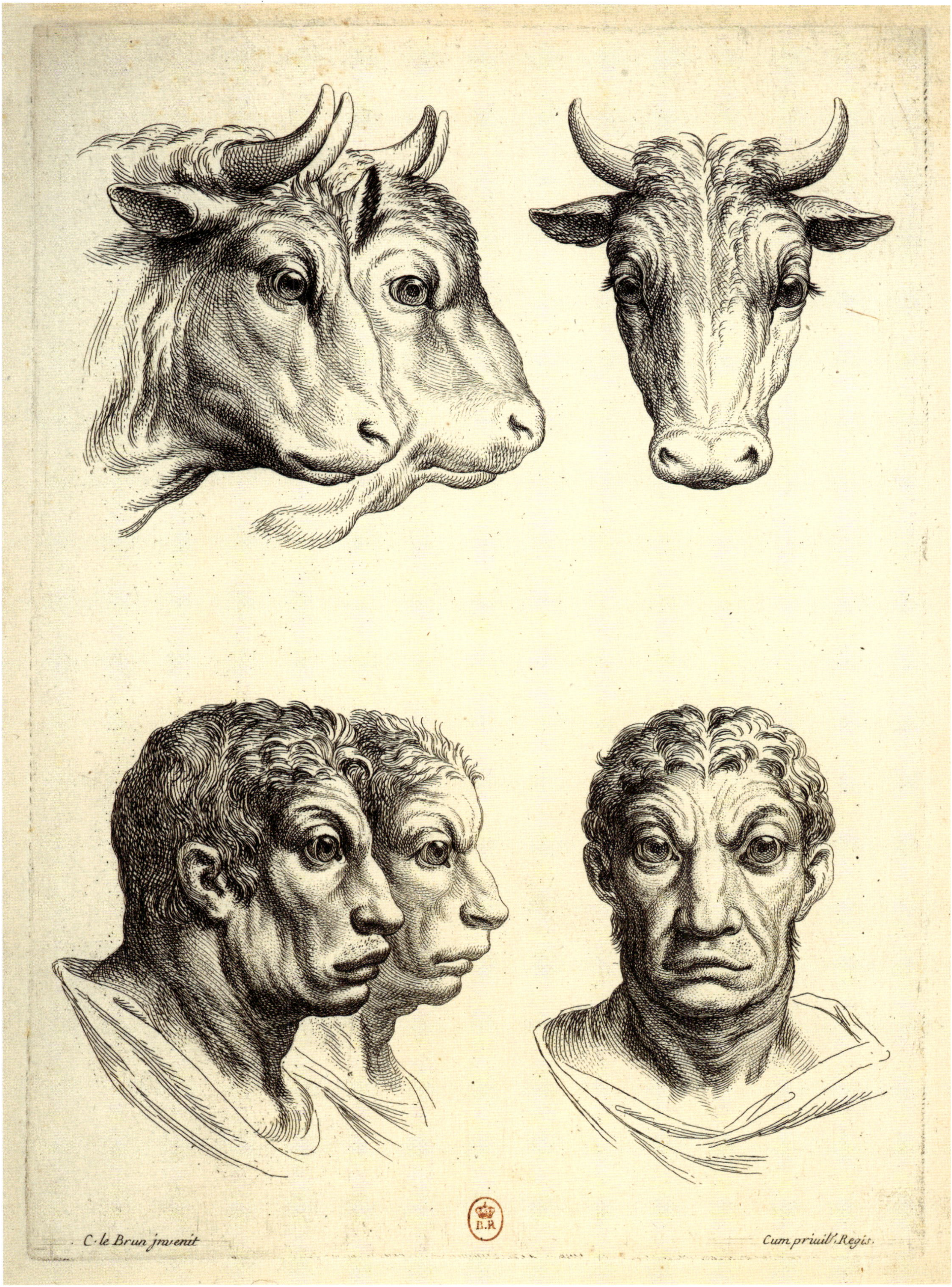

26

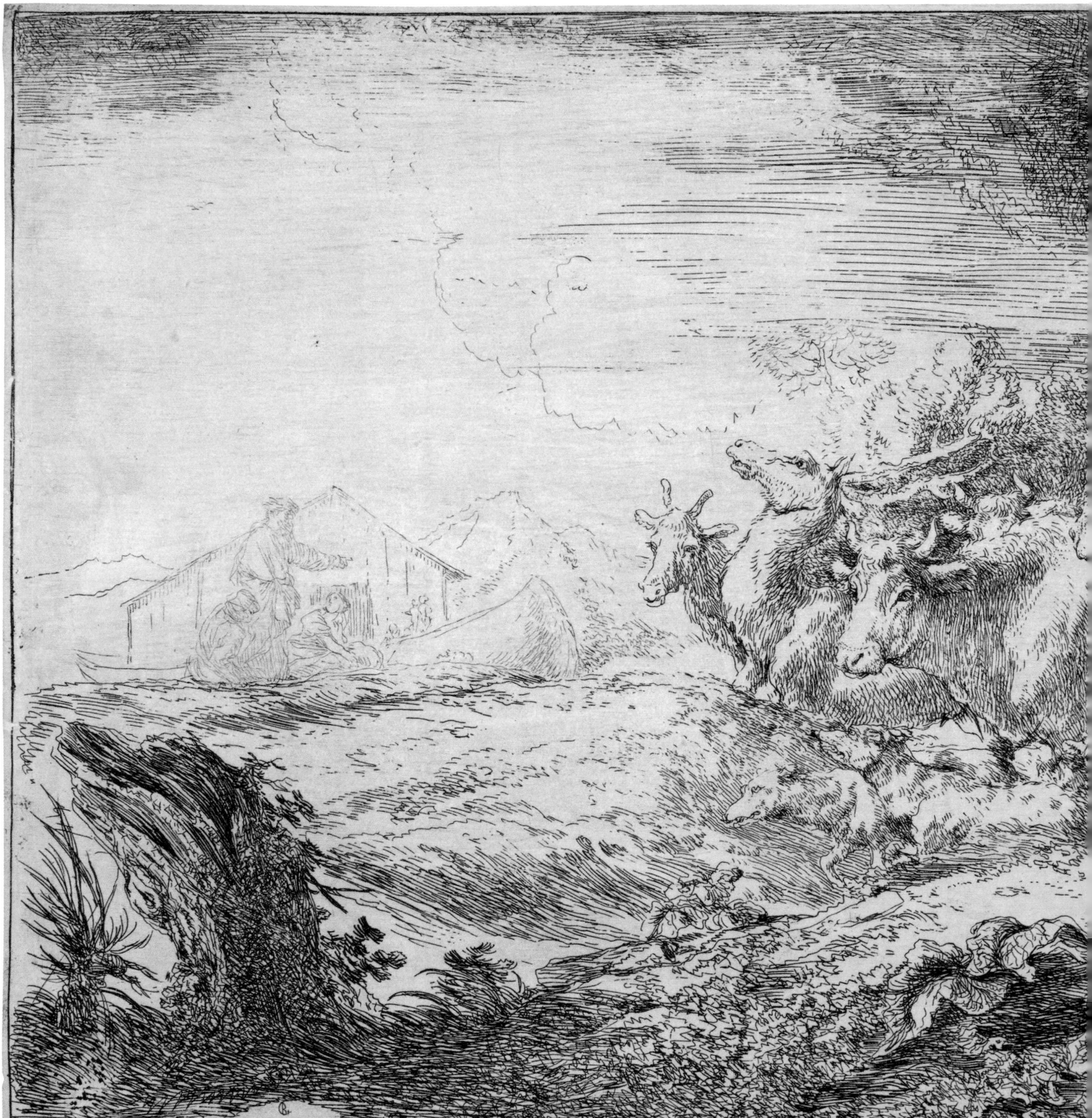

27

27 Giovanni Benedetto Castiglione, *Noah and the Animals Entering the Ark*, ca. 1650–1655

→ description on p. 56

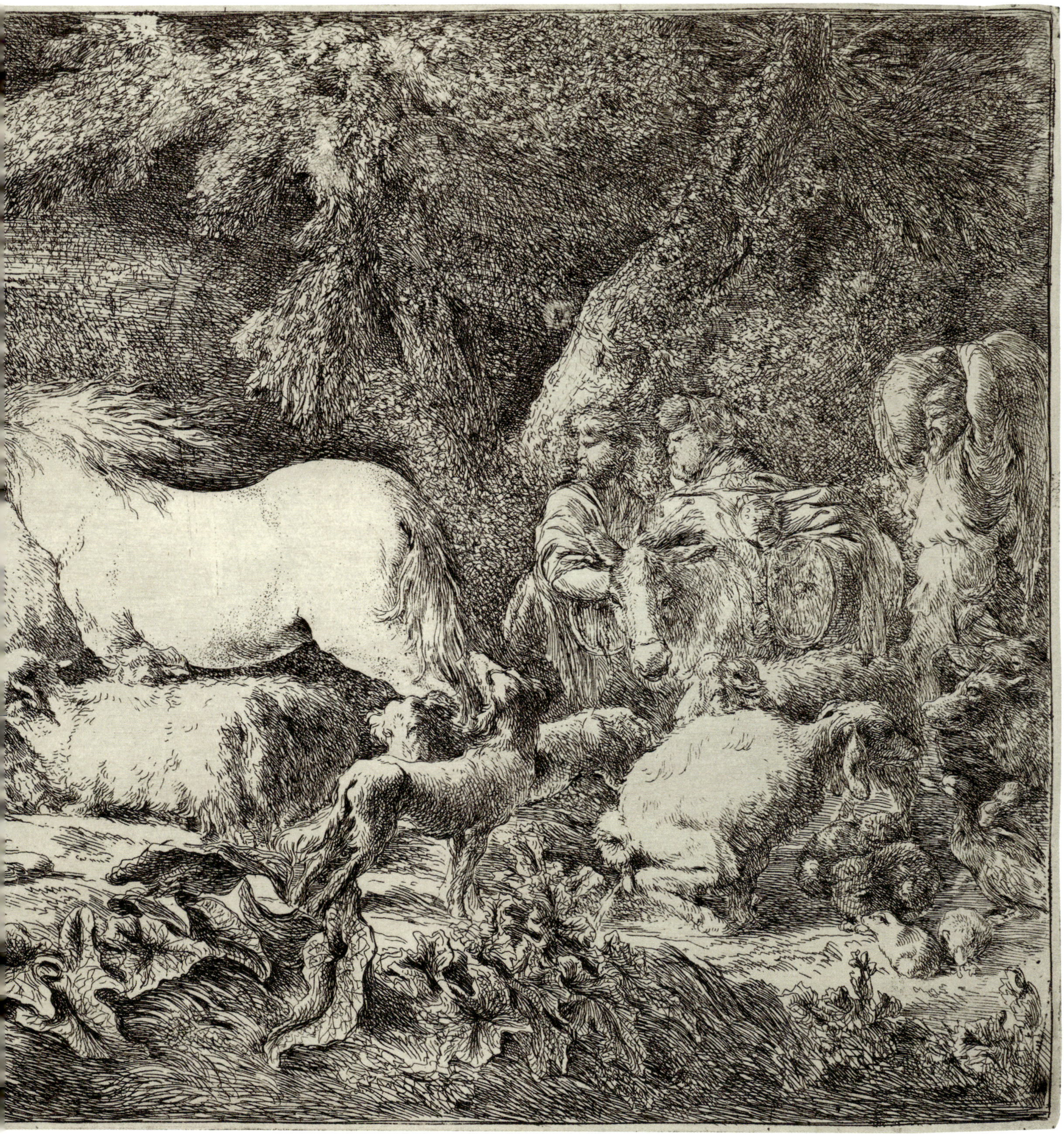

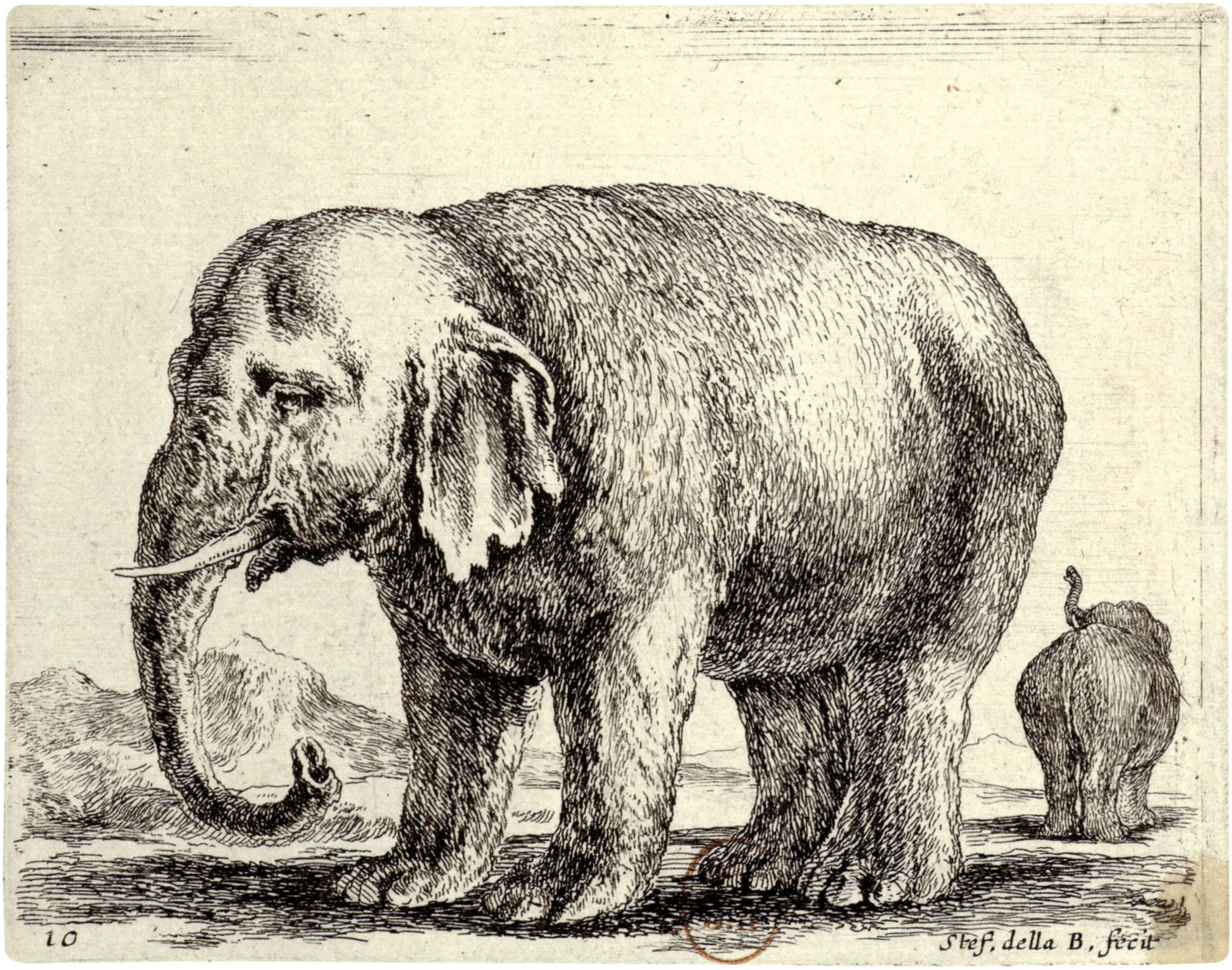

28

28 Stefano Della Bella, *Female Asian Elephant*, ca. 1643–1647

The Italian draughtsman Stefano Della Bella, known for his etchings, produced a series of small prints depicting animals. Some were copied from other engravings showing exotic species, but others were faithful likenesses drawn from life whenever this became possible. Such was the case with Hansken, the female elephant born in Ceylon in 1630, who travelled throughout Europe for about twenty years. She was a huge success, performing tricks of all kinds, famously handling a sword and a pistol! Hansken was portrayed in several prints during that period, and Rembrandt drew her on a number of occasions. Della Bella was also able to sketch her from life, either in 1643, when they were both in Paris, or in 1647 in Amsterdam. He drew her one last time in Florence in 1655 after her early death, which was due to malnutrition and inadequate care. V.S.

Etching | 8.5 x 10.8 cm (print area)

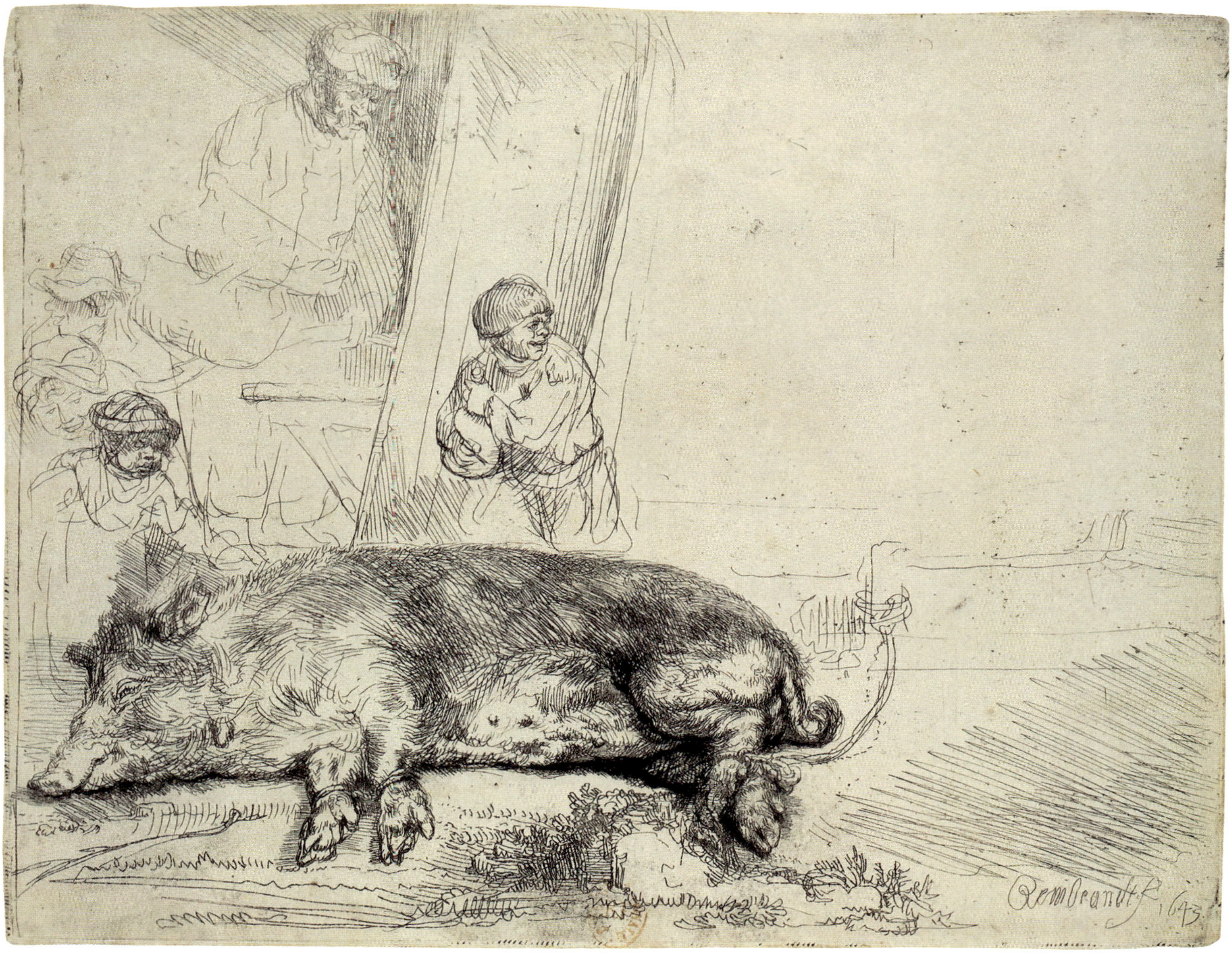

29

29 Rembrandt, *The Hog*, 1643

The slaughter of the pig in November forms part of the traditional portrayal of work carried out over the year. Rembrandt chose to give his image of this event an original slant. Instead of the traditional scene of cutting up the pig, he presented a timeless anatomical study of a recumbent sow, her eyes half-closed and her trotters bound. She is the only minutely engraved figure in the composition, drawing the gaze to the lower left-hand section of the print, while the upper right-hand side remains astonishingly white and blank. A few lightly etched figures can be seen in the background on the left; these are members of the family preparing to kill the animal. The child standing behind the pig is carrying an inflated bladder, a symbol of death in 17th century Holland. V.S.

Etching and drypoint | 14.5 x 18.4 cm (print area)

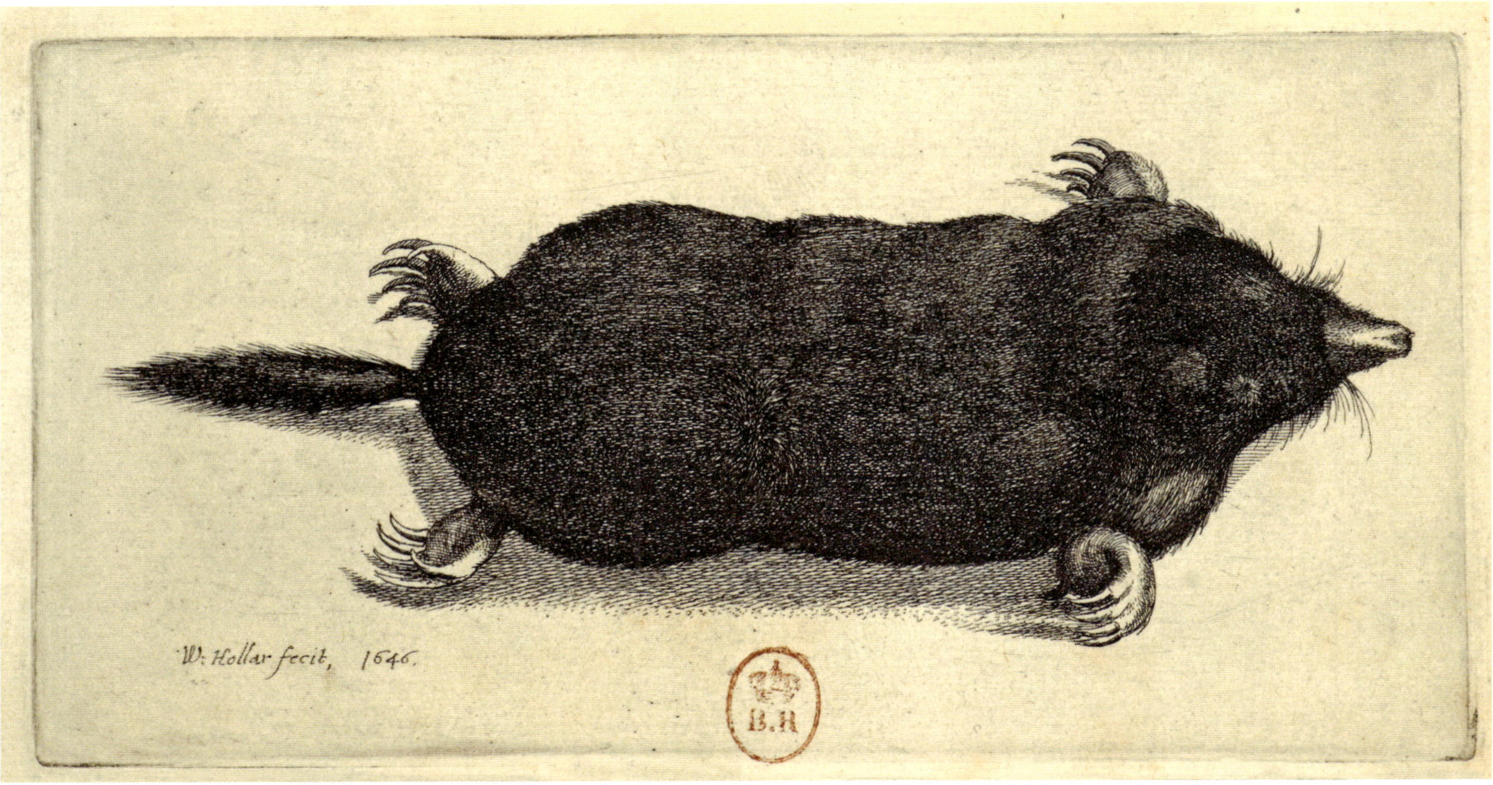

30

30 Wenceslas Hollar, *Dead Mole*, mid-17th century

Born in Prague in 1607, Wenceslas Hollar, a tireless traveller with an insatiable curiosity, produced a quantity of graphic work depicting his favourite themes: landscapes, city views, portraits, costumes and their adornments, animals and nature. He portrays all the animals in his images, from the insect to the large recumbent lion, with minute attention to detail, engraving them with great precision. He was particularly adept at reproducing the velvety sensuality of fur, as with this etching of a dead mole; his remarkably delicate portrayal has transformed a theoretically unappealing subject into an aesthetically pleasing image. V.S.

Etching | 7 x 3.8 cm (print area)

31 Anonymous, *Mice Attached to One Another by Their Tails*, 1683

During this period, curiosity was not confined to rare, large or unfamiliar animals. Monstrous specimens might be found in the corners of houses, and it was a much easier undertaking to record such events in printed images, given that they took place in localities nearer to print production centres. In this way, certain works were created in order to depict such phenomena, which served both as unusual news stories and as cases for scientific study.

This print records the astonishing discovery of six rats attached to one another by their tails, which were found in a cellar in Strasbourg in July 1683, shortly after the city had been taken by the French. Broadsides of this type, associated with actual events, rarely feature images of such fine quality and originality, in terms of both composition and execution. The sheet was issued by Johann Jonathan Felsecker, a printer from Nuremberg, who published another print on a similar theme; in that instance, the animals depicted attached by their tails were five cats! R.M.

Wunder-würdiger und seltzammer Scheusal eines entsetzlich und ominösen Ratten-Ungeziefers | Mezzotint and typographic content | 41.5 x 25 cm (sheet, trimmed)

Wunder-würdiger und seltzamer

Scheusal

Eines entsetzlich- und ominösen

Ratten-Ungeziefers/

So da den 4. und 14. Julii/ dieses mit GOtt tagenden 1683. Jahrs/ jüngsthin zu Straßburg in einem Keller gefunden worden.

Nach dem von guter Hand erhaltenen Original-Riß/ ihrer Gestaltung also in Kupffer-Bildniß/ zur Bewunder und Anschau vorgestellet.

6. Ratten welche mit den schwaiffen sehr ineinander verschlungen den 4/14 Juli in einen Keller zu Strasburg gefangen worden.

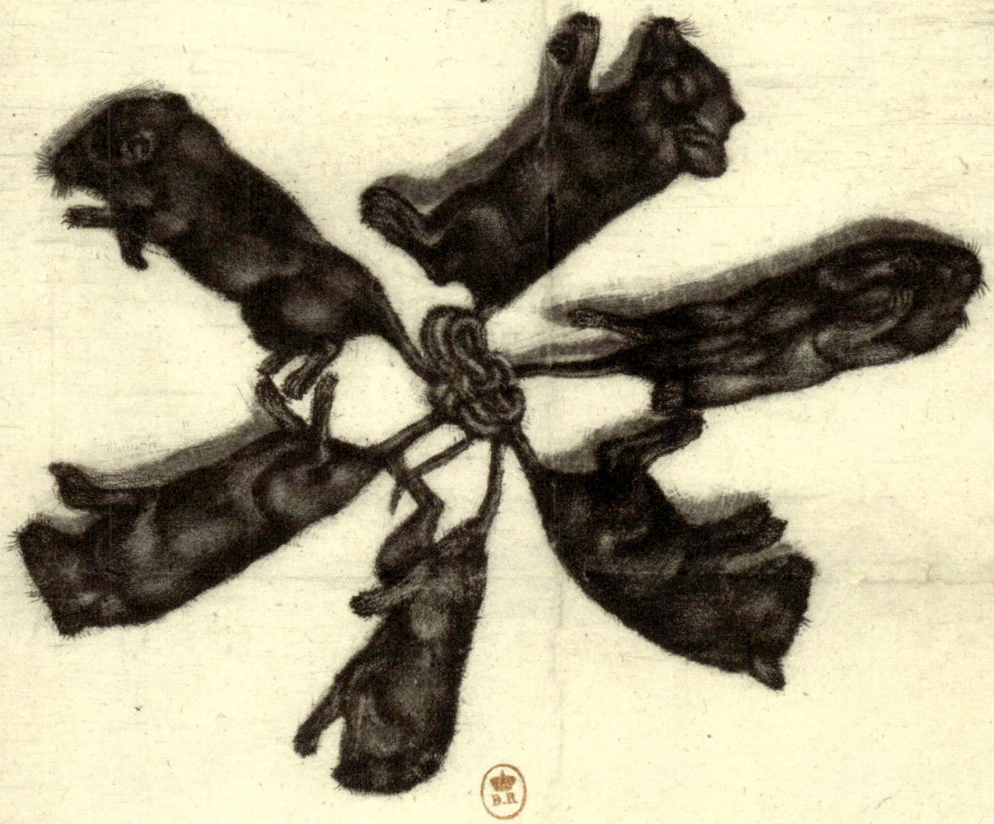

Zu finden bey J.J. Felsecker

Wann je und allewege die Abscheulichkeit unserer Sünden-Greule/ auch abscheuliche und greuliche Straffen/ (welche uns/ leider! zum Theil schon zimlich in die Hände gehen / und fast nahe herein rücken) verdienet und empfangen / so ist es ja auch kein Wunder / wann der grundgütige Wunder-GOtt uns auch vorhero/ noch zur gnädigen Erinnerung/ mit so abscheulichen Schrecken-Boten und Wunder-Begebenheiten heimsuchet. Wie allhier Conterfeylich / zu männigliches Nachsinnen und Erinnerung / vorgestellet ist; das garstige und unflätige Ratten-Ungeziefer/ welches zu Straßburg in Herrn Ammeister Würtzens Keller/ den 4. und 14. Julii/ mit jedermans Entsetzen/ und vieler Leute verwunderlichen Anschauen/ ist gefunden und vorgewiesen worden. Nemlichen sechs mercklich grosse Ratten/ so da mit den Schweiffen alle ineinander gewickelt und verwachsen/ daß sie nicht ohne Verletzung voneinander kommen kunten oder zu bringen waren/ sondern sich gleich einer Rose ausbreiteten/ deren einer hier / der andere dort hinaus wolte. Worüber es von vielen auch viel- und wunderliche Muthmassungen abgabe. So zwar auch nicht ohne: Dann die so vielfaltig gifftige/ widersinnig und unchristliche Anschläge / welche doch Christen wider Christen untereinander högen und ausbrüten/ deren einer hier/ und der andere dort/ als wutgierig und zwiespaltig hinaus will / sind eben auch ein solches gifftiges und Länder-verderbliches Unheil / als hier an diesem Ratten-Ungeziefer zu sehen / vorgestellet und gewiesen wird. Von einem guten Freund wird anbey berichtet / daß man dieses Ratten-Spectacul zu gedachten Straßburg nach der Pfaltz oder dem Rahthaus allda selbige verwunderlich zu weisen gebracht / und indeme man sie hernach alle erschlagen wollen / seye jedoch einer darvon entkommen/ die andern aber wohl-getroffen ligen blieben. GOtt zerstreue und verstöre also alle böse und gifftige Anschläge / wider sein Christliches Häuflein / daß solche nicht überhand nehmen / und in dem tieffen Abgrund Blut-begieriger Hertzen einwurtzeln mögen.

Die Ratzen-Art/ der Wider-Sinn/ der Rach-Wut vollen Menschen-Hertzen/
Die nur Zwiespalt und Strittigkeit/ und Blutvergiessen richten an/
Erwecken eben so viel Scheu/ als leider! Schad und Länder-Schmertzen/
Und sind/ gleichwie die Ratzen-Brut/ so Sünd-verwickelt übel drau/
Biß daß die GOttes-Rach erwacht / entdecket ihren Gifft und Grausen/
Und gibet den verdienten Lohn/ mit Spott und Tod/ auf ihre Köpff/
Daß ihnen selbsten es ergeht / wie sie mit andern wollen hausen/
Und dieses weist zur Spiegel-Schau / hier / dieses Natur Scheu-Geschöpff.

32 Anonymous, *Giant Squid, Found Dead in Ireland,* 1674

Despite the descriptions given by Pliny the Elder and the Scandinavian myth of the Kraken, giant deep-water cephalopods were long thought to be imaginary creatures as they were so rarely encountered by humans. In the 17th century, however, it was recorded that the remains of at least five giant squid or cuttlefish were found on various Northern European coasts. The discovery of one such specimen in October 1673, following a storm in Dingle-I-cosh, County Kerry in the south-west of Ireland, was reported a few months later in this English broadside issued by Francis Smith, a London bookseller. Unlike a number of other publications reporting the existence of such monstrous creatures, this makes no mention of God, but endeavours to provide a very precise description of the animal, including its strange, retractable, trunk-like mouth, which is presented in the image as a second head, equipped with eyes.

Shortly afterwards, an eight-page booklet developing details of the discovery appeared in London; it included a faithfully reproduced woodcut of the illustration on the broadside. It was indicated that this had originated from a painting on canvas that had brought the image of the squid to London, as it was impossible to preserve the animal. V.S.

A True Relation of a Strange Monster | Etching | 48.5 x 37.5 (print area)

A true Relation of a ſtrange Monſter that lately was by a Storm, driven a ſhore at *Dingle-I-coſh* in the County of *Kerry* in *Ireland*, with Letters Teſtimonial, under the hands of credible Eye-witneſſes.

To Mr. John Wickins *at the* Mearmaid *in* Milkſtreet, *London.*

LOving Friend, I had heard of this following Relation yeſterday, but not knowing the certainty of it, did not regard the writing of it: But this evening ſent to a very worthy man, who tels me he ſpake with the Perſon that is the Author, and that took the Fiſh (it is this.) One Mr. *James Steward*, whom I know, and Alderman *Aſhurſt* I think knows, was a Trader of a long ſtanding, travelling on the Sea-ſide, at a place in the weſt of *Ireland* called *Dingle-I-coſh*, where there is great fiſhing for Pilchers, ſaw a great Fiſh come ſwimming on the top of the water, towards the ſhore, at laſt it came quite to Land, he marked it and made towards it, and laid hold on the horns of it, and the Crowns on the Horns, had like to have taken off his fingers; it had two Heads, one great one, and a ſmall one coming out of that, the ſmall one had two tongues, and was like the head of an Eagle; on the great head ſtood ten horns, two were nine and eleven foot a peece, others which were wreathed, four of them about each great horn; the wreathed horns were full of Crownes; many hundreds of them, about the bigneſ of a Cloak-button, and like teeth under the Crownes: The bigneſ of the Monſter, was as big as a horſe; he hath brought to Town two of the wreathed horns and the ſmall head, and the reſt are coming up, and will be here the next week, and expoſed to view.

This Relation the man himſelf, who is a ſober Perſon told to a very good man, from whom I have it, and who ſaw the picture of it, which Picture he hath brought to *Dublin*, but the ſhape of the great head, this perſon cannot tell me, This ſtory for the unuſualneſ of it, I take notice of, and ſeems to be worth writing, if when it appears it anſwer the relation, which I have alſo ſent to Alderman *Aſhurſt*, I reſt.

Dublin, Decemb. 13, 1673. *your very loving friend* Thomas Hooke.

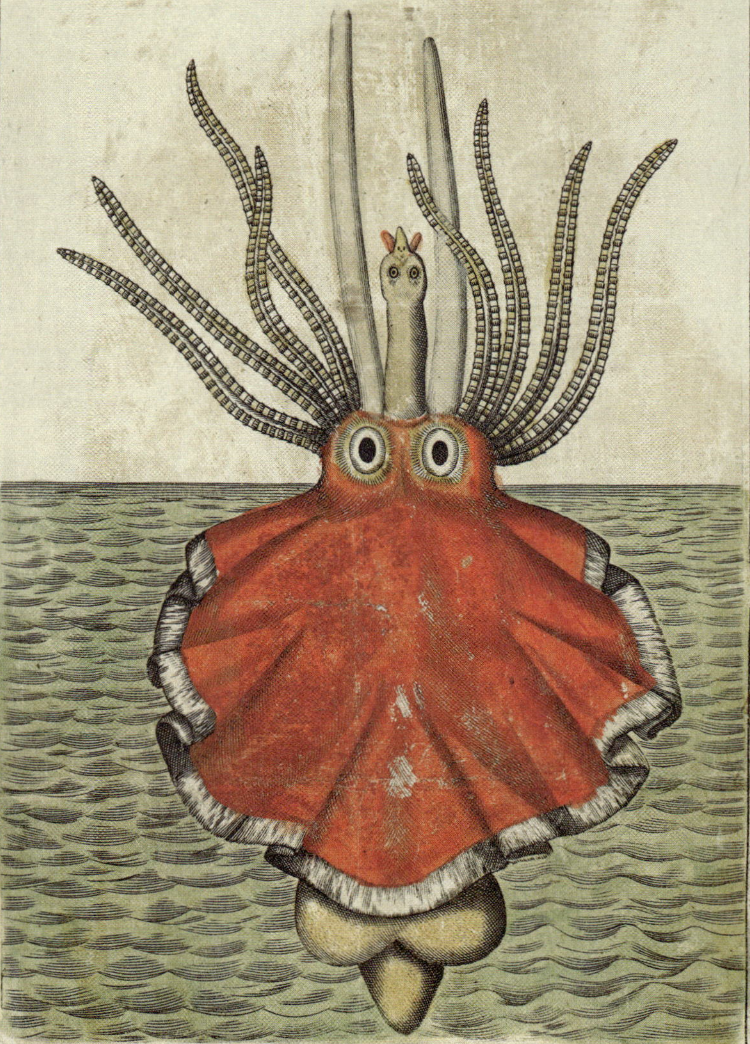

The Monſter Deſcribed.

THis Monſter was taken at *Dingle-I-coſh* in the County of *Kerry*, being driven up by a great ſtorm in the Month of *October* laſt, 1673; having two heads, one great head, (out of which ſprung a little head two foot, or a yard from the great head) with two great eyes, each as big as a pewter diſh, the length of it being about nineteen foot, bigger in the body then any horſe, of the ſhape repreſented by this figure, having upo[illegible] great head ten horns, ſom[illegible] ſome of eight or ten[illegible]n foot long, the bi[illegible] as a mans Le[illegible], which h[illegible]th ſides; A[illegible]end it ſelf h[illegible] horns plain, an[illegible]e the biggeſt and midd[illegible], the other eight had o[illegible]ndred Crowns a peece, placed by two and two on each of them, in all 800 crowns, each Crown having teeth, that tore any thing that touched them, by ſhutting together the ſharp teeth, being like the wheels of a watch, The Crowns were as big as a mans thumb or ſomething bigger, that a man might put his finger in the hollow part of them, and had in them ſome thing like a pearl or eye in the middle; over this Monſters back was a mantle of a bright Red Colour, with a fringe round it, it hung down on both ſides like a Carpet on a table, falling back on each ſide, and faced with white; the crowns and mantle were glorious to behold: This monſter had not one bone about him, nor fins nor ſcales, or feet, but had a ſmooth skin like a mans belly. It ſwoom by the lappits of the mantle; The little head it could dart forth a yard from the great one, and draw it in again at pleſure, being like a hawks beak, and having in the little head two tongues, by which it is thought it received all its nouriſhment; when it was dead and opened the liver wayed 30 pound. The man that took it came to *Clonmel* the 4th. of this inſtant *December*, with two of the horns in a long box with the little head, and the figure of the fiſh drawn on a painted-cloth, which was the full proportion of it, and he went up to *Dublin*, with an intent to ſhew it to the Lord Lieutenant.

Loving Friend, *Dublin December* 23, 1673. To Mr. *John Wickins* at the *Mearmaid* in *Milk-ſtreet, London.*

I ſend you this onely purſuant to my former of the Fiſh, which I now confirm to be as I gave you the firſt Account with this addition of certainty, that knowing the man by name *James Steward*, and hearing two or three nights ſince of his being at a Printers neer our houſe to get the Lord Lieutenants Order Printed, which he gave him for expoſing what he hath of the fiſh to view, I ſent, deſiring to ſpeak with him, and he came, having then the Picture with him of the Fiſh, and he gave me himſelf the full account of it. *viz.*

That in the month of *October* laſt, I think about the 15th. day he was alone riding by the Seaſide, at *Dingle-I-coſh*, and ſaw a great thing in the Sea, which drew his eye towards it, and it came juſt to him; when he diſcerned the horns it began to look frightfully, he ſaid he was ſometimes afraid to look on it, and when he durſt look on it, it was the moſt ſplended ſight that ever he ſaw; The Horns were ſo beſpangled with thoſe Crowns, as he calls them; they ſhewed he ſaith like Pearls or precious Stones; the Horns it could move and weild about the Head as a Snail doth, all the Ten; the two long ones it moſtly bore forwards, the other eight mov'd too and fro every way: When it came to ſhore its foreparts reſted on the ſhore, and there lay; He got help after a while, and when he ſaw it ſtirred not to fright them, he got ropes and put them about the hinder-parts, and began to draw it on ſhore, and ſaw it ſtir'd not to hurt them, they grew bold, and went to pull with their hands on the Horns, but theſe Crowns ſo bit them, that they were forced to quit their hold; the crowns had teeth under every one of them, and had a power to faſten on any thing that touched them; they moved the Horns with hand-ſpikes, and ſo being evening they left it on the ſhore, and came in the morning and found it dead. The two long Horns are about one 11 foot, the other 9; the other 8 Horns, about 6 and 8 foot long a peice, and as thick as a mans arm every one of them. He hath brought up to *Dublin* but two ſhort Horns of the Crowned ones, and the little Head, being not able to bring the reſt the way is ſo long.

The certainty is atteſted by many at the place, and is no doubt a very certain truth, the mantle was all red on the out-ſide, which for the colour ſake he kept a peice of it, it was five inches thick, and white under; when they cut the Fiſh it had not a drop of blood, nor ſcale, nor fin, my man took a draught of the Picture which I have here encloſed he ſaid it was as big as any horſe as ever he ſaw, it had no leggs.

Your loving friend, Thomas Hooke.

Drangon neer *Clonmell, Decemb.* 19, 1673.

Dear Son,

I Did the laſt week write to you, which I hope you have received, to which I refer you. This incloſed paper is a form of a ſtrange and monſtrous Fiſh, that was caſt on ſhore in the County of *Kerry* in *Ireland*, about a month ſince by a ſtorm, you need not doubt the truth of it, for I have my ſelf ſeen part of it, and have one of the Crowns by me to produce, I refer you to the paper for a relation of it; remember your duty both to God and man; be carefull in both, and the Lord direct you with all our Dear love to you and all friends, concludes him that is your very affectionate loving Father.

Thomas Clear.

LONDON, Printed for *Francis Smith* at the *Elephant* and *Caſtle* near the *Royal Exchange* in *Cornhil.*

Publiſhed with allowance.

32

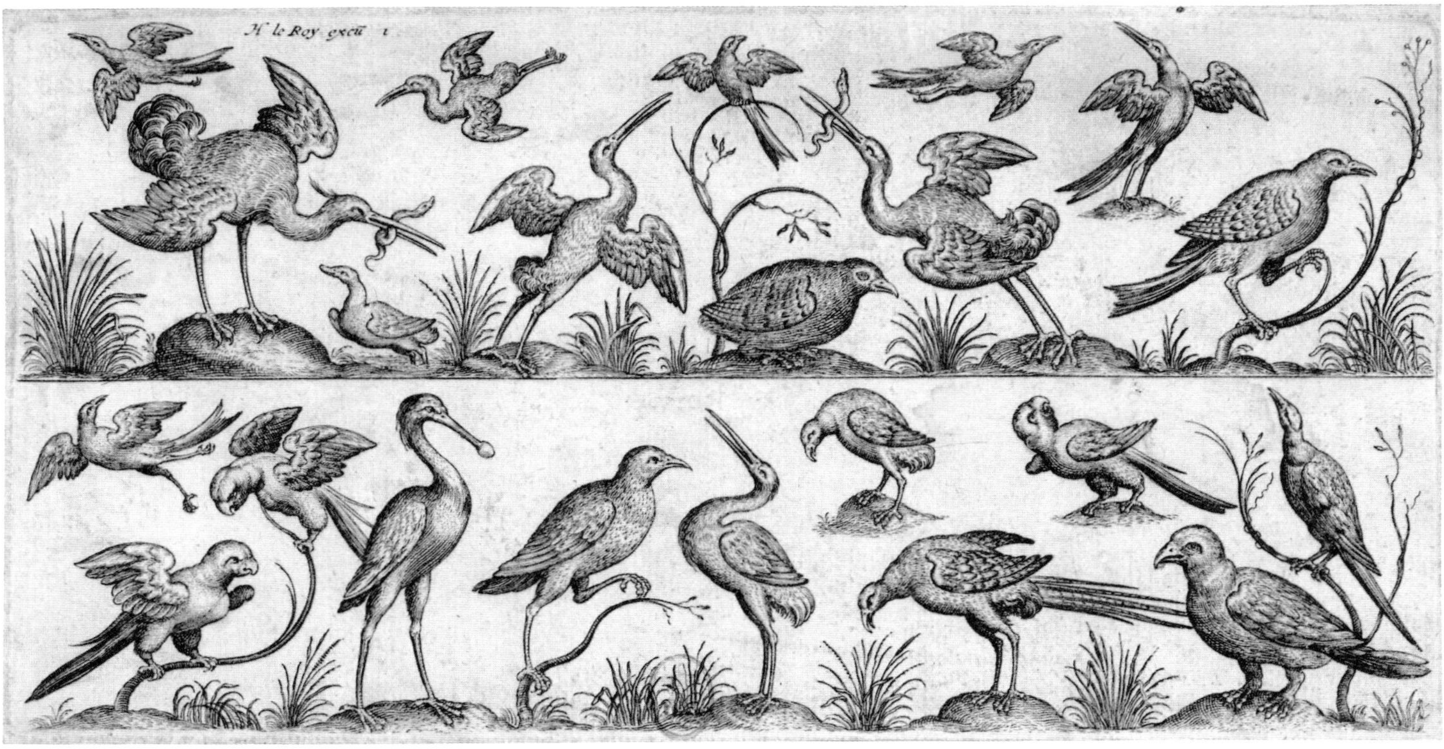

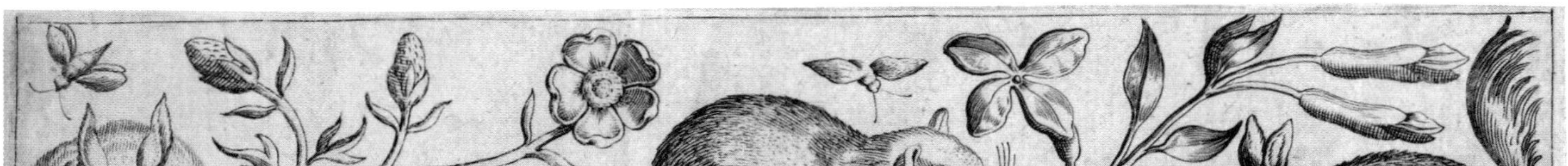

33

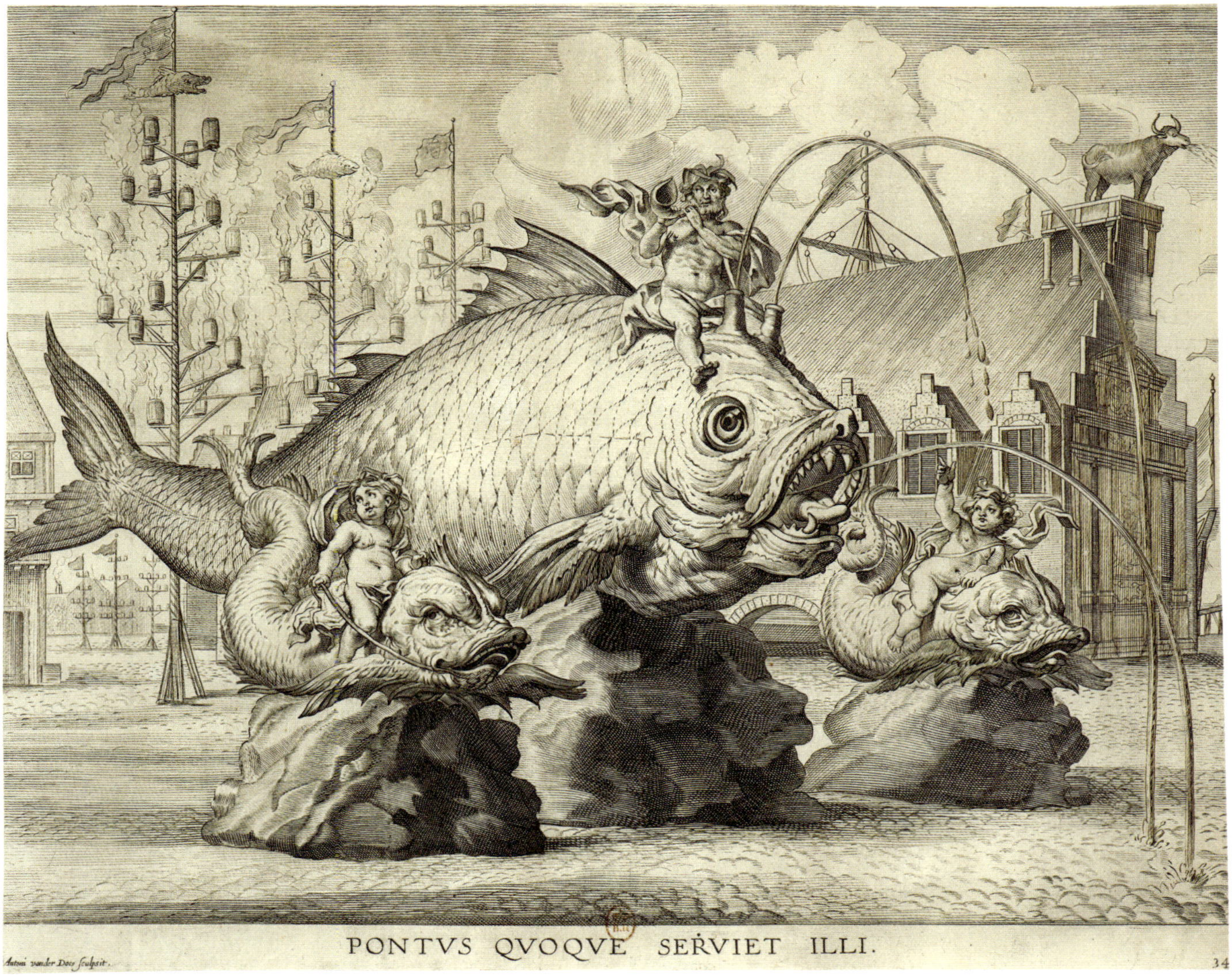

34

33 Henry Le Roy (?), *Prints Showing Birds and Small Animals*, ca. 1630–1640

Images of animals were used in the Middle Ages as decorative features for the borders and margins of books. Later, during the Ancien Régime, a similar vocabulary was adopted for the ornamental elements appearing at the beginning of each new chapter. These small animals introduced an entertaining and fanciful aspect to a large number of decorative arts besides those associated with the domain of books. Collections of models were available to fuel artists' imaginations; these could be adapted to decorate cabinets, tapestries or indeed other prints!

The example we have shown here is a burin engraving by Henry Le Roy of Holland, who had settled in Paris near the rue Saint-Jacques, a locality where this technique was being developed. Le Roy depicted elegant birds – particularly wading species – in various situations, some in flight and some perched on branches, as well as other, more original animals, such as rabbits, squirrels or carp, which in certain cases were copied from older models. This clearly did not affect the popularity of the series, which was re-published a few years later by Herman Weyen. R.M.

Burin engraving | 18.5 x 9.5 cm (print area)

34 Anthony Van der Does, *Decoration for the Joyous Entry of Ferdinand of Spain into Ghent*, 1635

This gigantic fountain in the form of a fish was one of the spectacular types of mechanisms that were a particularly popular feature of celebratory occasions during the baroque period. It was included among the temporary decorations that lined the processional route of the young Prince Ferdinand's 'joyous entry' into Ghent in 1635. An Infante of Spain, the prince had been named Governor of the Low Countries in 1630, and arrived there only after his triumph at the Battle of Nördlingen, when, at the head of his imperial troops, he achieved an outstanding victory over the Swedish Protestant army. The city authorities called upon the intellectual élites and leading painters and technicians of the day to devise the programme of events and the sovereigns' ceremonial arrival. Costly booklets and prints were subsequently produced in commemoration of these prestigious celebrations, many of which were ruinously expensive. V.S.

Burin engraving | 30 x 37.5 cm (print area)

35 Pieter Soutman, after Pieter Paul Rubens, *The Hunting of the Crocodile and Hippopotamus*, between 1642 and 1657

Rubens's predilection for dramatic action, heroic endeavour, vigorous movement and intensity of countenance achieved its fullest expression in the series of hunting scenes he was commissioned to paint by Maximilian I of Bavaria. Rubens breathed new life into this genre, which had been neglected since the Renaissance, using an Oriental setting for his scenes and depicting his hunters wearing turbans.

This hunt, the reproduction of a painting held in Munich, includes the first realistic representation of a hippopotamus since the days of Antiquity. Rubens may have been able to see stuffed examples of this animal in Rome in 1601, during an exhibition that had caused a certain amount of consternation, as these hippopotamuses did not correspond to the descriptions given by Aristotle or Herodotus. However, the text accompanying the print takes up an old classical theme, according to which the hippopotamus throws all caution to the wind when fighting its mortal foe, the crocodile, and finds itself at the mercy of man.

It is to the engraver Pieter Soutman of Haarlem, a student of Rubens from 1615 to 1620, that we owe the most impressive prints of these hunts that fascinated Delacroix. Vigorously etched rather than being engraved with a burin – a technique always imposed by Rubens for interpretations of his work – these works probably date from after 1640, when the painter died. V.S.

Etching | 46.7 x 63 cm (print area)

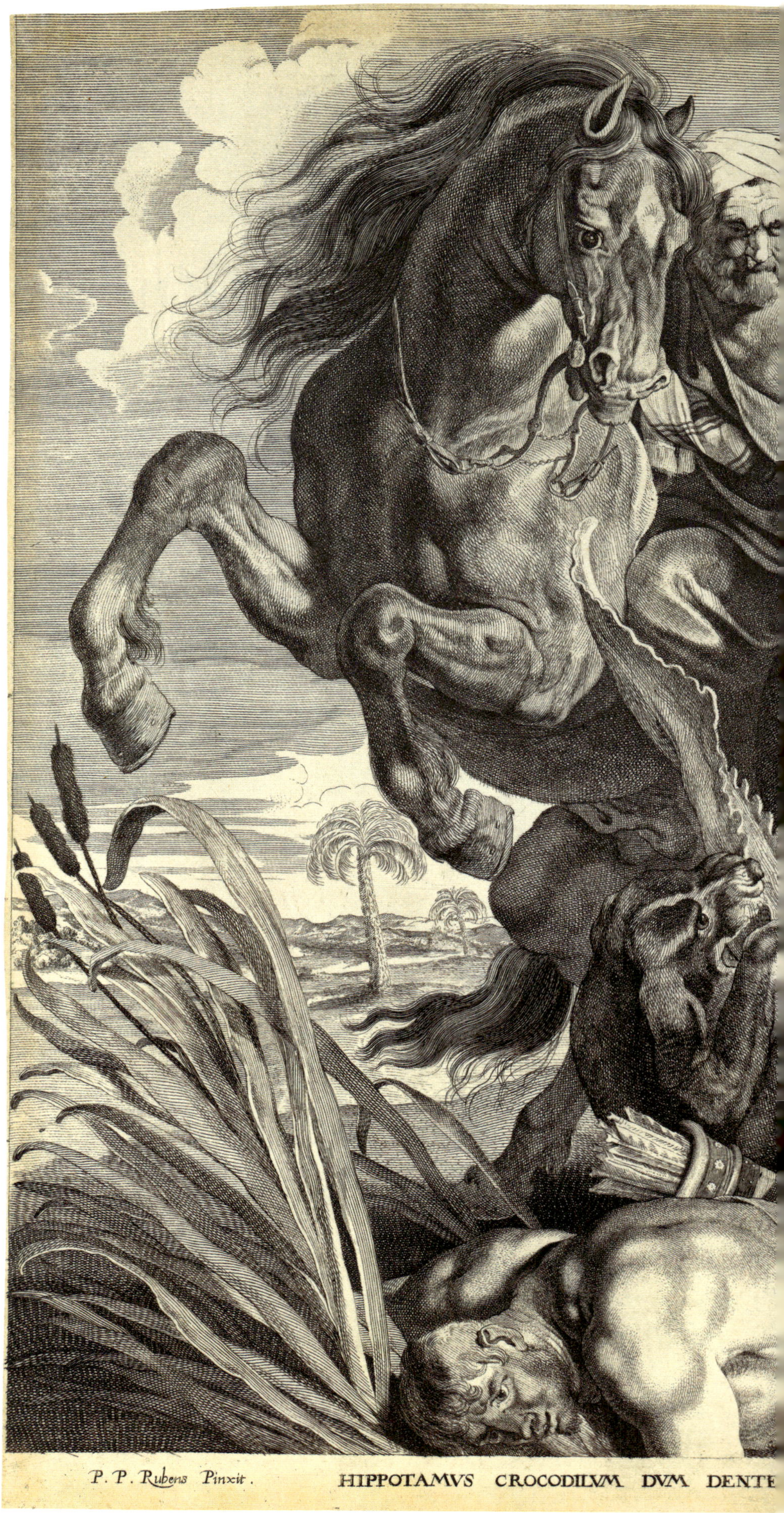

35

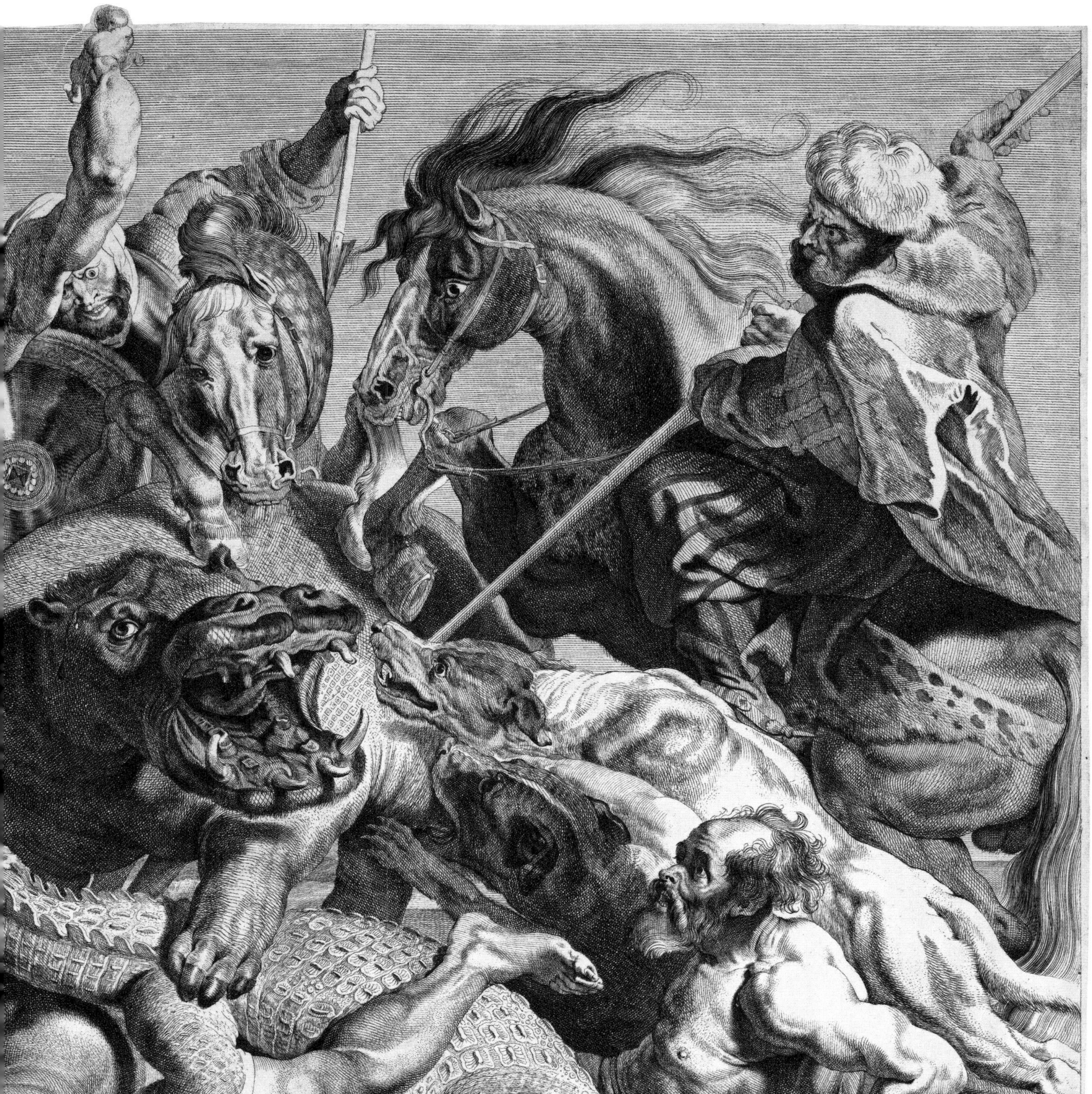
CTIT HOSTEM, IMPROVIDVS HOMINIS DEFICIT IPSE MANV.
P. Soutman. Inuenit Effigiauit et Excud. Cum Priuil.

36 Jan Saenredam, *Beached Sperm Whale Near Beverwijk in 1601*, 1602

The sight of rare animals sometimes became truly spectacular events. On 19 December 1601, a dead male sperm whale was washed ashore at Beverwijk, not far from Amsterdam. The phenomenon attracted curious onlookers from every social class, including Ernst-Casimir, Count of Nassau-Dietz, first cousin to the Prince of Orange; the young man held a handkerchief to his nose on account of the animal's powerful smell. The artist depicted himself drawing the whale, his presence at the scene testifying to the accuracy of the likeness.

However, images dating from this period cannot be viewed solely in terms of realistic representation. When the beached whale appeared, the war between the future United Provinces (now the Netherlands) and Spain had already been raging for twenty years. One week later, on 24 December 1601, a solar eclipse occurred in Northern Europe; seen as an ill omen, this was depicted in the cartouche frame at the top of the image. In a later version of the engraving, Death is shown firing arrows directly at the figure of Amsterdam: the image has both moral and political connotations.

This print therefore reminds us that in the 17th century, animals were not simply viewed with the dispassionate eyes of science, but were still associated with contexts and symbolism often rooted in ancient times. R.M.

Burin engraving | 40.7 x 59.6 cm (boundary line)

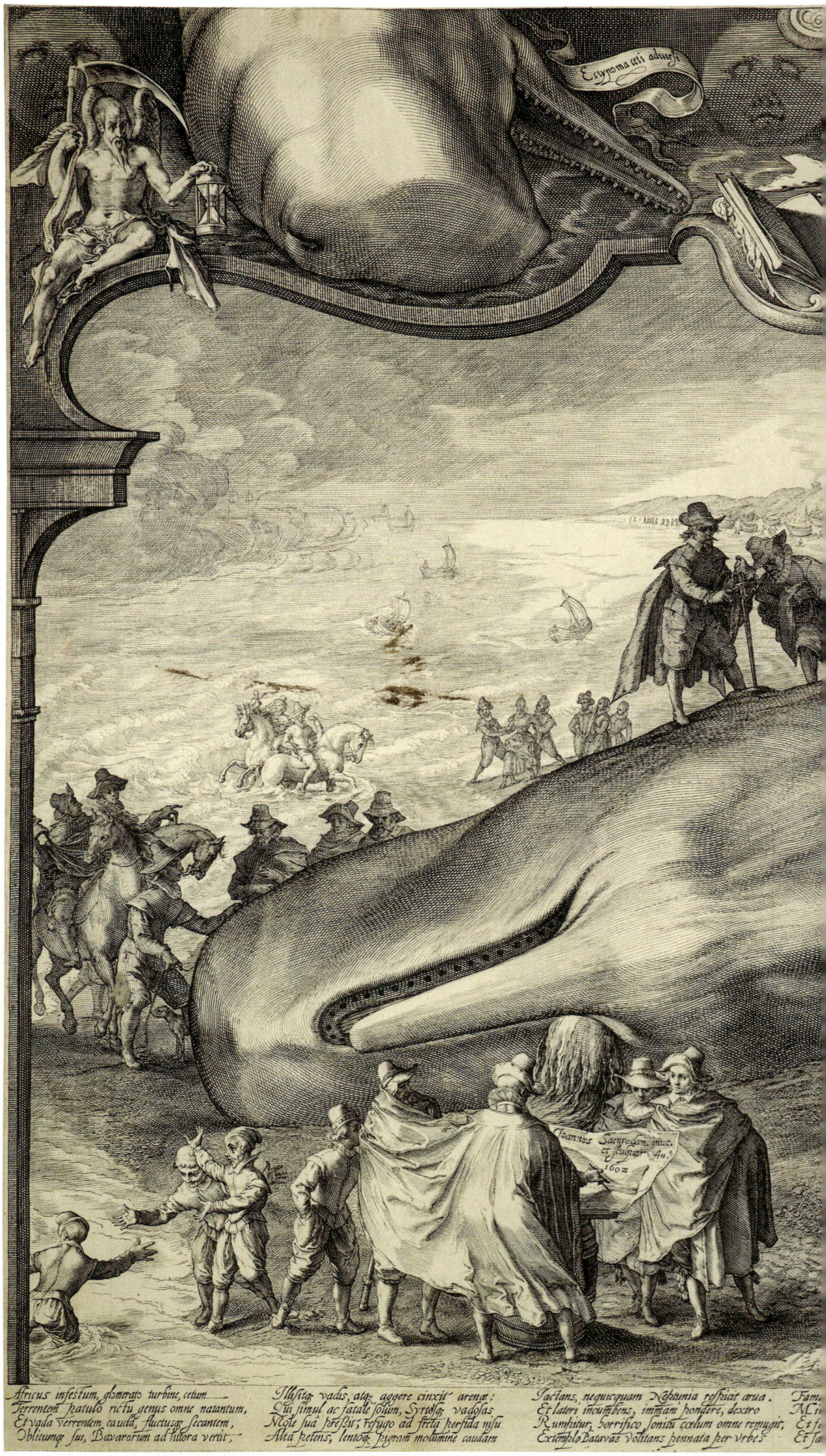

36

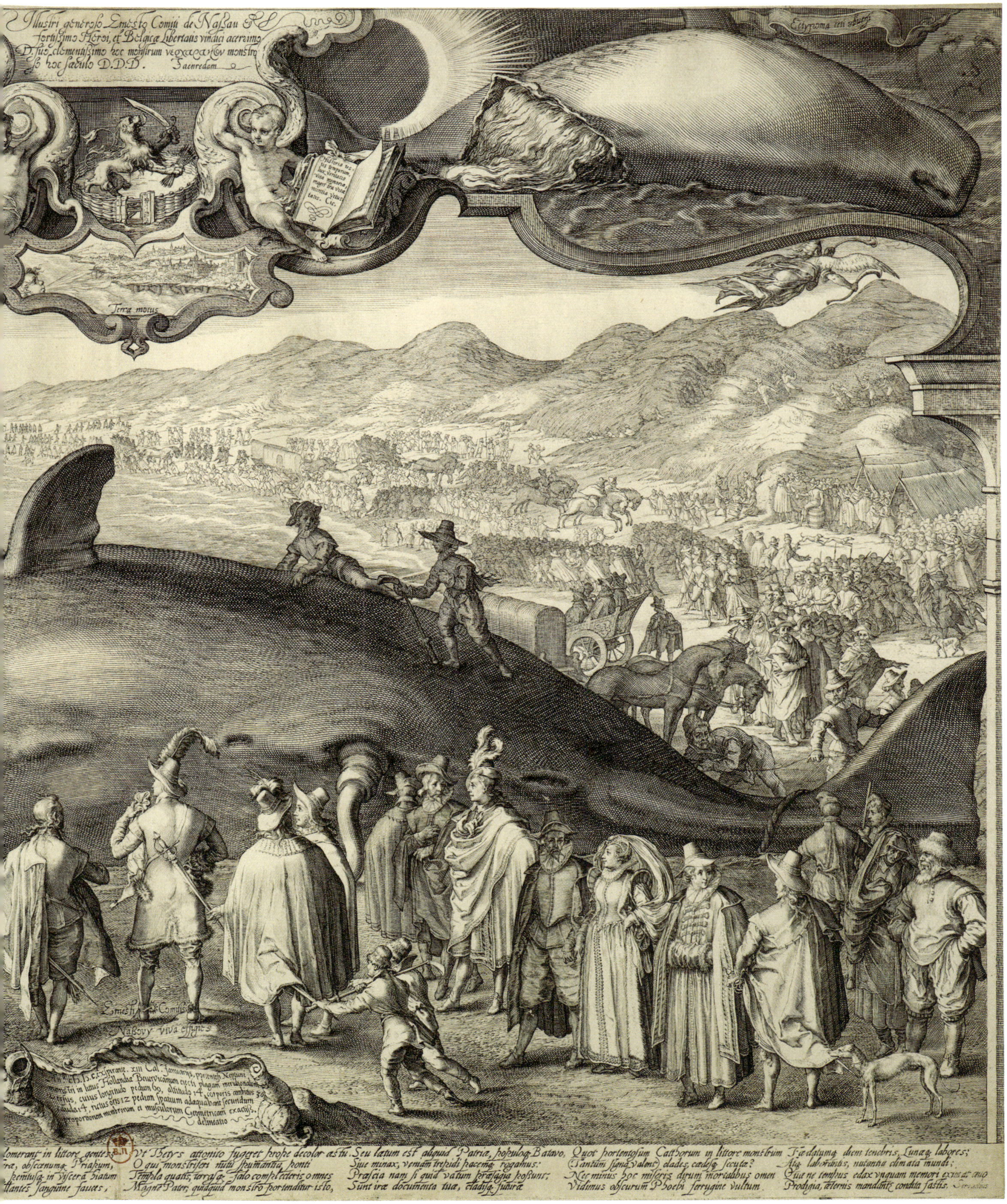
Illustri generoso Ernesto Comiti de Nassau &c.
fortissimo Heroi, et Belgicæ Libertatis vindici acerrimo
D. suo clementissimo hoc monstrum
hoc sæculo D.D.D. Saenredam
Terra motus
Nassovy viva effigies
Vt Thetys attonito fugeret prope decolor æstu.
O qui monstriferi nutu spumantia ponti
Templa quatis, terrasq; salo complecteris omnes
Magne Pater, quidquid monstro portenditur isto,
Seu lætum est aliquid Patriæ, populoq; Batavo,
Siue minax, veniam trepidi pacemq; rogamus:
Præscia nam si quid vatum præsagia possunt:
Sunt iræ documenta tuæ, cladisq; futuræ
Quot portentosum Cattorum in littore monstrum
(Tantum signa valent) clades, cædesq; secutæ?
Nec minus hoc miseris dirum mortalibus omen
Vidimus obscurum Phoebi ferrugine vultum
Fœdatumq; diem tenebris, Lunæq; labores;
Atq; laborantis, nutantia climata mundi;
Quæ ne tempus edax vnquam memori eximat ævo
Prodigia, æternis mandantq; condita fastis.

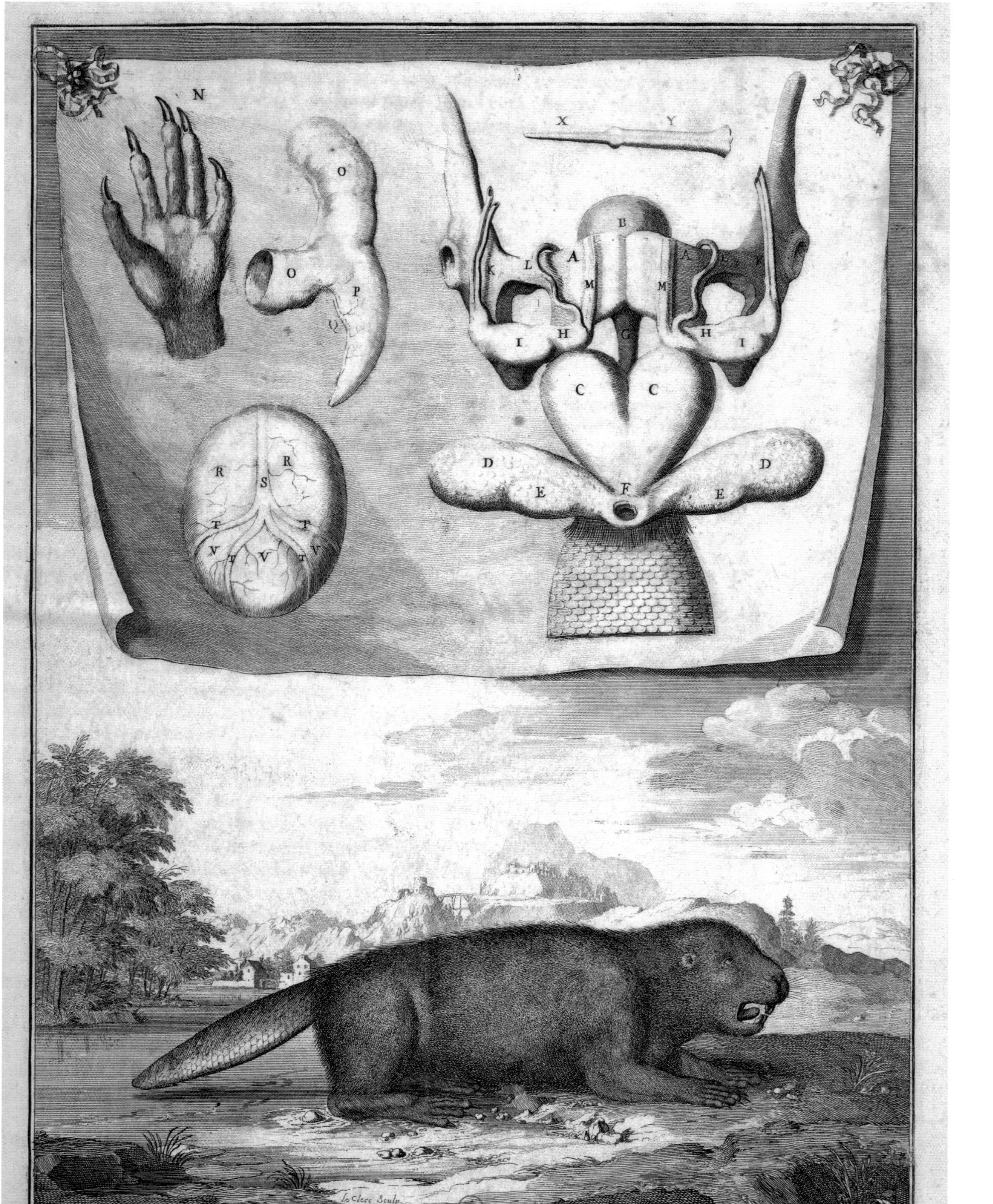

37

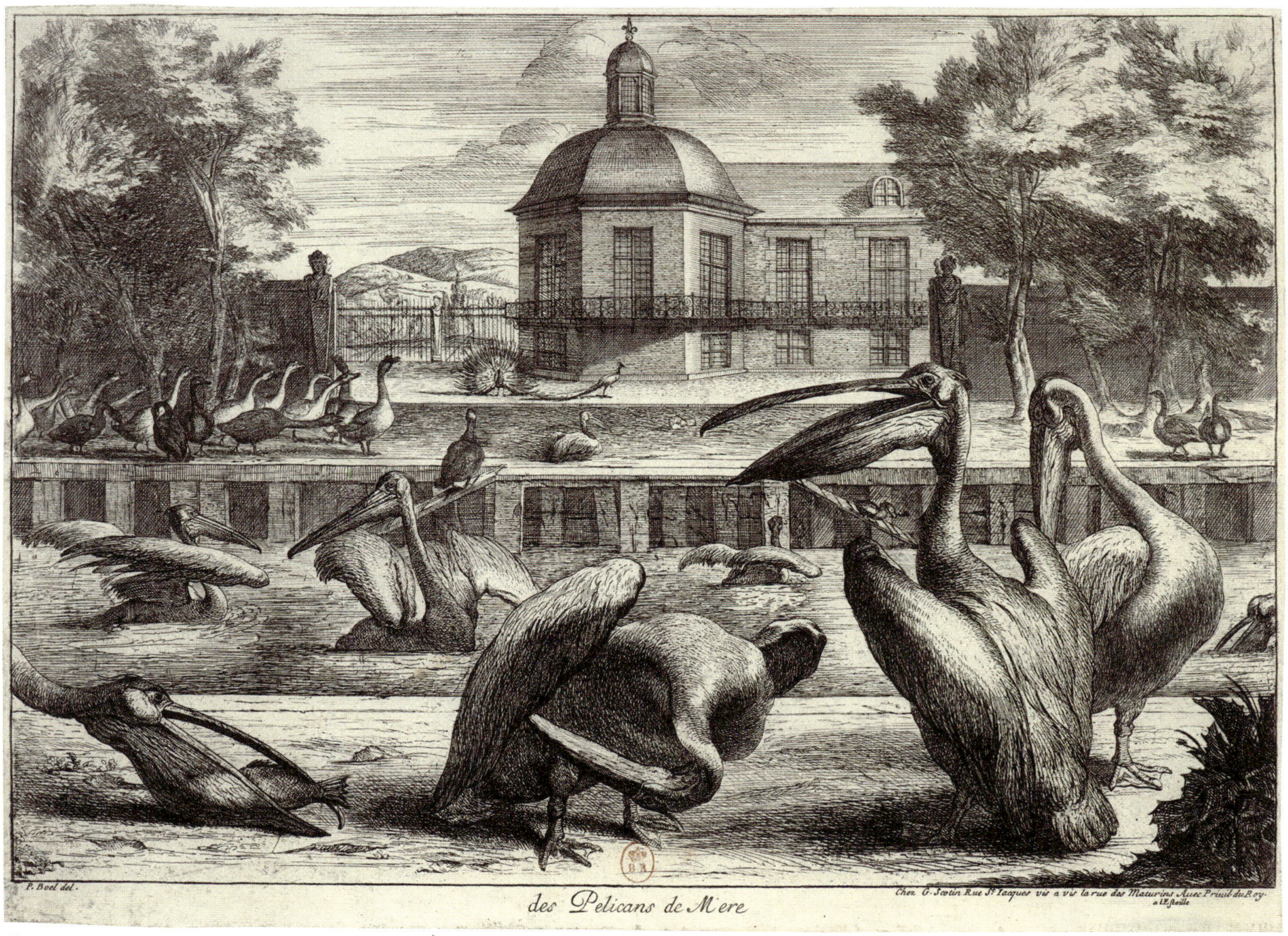

38

37 Sébastien Leclerc, *Beaver*, 1671

The reign of Louis XIV witnessed rapid advances in the domain of zoology, thanks to the new knowledge of animal anatomy obtained through dissections. The King himself raised exotic animals in his ménagerie at Versailles, and these were studied by members of the Académie des sciences, founded in 1666. Their work culminated in the *Mémoires pour servir à l'histoire naturelle des animaux*; this innovative book written by Claude Perrault and published by the Royal Printing House in 1676 described fourteen different species. The descriptions were accompanied by prints showing the animals in their natural habitats, together with images of some of their organs, all made by Sébastien Leclerc, one of the leading engravers of the time.

Very little was known about the beaver, which was not included among accounts given by the Ancients, and was difficult to classify according to traditional scientific principles. In the Middle Ages, images showing the animal with its tail dipped in water led to its association with fish; for this reason, it was even permitted as food during Lent! As a beaver had been brought directly from New France, Perrault had the opportunity to see an example of the species for himself. Despite the fact that its eyes had been devoured by rats, he was able to produce the first full description of the animal, completed by a print showing the most notable elements of its anatomy. R.M.

Compiled by Claude Perrault, *Mémoires pour server à l'histoire naturelle des animaux*, Paris, Imprimerie royale (Royal Printing House), 1671 | Etching | 29.5 x 41 cm (platemark)

38 Gérard Scotin, after Pieter Boel, *Pelicans*, late 17th century

In 1662 Louis XIV ordered the building of a ménagerie at Versailles, so that all his exotic animals could be kept in one place. These included flamingos, ostriches, gazelles, camels, mongooses, Canadian beavers, lynxes and serval cats. Members of the Académie des sciences delighted in studying these prestigious species. Some of the animals were purchased, while others were diplomatic gifts, such as an elephant given by the King of Portugal and a tiger that was a present from the Sultan of Morocco. The ménagerie was composed of a central octagonal pavilion with a circular balcony, which can be seen in the background of the print. This afforded a view of all the animal yards, arranged in a fan shape around the building. One of these contained the pelicans, a bird still rare in Europe at that time. Pieter Boel, a painter from Antwerp who worked in Charles Le Brun's studio from 1668, specialized in still life and animal images. He made several studies of the animals in the royal ménagerie. V.S.

Etching | 25.2 x 35 cm (print area)

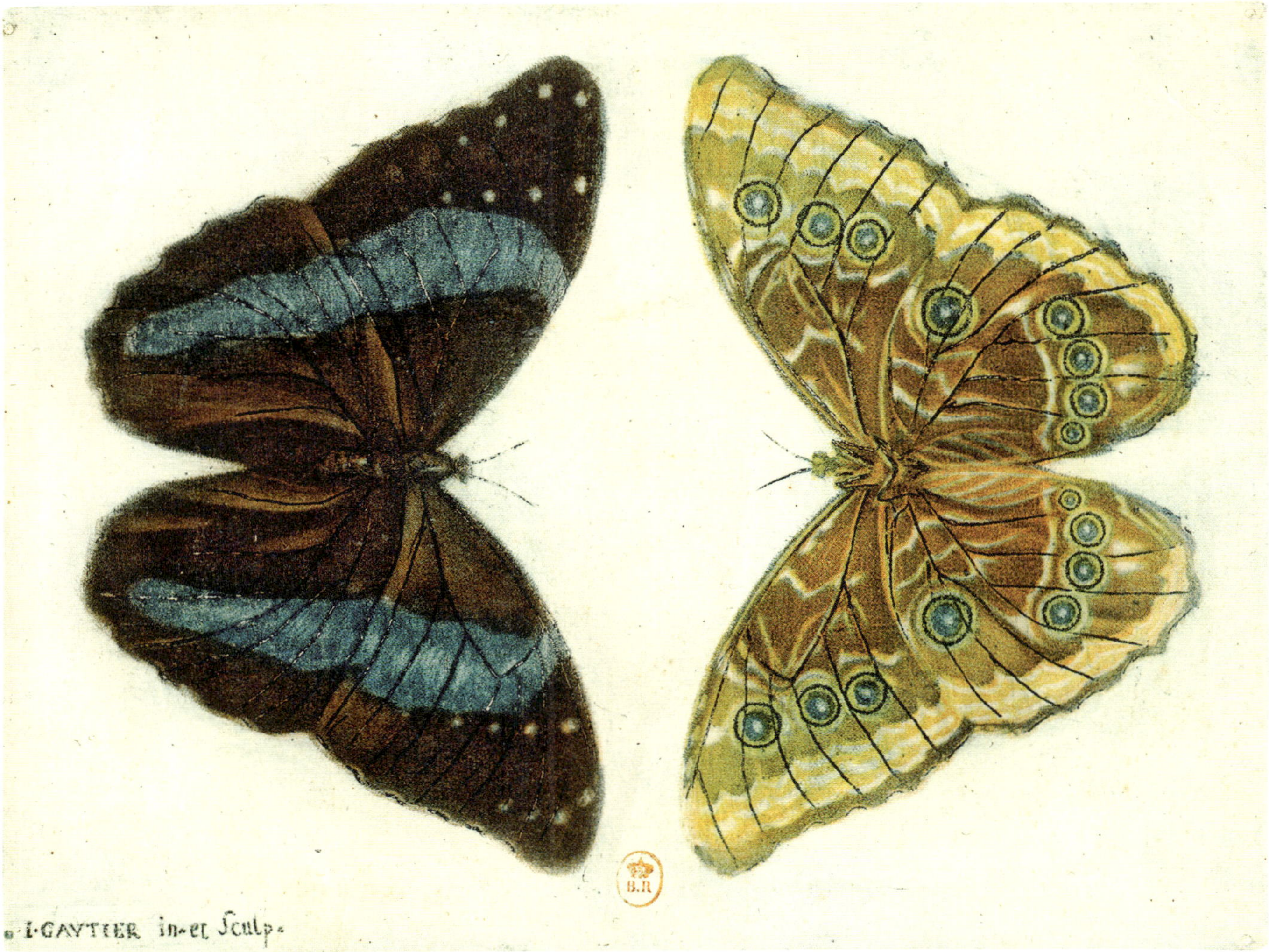

39

39 Jacques Fabien Gautier d'Agoty, *Two Butterflies Placed Opposite One Another*, ca. 1741

During the first third of the 18th century, the German painter and engraver Jacob Christoph Leblon (1667–1741) developed a technique of producing coloured prints by superimposing impressions using several plates, thereby inventing the four-colour printing process. Although when he embarked on this undertaking he had an inkling of the important effect the new procedure would have on publications devoted to natural history and anatomy, he only published one print relating to these domains. Gautier d'Agoty was a mediocre engraver and a somewhat unscrupulous businessman, yet he was passionately interested in science; after his master's death he attempted to exploit the latter's invention by publishing a number of scientific works that he illustrated with prints using Leblon's method. Although Gautier is principally known for his flayed anatomical human figures, strange and troubling images that fascinated the Surrealists, he also produced a small number of zoological plates, such as this work featuring two butterflies. C.L.B.

Mezzotint, colours printed using registration method | 18.9 x 25.1 cm (print area)

40 After Samuel Fallours, 231. *Devil-Fish. Type of Ray*; 232. *Devil-Fish*; 233. *Zeyl-Visch. Swordfish*, ca. 1719

In about 1719, Louis Renard published a work containing reproductions of some of the drawings made by Samuel Fallours, an employee of the Dutch East India Company who had been posted on Ambon Island in the Moluccan Archipelago in the early 18th century. This was one of the first attempts to depict tropical saltwater fish. Although in the book Renard insists on the authenticity of his engraved and coloured images, and on their superiority over the stuffed specimens on display in cabinets of curiosities, the vivid colours and fantastical forms of some of these fish present a startling sight. One such example is this 'devil-fish' resembling a monkfish, while the shape and blue colouring of the swordfish depicted on the same plate are closer to reality. The 'Agent of His Britannic Majesty', according to the title page of the publication, Louis Renard was in fact a publisher from Amsterdam, who at the same time worked as a commercial broker and a spy in the service of the British crown. C.L.B.

Plate from *Fishes, crayfishes and crabs of various extraordinary colours and shapes to be found around the Moluccan Islands and on the shores of lands in the Southern Hemisphere* by Louis Renard | Coloured etching | 28.1 x 20.5 cm (print area)

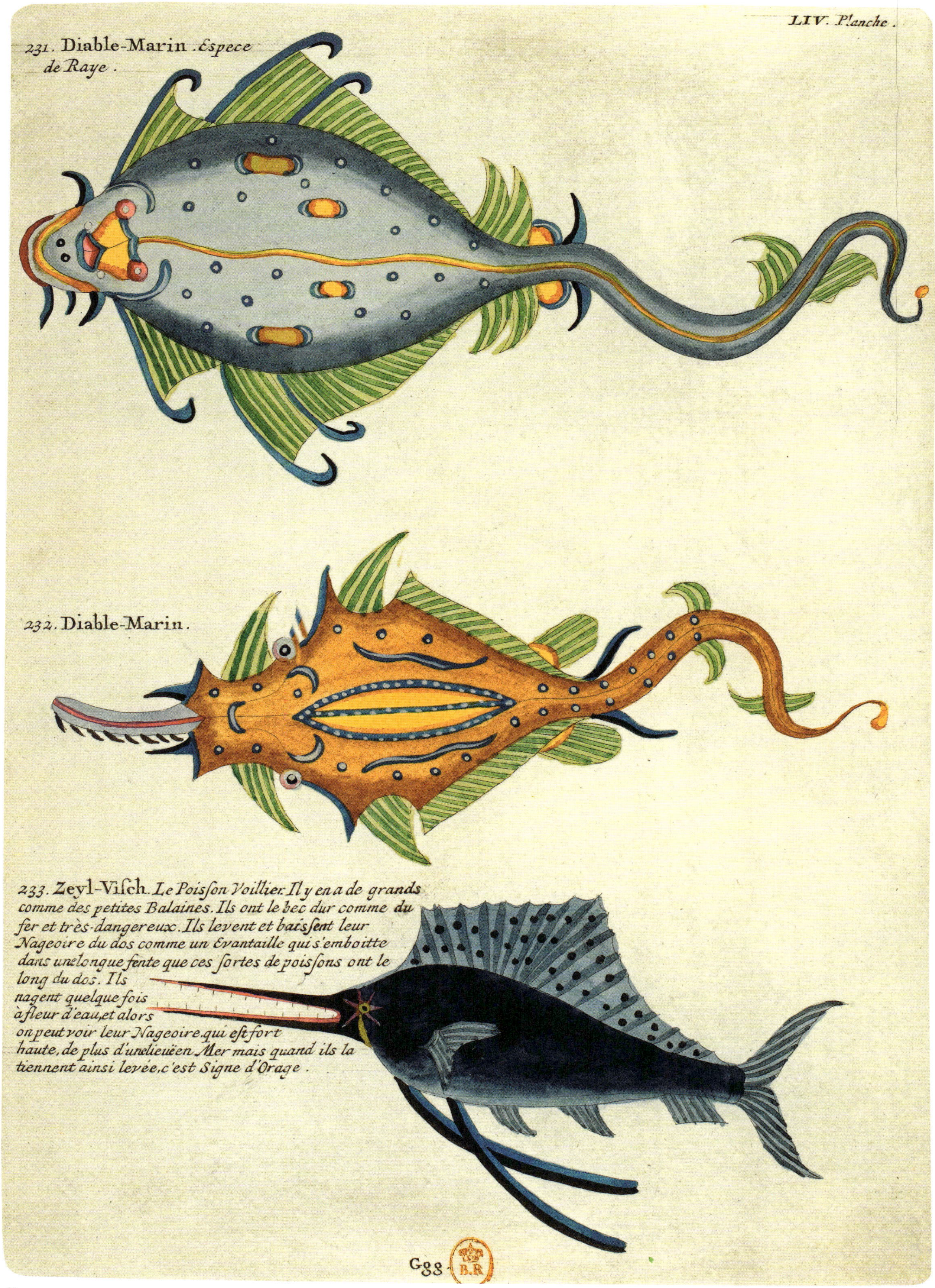
LIV. Planche.
231. Diable-Marin. Espece de Raye.
232. Diable-Marin.
233. Zeyl-Visch. Le Poisson Voillier. Il y en a de grands
comme des petites Balaines. Ils ont le bec dur comme du
fer et très-dangereux. Ils levent et baissent leur
Nageoire du dos comme un Evantaille qui s'emboitte
dans une longue fente que ces sortes de poissons ont le
long du dos. Ils
nagent quelque fois
à fleur d'eau, et alors
on peut voir leur Nageoire, qui est fort
haute, de plus d'une lieuëen Mer mais quand ils la
tiennent ainsi levée, c'est Signe d'Orage.
G 88
B.R.

40

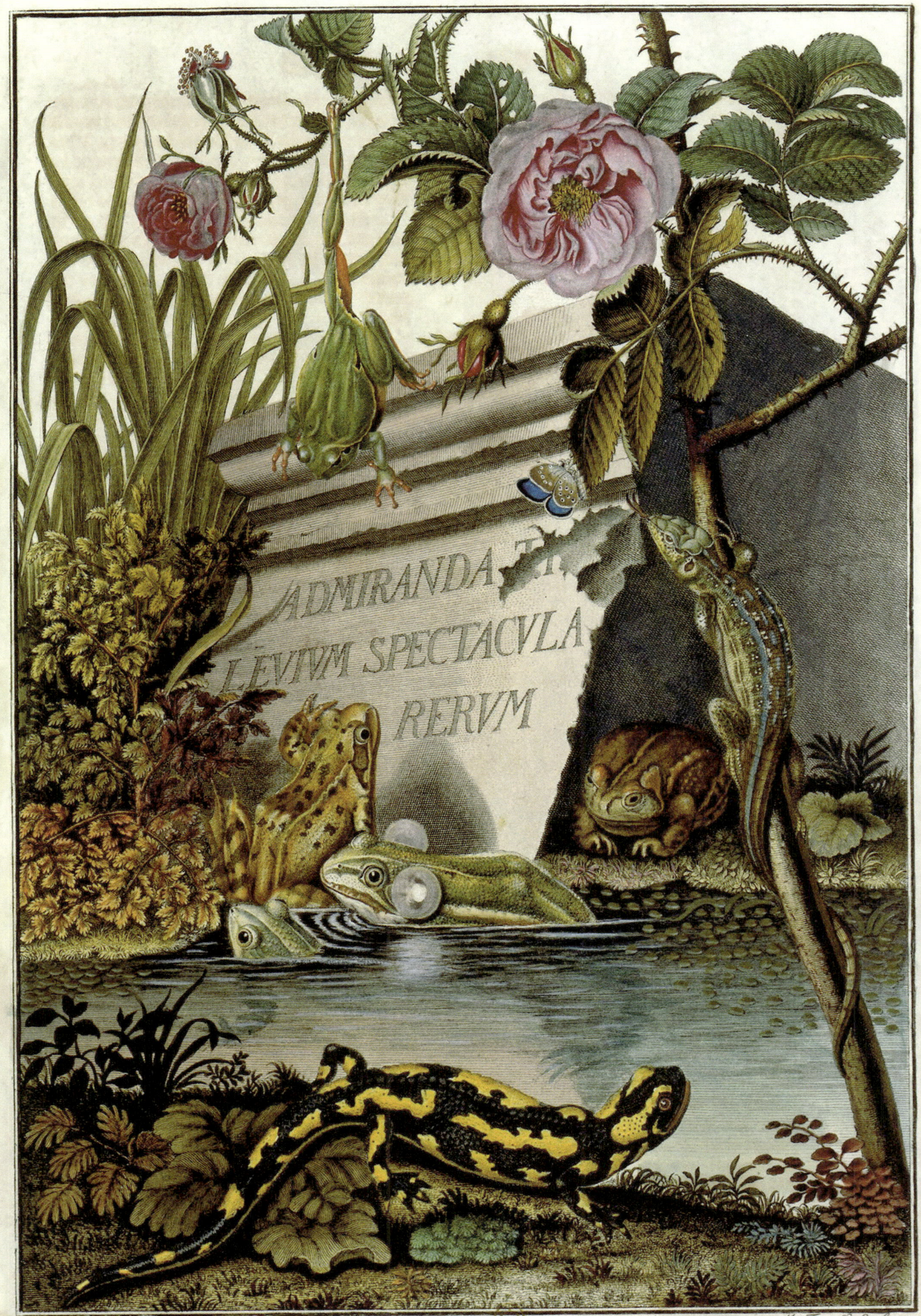

August Joh: Roesel Inv: et pinx: M. Tyroff sculp:

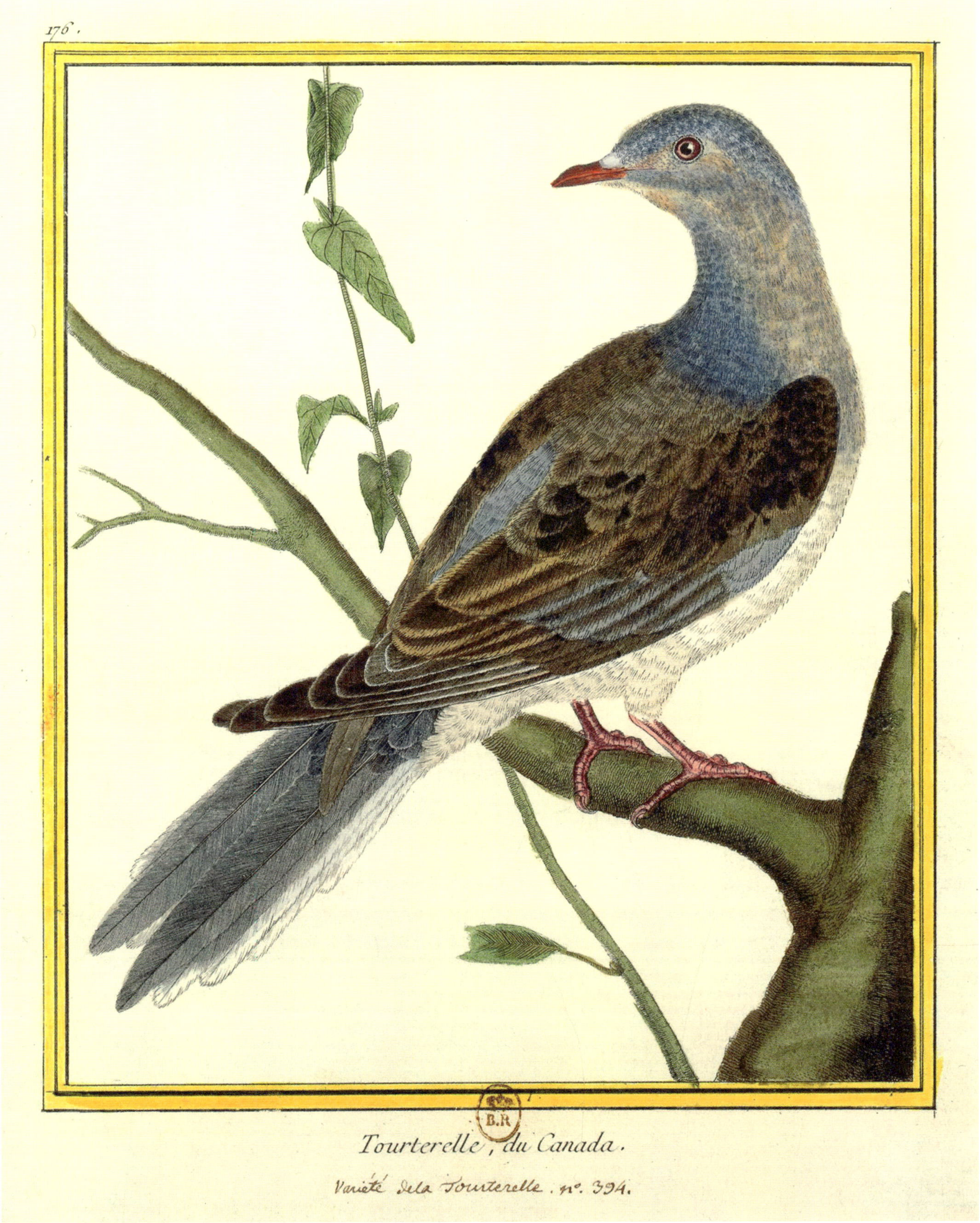

42

41 Martin Tyroff, after August Johann Rösel von Rosenhof, *Historia naturalis ranarum nostratium* (*The Natural History of the Frogs in Our Lands*), 1758

→ description on p. 78

42 François-Nicolas Martinet, *The Canadian Turtle-Dove*, ca. 1770

→ description on p. 78

41 Martin Tyroff, after August Johann Rösel von Rosenhof, *Historia naturalis ranarum nostratium* (*The Natural History of the Frogs in Our Lands*), 1758

→ Image on p. 76

A highly talented painter and miniaturist, Rösel von Rosenhof was fascinated by the study of insects, having been influenced by the work of Maria Sybilla Merian (1647–1717), a painter and naturalist. His interest also extended to frogs, which he observed, classified and drew before publishing his *Historia naturalis ranarum nostratium.* This is considered to be one of the most beautiful books on herpetology due to the exceptional quality of its illustrations. The volume begins with a magnificent frontispiece, depicting frogs and other amphibians in a luxuriant natural environment around a pond, above which is a stone slab inscribed with a verse from book IV of Virgil's *Georgics*: *Admiranda tibi levium spectacula rerum* (I will show you tiny things worthy of your admiration). C.L.B.

Coloured etching (watercolour, gouache highlights) | 38.4 x 6.3 cm (print area)

42 François-Nicolas Martinet, *The Canadian Turtle-Dove*, ca. 1770

→ Image on p. 77

In about 1770, Louis-Jean-Marie Daubenton, who collaborated with the comte de Buffon in his work on natural history, asked Martinet, an artist specializing in drawings of birds, to produce coloured illustrations of the collection of stuffed birds in the Jardin du Roi. This had just been extended thanks to the specimens bequeathed by the naturalist René Antoine Ferchault de Réaumur. Martinet produced 1,008 etchings, which were then painted in watercolour by various artists and sold as '*planches enluminées*' ('illuminated plates'). Buffon, engaged in the publication of his *Histoire naturelle*, decided to use these illustrations in the section devoted to birds; in the first edition of the work, this had contained only black and white prints, drawn by Jacques de Sève. In 1770, having now acquired experience, Martinet began work on his *Histoire des oiseaux, peints dans tous leurs aspects apparents et sensibles.* The birds in these images are shown in somewhat livelier poses than in the plates used for Buffon's publication, and are depicted in their natural environment. Martinet's birds were so successful that they may be found decorating a number of items in porcelain, having been used as models. C.L.B.

Plate illustrating *L'Histoire naturelle des oiseaux* by Buffon (1770–1783) | Coloured etching | 23 x 18 cm (print area)

43 Louis Jean Desprez, *The Chimera of Monsieur Desprez*, 1771

Although the architect and draughtsman Louis Jean Desprez did not produce a large number of engravings, they are outstanding for their inventive quality, as demonstrated by this image. A unique example of the artist's work, it depicts a three-headed chimera partly reduced to a skeleton. Emerging on either side of the monster's thoracic cage is the tortured body of a man whom it has swallowed. One head is devouring its victim's face with a long, bird-like beak, while the other two are tearing the hands of the unfortunate individual. Human and animal remains are strewn on the ground, where a giant insect is seen crawling while a snake slithers along a wall.

The print was an instant success; some twenty years later it served as the model for a revolutionary allegory where 'a three-headed Monster representing the three estates of the *Ancien Régime* is engaged in devouring the remains of the people's cadaver, which it has mercilessly dispatched into its carnivorous entrails'. C.L.B.

Etching | 27.5 x 35.5 cm (sheet)

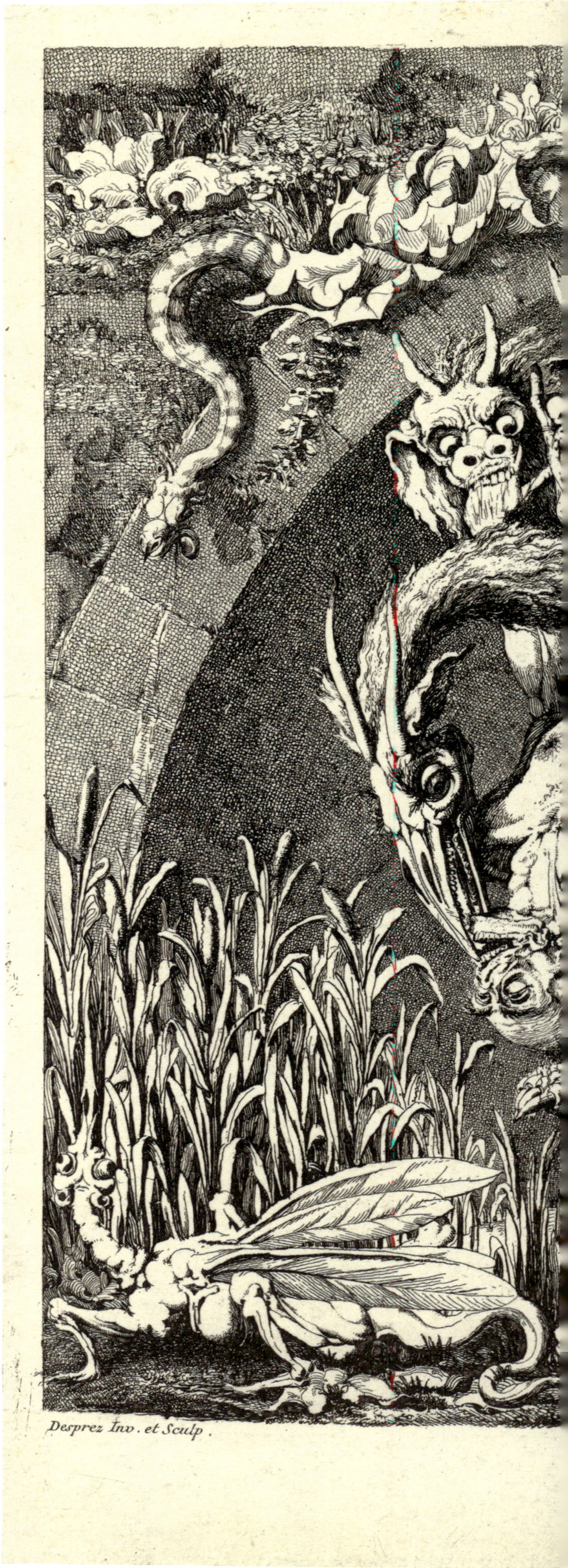

43

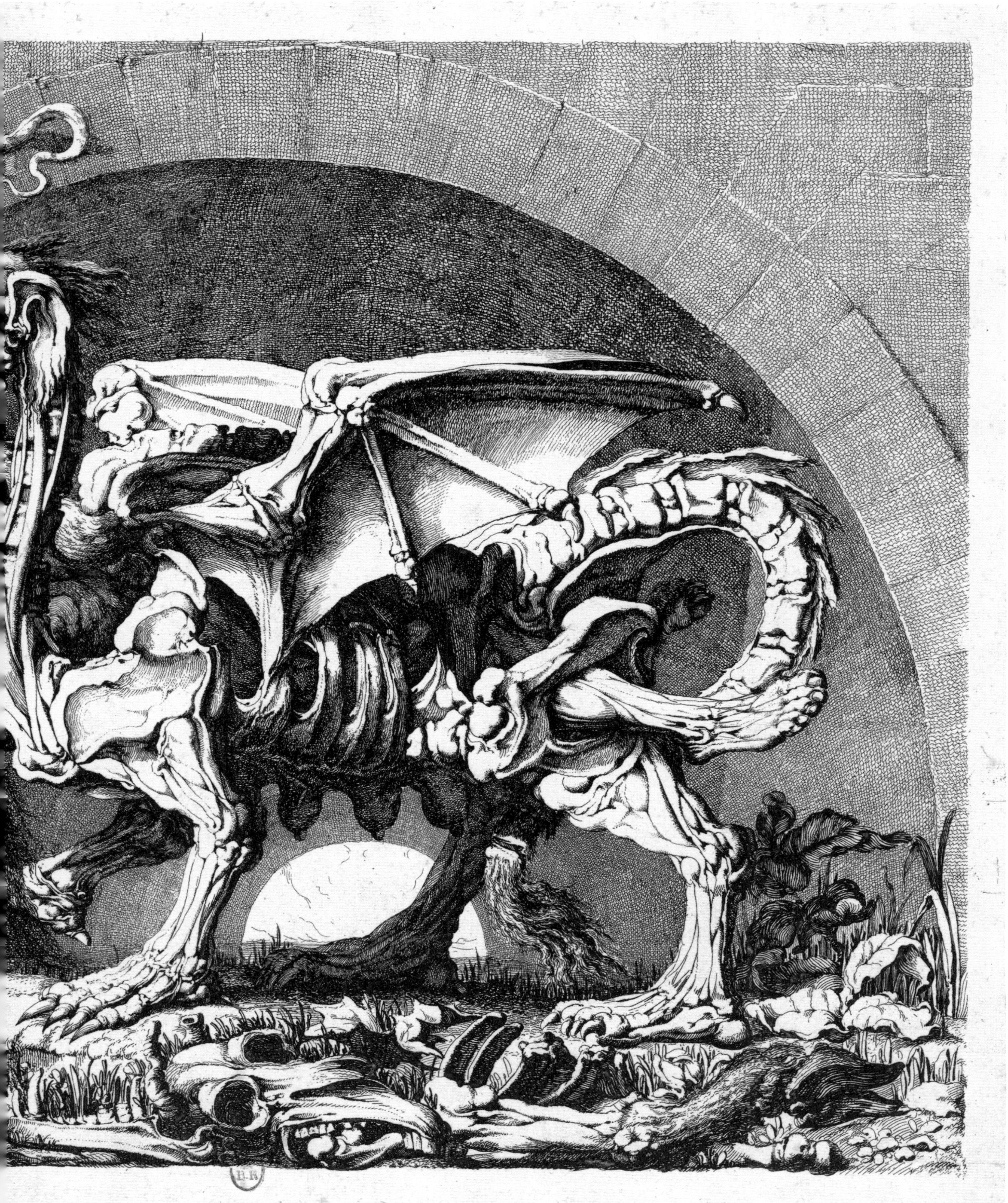

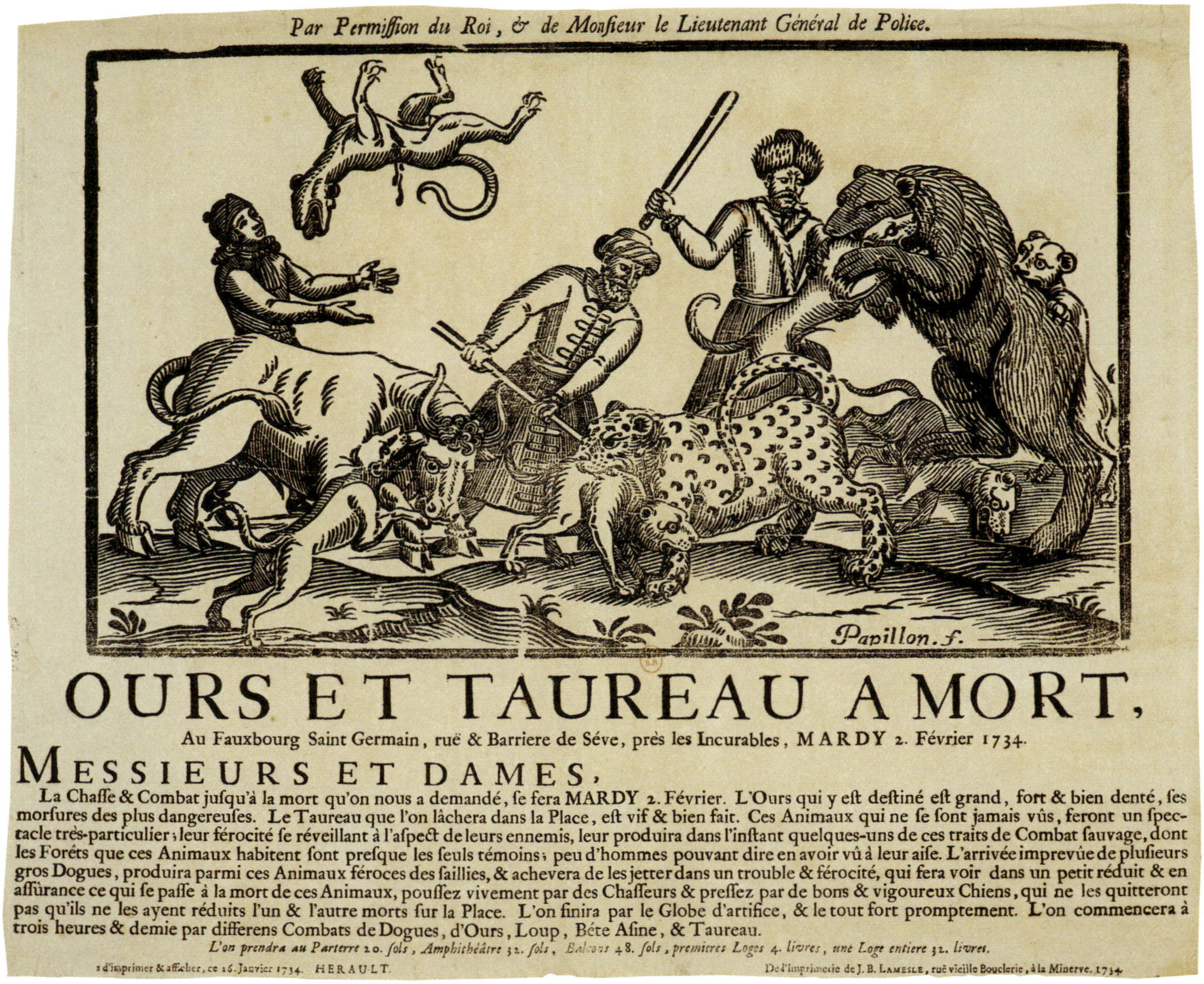

44

44 Jean Papillon, *A Bear and Bull Fight to the Death*, 1734

Two posters relating to these animal fights, which were public entertainment during this period, have been preserved. Although they show identical images they have different texts, and include mention of the authorization given to print and display each notice, dated 1734 and 1756, respectively. The two proofs were given to the Bibliothèque du roi by Jean-Michel Papillon, who descended from a dynasty of woodcut practitioners, and wrote in 1761: 'Still a very common sight seen on street corners [. . .] the poster announcing a Bull fight; this is from the drawing made by my late father, & and was engraved by my grandfather [. . .] normally two or three hundred posters a week would be pulled from this block; in this way, by 1734 it must have served to produce over five hundred and twenty five thousand proofs.' (From the *Traité historique et pratique de la gravure en bois*). Although Papillon's aim may be to demonstrate the superiority of 'engraving in wood', and his calculations are somewhat difficult to believe, these few lines testify to the longevity of the image. Economic reasons may well have played a part in this case, as posters were, of course, circulated free of charge. The few illustrated posters that have survived from the days of the Ancien Régime often served as 'all purpose' decorative features. The large image here functioned in the same manner, and was applied to different texts over the years as required. A.-M.S.

Poster, woodcut | 39 x 48 cm (sheet)

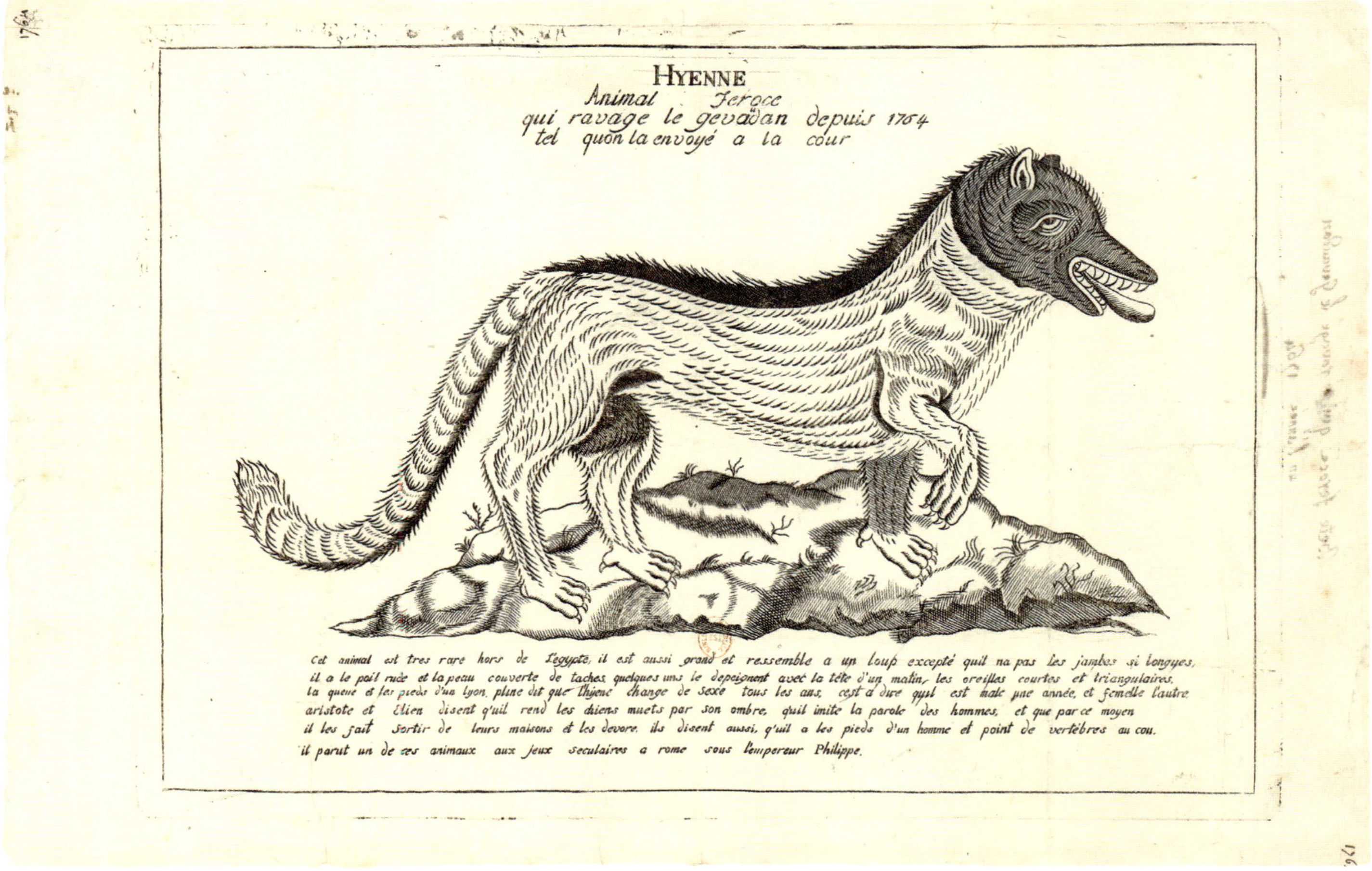

45

45 Anonymous, *The Hyena, a Ferocious Animal That Ravaged the Region of Gévaudan from 1764, as Sent to the Court*, ca. 1765

The region of Gévaudan was the scene of unexplained attacks from the spring of 1764 to 1767, when tens of women and children were killed by what was initially thought to be a pack of wolves, and subsequently a single 'beast' craving human flesh. The events were brought to the attention of readers at both the national and European level by various gazettes, and large numbers of images, often executed in a cursory fashion, purported to represent the 'true likeness' of the beast. It was shown in turn as a wolf, a fantastical monster or an exotic creature. This engraving presents the 'ferocious animal that ravaged Gévaudan' as a hyena, and, in an attempt at realism, its form has been borrowed from a plate illustrating a work on natural history. In an approach very unlike that of Buffon's *Histoire naturelle*, however, there is an emphasis here on the supernatural aspects of the beast, with references to Pliny the Elder, Aristotle and Elian being used to support these incredible details: the animal 'changed sex every year', 'struck dogs dumb at the sight of its shadow' and 'imitated human speech'. Yet in 1756, a Jesuit priest, Father Tolomas, denounced this 'childish nonsense that most Naturalists have adopted one after the other, and all with a tone intended to convince us that they believe what they say'. The engraving reflects the role played by the printed image, well into the Age of Enlightenment, in circulating information and rumours. While leading the public to believe that it is simply describing a mammal found 'very rarely outside Egypt' but nonetheless genuinely real, this print makes its own contribution to enriching the fabulous imagery associated with the Beast of Gévaudan. R.G.

Burin engraving | 23.5 x 44.5 (platemark)

46 Anonymous, *Pack of Belgian Tarot Cards with Animal Trump Scenes*, ca. 1755

The so-called animal tarot cards, which date from the latter half of the 18th century, originated in Bavaria. The genre spread through Belgium, Alsace and Russia before its popularity declined in the early 19th century. Bearing French suit symbols, these packs are characterized by a series of trump scenes representing domestic and exotic animals, and are established within the tradition of the moralistic and fabulous bestiary. The way in which these animals are represented is based more on their different natures than on their degree of domestication or exoticism. The donkey, sometimes reviled for having a libidinous and malevolent character, is shown here in a submissive state, bearing a packsaddle for transporting harvested crops; he still has a vigilant eye, however, albeit somewhat wistful. The other herbivores, a stag, a dromedary and a unicorn, are likewise depicted at rest, inactive and at most raising a leg. Only the goat, driven by curiosity, stands on its hind legs to reach some red fruits growing on a tree. The predators are shown bounding forward, their eyes alert, corroborating their images in fables; the fox has a bird in its mouth, the wolf is carrying off a lamb and the lion is threatening an invisible prey with his claws. The crocodile is the only reptile depicted; it stands in isolation, which somewhat negates the threat posed by its red mouth and lashing tail. Finally comes the bear, shown leaning on a staff and yet with open jaws, midway between a fairground animal and a wild beast. Always the 21st trump, it presides over both human and animal destinies.

The worn lines on these engravings suggest that many prints had already been made from this wooden block by 1755. These animals continued to survive until 1815, their features yet more altered, on packs printed from the same blocks by the cardmaker Servaes, still established in Brussels. J.T.

Woodcuts, stencil-coloured | 11.3 x 5.9 cm (card)

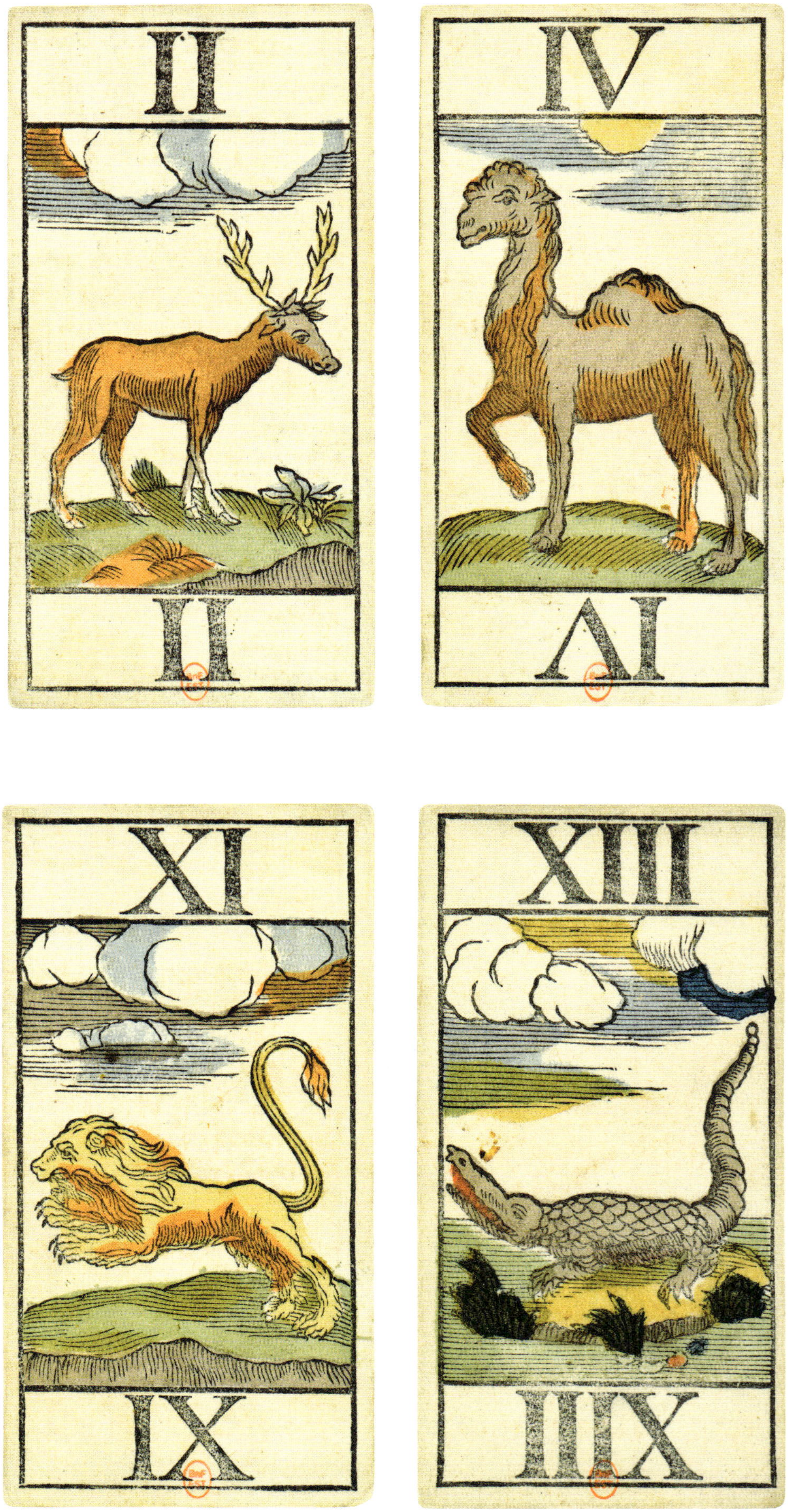

46

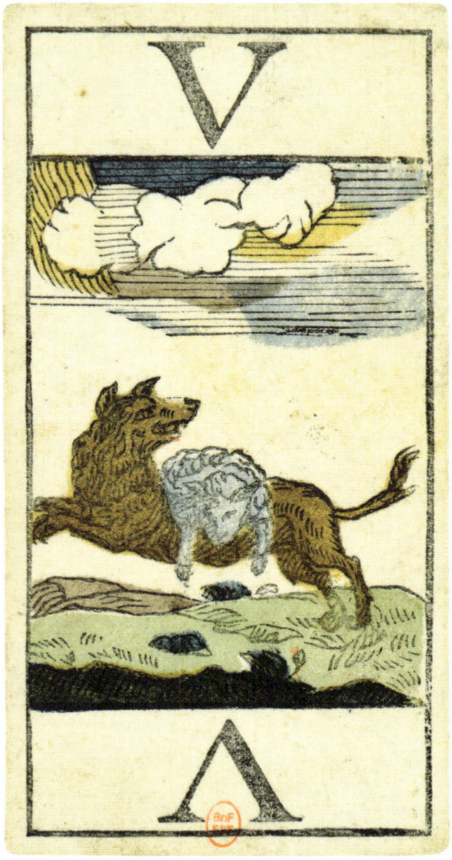
V

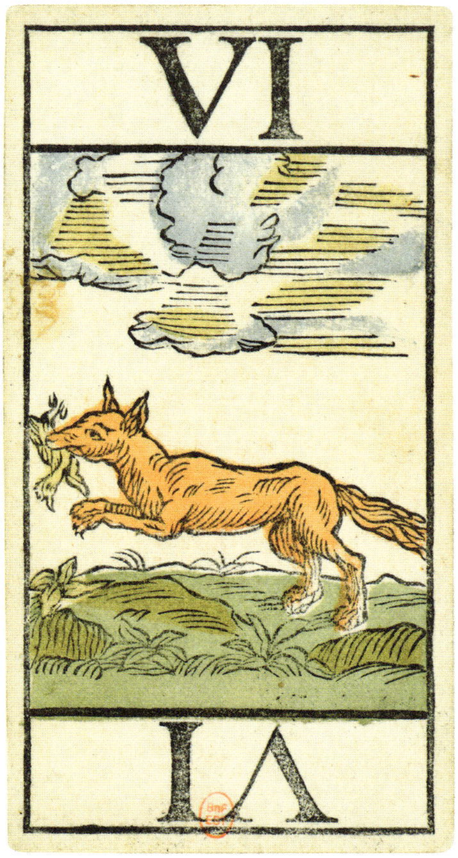
VI

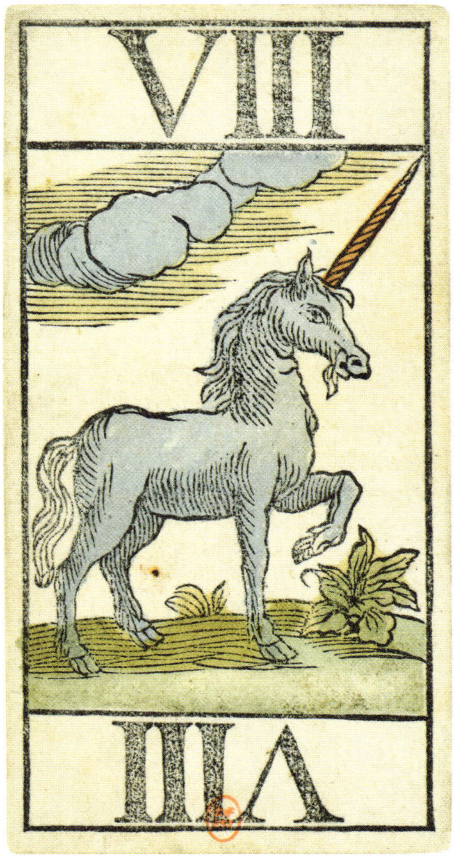
VIII

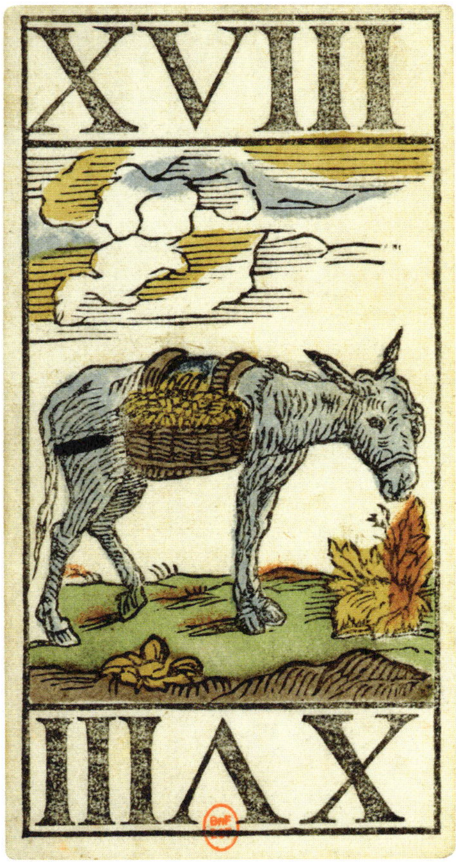
XVIII

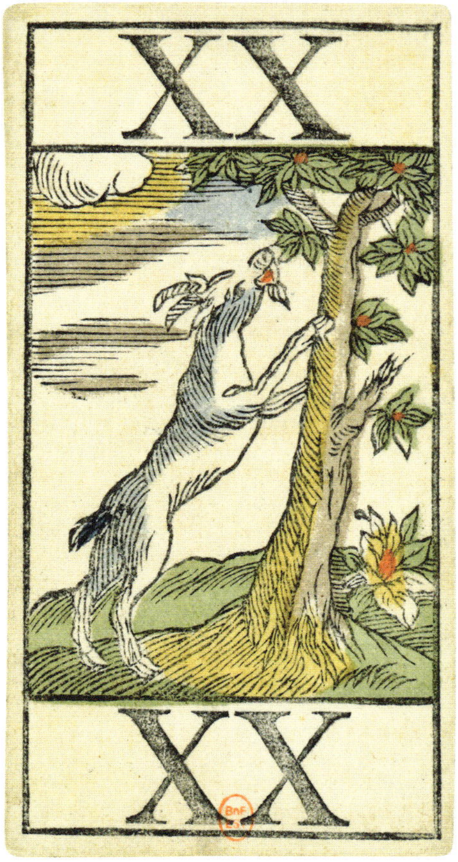
XX

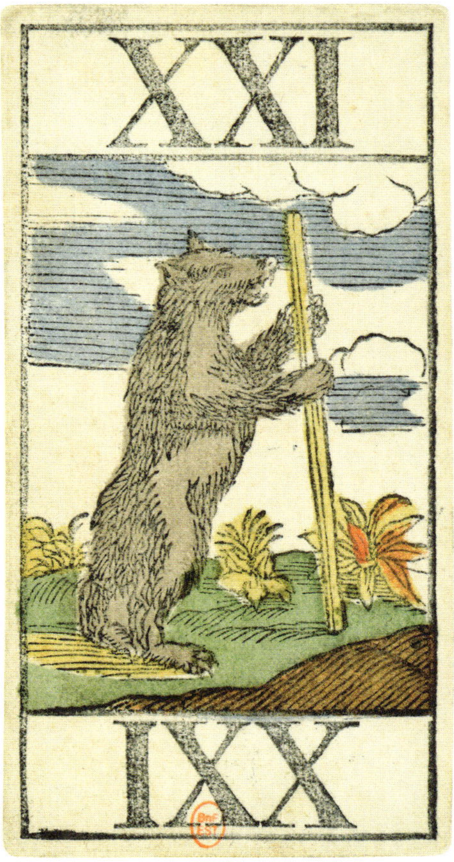
XXI

47 Charles-Germain de Saint-Aubin, *Pyrotechnia*, ca. 1760

The Saint-Aubin brothers left a body of work that reflects the refined and caustic spirit of 18th century France. In addition to the delicate portraits engraved by Augustin, his brother Gabriel, a painter, draughtsman and engraver, reproduced lively scenes set in the streets and *salons* of Paris. The eldest sibling, Charles-Germain, inherited their father's official position of embroiderer to the King, and it was he whom Diderot commissioned to create the plates for the section of the *Encyclopédie* devoted to the art of embroidery. Between 1750 and 1760, he published a work entitled *Essais de papillonneries humaines*, which comprised a few ornamental plates possibly intended as models for decorating textiles and porcelain. These featured anthropomorphic images of butterflies fighting duels, performing in the theatre and being assisted at their toilette. *Pyrotechnia*, created in the same vein as the *Essais*, shows them preparing to set off a firework.

The figure of the monkey was typically used in the decorative arts during the 18th century as a light-hearted way of portraying human occupations. Saint-Aubin's delicate insects, however, carry an additional message. Engaged in frivolous activities, they flutter around (the corresponding French verb '*papillonner*', from '*papillon*', a butterfly, dates from the 18th century), serving as metaphors for a charming, flighty aristocracy incapable of contributing to the construction of society. C.L.B.

Etching | 18.5 x 13.5 cm (print area)

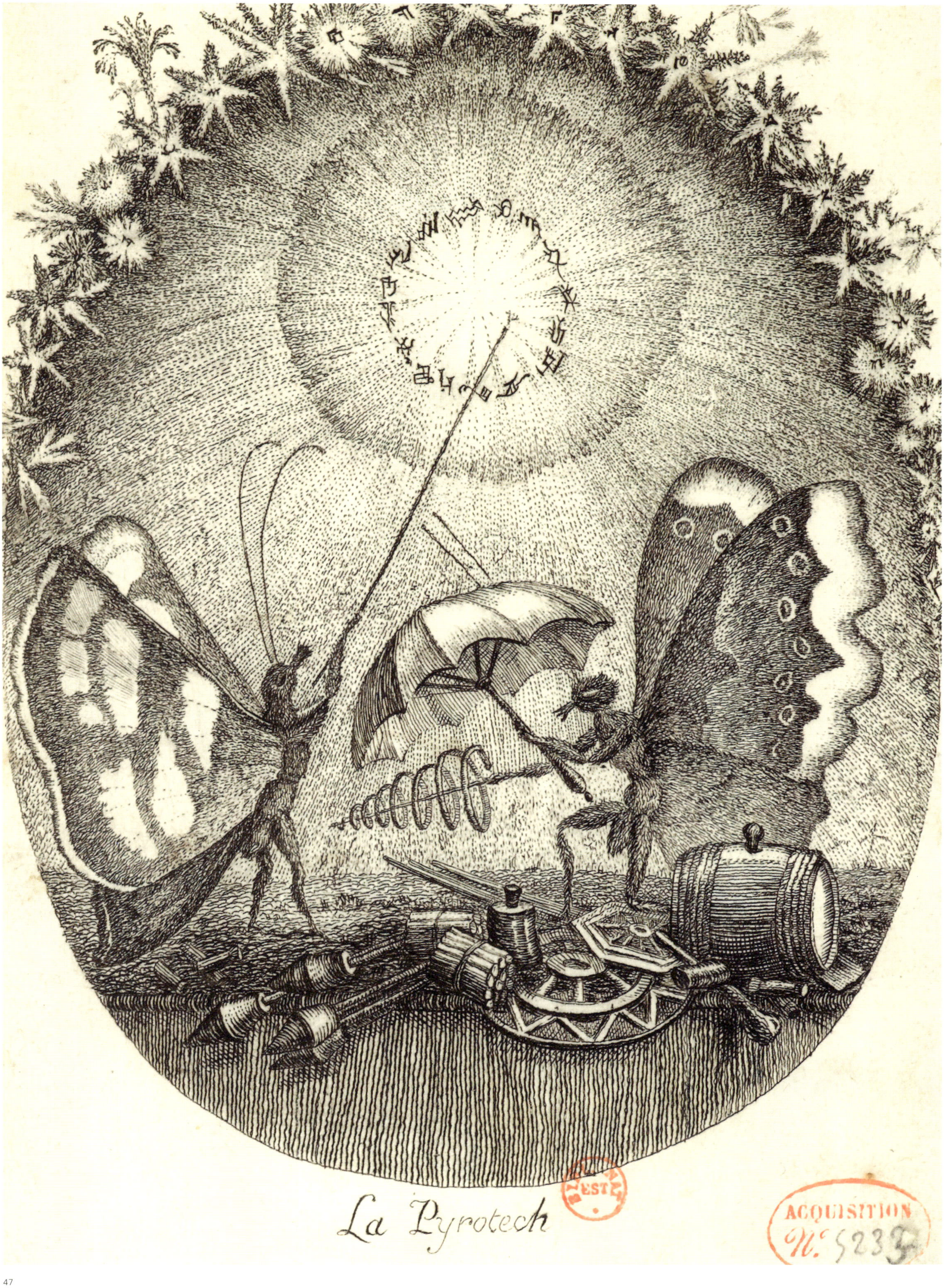

47

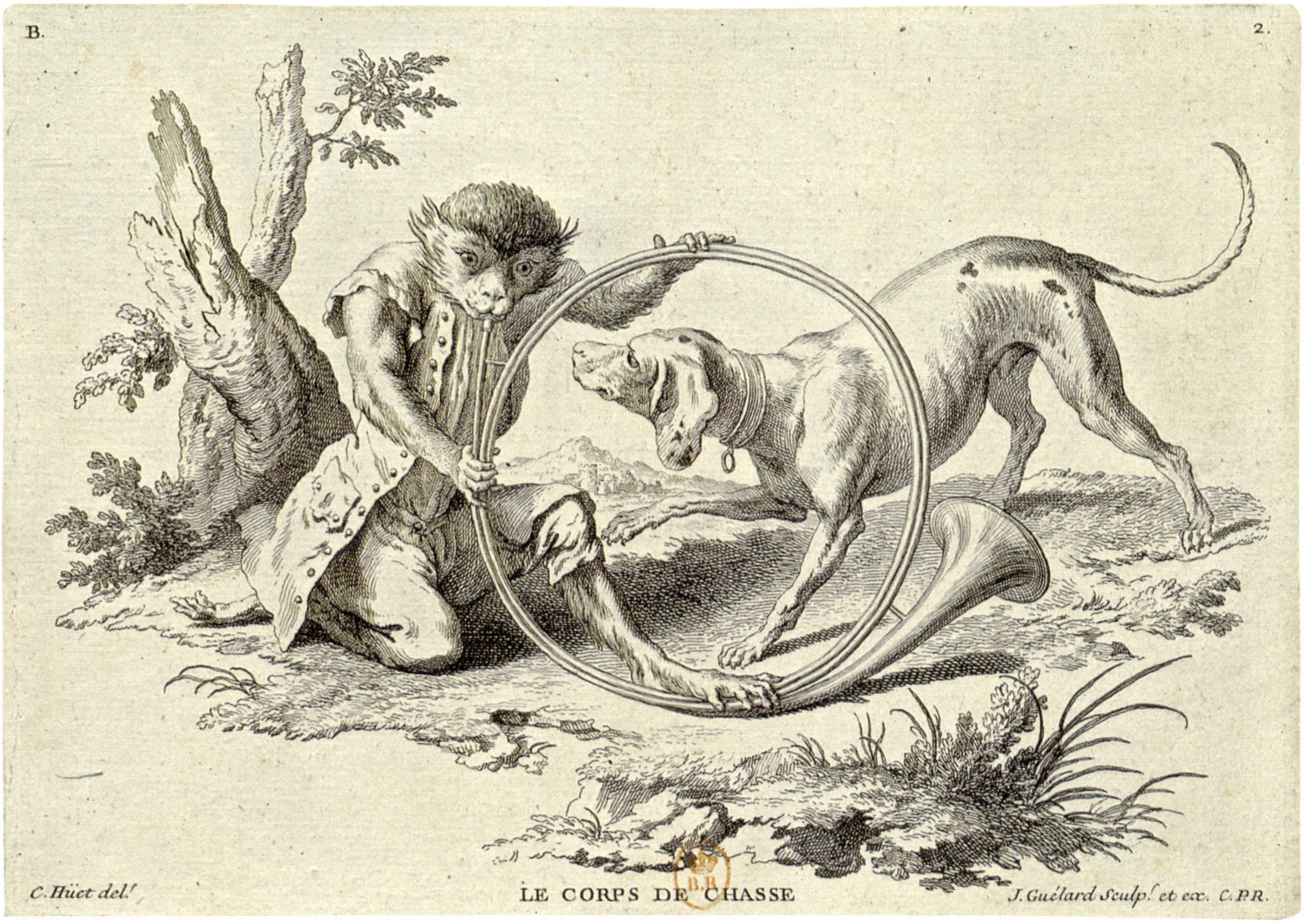

48

48 Jean-Baptiste Guélard, after Christophe Huet, *The Hunting Horn*, ca. 1741

The practice of denouncing man's vanity and idiosyncrasies by replacing human figures with anthropomorphic images of monkeys, often in burlesque scenes, originated in 17th century Flemish painting. During the first half of the 18th century, the rococo style, with its curves and sinuous lines, lent itself perfectly to depicting the slender silhouette of the monkey, and decorative artists included them in adornments for wall panels and painted ceilings. Christophe Huet created three ornamental pieces featuring monkeys that can still be seen today: the *Petite* and *Grande Singeries* at the Château de Chantilly, a sitting room at the Château de Champs-sur-Marne, and the *Cabinet des Singes* at the Hôtel de Rohan in Paris. In 1743 he joined forces with the engraver Guélard in order to disseminate his entertaining scenes in print form; these depict monkeys dancing, playing the organ, teaching music or, as with the example here, hunting. C.L.B.

Extract from *Singeries ou Différentes actions de la vie humaine représentées par des singes* | Etching | 15 x 19 cm (sheet)

49 Anonymous, *The Large Troupe of Curious Animals That Entertained the City and the Court on 11 July 1784*, 1784

The first hot-air balloon ascensions made by the Montgolfier brothers in 1783 attracted huge public interest and led to numerous successive attempts at operating aerostats. On 11 July 1784, the Abbé Miollan, a teacher of physics, and the engraver Jean-François Janinet prepared to take off from the Observatory Gardens in Paris in an enormous balloon. Unfortunately, however, the weather was hot and the balloon could not be inflated. The huge crowd of people who had arrived to witness the spectacle, which they had contributed to funding through subscriptions, felt cheated. Breaking down the barriers in their anger, they smashed the mechanism to pieces, which caused it to catch fire. For weeks, Miollan and his partners were the butt of mockery in songs and pamphlets. A number of images circulated in which they were caricatured as animals. The Abbé and Janinet were represented as two cats called 'Miaullant' and 'Jean Minet', respectively; Bredin, the mechanic, was depicted as a dog named 'Gredin', meaning 'scoundrel', while the Marquis d'Arlandes, the fourth member of the party, was shown as a monkey. C.L.B.

Coloured etching | 20 x 18.7 cm (print area)

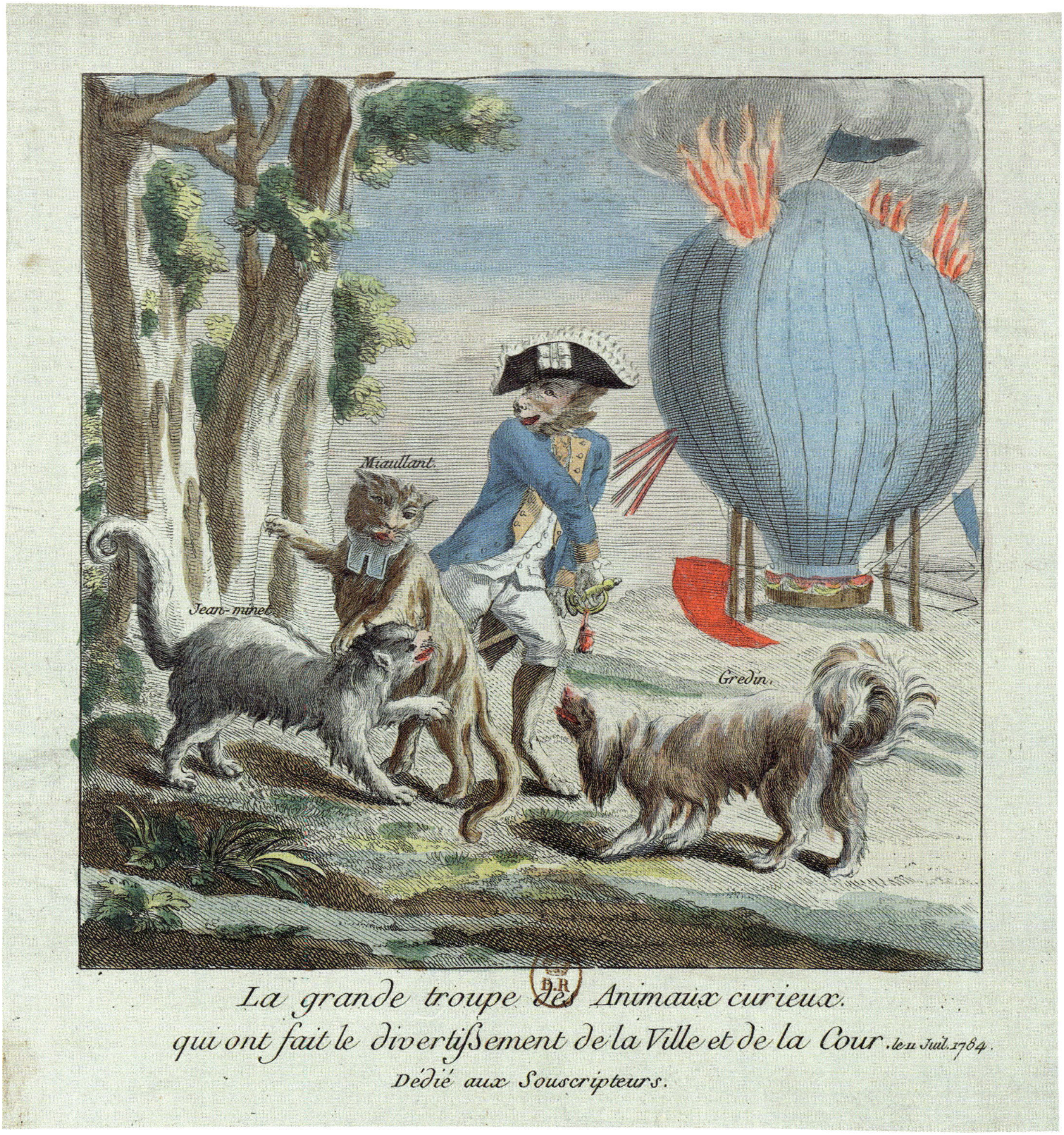
Miaullant.
Jean-minet.
Gredin.
La grande troupe des Animaux curieux.
qui ont fait le divertissement de la Ville et de la Cour. le 11 Juil. 1784.
Dédié aux Souscripteurs.

49

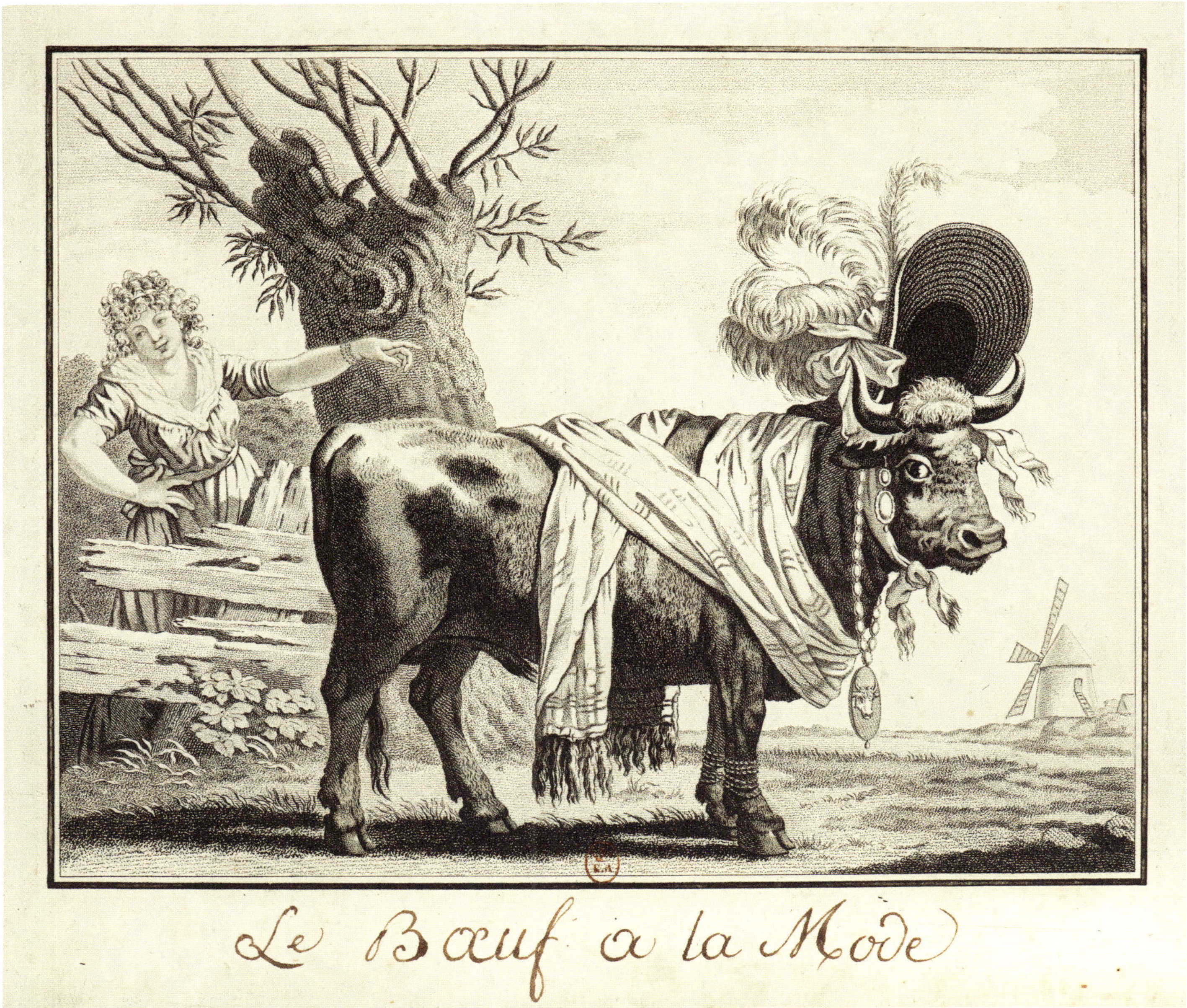

50

50 Louis-Charles Ruotte, after Frans Swagers, *The Fashionable Ox*, 1797

In 1797 a collection of caricatures deriding the sartorial extravagance of fashionable women during the Directoire period was published in Paris. These include an ox wearing a hat adorned with feathers and covered with jewellery and ribbons. Some versions show the front half of the animal decked out as a '*Merveilleuse*', whilst its back half is wearing the costume of an '*Incroyable*', thus mocking both male and female fashions of the day. The image was so popular that it became a restaurant sign. Established in 1792 near the Palais-Royal by two brothers from Marseille, *Le Boeuf à la mode* enjoyed resounding success until its closure in 1936. The sculpted sign of the ox wearing its finery may still be seen above the door of no. 8 rue de Valois, the location of the former establishment. C.L.B.

Stipple engraving | 28.1 x 36.7 cm (print area)

51 Anonymous, *The New 'Incroyable', or the Fashionable Goose*, 1797

Engraved caricatures played a major role in exhibiting the highly elaborate costumes worn by the 'gilded youth' during the Directoire period, as emphasized by Louis-Sébastien Mercier in *Le Nouveau Paris* (1797): 'Crowds of passers-by stopped in front of print-sellers' windows to gaze at the *Incroyables* and the *Merveilleuses* [. . .] the folly of the day, the anarchy, the danger presented by wigs'.

In the same satirical style as the engraving of *The Fashionable Ox* (no. 50), this image presents a goose clad in the costume of an '*Incroyable*', who glares at the world with the haughty and aloof air of a dandy; he is ready to use his knobbled cane to fight off revolutionaries and Jacobins. C.L.B.

Coloured etching | 20.5 x 15.2 (boundary line)

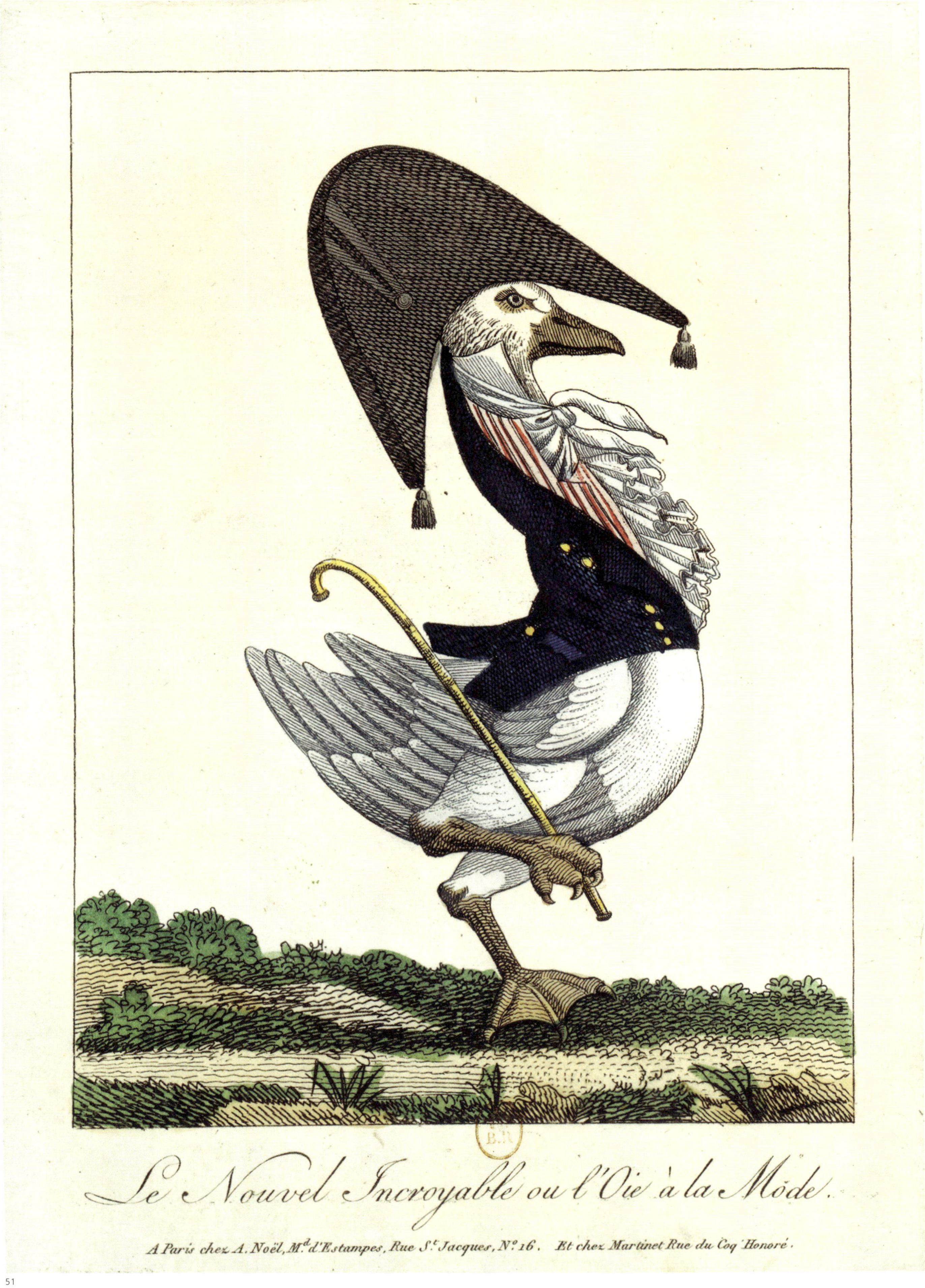

Le Nouvel Incroyable ou l'Oie à la Môde.
A Paris chez A. Noël, Md. d'Estampes, Rue St. Jacques, No. 16. Et chez Martinet Rue du Coq Honoré.

51

52 Gabriel Huquier, *Plate Showing Chinese-Inspired Ornamental Motifs*, ca. 1740

Interest in China began to develop in France towards the end of Louis XIV's reign, and Chinese *objets d'art* gradually found their way into the interiors of royal and noble houses. In the first half of the 18th century, the decorative arts adopted the scrolled shapes characterizing this style of ornamentation; undulating and elaborate, they were easily integrated into the sinuous lines of the rococo. Artists and craftsmen required reference models that they could then develop into a Western form of *chinoiserie*, prompting designers and engravers to publish a series of prints 'in the Chinese style' to serve as inspiration for cabinet-makers, fabric manufacturers, porcelain painters and so on. Gabriel Huquier, a prolific publisher of engravings depicting such decorations, specialized in producing collections of this type, the *Livre des différentes espèces d'oiseaux* being a very beautiful example. The plate partially reproduced here incorporates several motifs, some in the form of animals, such as this figure of an elephant. C.L.B.

From *Livre des différentes espèces d'oiseaux, fleurs, plantes et trophées de la Chine tirés du cabinet du Roy* | Etching | 32.4 x 49.3 cm (print area)

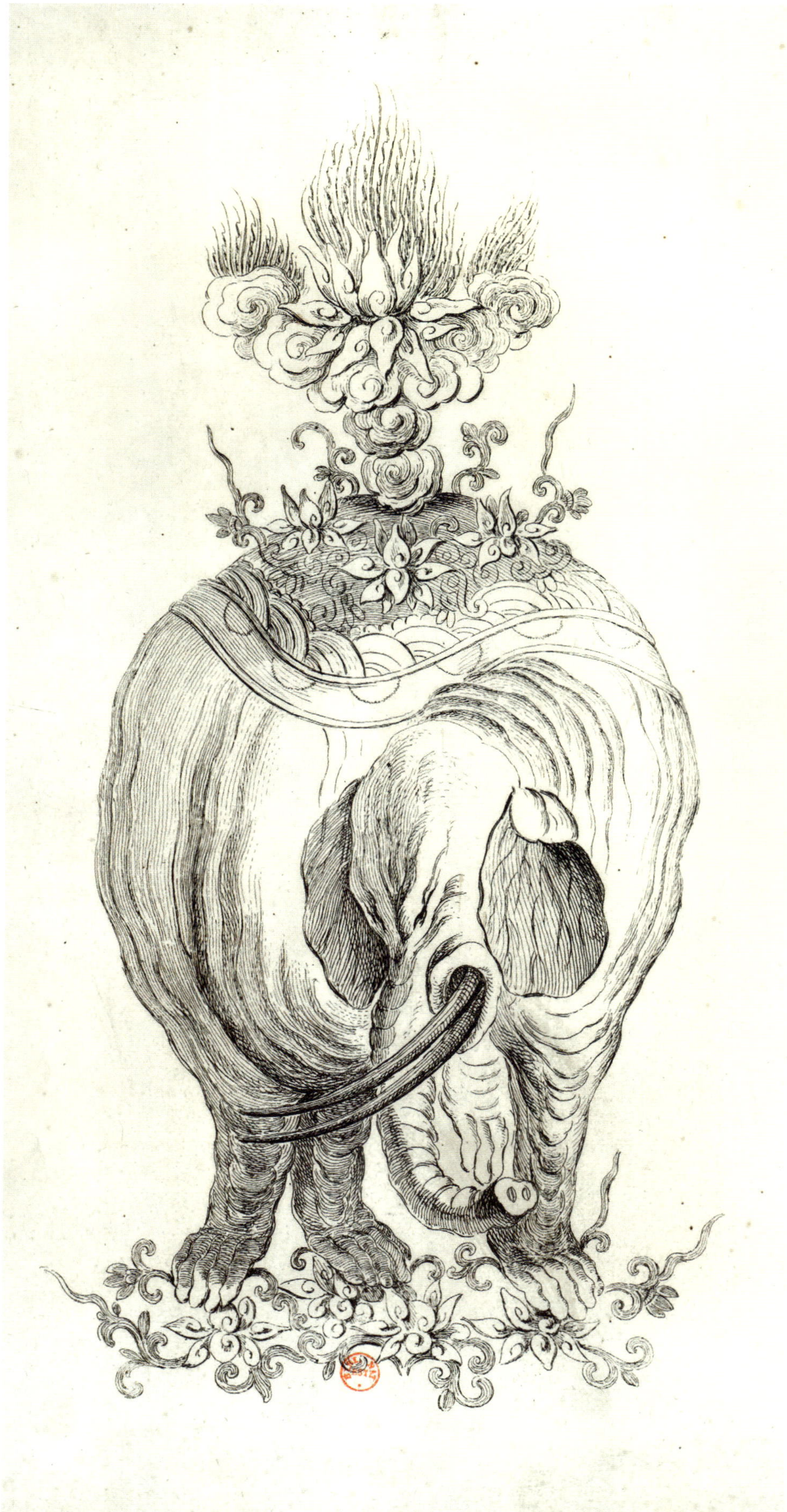

52

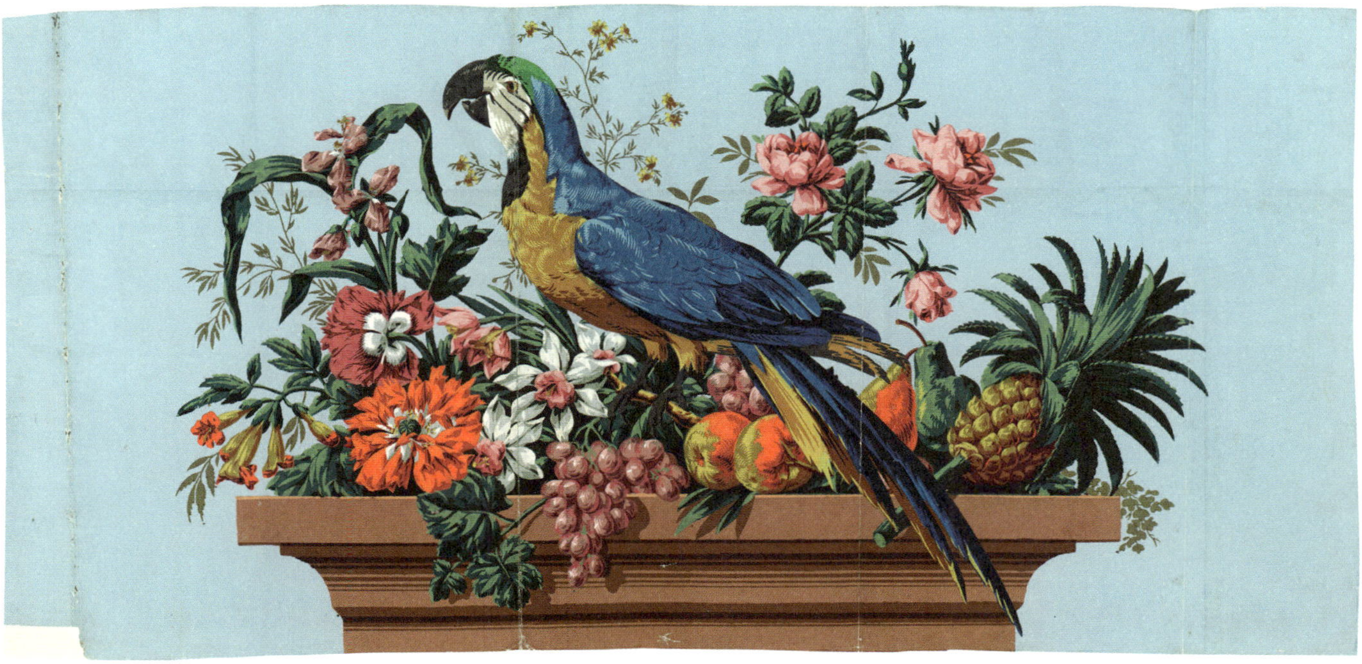

53

53 Hartmann Risler & Cie Manufacturing Company, after Joseph Laurent Malaine, *Lintel Decoration, Parrot Perched on a Natural Arrangement of Fruits and Flowers*, 1799

The latter half of the 18th century witnessed the development of the fashion for wallpaper, first in England and then in France. The most private living areas, including rooms in the mansions belonging to the nobility, were papered with very brightly coloured sheets featuring combinations of the decorative themes then in vogue: flowers, fruits, animals, pastoral scenes and *chinoiseries*. Here, perched on a basket filled with flowers and fruits (grapes, pineapples, pears and peaches), a parrot with superb plumage appears about to speak. During this period, wallpaper was produced in single sheets from engraved wooden blocks, and successively printed with different colours. This process required a large labour force, who worked in factories run in a manner that heralded the industrial 19th century. It was doubtless no coincidence that, in April 1788, one of the first riots of the French Revolution broke out in the wallpaper factory owned by Jean-Baptiste Réveillon and located in the faubourg Saint-Antoine in Paris. The Hartmann Risler & Cie Manufacturing Company factory was established in Mulhouse in 1799 and later installed at Rixheim; this was the founding company of the Maison Zuber, which continues to produce very high-quality wallpaper. C.L.B.

Wallpaper, pieced together, designs printed using engraved wooden blocks, colour applied using block printing method | 56.5 x 117.5 cm (sheet)

54 Jean-Charles Baquoy, after Jacques de Sève, *The Wolf*, 1758

The monumental *Histoire naturelle, générale et particulière* is the best-known work by the comte de Buffon, whose aim was to present a systematic inventory of 'the vast spectacle of nature'. This undertaking was left unfinished, however, the only sections to be published being those devoted to minerals, quadrupeds and birds. The scientific scope of the work remains limited, as Buffon refused to use the taxonomy developed by Carl Linnaeus a few years earlier, which was universally adopted as a system of classification in the 19th century. According to Buffon – who supported the principles of empirical method – in order to study nature one should 'observe much and observe again frequently'. His work therefore included a great many illustrations, made by Jacques de Sève and Buvée L'Amériquain, with 'portraits' of animals as well as images of their internal organs and skeletons.

Depicted with varying accuracy, the animals in the *Histoire naturelle* are somewhat artificially placed in profile, stiffly posed, against assorted backgrounds. These images do not differ greatly from already antiquated pictorial traditions. C.L.B.

Plate from *Histoire naturelle, générale et particulière* (1749–1788) by Buffon | Etching and burin work | 19.5 x 15 cm (boundary line)

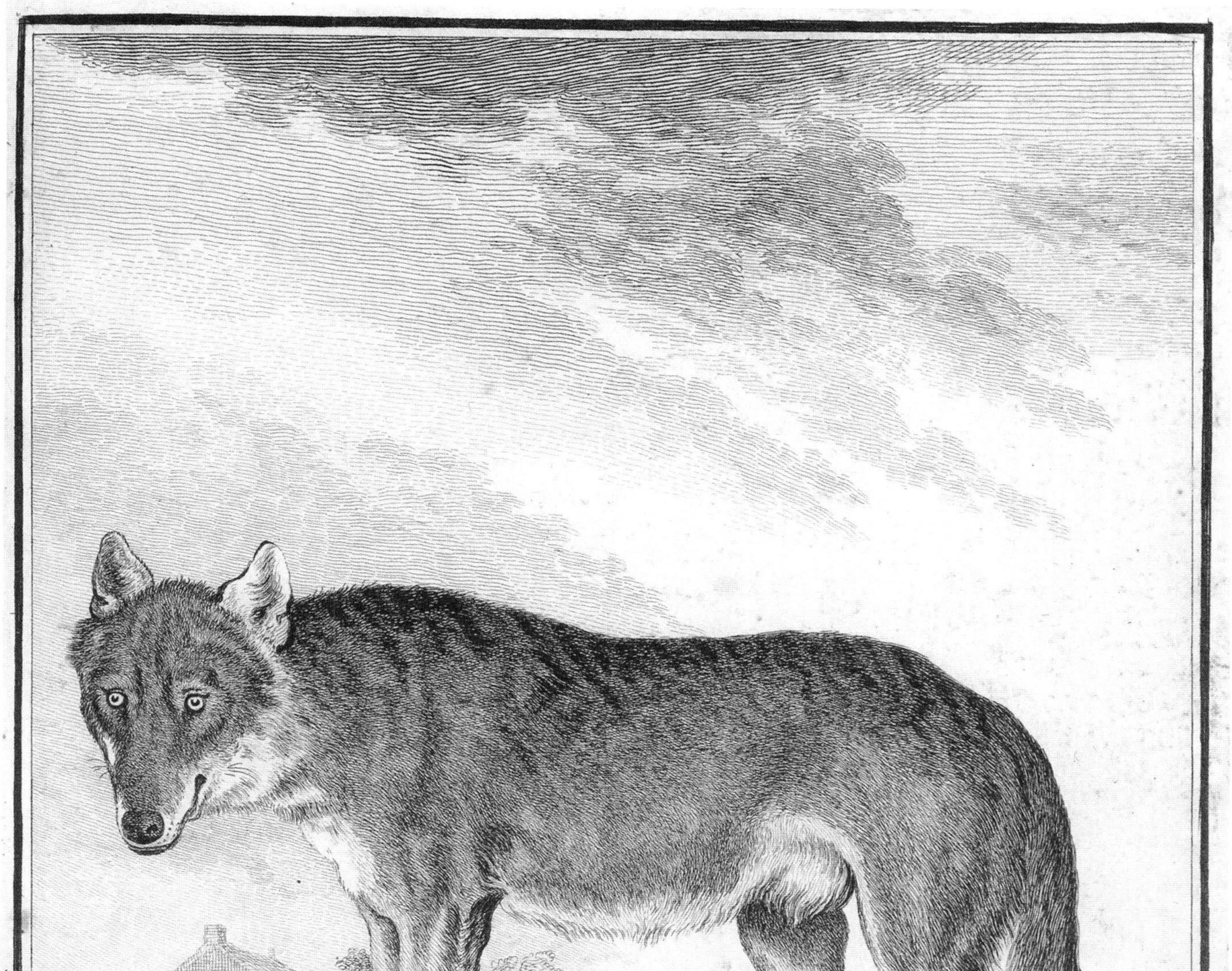

54

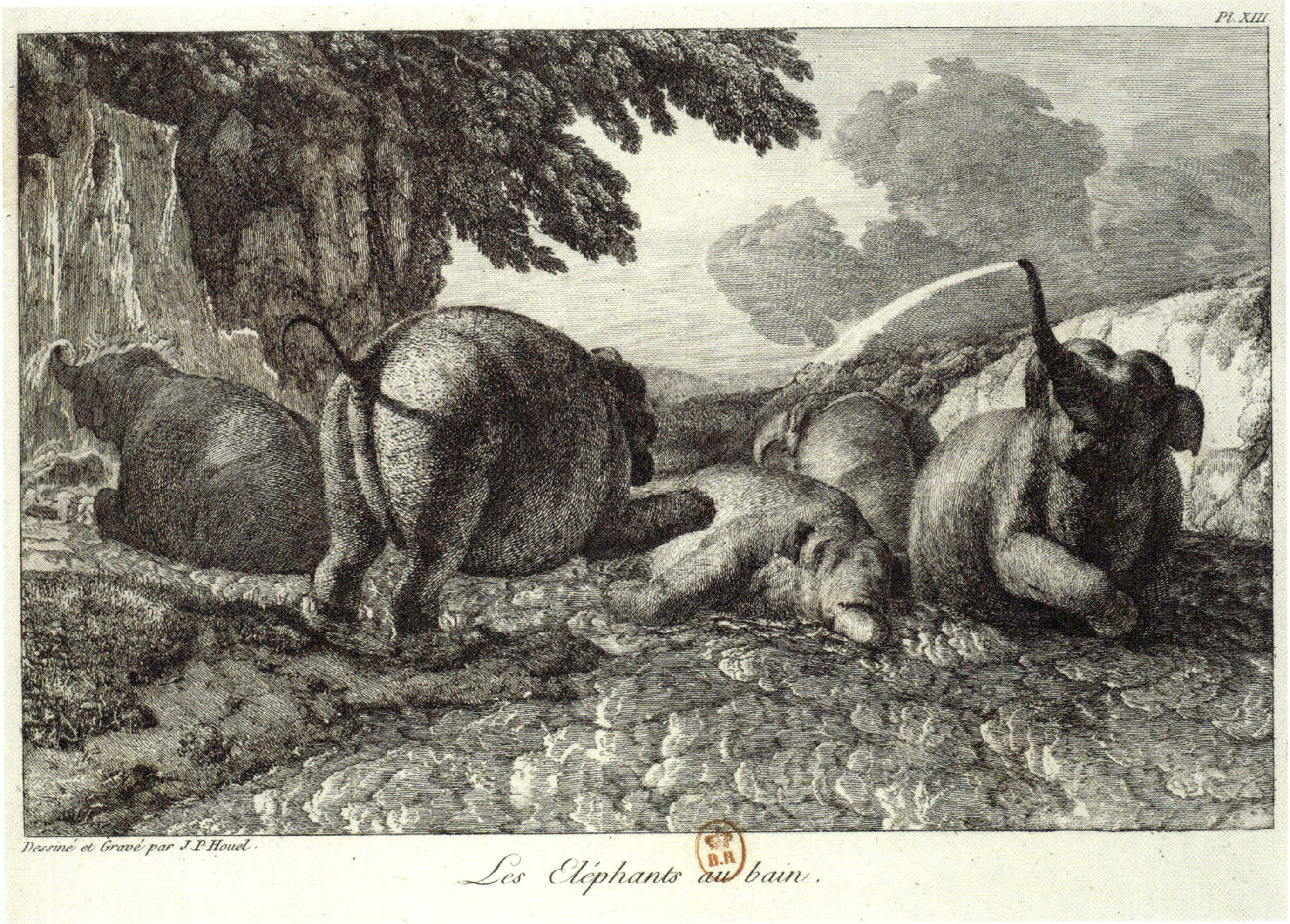

55

55 Jean-Pierre Louis Laurent Hoüel, *Elephants Bathing*, 1803

The pair of elephants known as Hans and Parkie (who was later re-baptized Marguerite) were confiscated by the armies of the French Republic after their victory in 1795 over the troops of William V, Stadtholder of Holland. The animals left the royal ménagerie at Het Loo in Guelders, and in 1798, after a highly eventful journey lasting over a year, they arrived at the Muséum d'histoire naturelle in Paris, where they became the chief attraction. The public were fascinated by Hans's irascible character and by the fondness the animals evidently felt for one another.

Using his good relations with museum staff, the painter, engraver and draughtsman Hoüel was able to spend eight weeks in the company of the pachyderms, even observing them while they slept at night. The result of these studies was a collection of twenty prints, which he created from his drawings and accompanied with commentaries. In each of these small images, he places the animals in what he imagined to be their natural environment. Hans died in 1802. His remains were stuffed, a practice that had not been extensively developed for animals of his size during that period. In 1931, he was added to the collections in the natural history museum at Bourges, where he can still be seen today. C.L.B.

Etching | 14.7 x 22.8 cm (boundary line)

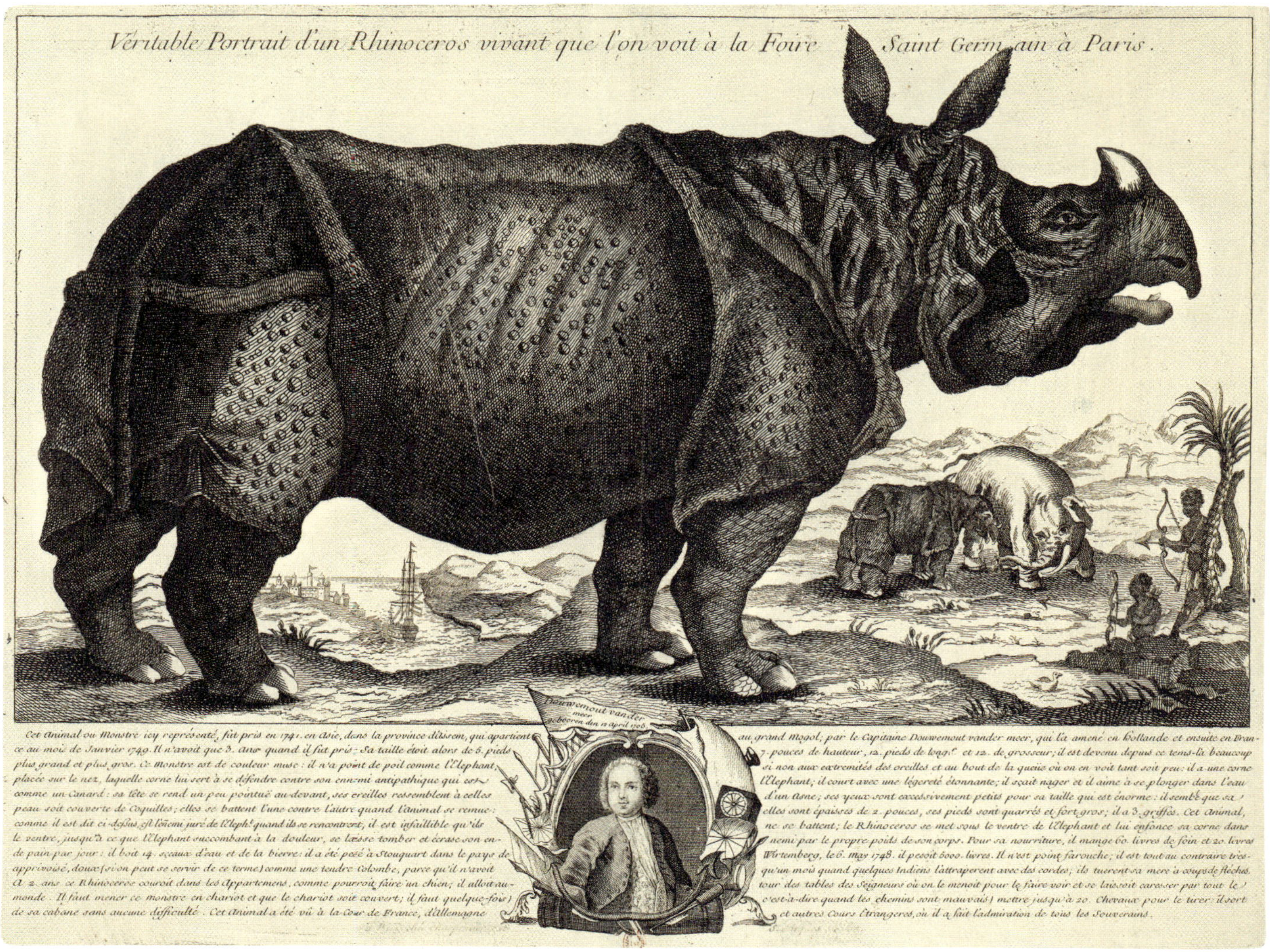

56 Anonymous, *Genuine Portrait of a Live Rhinoceros on Show at the Saint-Germain Fair in Paris*, 1749

Clara, a female rhinoceros, was captured in Bengal when very young and adopted as a pet by a director of the Dutch East India Company. She was brought to Europe in 1741 by her new owner, Captain Douwemout Van der Meer, who exhibited her in fairs throughout Europe until 1758. In this way, Clara was shown to Louis XV in 1749 and may have been admired at the Saint-Germain fair, where Giacomo Casanova confirmed that he had seen her. The star attraction of the day, the animal was painted or drawn by a number of artists, including Jean-Baptiste Oudry (1686–1755) who depicted her in Paris, and Pietro Longhi (1701–1785) who painted her in Venice in 1751. Clara then lost her horn. The rhinoceros theme was also adopted by practitioners of the decorative arts and the world of fashion: clocks, ribbons and even hairstyles '*au rhinocéros*' appeared in France.

An astute businessman, Van der Meer had several posters and prints of the animal made, all featuring the same iconography but with inscriptions that varied according to location. This representation of Clara reflects the enduring influence of the woodcut by Albrecht Dürer, which served as a reference for images of the rhinoceros during the 16th and 17th centuries. C.L.B.

Etching and burin work | 40.5 x 54.5 cm (print area)

57 Jean-Baptiste Oudry, *Deer Attacked by Dogs*, 1736

A multi-talented painter, Jean-Baptiste Oudry is principally known for his still lifes and scenes depicting animals, particularly his famous series illustrating La Fontaine's *Fables*. This very frequently served as a model for tapestries, as well as for the engraved plates illustrating the large edition of the *Fables* from 1755–1760.

In 1724, Louis XV commissioned Oudry to create paintings of three hunting scenes representing the kill, which were intended to decorate the guard-room at the Château de Chantilly – two of them may still be admired there. In 1725, Oudry published a series of etchings from these paintings, which were re-issued in 1736.

Here we see the deer having been caught by four dogs that are biting its legs, and from which it cannot escape. Despite the violence of the scene, the image celebrates the pleasure and nobility of the hunt; the painter has portrayed the deer in a proud and elegant pose, full of grandeur, reflecting all the respect owed by the hunter to the vanquished animal about to die. C.L.B.

Etching and burin work | 36.6 x 26.4 cm (print area)

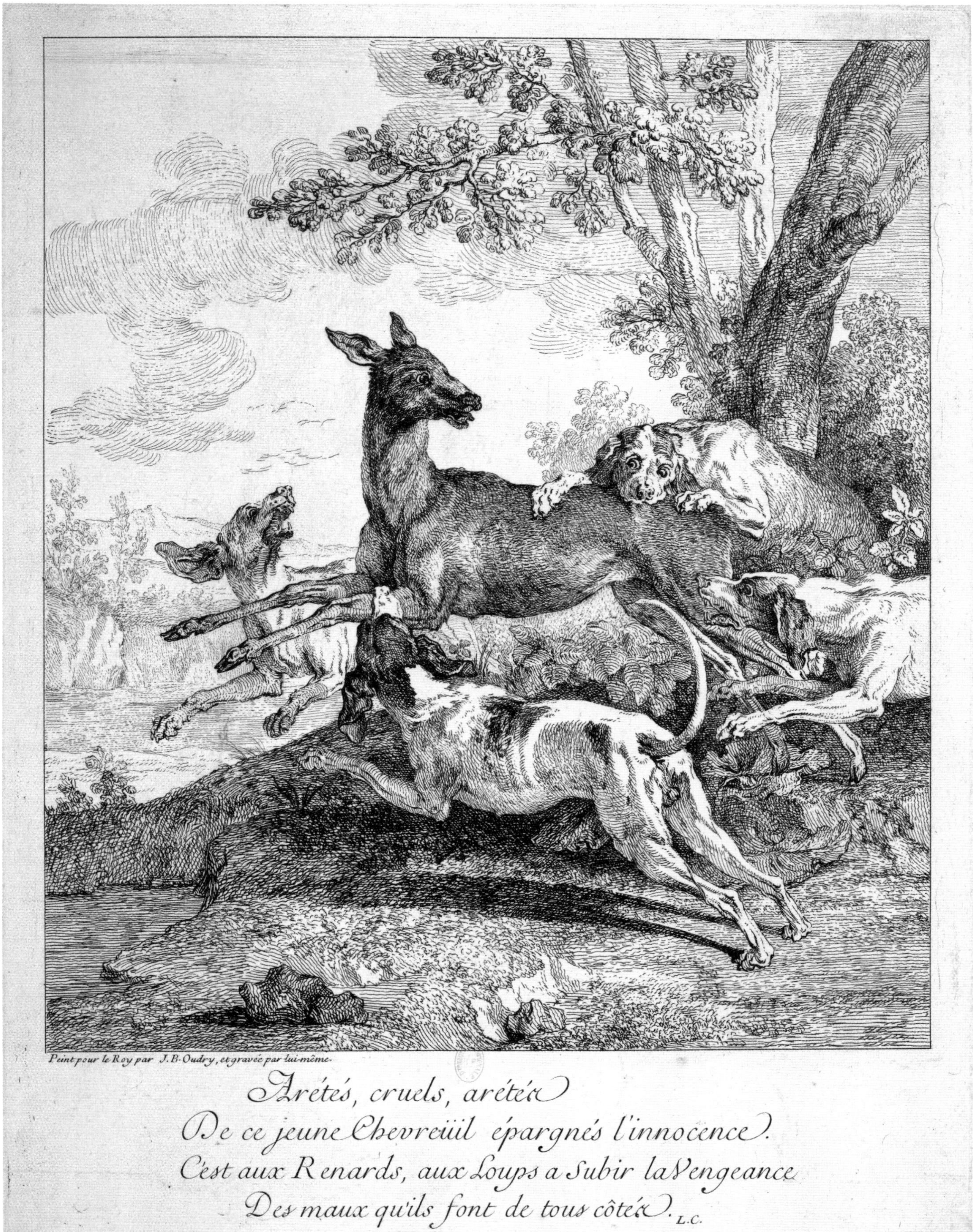
Peint pour le Roy par J.B. Oudry, et gravée par lui-même.
Arétés, cruels, arétés
De ce jeune Chevreüil épargnés l'innocence.
C'est aux Renards, aux Loups a subir la Vengeance
Des maux qu'ils font de tous côtés. L.C.

57

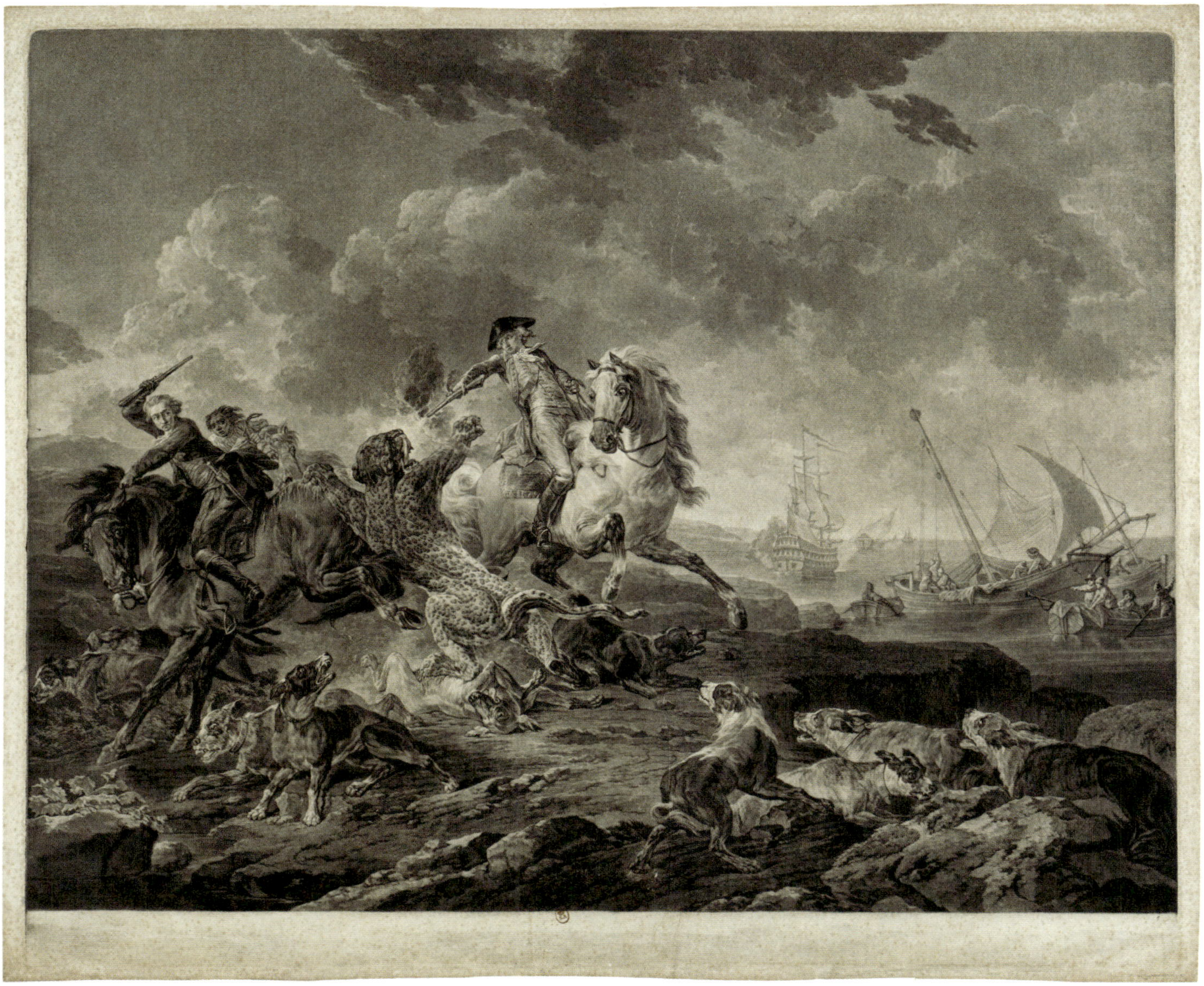

58

58 Johann Alexander Gottfried Jacobé, after Francesco Casanova, *Jaguar Killed in America by the Prince of Nassau-Siegen*, 1787

A military man who led an adventurous life, the Prince of Nassau-Siegen abandoned his arms for a time to follow Louis-Antoine de Bougainville on his voyage of discovery across the Pacific (1766–1769). In 1766, while the expedition was making a temporary sojourn in Latin America before passing through the Straits of Magellan, he encountered a jaguar in the heart of the Brazilian jungle. The ensuing confrontation, which amounted to hand-to-hand combat, established the Prince's reputation as a tamer of ferocious beasts. The scene was immortalized a few years later by the artist Francesco Casanova, brother of the famous adventurer, in a large painting that was engraved by Jacobé and entitled *Tiger Killed in America by His Highness Monseigneur the Prince of Nassau-Siegen.* The animal depicted is unquestionably a jaguar, however; shown rearing on its hind legs in the manner of a mythical creature, it instills terror into the pack of dogs before being struck down by Nassau. A painter of battle scenes, Casanova presented the episode as a fight to the death between two foes. C.L.B.

Mezzotint | 64.5 x 79.5 cm (print area)

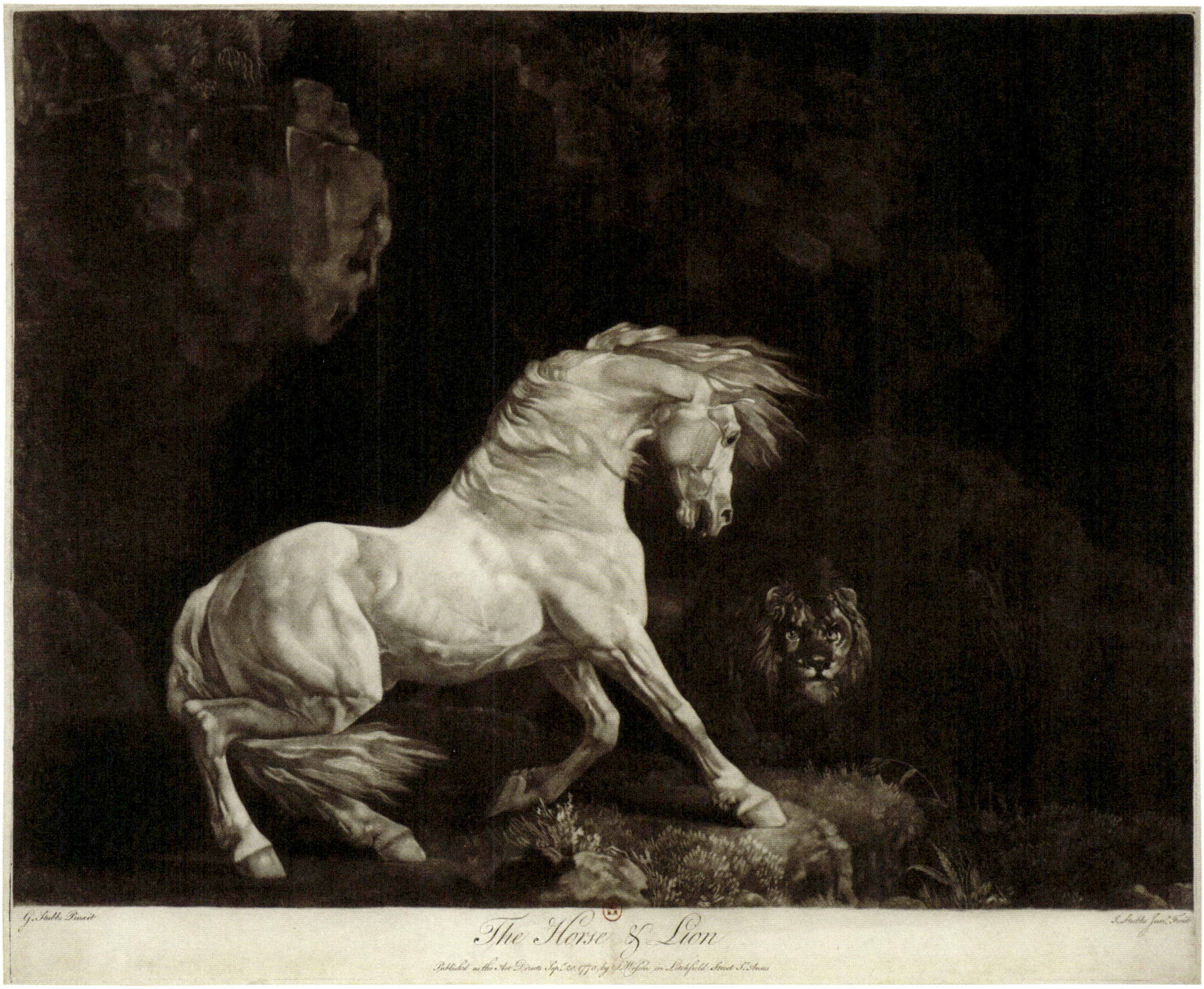

59

59 George Townley Stubbs, after George Stubbs, *The Horse and Lion*, 1770

The theme of a horse attacked by a lion frequently recurs in the works of English artist George Stubbs. He produced no fewer than seventeen versions of this fabled combat, painted on canvas or in enamel and possibly inspired by antique statuary that he had seen in Rome.

Although he was an engraver himself, Stubbs entrusted the work of portraying the horse's fear through the deep and subtle tones of mezzotint to his son, George Townley. The white form and musculature of the animal stand out against a wild, nocturnal landscape as it faces a crouching lion, ready to pounce. The image fully reflects Stubbs's great interest in the anatomy of the horse, a subject on which he published a work in 1766; in this case, however, we are particularly struck by the almost human expression of terror on the horse's face and by the tension pervading the scene. These compositions, popularized by prints, enjoyed great success both in Great Britain and in France, and influenced certain Romantic painters such as Eugène Delacroix. C.L.B.

Mezzotint | 46 x 55.8 cm (print area)

60 Gilles-Antoine Demarteau, after Carle Vernet, *Front View of a Horse's Head*, 1800

The name of Vernet remained associated with the history of French painting for three generations. The son of Joseph (1714–1789) and the father of Horace (1789–1863), Carle Vernet was the least renowned of the three artists. More accomplished as a draughtsman than as a painter (although it should be noted that his *Morning of Austerlitz* was admired by Napoleon), he left a body of work characterized by satirical social commentary and equine scenes. A passionate equestrian, he sketched horses of every breed, although thoroughbreds remained his favourites. He loved to ride these animals, and depicted them in cartoons that were used by engravers in the late 18th century, before he himself reproduced some in the form of lithographs. Engraved by Gilles-Antoine Demarteau in 1800, his *Horse's Head* presents an animal displaying almost human sensitivity, whose pricked ears, flaring nostrils, strained neck and wide-open eyes express an anxiety full of nervous tension.

The engraving technique used here is the 'crayon manner'; through this process, which was developed in France during the late 1750s by Gilles Demarteau, uncle of Gilles-Antoine, it was possible to produce striking facsimiles of charcoal or red chalk drawings. C.L.B.

Crayon manner, printed in black | 56 x 38.7 cm (print area)

61 Francisco de Goya, *Animal Follies. Other Laws for the People*, 1819–1824

→ Image on p. 102–103

This plate belongs to the unfinished series entitled '*Los Disparates*', otherwise known as the '*Proverbios*'. Goya himself wrote the caption '*Disparate de Bestia*' on the only known proof pulled for him. *Disparate* translates into English as 'folly' or 'absurdity', which links this series to that of the '*Caprichos*' (caprices), one of which is entitled the 'sleep of reason produces monsters'.

Some time elapsed before the publication of this etching, which has recently been acquired by the Louvre's Chalcographic Department. It finally appeared in the magazine *L'Art* in 1877 bearing the new title '*Otras leyes por el pueblo*' ('Other laws for the people'). This did nothing to elucidate the mysterious nature of the subject drawn by Goya. Is the sculptural elephant, standing out so strongly against the perfectly circular arena and seemingly challenged by four strange characters presenting him with an open book, intended to symbolize the people? V.S.-H.

Etching, drypoint, aquatint | 24 x 35 cm (print area)

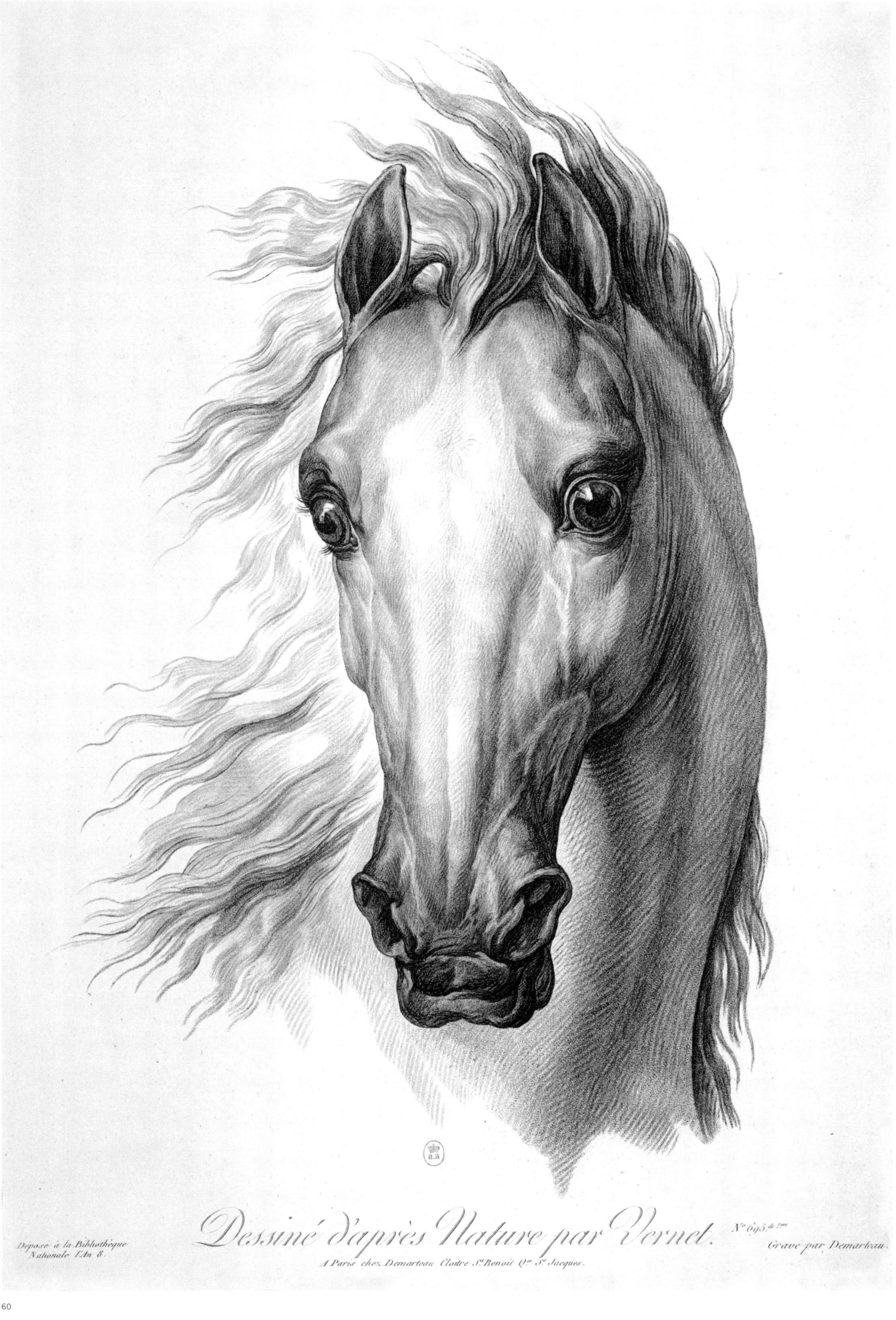
Dessiné d'après Nature par Vernet.
N° 695. de 1ere
Déposé à la Bibliothèque Nationale l'An 8.
Gravé par Demarteau.
A Paris chez Demarteau Cloître St. Benoit Qer St. Jacques.

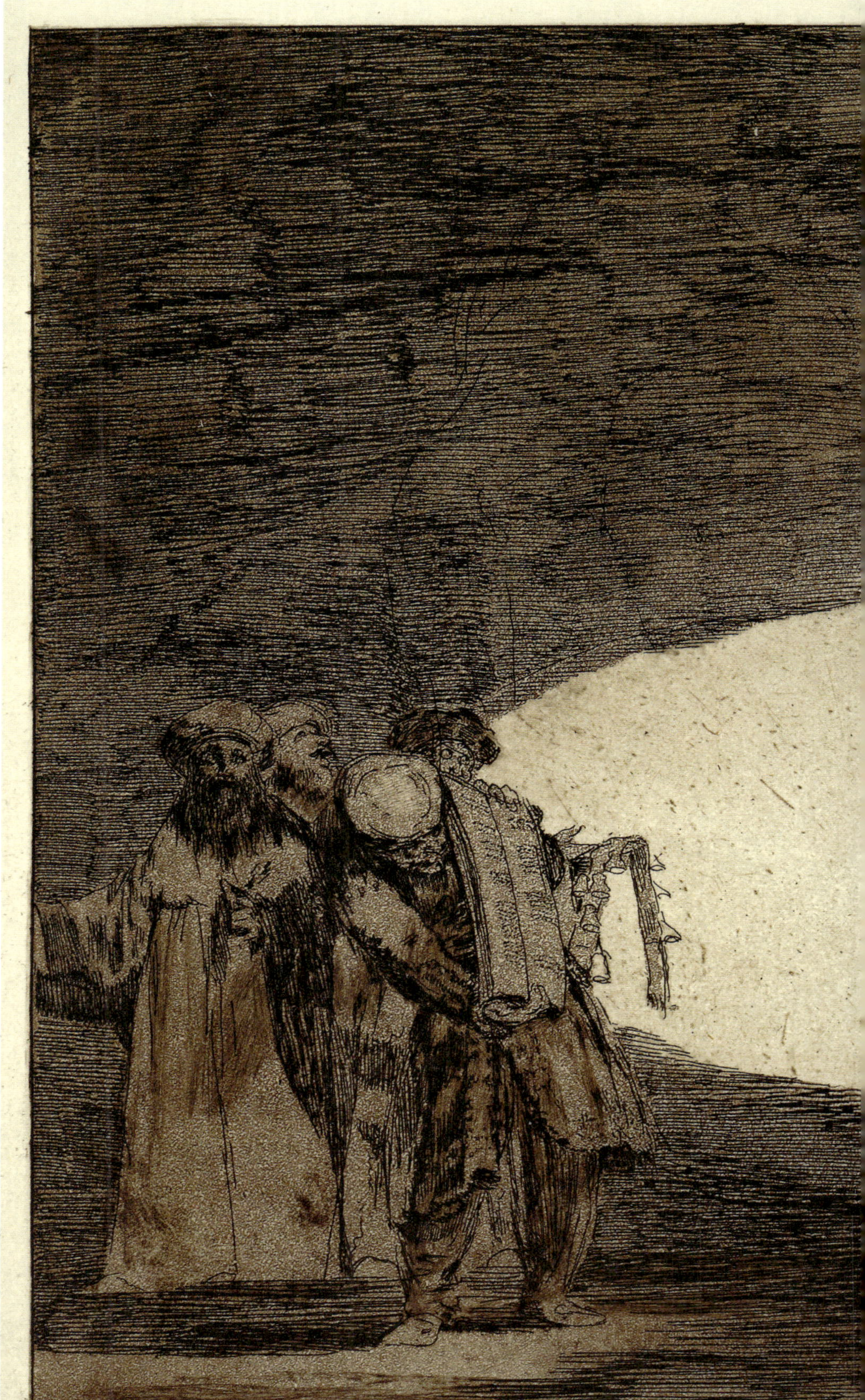

61

61 Francisco de Goya, *Animal Follies. Other Laws for the People*, 1819–1824

→ description on p. 100

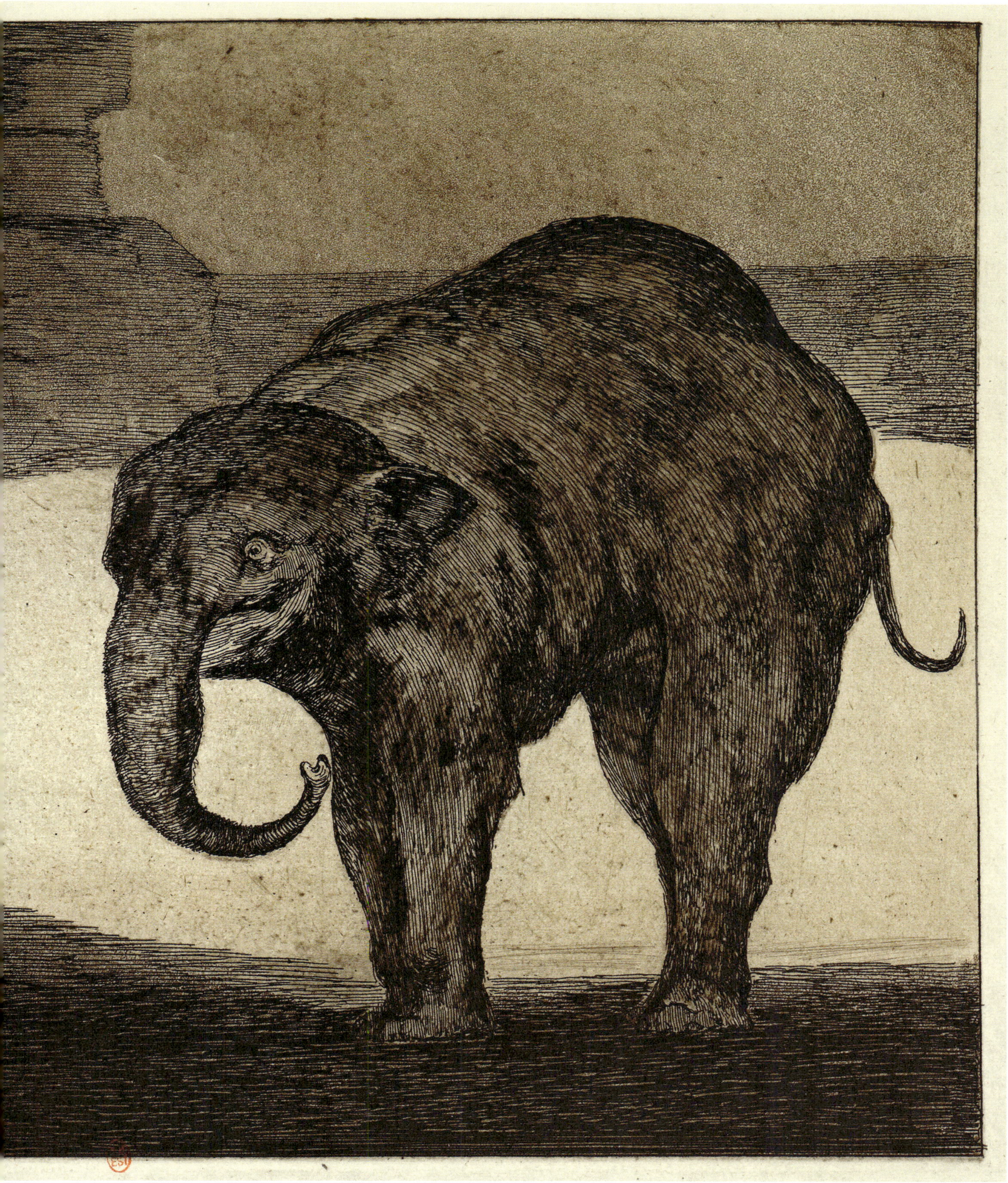

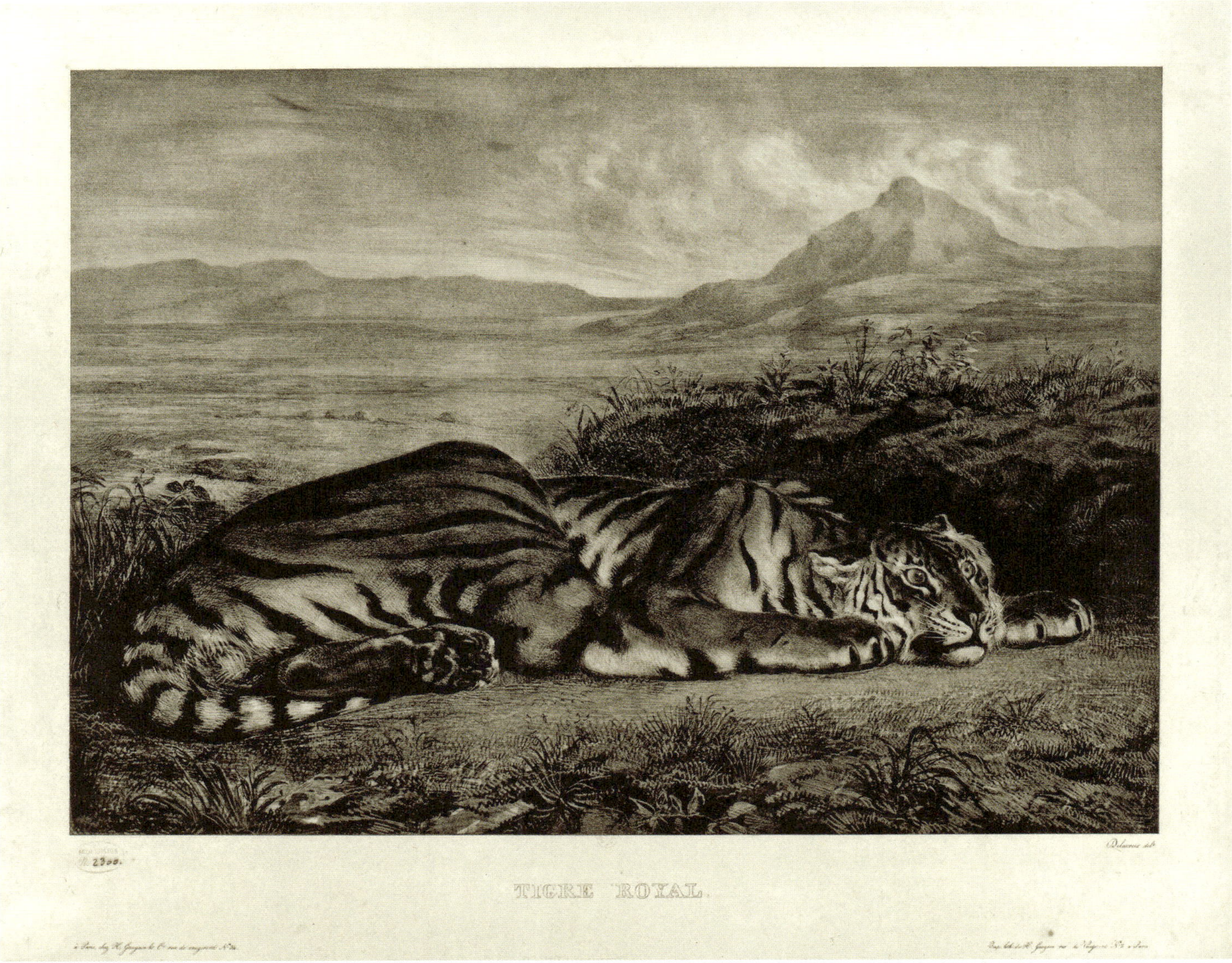

62a

62 Eugène Delacroix, Royal Tiger and Lion of the Atlas, 1829–1830

Royal Tiger and *Lion of the Atlas*, which were printed by Gaugain and both published in January 1830, should be seen as companion pieces. They were created following the intense studies carried out by Eugène Delacroix, together with Antoine-Louis Barye, during the late 1820s. In particular, they attended the dissections of the lions donated by Admiral de Rigny, which were carried out in Georges Cuvier's laboratory at the Jardin des Plantes in 1829. Although the power of these works certainly lies in their accuracy of anatomical portrayal and in their realism of expression, they are equally striking as masterly examples of the lithographic technique. This is particularly evident in the depiction of the animals' fur and in the use of the engraving tool to recreate their whiskers. M.M.

Lithographs | 32.7 x 46.7 cm (image)

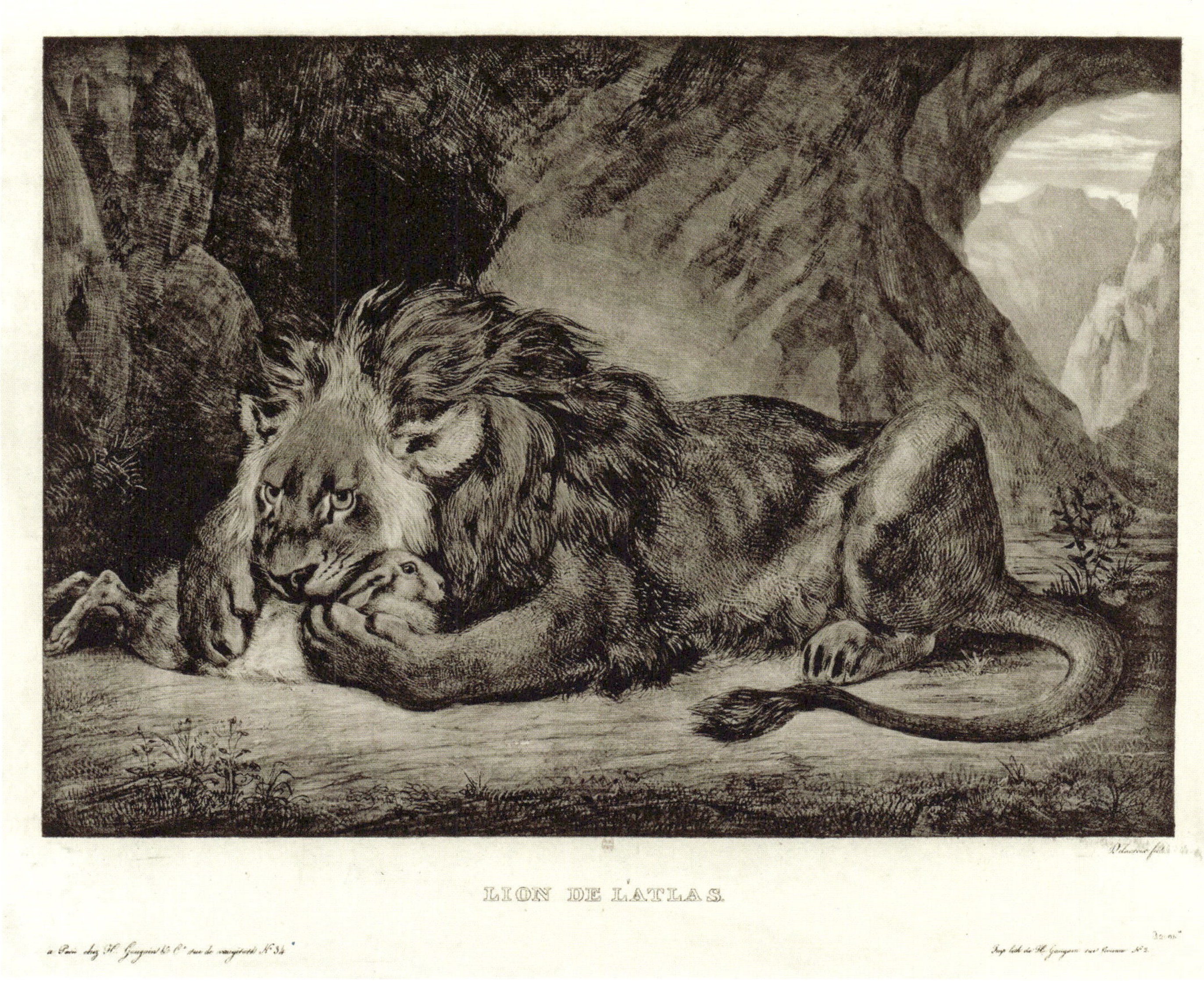

62b

63 John James Audubon, *Snowy Owls*, ca. 1830

This pair of snowy owls, painted by Audubon in the far north of America, displays his customary minute attention to detail. The dead birds, shown in their native habitat, are fixed into natural-looking positions with wire supports, so that they appear alive. Trained by the painter David and already passionately interested in natural history, Jean-Jacques Audubon fled conscription into Napoleon's armies and settled in the United States. There, now known as John James Audubon, he led a wandering life as a hunter, ornithologist and painter. Paradoxically, this precursor of the environmental movement was capable of killing around a hundred birds a day – although this was a period when the natural world was thought to have infinite resources. In order to keep track of his numerous hours of observation, he accumulated paintings that are of interest both for their documentary value and as works of art. Thanks to the engraver Robert Havell, he was able to publish *Birds of America* in England from 1827 to 1838. This four-volume work comprises 435 plates in 'double elephant' format. It was followed by volumes of textual descriptions entitled *Ornithological Biography*. Publication was first funded through subscription; the Kings of England and France were included among the subscribers, together with the naturalist himself, through whom the Bibliothèque nationale acquired the most beautiful plates. To this day, several new editions of the work have been produced. M.M.

Etching and aquatint, coloured | 96.7 x 64.6 cm (print area)

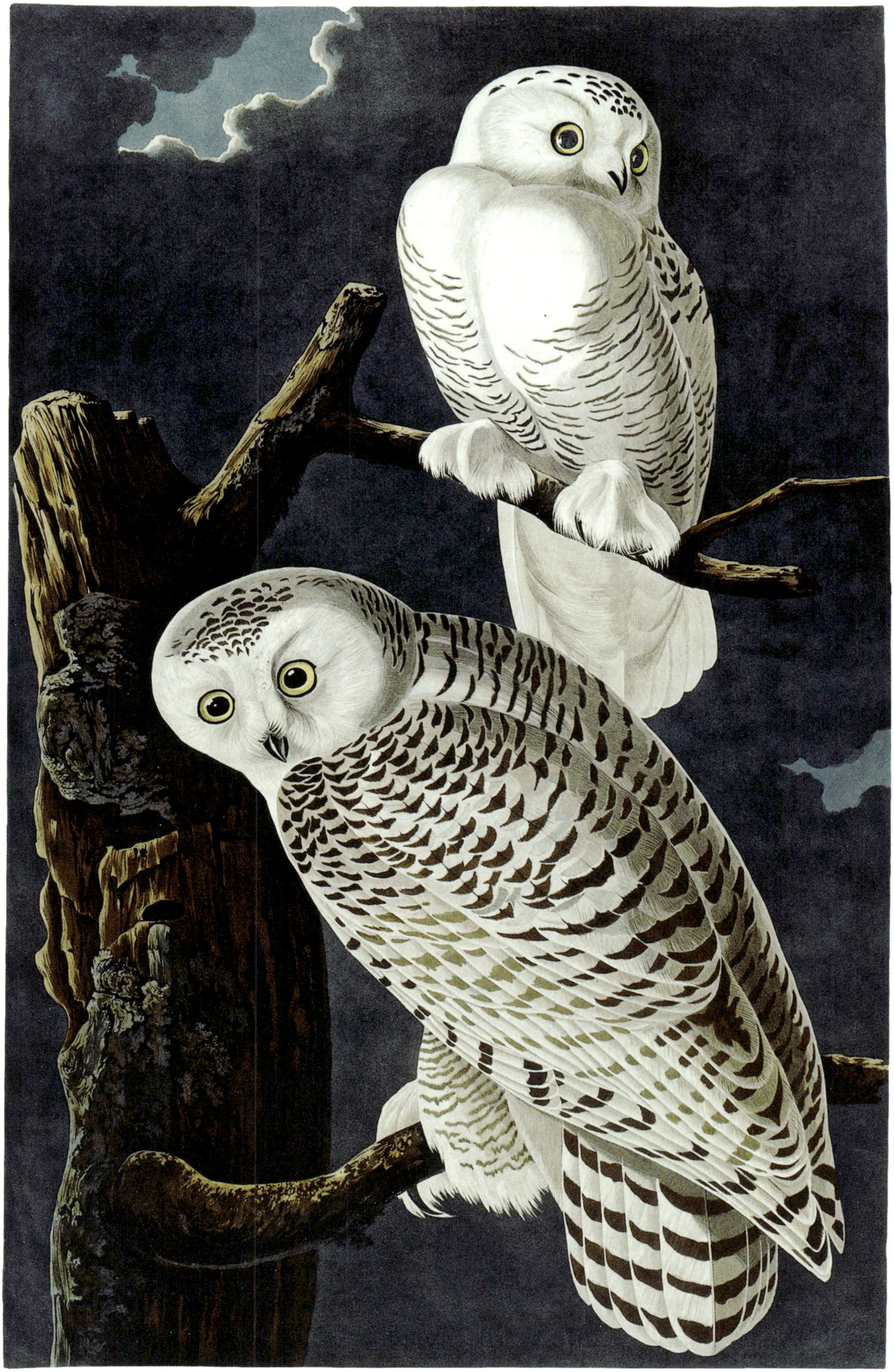

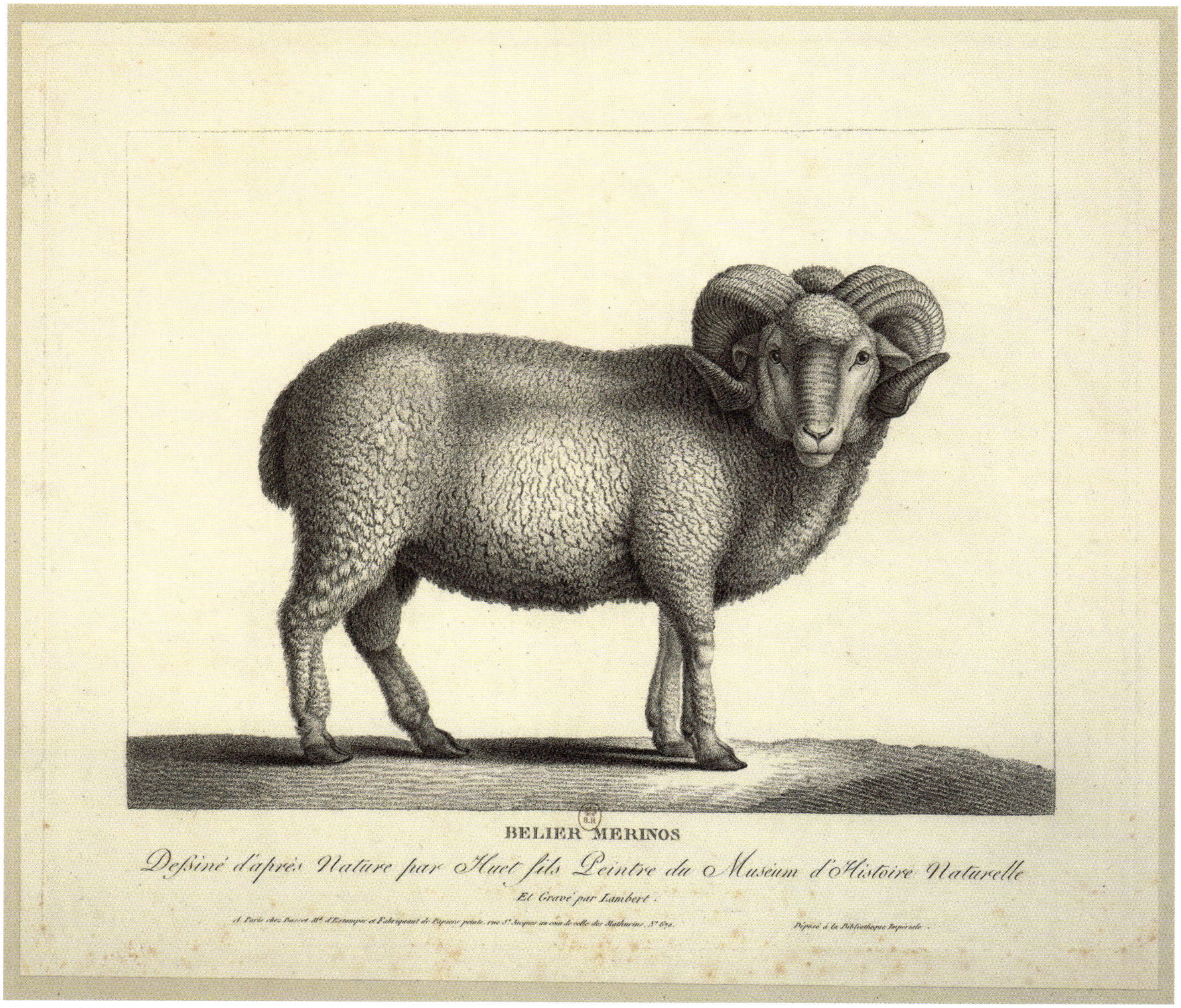
BELIER MERINOS
Deſsiné d'après Nature par Huet fils Peintre du Muséum d'Histoire Naturelle
Et Gravé par Lambert.
A Paris chez Basset Md. d'Estampes et Fabriquant de Papiers peints, rue St. Jacques au coin de celle des Mathurins, N.o 670.
Déposé à la Bibliothèque Impériale.

64

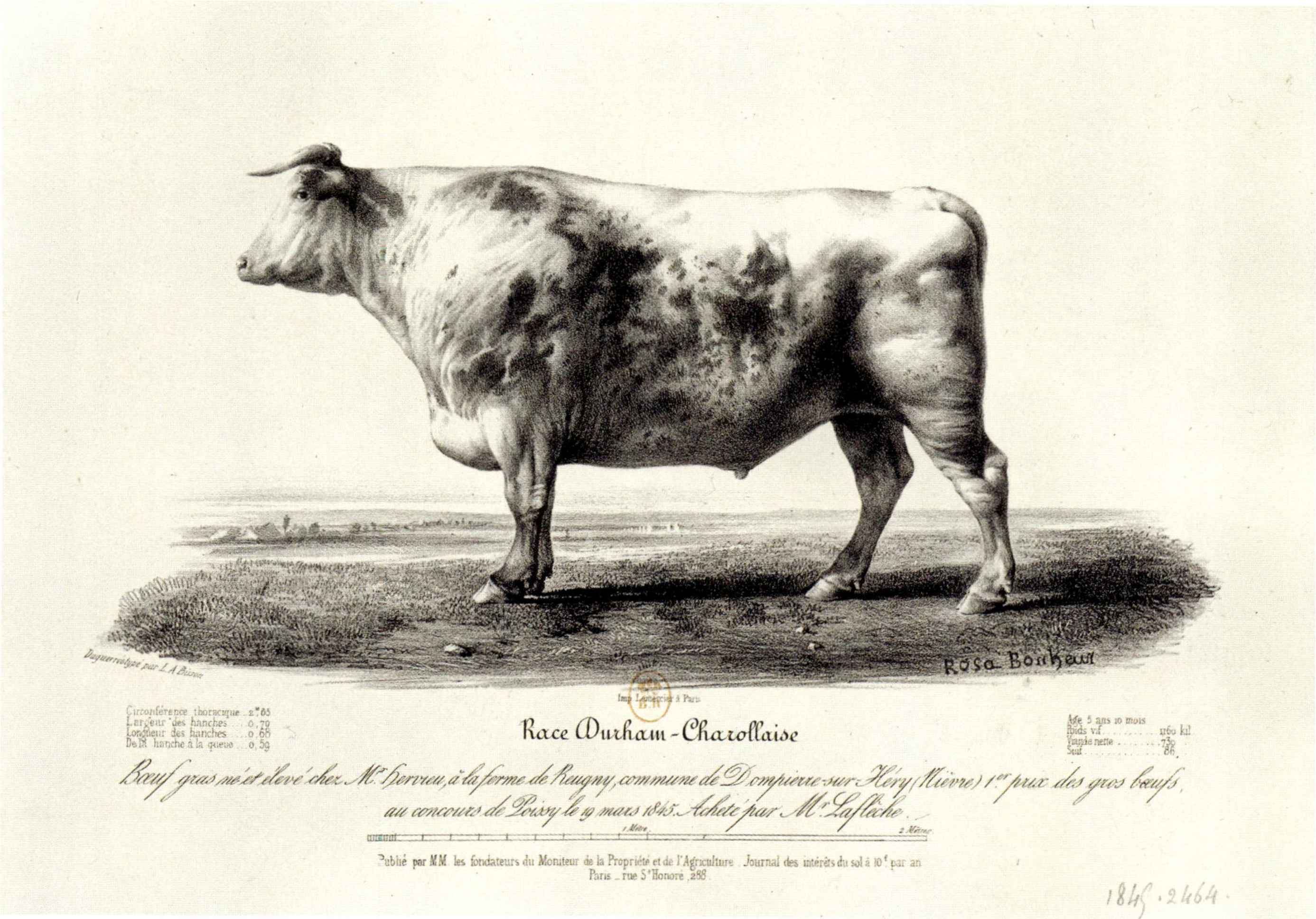

65

64 The Lambert brothers, after Jean-Baptiste Huet, *Merino Ram*, 1805

Jean-Baptiste Huet, known as *Huet fils*, was born into a family of artists and inherited his talent for animal drawing from his father, whose work includes a wealth of images of the ovine species. His brothers, Nicolas and François, likewise won renown as animal artists. Like the majority of animals that Jean-Baptiste Huet drew from life, this merino ram was probably kept in the ménagerie at the Jardin des Plantes, to which the artist had privileged access as a painter attached to the Natural History Museum.

His drawing was entrusted to the Lambert brothers, who created an engraving from the work using the stippling technique; still in vogue in the first decade of the 19th century, this process realistically reproduced the animal's physical characteristics. V.S.-H.

Stipple engraving | 35 x 42.8 cm (print area)

65 Rosa Bonheur, *The Durham-Charolais Breed*, 1845

In 1845, at only twenty-three years of age, Rosa Bonheur had just been awarded a bronze medal at the Salon and was already winning renown as an animal artist. This lithograph demonstrates her great skill at depicting oxen, a subject she adopted on numerous occasions. The impeccably realistic drawing was executed from a daguerreotype by Louis Auguste Bisson and was published by the *Moniteur de la propriété et de l'agriculture*.

This is the portrait of a hefty Durham-Charolais ox, a race that had been obtained by crossing Charolais cattle with an English breed in the Nièvre region. The printed information accompanying this quasi-photographic image provides specific details relating to the superb physique of this animal, which would attract the attention of many a butcher: aged 5 years and 10 months, this ox already weighs 1160 kilos and has a chest measurement of 2.65 metres! V.S.-H.

Lithograph | 19.4 x 27.7 cm (image)

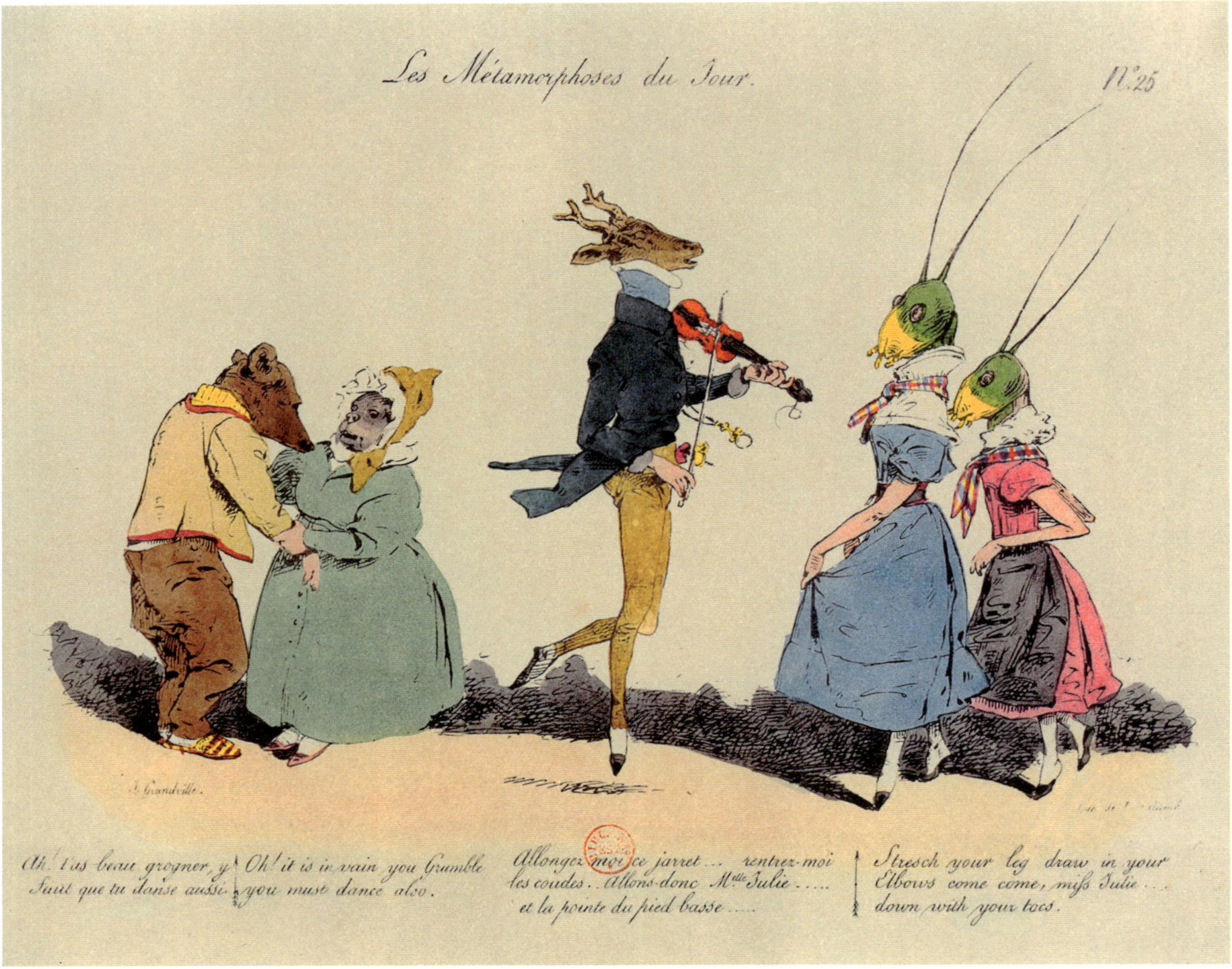

66

66 Jean Ignace Isidore Gérard, known as Grandville, *The Dancing Lesson*, 1828

We are in the home of the Durognon family, highly prosperous butchers who have enlisted the services of a sprightly dancing-master to teach their two lanky daughters, shown as here as grasshoppers, graceful posture and movement. The text accompanying the composition describes the scene in cruel terms: 'The daughters are uncomely, the parents ridiculous. The mentality of these four individuals lies more or less at the physical level, in other words, below zero . . . but they are rich!' In this way, metaphors and metamorphoses become vehicles for social satire, as with the fables of Ovid and La Fontaine. Firstly, Grandville lowers man to the level of animals. He then creates lively images in which they are shown speaking, dressed in human clothing and walking on their hind legs, thereby transforming them into recognizable characters and lampooning human idiosyncrasies. This approach is the hallmark of Grandville's fanciful yet naturalistic style, and explains the great success achieved by the *Métamorphoses du jour*, a series of seventy-one lithographs that brought fame to the artist, who is sometimes known as the 'Buffon of satire'. M.M.

Plate no. 25 of *Les Métamorphoses du jour* | Coloured lithograph | 23.3 x 28.7 cm (sheet)

67 Anonymous, *The Vanity of the Peacock, or the New Panegyric to 100 Parisian Coquettes*, 1821

This lithograph, which dates from 1821, is accompanied by a lengthy text addressed to 'husbands and mainly young men', in the form of a virulent (and anonymous) warning against 'Parisian society women': 'Although ignorant and empty-headed, they are extremely pedantic, proud, ambitious and very jealous of other females.' The description goes on to condemn them as 'talkative, sharp-tongued and maligning all their friends', as well as 'greedy, untruthful and excessively covetous, volatile, unreasonable and capricious from morn til night!'

This hate-filled indictment appears beneath the image of a peacock, a bird that symbolizes their major shortcoming: 'vanity is the principal fault that these coquettes share with the peacock, the emblem of practically all their imperfections'. The peacock illustrating this diatribe is shown fanning out its tail, which is set with women's heads instead of 'eyes'. Their various hair styles serve as a reminder that, whether 'brunettes, blondes or even redheads', all are 'prouder than the peacock!' V.S.-H.

Coloured lithograph | 38.7 x 38.7 cm (sheet)

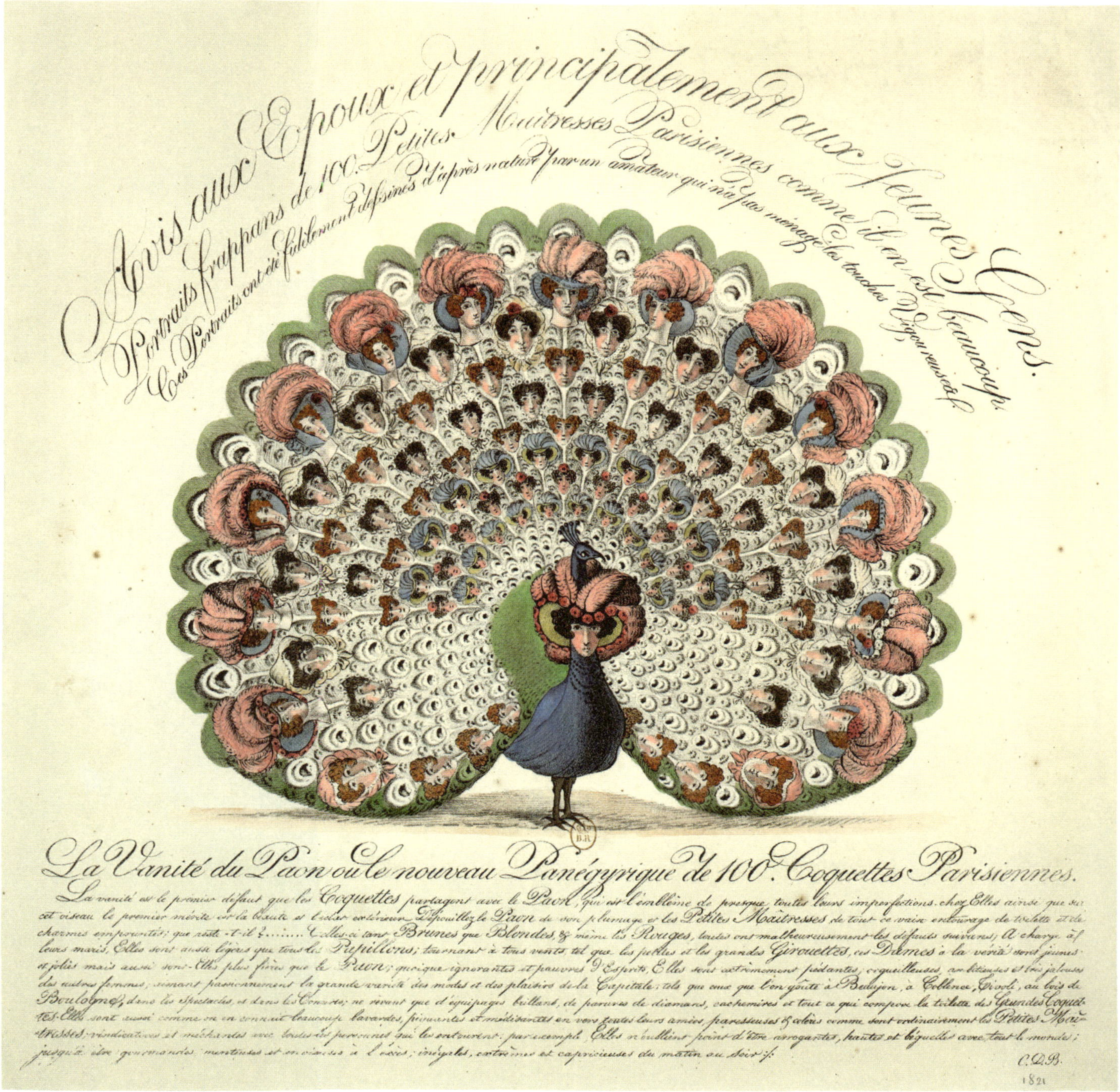

Avis aux Epoux et principalement aux Jeunes Gens.
Portraits frappans de 100. Petites Maîtresses Parisiennes comme il en est beaucoup
Ces Portraits ont été fidèlement dessinés d'après nature par un amateur qui n'a pas ménagé les touches vigoureuses
La Vanité du Paon ou le nouveau Panégyrique de 100. Coquettes Parisiennes.
La vanité est le premier défaut que les Coquettes partagent avec le Paon, qui est l'emblême de presque toutes leurs imperfections. chez Elles ainsi que sur
cet oiseau le premier mérite est la beauté et l'éclat extérieur. Dépouillez le Paon de son plumage et les Petites Maîtresses de tout ce vain entourage de toilette et de
charmes empruntés; que reste-t-il?...... Celles-ci tant Brunes que Blondes, & même les Rouges, toutes ont malheureusement les défauts suivans; A charge à
leurs maris, Elles sont aussi légères que tous les Papillons; tournant à tous vents, tel que les petites et les grandes Girouettes, ces Dames à la vérité sont jeunes
et jolies mais aussi sont-Elles plus fières que le Paon; quoique ignorantes et pauvres d'Esprits, Elles sont extrêmement pédantes, orgueilleuses, ambitieuses et très jalouses
des autres femmes, aimant passionnement la grande variété des modes et des plaisirs de la Capitale: tels que ceux que l'on goûte à Beaujon, à Coblence, Tivoli, au bois de
Boulogne, dans les Spectacles, et dans les Concerts; ne rêvant que d'équipages brillans, de parures de diamans, cachemires et tout ce qui compose la toilette des Grandes Coquet-
tes. Elles sont aussi comme on en connait beaucoup bavardes, piquantes et médisantes envers toutes leurs amies, paresseuses & colères comme sont ordinairement les Petites Maî-
tresses; vindicatives et méchantes avec toutes les personnes qui les entourent: par exemple, Elles n'oublient point d'être arrogantes, hautes et bégueules avec tout le monde;
jusqu'à être gourmandes, menteuses et envieuses à l'excès; inégales, extrêmes et capricieuses du matin au soir.
C.D.B.
1821

67

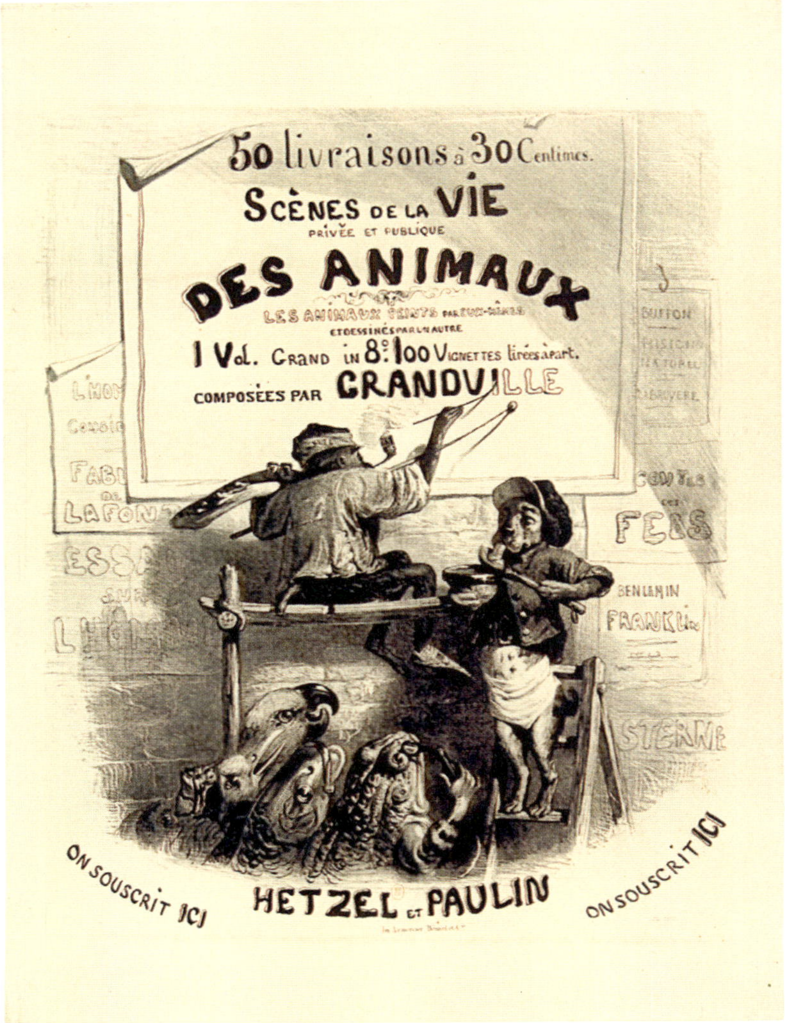

68

68 Jean Ignace Isidore Gérard, known as Grandville, *Scenes of the Private and Public Lives of Animals*, 1840

This poster advertises the launch of a subscription for a publication that comprised various texts by different writers (including Stahl and Balzac) and was exclusively illustrated by Grandville. He is described in the frontispiece as the 'La Bruyère of animals and the La Fontaine of artists', for his unfailing ability 'to seize upon the curious analogies that exist between man and animals'. This poster, which takes the form of an image within an image, depicts the painter as a monkey. It echoes the illustration that introduces the work, while the poster adds the subtitle '*Les animaux peints par eux-mêmes*'. This refers to another publication of the day, '*Les Français peints par eux-mêmes*' ('The French painted by themselves'), which may have provided the inspiration for this venture. The practice of issuing literary works in 'installments' was devised by publishers during the Romantic period and enabled payments to be staggered. Known as 'bookshop posters', these notices mainly featured lithographic images, the technique being another novelty of the day, and were the first illustrated commercial posters to be produced in large numbers. However, although the book's prologue facetiously declares that they are 'affixed to every wall', including 'the Great Wall of China itself', the posters were actually intended for interiors, and were put up in bookshops and reading rooms. A.-M.S.

Poster, lithograph | 70 x 53 cm (sheet)

69 Gustave Doré, *The Monkey and the Dolphin*, 1868

After Jean-Baptiste Oudry and Grandville, and before Chagall, Gustave Doré applied his talents to the literary genius of La Fontaine. His drawings combine realism with vision. In 1855 he drew up a list of the literary masterpieces he wished to illustrate, which included the *Fables*. The two volumes published by Hachette in 1867 were decorated with several in-text vignettes, in addition to eighty-five full-page images executed by Doré in pen, ink wash and gouache directly onto a wood block, and entrusted to the most skillful endgrain wood engravers of the day.

Although in the fable of the monkey and the dolphin there is such a strong resemblance between man and monkey that the dolphin is taken in, Doré portrays the animal in a more realistic manner. Paradoxically, it is in the image of the dolphin that he gives free rein to his imagination, abandoning accurate depiction to create a type of sea monster with a dragon's tail and anthropomorphic head. V.S.-H.

Wood engraving by A. Ligny from a drawing by Gustave Doré | 23.8 x 19 cm (boundary line)

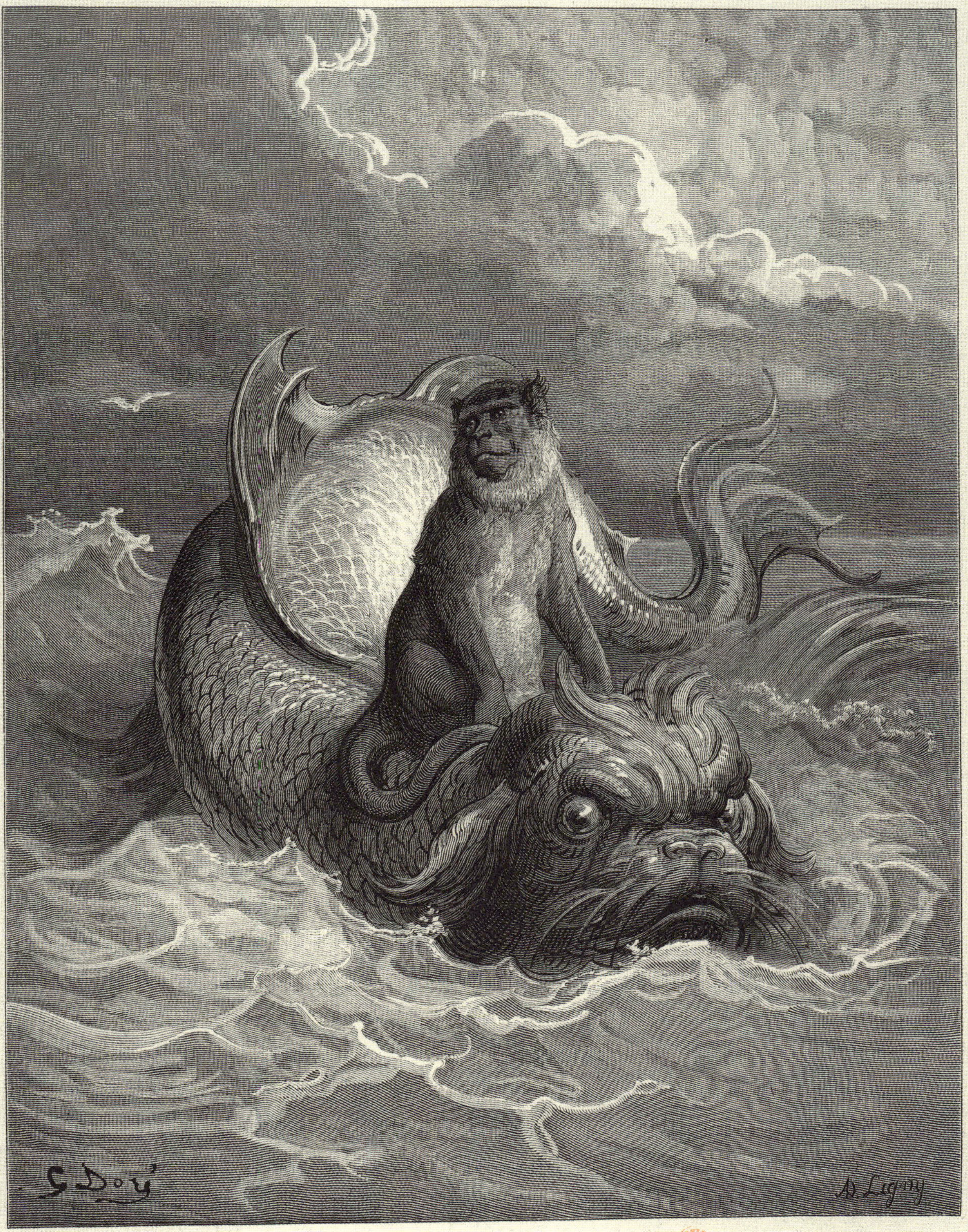

LE SINGE ET LE DAUPHIN.

69

LA GIRAFE,

Agée de 2 ans et demi, haute de 13 pieds, envoyée au Roi de France par le Pacha d'Egypte. Elle est la première amenée vivante en Europe; elle a été présentée au Roi le 9 juillet 1827, à Saint-Cloud.

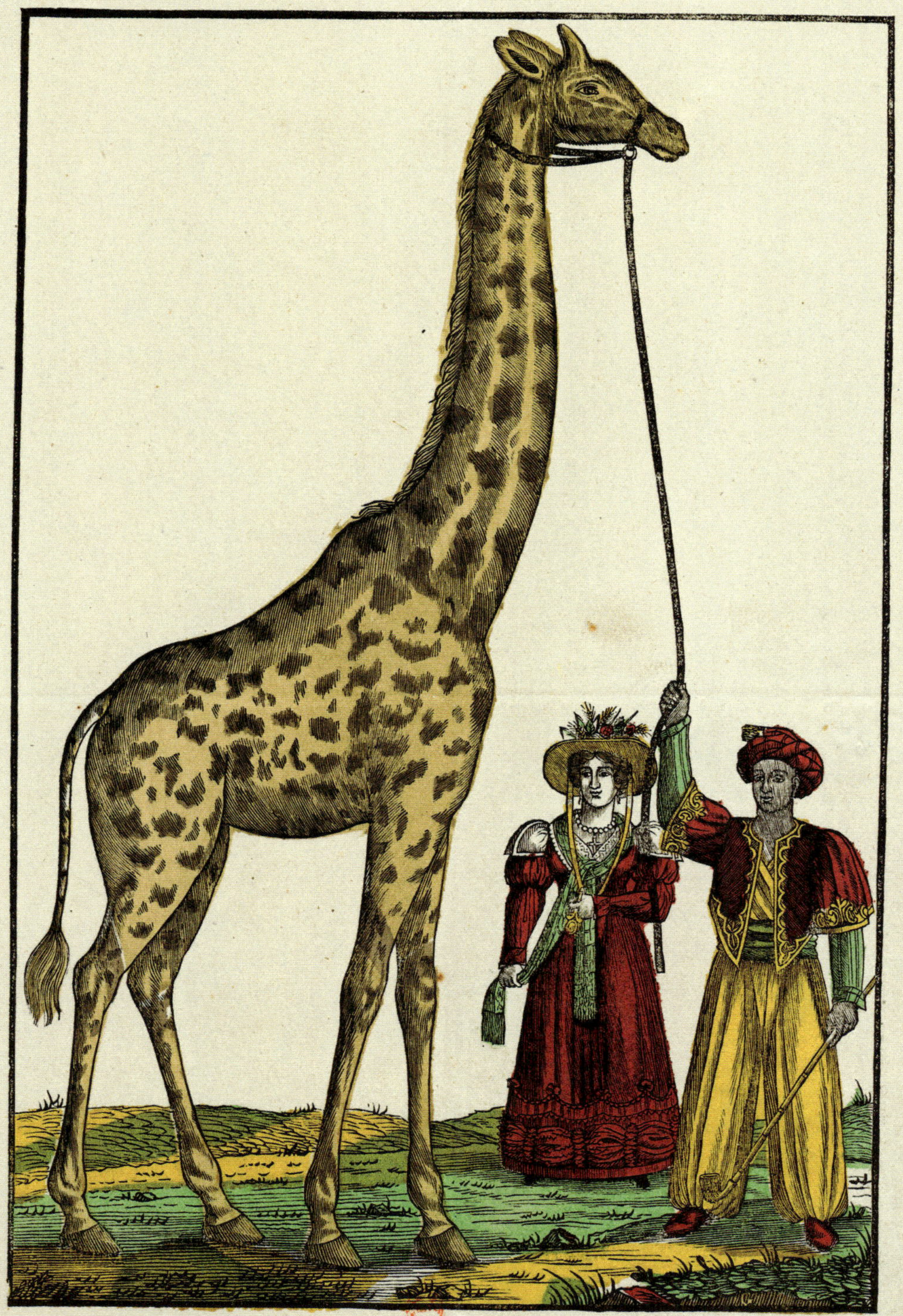

LA GIRAFE A LA MODE. — Air : *A la façon de Barbari.*

On parle souvent aujourd'hui
De nouvelle méthode;
A la Girafe, chacun dit :
Faut se mettre à la mode;
Tout le monde prend le bon ton,
La faridondaine, la faridondon,
On s'met à la Girafe ici, biribi,
A la façon de Barbari, mon ami.

On n'est jamais bien habillé
Dans le siècle où nous sommes,
Si l'on n'est pas bien costumé
Au genre qu'on renomme,
A la Joco n'est plus de saison,
La faridondaine, la faridondon,
A la Girafe on brille ici, biribi,
A la façon, etc.

Des toiles de toute façon
On imprime au plus vite;
Robin des bois n'est plus d'saison,
Tout un chacun le quitte;
Grand falbala, et grands frisons,
La faridondaine, la faridondon,
Ajoutez la Girafe aussi, biribi,
A la façon, etc.

Filles et femmes d'aujourd'hui
Ont-très-belle tournure,
Tout un chacun en est séduit
Voyant leur chevelure:
On peigne beaucoup de frisons,
La faridondaine, la faridondon,
Tout est à la Girafe ici, biribi,
A la façon, etc.

Chapeau de paille surmonté
De rubans, de panaches,
Colerette, corset monté
Qui bien souvent rien ne cache.
On croit quelquefois qu'c'est du bon ton,
La faridondaine, la faridondon :
Tout c'fait à la Girafe ici, biribi,
A la façon, etc.

Pour les modes en vérité
On ne sait plus que faire;
On a toujours beau rechercher,
L'on ne sait comment plaire.
Café, musique et chanson,
La faridondaine, la faridondon,
Enseigne à la Girafe aussi, biribi,
A la façon de Barbari, etc.

ÉPINAL, IMPRIMERIE DE PELLERIN.

70

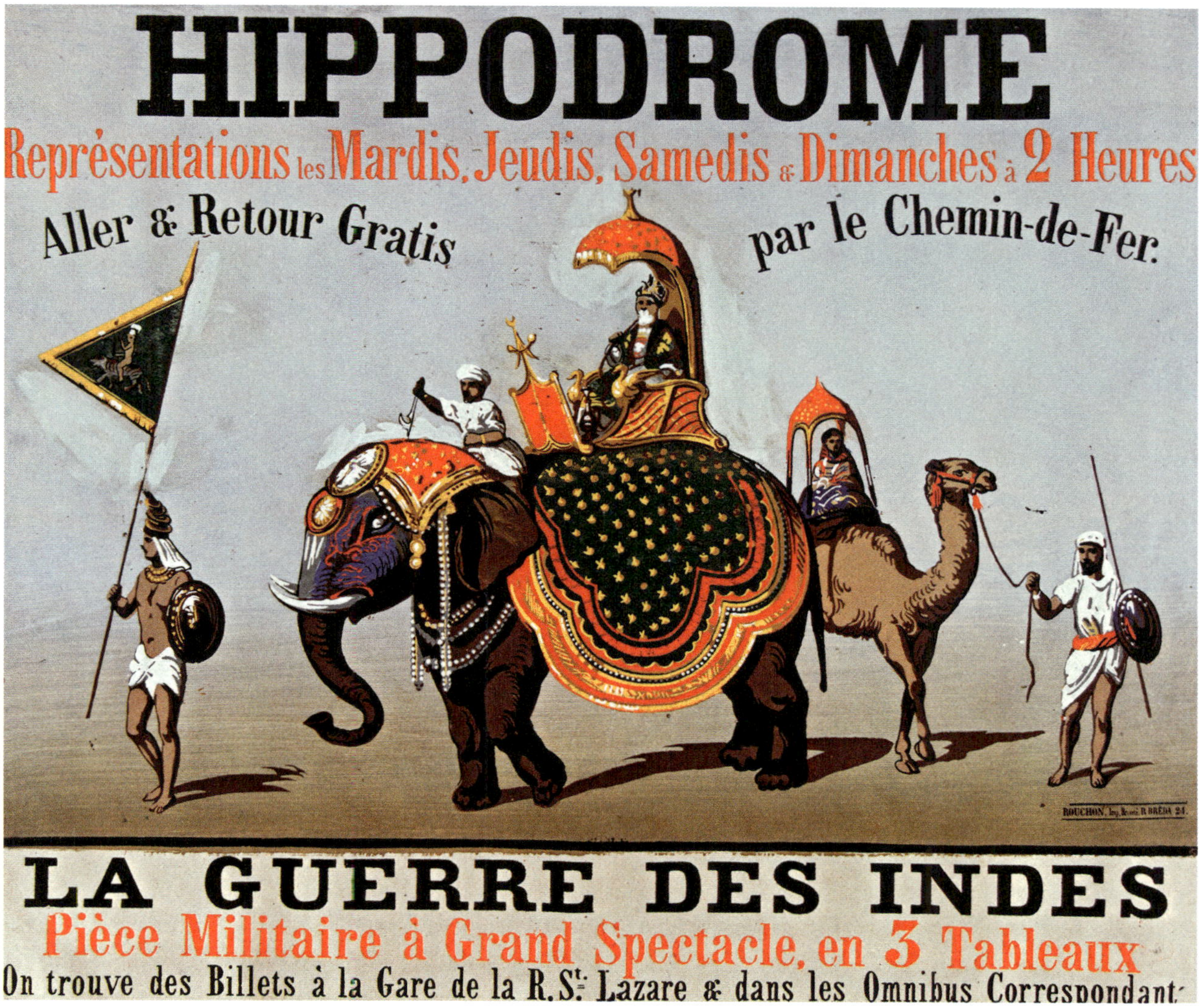

71

70 Anonymous, *The Giraffe*, 1828

Issued by the Pellerin publishing house in Épinal, this print commemorates the arrival in Paris of an animal never before seen in France, a gift from Muhammad Ali to Charles X. The event is summarized in the inscription: 'The giraffe, aged 2 and a half and measuring 13 feet high, sent to the King of France by the Pasha of Egypt. She is the first of her kind to be brought to Europe alive. She was presented to the King on the 9th of July 1827, at Saint-Cloud.' And indeed, after having crossed the Mediterranean from Alexandria in a specially adapted boat, the giraffe disembarked at Marseille in November 1826, from where she walked to the capital escorted by Geoffroy Saint-Hilaire in person. Arriving in Paris on 30 June 1827 and already famous in all the regions through which she had passed, the giraffe was presented to the King and installed in the ménagerie at the Jardin des Plantes. She became one of the capital's chief attractions and was seen by six hundred thousand visitors that summer. Her popularity was reflected in a number of texts, theatre plays, pamphlets and songs, such as the '*Girafe à la mode*' printed under the image shown here. There were fashions and hairstyles known as '*à la girafe*', and prints too played their part, as images of her tall silhouette were circulated far and wide. Following the giraffe's death in 1845 she was stuffed; she can still be seen today at the Natural History Museum in La Rochelle. V.S.-H.

Woodcut, stencil-coloured | 41 x 25 cm (sheet)

71 Anonymous, *Hippodrome*, '*The War of the Indies*', 1858

The poster shown here advertises the Porte Dauphine hippodrome, these being areas where equestrian spectacles and other entertainments were held. The show put on by Monsieur Arnault the elder, with music by Monsieur Varney, was presented for the first time on 29 May 1858. The programme, which lists the elephant among the cast members, reveals that the star shown on the poster was named Betsy. We learn that in the third scene of the second tableau, 'after the performance from the Indian dancers, the sultan's favourite elephant, led by her *mahout* (keeper) makes her entrance and takes centre stage'. Initially censored, the show was altered and its exotic character was accentuated. The poster depicts a procession (the camel possibly being an imaginary element) suggesting the scale and splendour of this 'huge spectacle'.

Rouchon was the only printer in the mid-19th century to produce these types of illustrated posters. Large engravings made from coloured wood blocks following a technique similar to wallpaper printing, they were used to publicize entertainments, books and shops selling fashions and accessories. They appeared several decades before the modern, coloured lithographic posters that were first created by Jules Chéret and enjoyed great success during the 1890s. Thanks to the Legal Deposit system, the Bibliothèque nationale has an exceptional collection of Rouchon's works. A.-M.S.

Poster, coloured wood engraving | 100 x 119 cm (sheet)

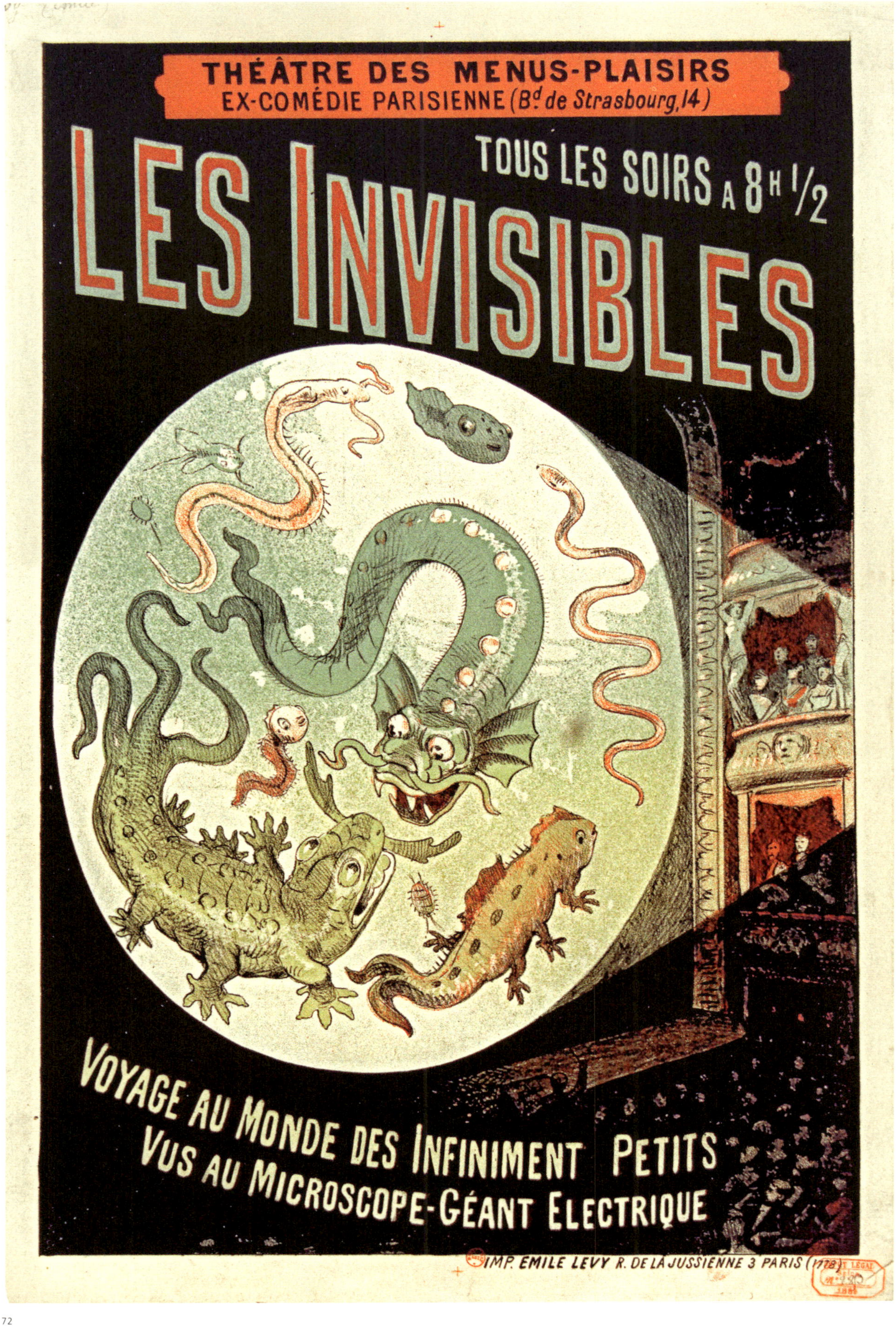

72

72 Anonymous, *The Théâtre des Menus-Plaisirs, Invisible Creatures*, 1883

→ description on p. 118

73 Anonymous, *The World Before the Creation of Man*, 1885

→ description on p. 118

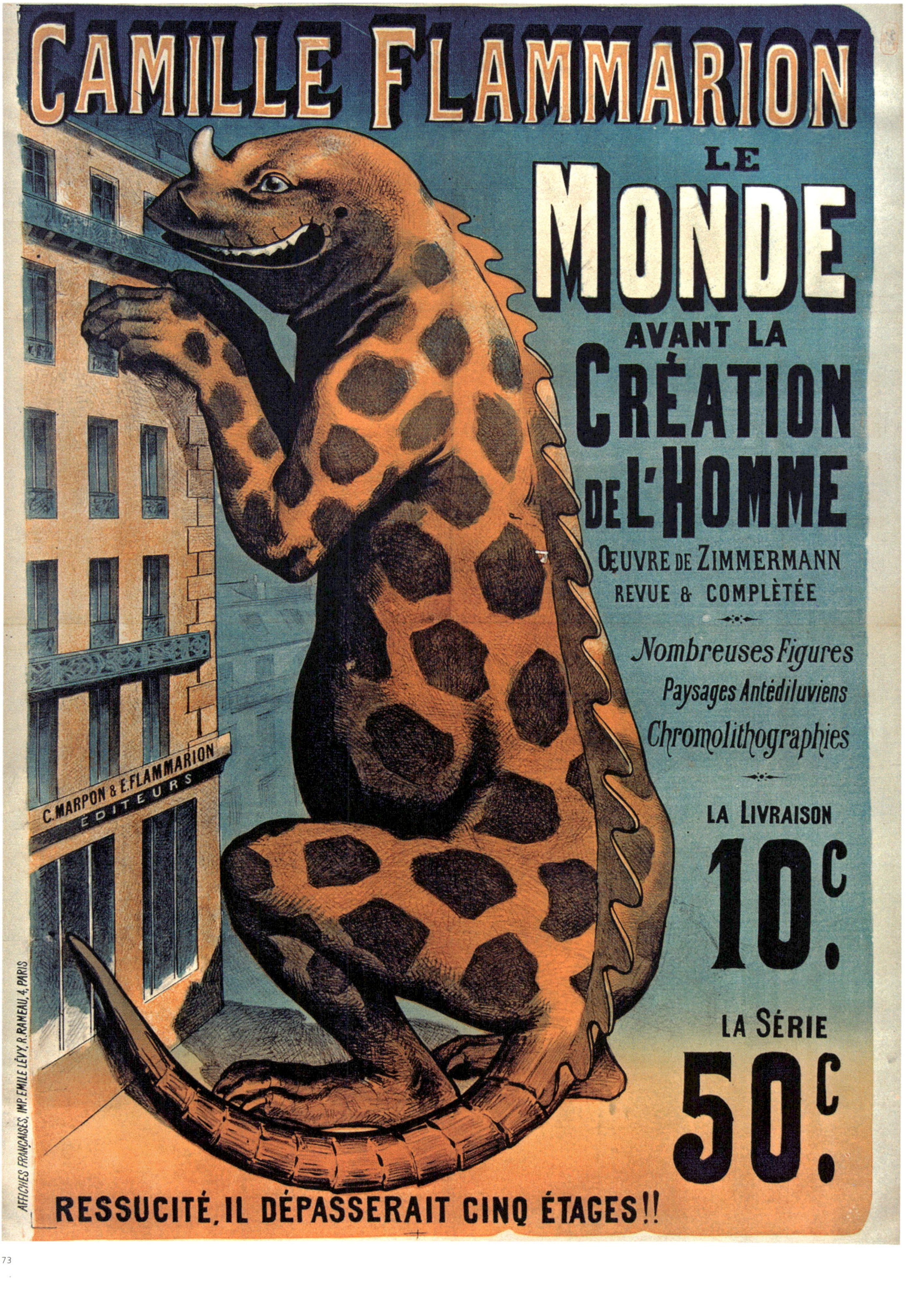
CAMILLE FLAMMARION
LE
MONDE
AVANT LA
CRÉATION
DE L'HOMME
ŒUVRE DE ZIMMERMANN
REVUE & COMPLÉTÉE
Nombreuses Figures
Paysages Antédiluviens
Chromolithographies
LA LIVRAISON
10C.
LA SÉRIE
50C.
C. MARPON & E. FLAMMARION
ÉDITEURS
AFFICHES FRANÇAISES, IMP. EMILE LÉVY, R. RAMEAU, 4, PARIS
RESSUCITÉ, IL DÉPASSERAIT CINQ ÉTAGES!!

73

72 Anonymous, *The Théâtre des Menus-Plaisirs, Invisible Creatures*, 1883

→ Image on p. 116

In 1883, the French periodical *Les Annales du théâtre et de la musique* stated that the Théâtre des Menus-Plaisirs, which was experiencing financial difficulties, would be opening its doors on 31 October, but only 'for a spectacle which has nothing to do with the theatre in the strict sense of the word: it is presenting "Invisible Creatures", seen under a microscope lit by an electric light'. In the following year, it was clear that theatre audiences were generally unimpressed: 'the theatre is taken over by a passing impresario who exhibits scenes from the invisible world by means of magnifying mechanisms.'

Although one might have expected that these illuminated screenings were educational in nature, with their references to science and to efficient technical procedures, the images actually shown were more suggestive of fairground amusements than of popular education. The microscopic world that was displayed took the form of fantastical animals intended to appear frightening in order to attract a public eager for sensation. A very similar poster to the one shown was produced by the same printer in 1887. Proclaiming: 'Coming very soon, invisible worlds', it would indicate that this type of spectacle continued to be presented.

Émile Lévy, who opened his printing establishment in 1872, was quick to follow the example of Jules Chéret and supplied a great many theatre entrepreneurs with coloured lithographic posters. A.-M.S.

Coloured lithographic poster | 60 x 40 cm (sheet)

73 Anonymous, *The World Before the Creation of Man*, 1885

→ Image on p. 117

Camille Flammarion (older brother of Ernest, who founded the Flammarion publishing house) was the father of popularized science, particularly in the domain of astronomy. Here he adapts the French translation of the work by W.F.A. Zimmerman, *Die Wunder der Urwelt*, which was published in the early 19th century. In the preliminary chapter, entitled 'The first days of the Earth' Flammarion presents a general description of the wildlife: 'Iguanodons, similar in form to kangaroos, reached up to 14 metres in length: if they leant their arms on one of our tallest houses, they would be able to eat from a fifth-floor balcony.' This sentence was used as the caption of the illustration on page 21; reproduced as coloured lithograph for the poster, it heralded the popular interest in dinosaurs in spectacular fashion. In Flammarion's view, 'these fantastic creatures are just as extraordinary as those conceived by the human imagination, such as centaurs, fauns, griffons and chimeras [. . .] Moreover, they were real; they lived in the heart of primeval forests'. Publications in the 1880s, which still relied on sale by installments, began to use coloured lithographic posters that were enlarged for street display. A.-M.S.

Coloured lithographic poster | 130 x 96 cm (sheet)

74 Jean Carlu, '*Aquarium de Monaco*', *Oceanographic Museum*, 1926

As emphasized by Jean Carlu himself, rather than showing a 'swarming', scattered mass of fish, his image of an aquarium 'is concentrated into a few typical shapes, which are brought together and solidly established along two diagonal lines'. His aim was to 'translate, through use of line, the essential characters of these three fish: the insidious moray eel is depicted with an undulating line, the sunfish, rotund and inoffensive, with curves, and the ill-natured scorpion fish with a series of sharp points' (*Vendre*, 1930). Rigorous scientific accuracy is not important here, neither is the evident disproportion displayed in the image, where the different underwater species are shown superimposed on one another: this is a form of vision. For, when creating a poster, 'simplification is vital'; the artist must 'convey his message instantly'. (*L'Affiche*, 1927). Carlu belonged to the avant-garde group of poster designers, which included A. M. Cassandre, Charles Loupot and Paul Colin, who in the 1920s championed functionalism and created pared-down, synthetic images. According to Carlu, this poster also constituted a 'lithographic performance', as it demonstrates the ability of this technique to create the grained finish and the colours seen in his drawing. Despite the use of an inking process that enabled several colours to be printed simultaneously, a dozen impressions were needed in order to create the image (*Interview*, 1980). A.-M.S.

Coloured lithographic poster | 106 x 76 cm (sheet)

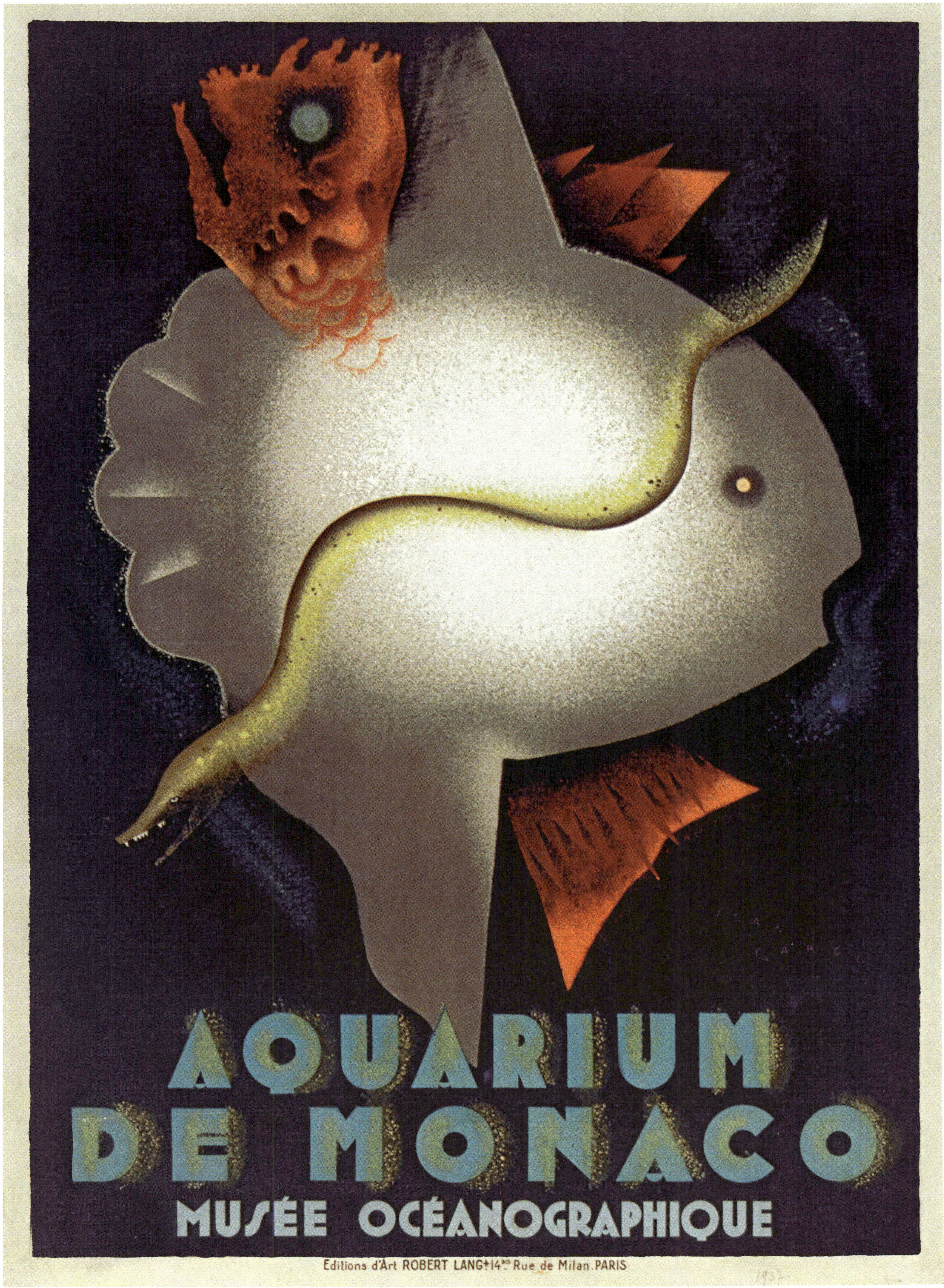
AQUARIUM
DE MONACO
MUSÉE OCÉANOGRAPHIQUE
Editions d'Art ROBERT LANG 14bis Rue de Milan. PARIS

74

75 Benjamin Rabier, *La Vache qui rit*: '*The Laughing Cow*', 1927 (9th edition)

Benjamin Rabier began creating his animal world and 'making laughing animals' for the illustrated press and children's comic books in the very early 20th century. During the First World War, he devised the logo for the unit delivering fresh meat supplies to the French troops; the jovial cow he created was sometimes known as the 'Wachkyrie' in a facetious reference to the German Valkyries. She was subsequently used to illustrate the music score for the 'Valkyrie Foxtrot', which was composed by a former soldier from the fresh meat supply unit and sent by him to all his former war comrades. These included Léon Bel, a producer of processed cheese. In 1921, Bel trademarked the brand, known as '*La Vache qui rit*', together with a drawing he made inspired by Rabier's. In 1923 he commissioned and paid Rabier to produce a new version of the cow. However, he had this edited by the printer Vercasson, who altered the animal's colour and added earrings in the form of boxes of cheese. Vercasson secured a copyright on the drawing under his own name, with the title '*la vache rouge*' (the red cow), so that the laughing cow could not legally become bright red until 1952! Rabier gave the animal a human expression; her eyebrows raised, she wrinkles up her face in a beaming smile. His signature long remained appended to the brand image, which appeared in multiple formats and media, and achieved an exceptional level of fame. A.-M.S.

Coloured lithographic poster | 160 x 120 cm (sheet)

76 Charles Rambert, *Usury*, 1850

→ Image on p. 122

Usury forms part of a series of lithographs depicting various allegories (*War, Civil War, Drunkenness, Debauchery and Lust, The Duel, The Slanderer* and *Money*). Published in 1851, these images combine a denunciatory tone with a fantastical perspective. Now largely forgotten, Charles Rambert – 'part artist, part philosopher and part preacher' – achieved fleeting fame for his strange compositions. According to Henri Beraldi, these were suffused with the 'allegorical-religious-mystical-socialist' tendencies then in vogue.

Rambert was obsessed by poverty, which blighted his entire life, and extolled the principle of charity. Here he condemns the evils of usury through this dramatic image of a man held captive in a web made by a giant spider. The creature, whose body is marked with the words 'Interest on interest', is preparing to suck the blood from its victim's neck. V.S.-H.

Lithograph | 42.5 x 30.7 cm (sheet)

77 Félix Braquemond, *The Duck* (*The Newspaper*), 1856

→ Image on p. 123

Unrivalled as a practitioner, Félix Braquemond was also a theoretician and championed the etching revival that occurred in the 1860s. This duck belongs to a series of prints that included a magpie, a crow, a heron and storks. These realistic studies of birds served a satirical purpose, following the theories of Auguste Comte, who advocated the analysis of animal groups as a means of gaining insight into the human species. The satire in this case lies in the pun on the name used to denote a sensationalist paper ('*un canard*', or duck) and the bird itself. The image emphasizes the trivial nature of these printed sheets, full of false news and misleading information. The word 'journal' here is partly concealed by the boundary line, and on the left-hand side, just above the horizon, the engraver has written the words '*horizon politique*'. The fourth state of the print, published in *L'Artiste* on 7 September 1856, also contains a quatrain by Edmond About, placed between the duck's wings: '*Merveille! Merveille! Merveille! Bonnes gens ouvrez l'oreille! / Je vais vous dire un récit / Qui s'est passé loin d'ici*'. ('Sensation! Sensation! Sensation! / Listen up, good folk! / And I'll tell you a tale / Of something that happened far away'.)

The original page layout, which made use of the boundary line and the framed image of the animal shown in flight, beak open to cry out its sensational news, contributes to the powerful and modern character of the work. V.S.-H.

Etching | 26 x 21.5 cm (image)

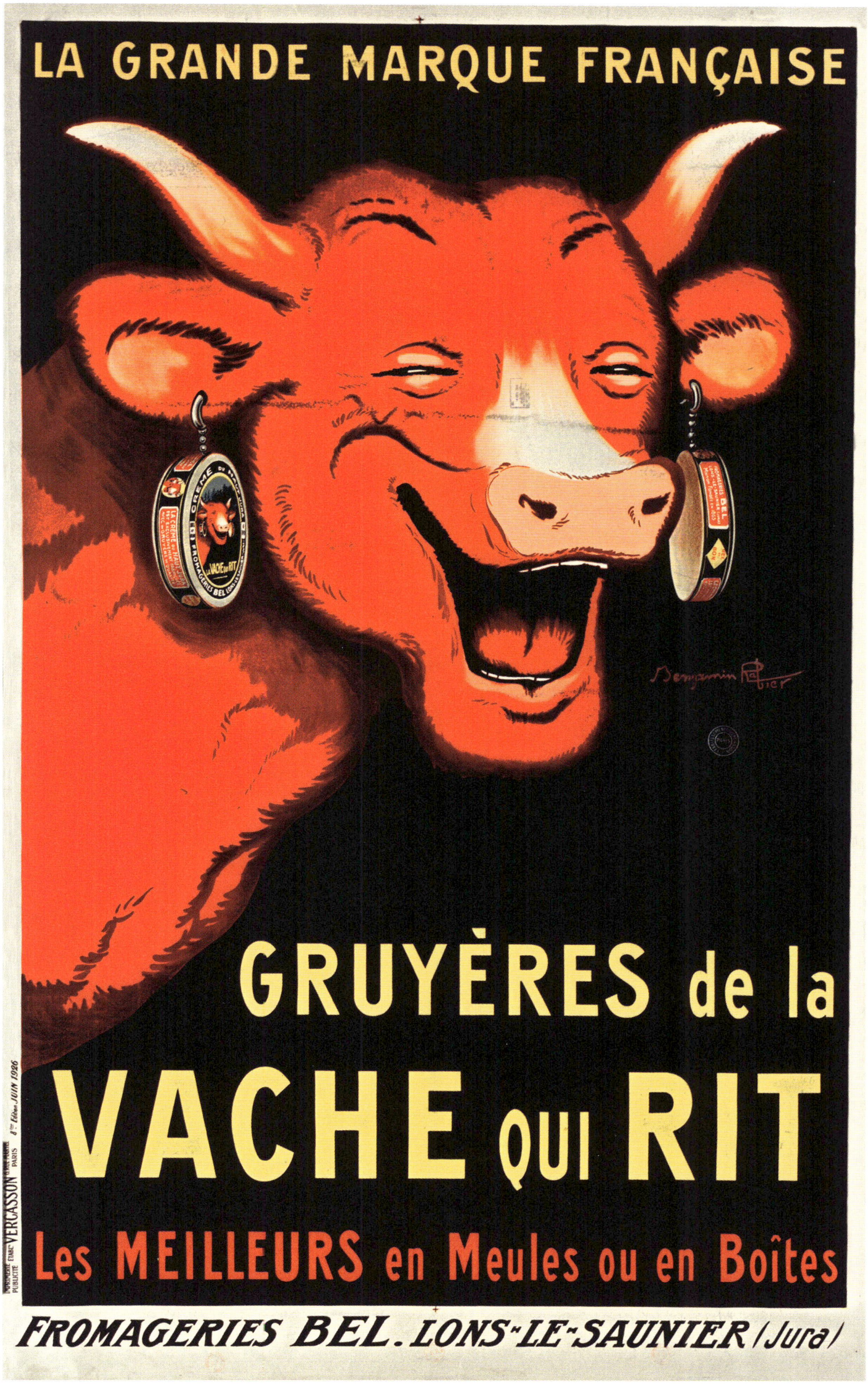
LA GRANDE MARQUE FRANÇAISE
GRUYÈRES de la
VACHE QUI RIT
Les MEILLEURS en Meules ou en Boîtes
FROMAGERIES BEL. LONS-LE-SAUNIER (Jura)

75

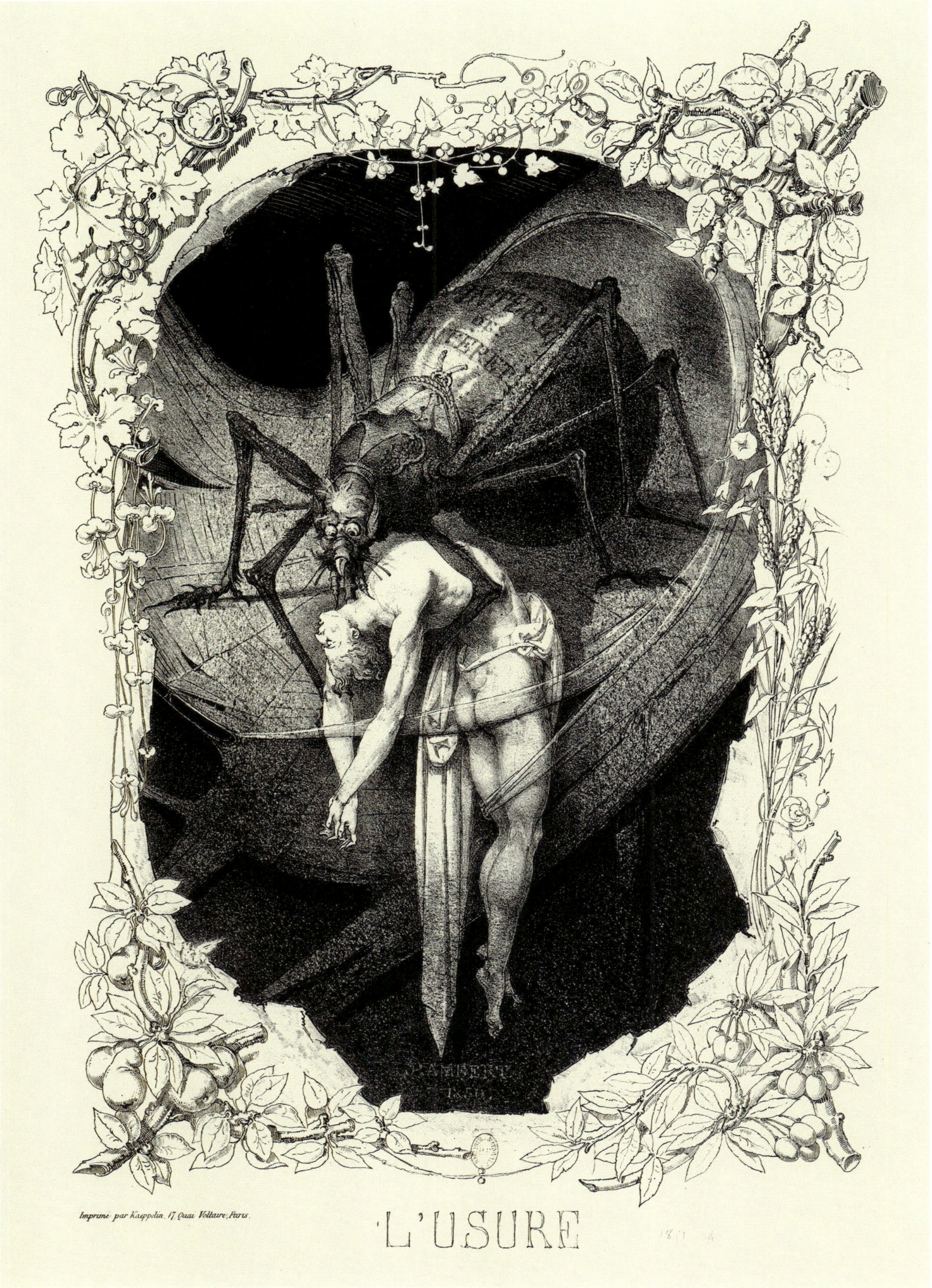

76

76 Charles Rambert, *Usury*, 1850
→ description on p.120

77 Félix Bracquemond, *The Duck* (*The Newspaper*), 1856
→ description on p. 120

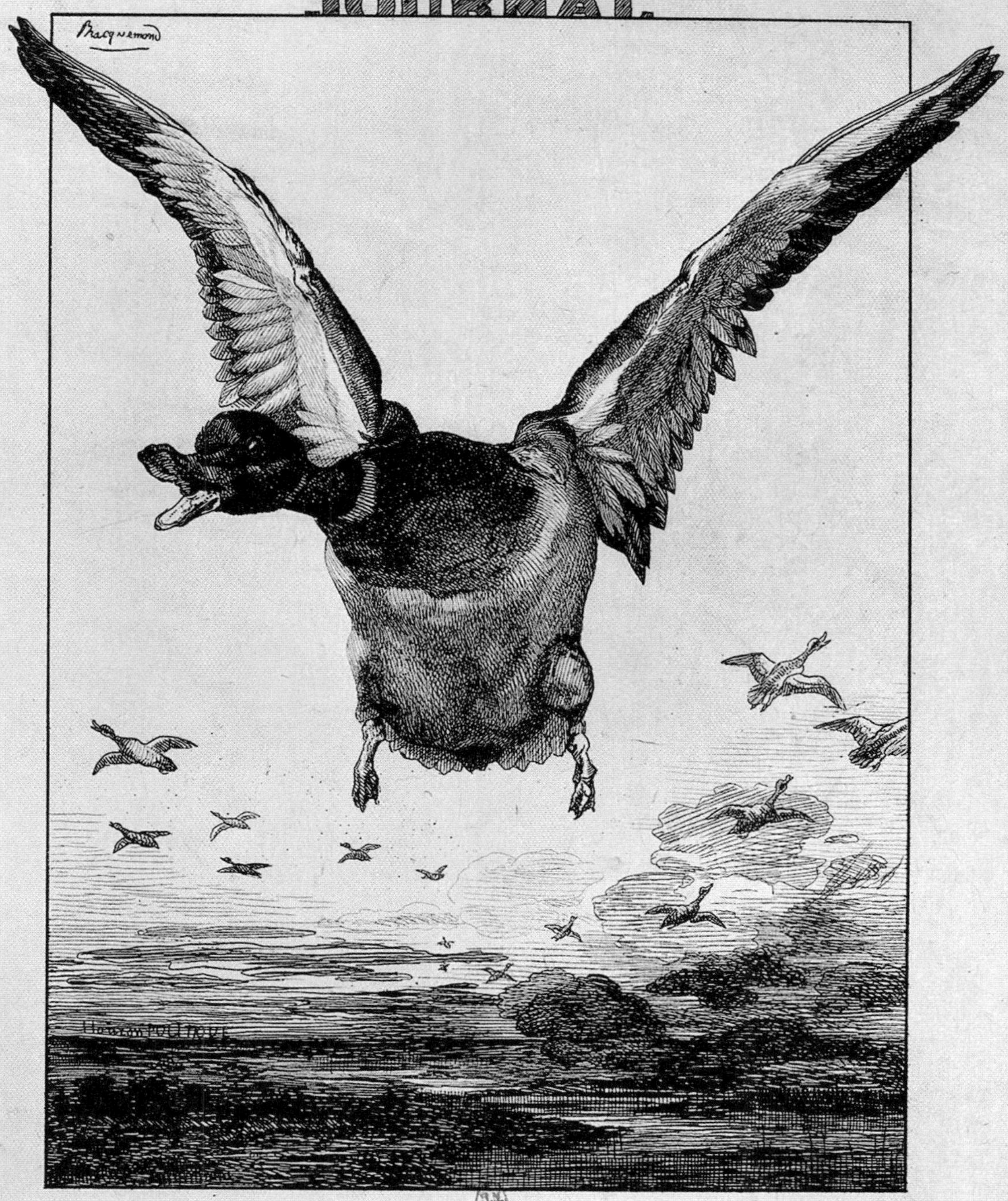

77

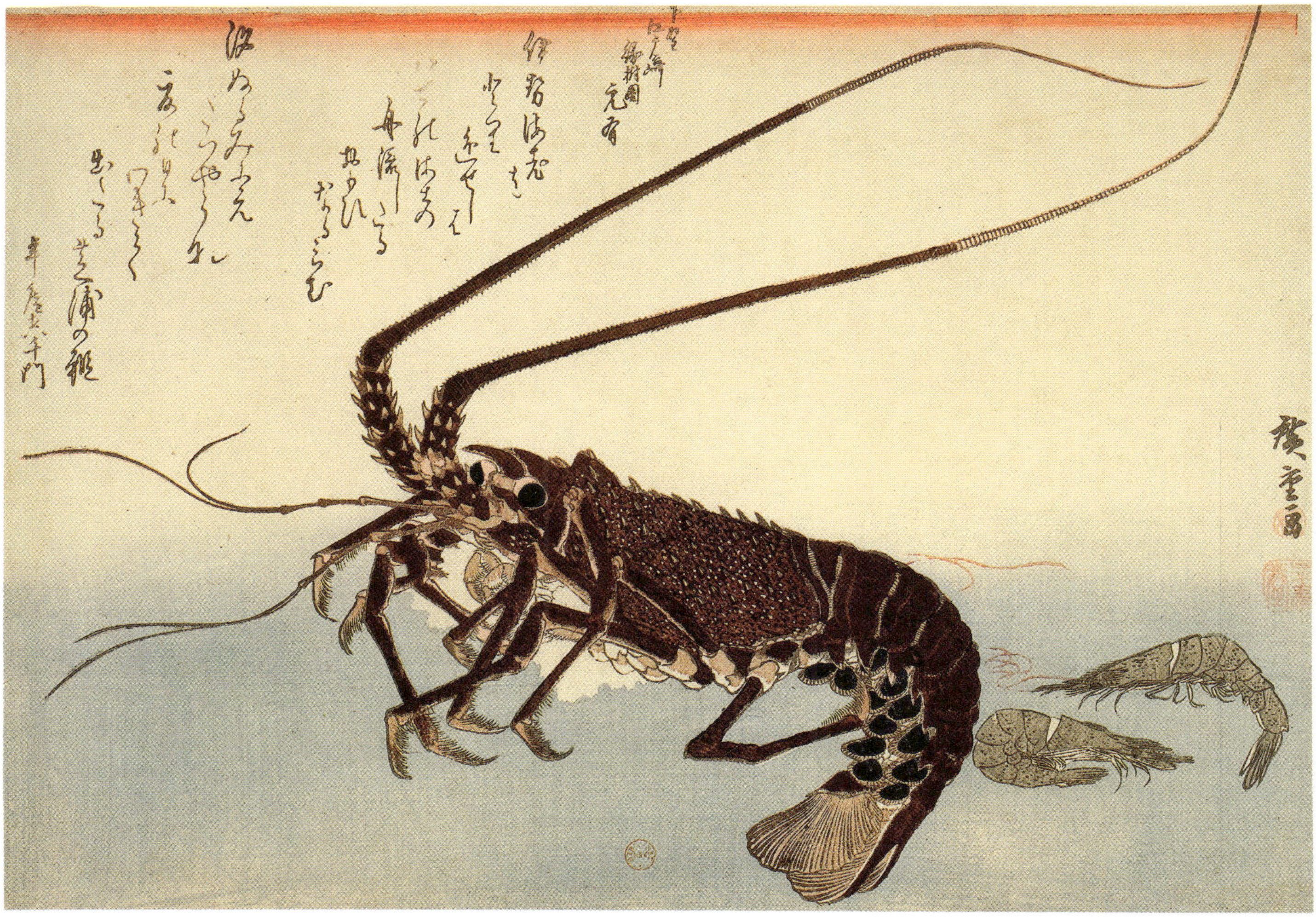

78

78 Hiroshige, *Spiny Lobster and Prawns*, ca. 1832

Hiroshige, the famous master of the *ukiyo-e* style, devoted two series of ten prints to images of large fish and crustaceans, including this startlingly realistic spiny lobster. These still-life prints, which are highly refined in execution, are used to illustrate examples of the *kyōka*, short poems that are very free in both their style and content. In this way, the lobster and the two prawns were accompanied by the following text: 'Failing to catch a lobster is like watching the departure of a boat you have missed. Even if the ocean seems to smoke in the mid-day heat, a prawn leaps from the depths as if during a frozen spring.' Japanese prints, with their naturalistic motifs, exerted a considerable influence over French artists, who often copied such works. Hiroshige's lobster may therefore be found, reinterpreted by the engraver Félix Bracquemond, decorating the large serving dish produced by Eugène Rousseau and made at the Creil and Montereau factory. V.S.-H.

Print from the *Large Fish* series | Coloured woodblock print | 26 x 37 cm (image)

79 Hiroshige, *Suidobashi Bridge at Surugadai*, 1857

The carp boldly occupying the foreground of one of Hiroshige's *One Hundred Famous Views of Edo* is a streamer known as a *koinobori*, placed high on a bamboo mast to celebrate the Boys' Festival. This occasion is marked in every household; originating from China, it takes place each year on the fifth day of the fifth month.

Floating on the breeze, these windsocks made of paper or cloth in the form of a carp (the black carp, or *magoi*, represents the father) refer to a Chinese legend according to which a carp swam courageously up the Yellow River against the current, and was transformed by the gods into a flying water dragon. This symbol of strength and perseverance ensures that the boys' destinies are placed under the best possible auspices. V.S.-H.

Coloured woodblock print | 33.7 x 22.2 cm (image)

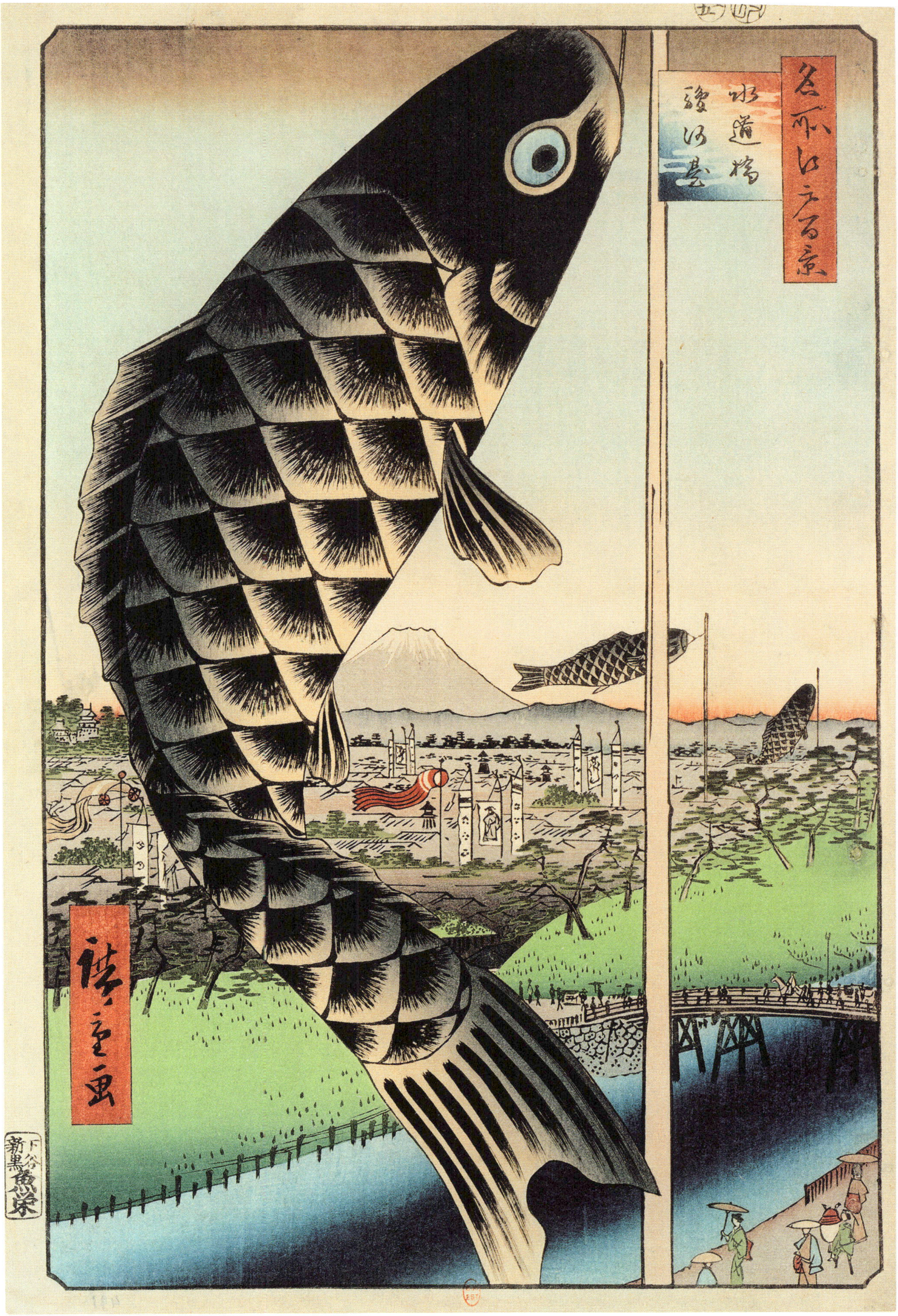

79

80 Édouard Manet, *The Cats' Rendez-Vous*, 1868

In 1868, the walls of Paris were covered in copies of an illustrated poster created by Manet and commissioned by Champfleury in order to publicize his book *Les Chats, histoire, mœurs, observations, anecdotes.* The first poster to constitute a genuine work of art, it enjoyed great success. Manet's lithograph, which resulted from a watercolour and gouache study, was placed in the centre. Manet was fascinated by cats, which appear in his etchings *Olympia*, *Les Chats et les fleurs*, and in preliminary sketches. Here he portrays two cats engaged in a voluptuous dance on the rooftops of Paris; the contrast between black and white, the composition with its opposing movements and the linear stylization all produce tension within the image. The interplay between the concisely drawn silhouettes reflects the influence of Japanese art on Manet's work. He admired Hokusai's *Manga*, with its portrayal of twenty or so mischievous cats, and Kuniyoshi's fan, decorated with feline figures. M.M.

Lithograph | 43.5 x 33.2 cm (image)

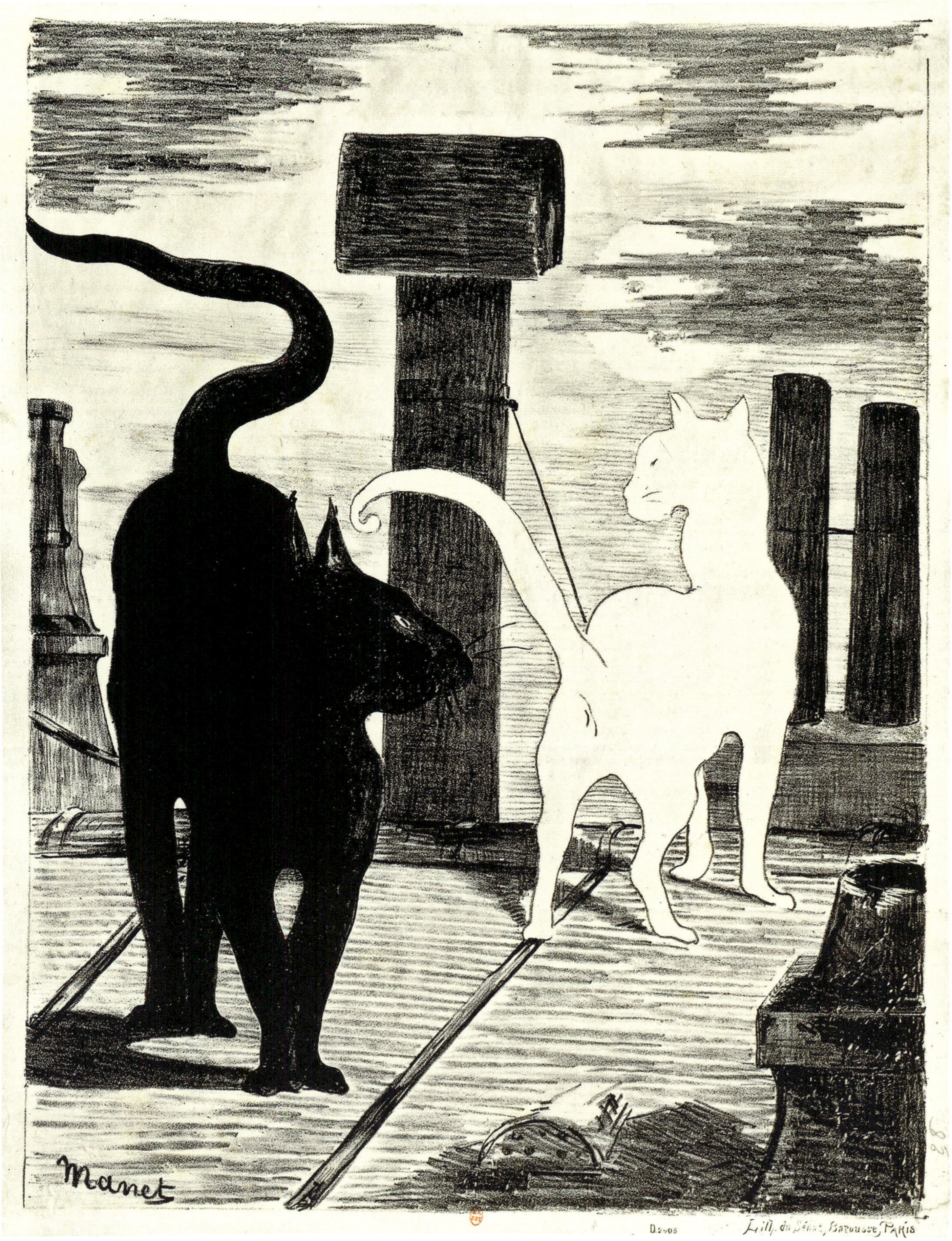

80

81 Odilon Redon, *Spider*, 1887

This lithograph of a smiling spider was created by Redon from a drawing he made in 1881, when he also produced its companion piece, *L'Araignée en pleurs* (The crying spider). Knowledge of arachnoids had advanced as a result of numerous scientific studies conducted by naturalists; some of these, publicized in popularized articles, provided Redon with sources of information. Spiders were frequently compared to human beings in features published by the periodical *La Nature*; this tendency towards anthropomorphism echoed that of the previous generation, an example being the works of Grandville, with which Redon was very familiar.

Besides the spider's 'human face', as the artist himself described it, the image also owes its strange quality to the disproportionate size of the animal in relation to the tiling – as if it had been magnified by a microscope – and to the unrealistic depiction of its ten legs, only some of which brush the ground. The reproduction of the black down on the spider's body, which is evident in the original charcoal drawing, and the subtle suggestion of the nuances of texture on the ground and the wall, testify to Redon's skillful use of the lithographic chalk. V.S.-H.

Lithograph on China paper applied to vellum | 26 x 21.5 cm (image)

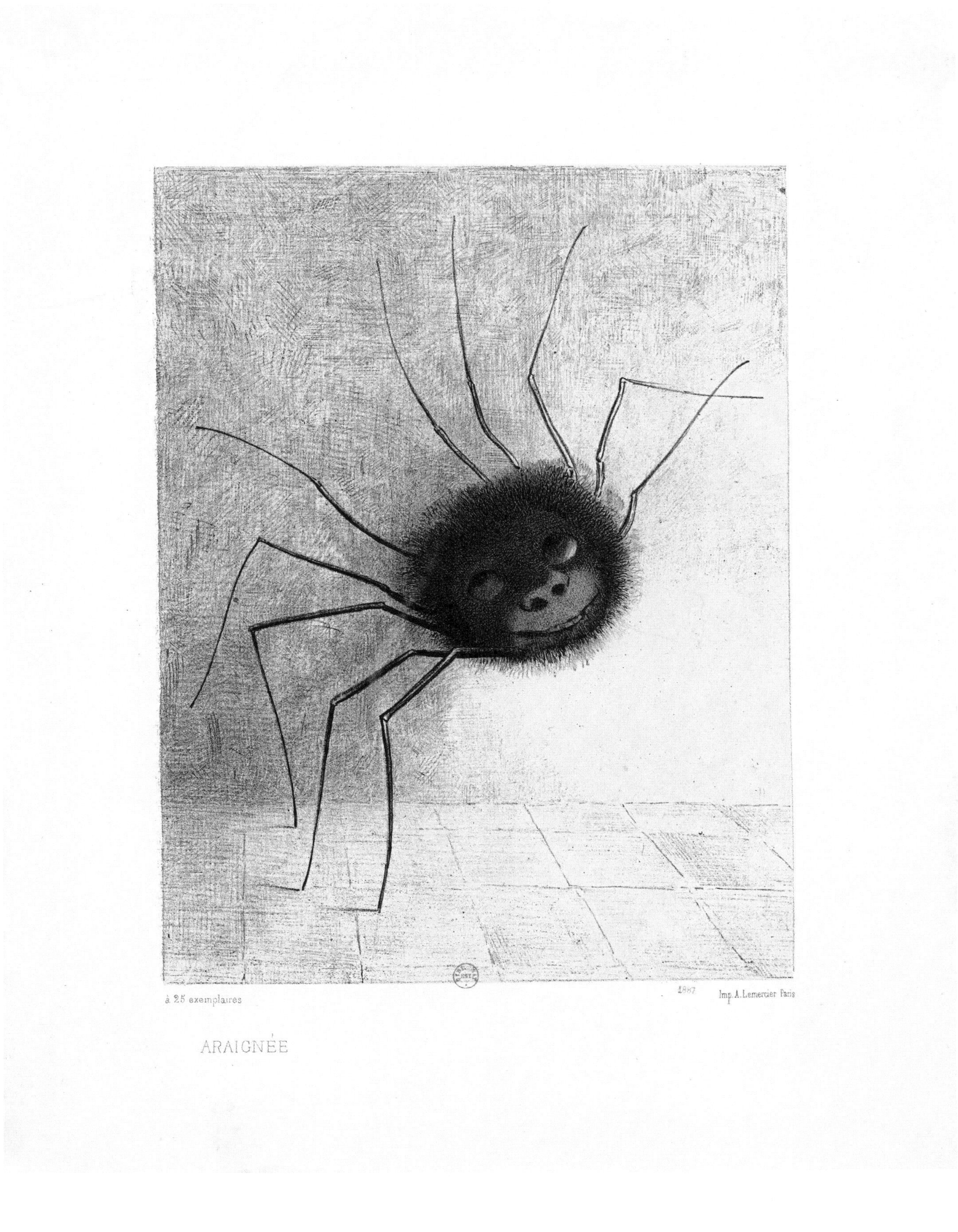
à 25 exemplaires
1887
Imp. A. Lemercier Paris
ARAIGNÉE

82 Henri de Toulouse-Lautrec, *The Waltz of the Rabbits*, 1895

Toulouse-Lautrec produced images of a circus bear, a pet dog, a crocodile and a mouse (who found their way onto a dinner menu), as well as a number of horses, whose anatomy he studied with intense fascination. Most notably, he created twenty-two plates for the illustrated edition of Jules Renard's *Histoires naturelles*, published in 1899. Although he cannot be categorized as an animal artist, these works confirm the genuine interest he had in animals, some of which he observed in the Jardin de l'Acclimatation.

The illustration shown here features on the cover of the song sheet for '*La Valse des Lapins*' ('The Waltz of the Rabbits'), a popular song by Léon Durocher, with music by Désiré Dihau, one of Toulouse-Lautrec's relatives. Dating from 1895, it marks the beginning of that interest, which became particularly evident at the end of his life. V.S.-H.

Lithograph | 31.7 x 24 cm (image)

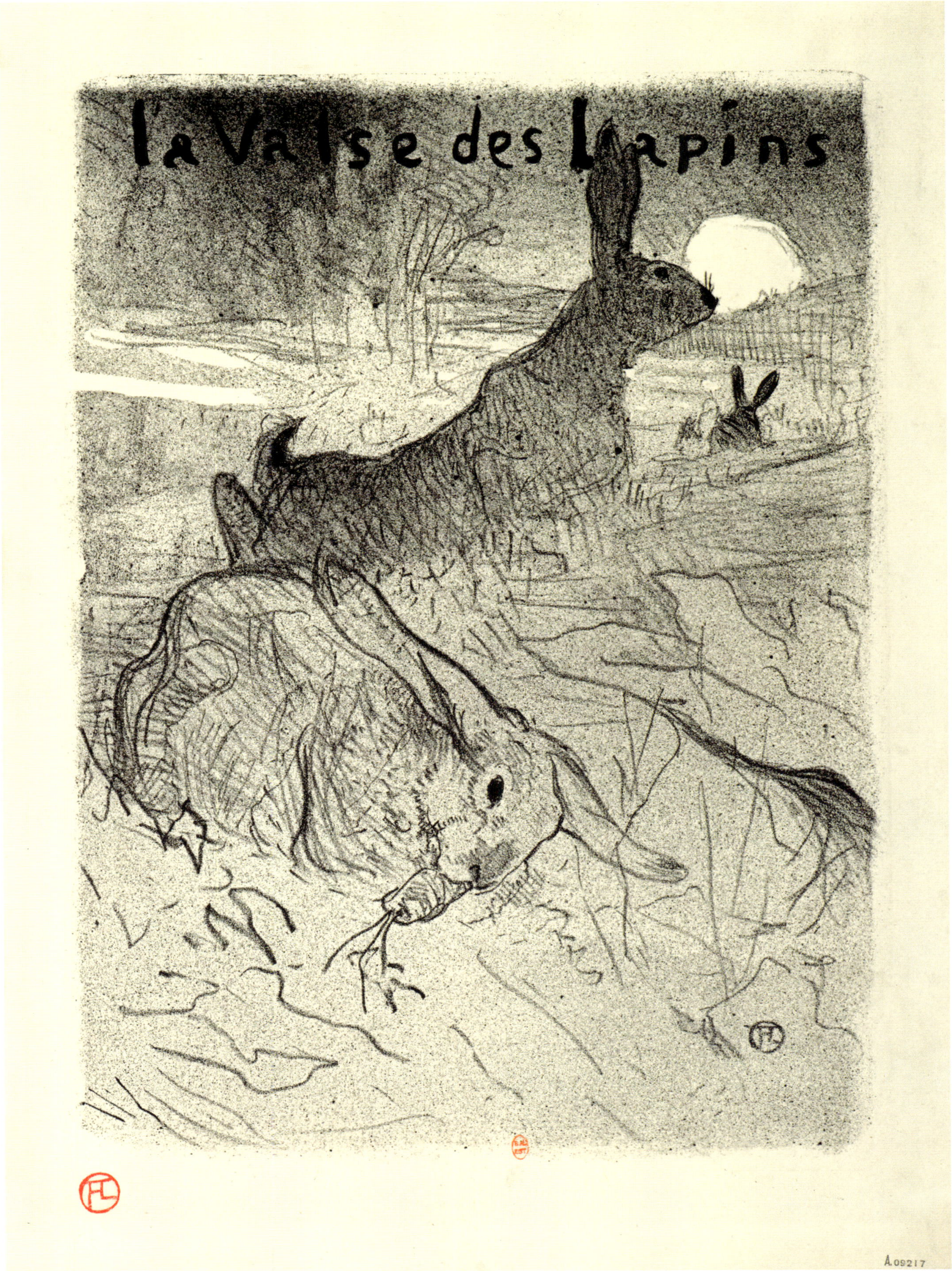

82

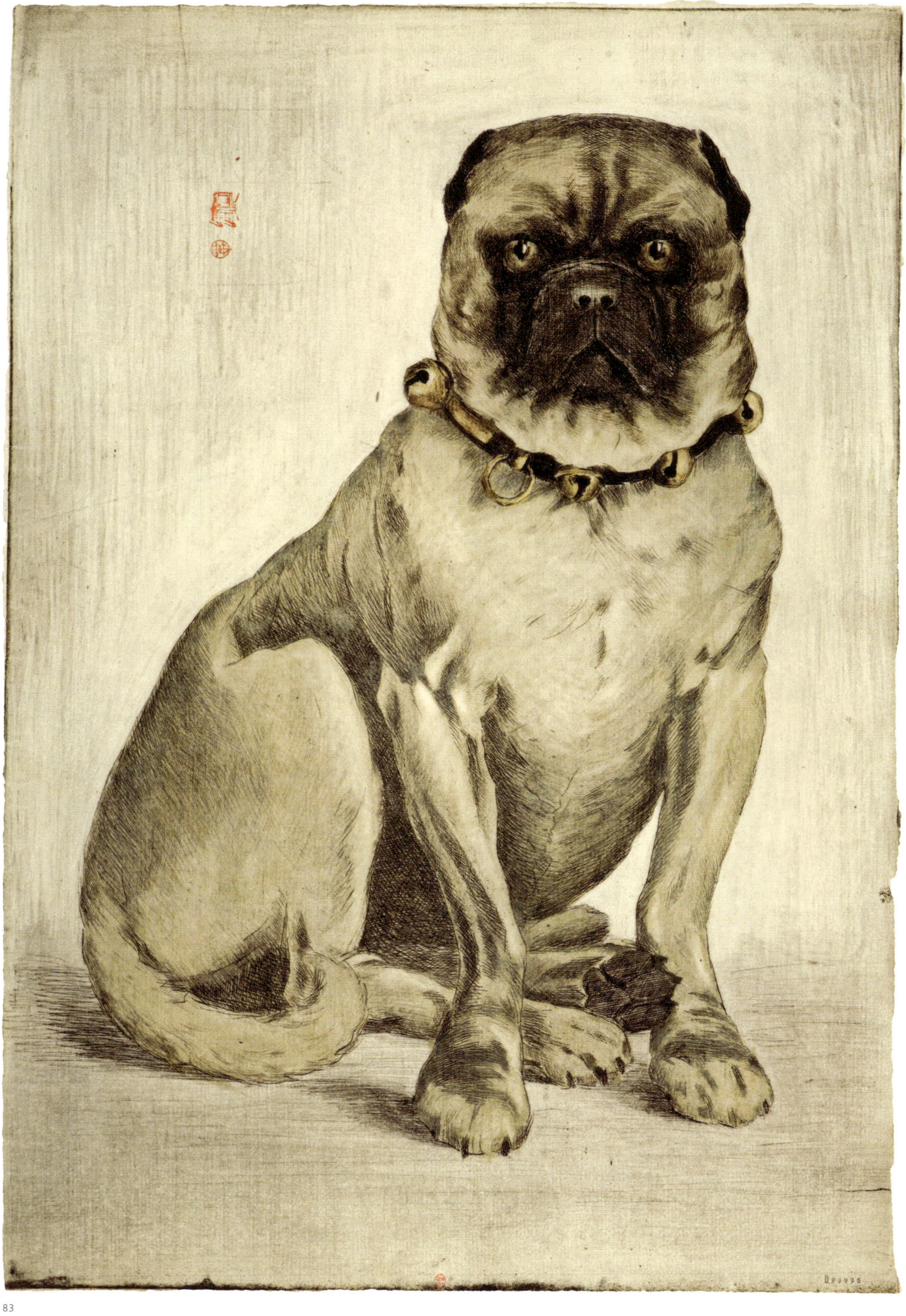

83

83 Henri Guérard, *Azor*, ca. 1888

→ description on p. 134

84 Théophile Alexandre Steinlen, *The Black Cat Tour*, ca. 1896

→ description on p. 134

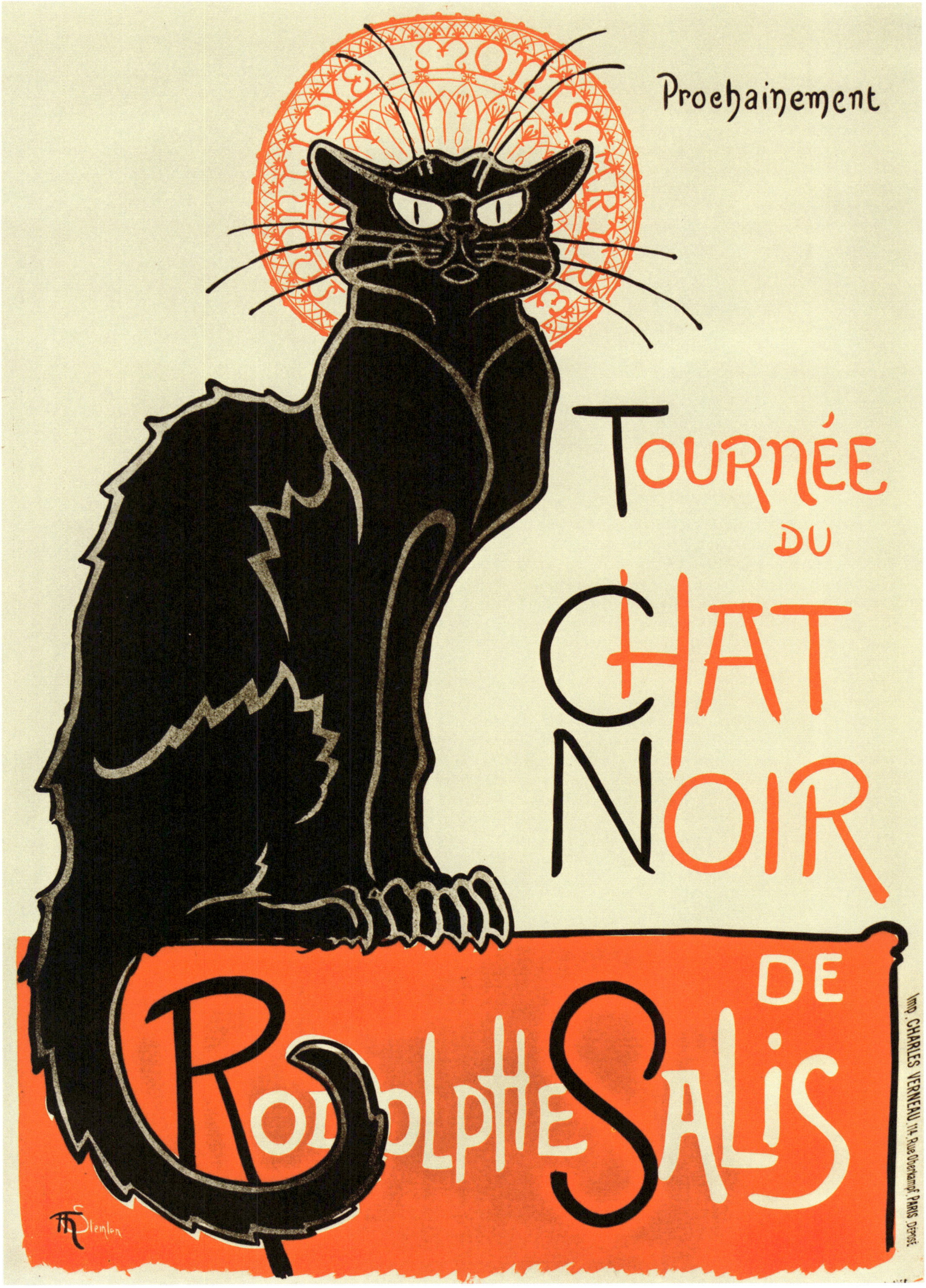
Prochainement
Tournée du Chat Noir
de Rodolphe Salis
Imp. Charles Verneau, 114, Rue Oberkampf, Paris. Déposé
Steinlen

84

83 Henri Guérard, *Azor,* ca. 1888

→ Image on p. 132

Henri Guérard started etching in 1872, working in a spectacularly untidy studio that he shared with a monkey and a few cats and dogs (most likely including Azor, shown here), amidst piles of worn-out shoes, frayed old books and dented watering cans. There was also a collection of lanterns, which were constantly threatening to topple from shelves or to emerge from under the bed, as well as disused pieces of guttering that the artist flattened out to serve as fine etching plates. Guérard was an original character, a dreamer and a multi-talented practitioner, who fashioned fans, medals and even keyhole escutcheons! Above all, he was a virtuoso engraver who excelled in every medium. Inventive and curious, he experimented with every type of engraving and brought new approaches to old techniques. Like his friend Félix Buhot, he was one of the most outstanding printmakers of the late 19th century. Here Guérard used two plates, one for the black outline, the other for the aquatint. M.M.

Coloured etching | 51.3 x 35.3 cm (print area)

84 Théophile Alexandre Steinlen, *The Black Cat Tour,* ca. 1896

→ Image on p. 133

The famous *Black Cat* cabaret establishment, founded in Montmartre by Rodolphe Salis in 1881, was the centre of bohemian, artistic and literary life. It was a meeting place for singers, including Aristide Bruant, poets (former members of the '*Hydropathes*' society), musicians (Claude Debussy and Éric Satié) and artists such as Caran d'Ache and Henri Rivière, with his famous shadow theatre. The venue may have owed its name to a black cat spotted nearby at the time of its opening; it immediately conjures images of an ambivalent figure, suggesting an animal familiar and a creature born of medieval sorcery. Steinlen, who was fond of cats, lived in the district and regularly illustrated the eponymous review. In 1896 he created a poster for the cabaret's summer tour. In his somewhat tongue-in-cheek interpretation, the black feline, with its traditionally diabolical connotations, is associated with sainthood, being depicted with a halo bearing Salis's motto, '*Montjoye-Montmartre*'. The use of flat tints and the outline of the animal's silhouette recall the zinc figures of the shadow theatre and the cabaret signs designed by Willette and Grasset. Several versions of this poster, with variations in the accompanying text, have been produced over the years. Thanks to the renowned creations of Lautrec, Mucha and Steinlen, the 1890s were a true golden age of poster art. A.-M.S.

Coloured lithographic poster | 140 x 100 cm (sheet)

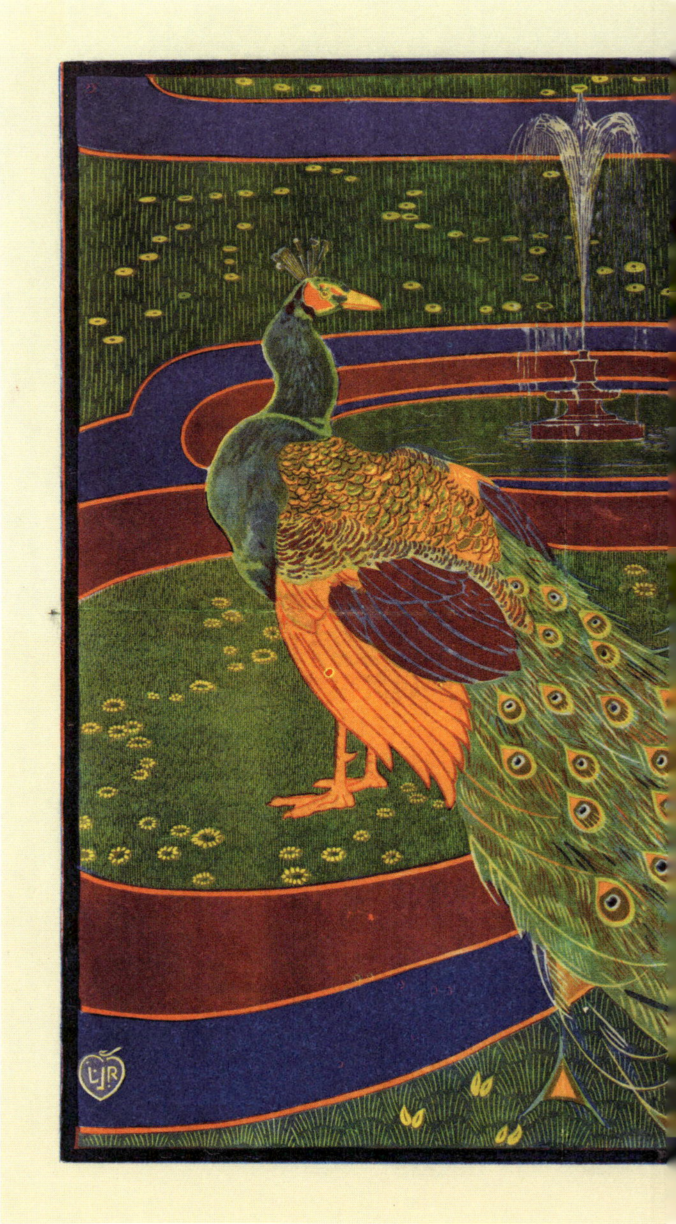

85

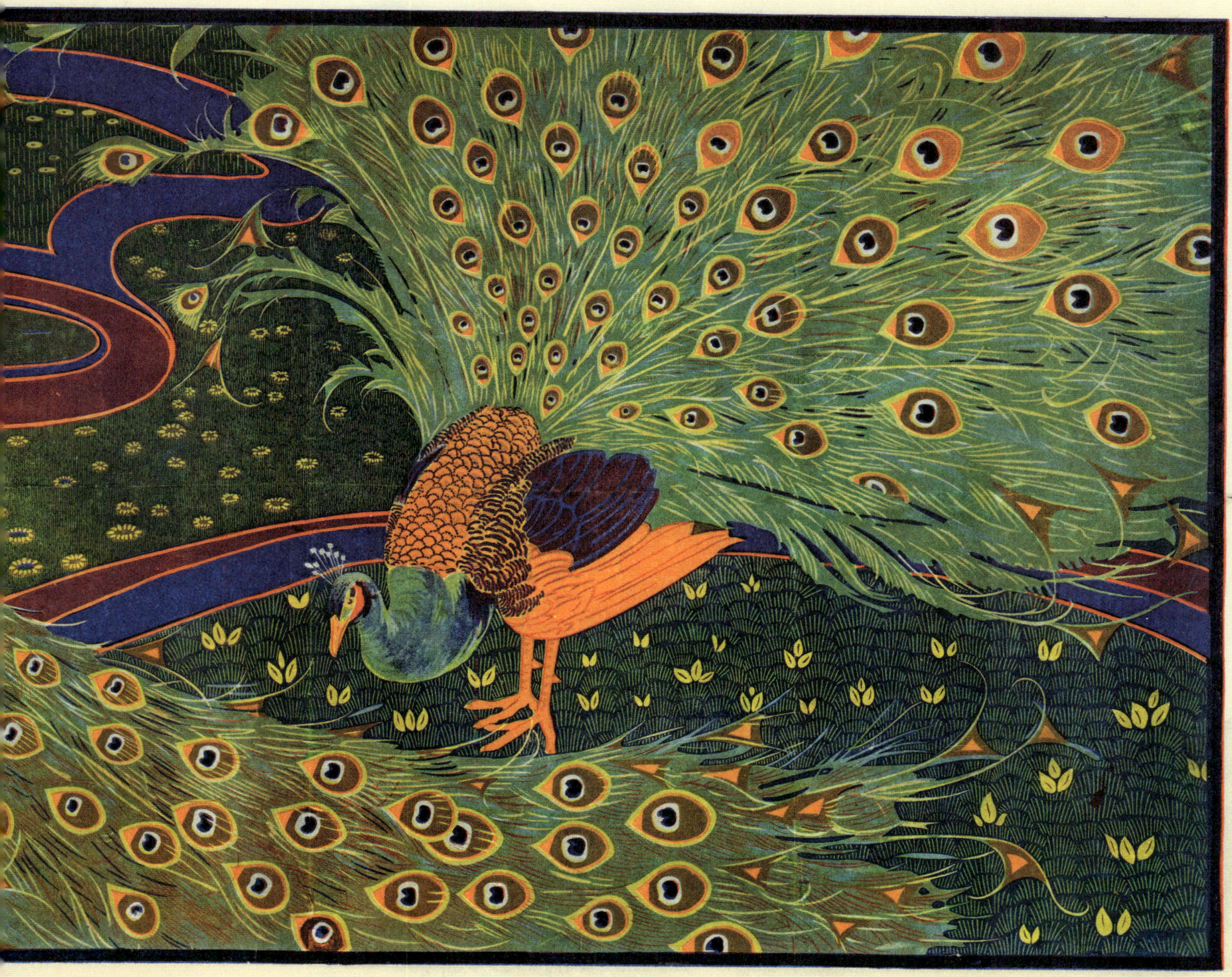

85 Louis-John Rhead, *Peacocks*, 1897

Born in England, Rhead settled in the USA in 1883. Following in the wake of Walter Crane, William Morris and Eugène Grasset, he was interested in the applied arts and was involved in book and magazine illustration, bookbinding and producing models for embroidery and ceramics. He also created posters, an art for which France was renowned in the late 19th century. After showing his work in New York (1895) and London (1896), he was invited to exhibit in Paris in 1897. The request was made by *La Plume*, a 'literary, artistic and society' review, which published two decorative panels, *Peacocks* and *Swans*, to mark the occasion. Throughout the 1890s Léon Deschamps, who edited *La Plume*, was busy actively promoting contemporary artistic and literary works through his review, but he also organized exhibitions (such as the *Salon des Cent*), and published books, prints and posters. Inspired by the natural world, these two large companion pieces are characteristic of the art nouveau style and present a contrast between the glowing colours of the peacocks and the pure whiteness of the swans, set in sinuous curves. They reflect a time of intense creativity in the graphic arts and demonstrate the popularity of coloured lithographs, which were used for artistic posters and decorative prints. Another version of *Peacocks* was used as an advertising poster in the *Journal de la beauté*. A.-M.S.

Coloured lithograph | 85 x 150 cm (sheet)

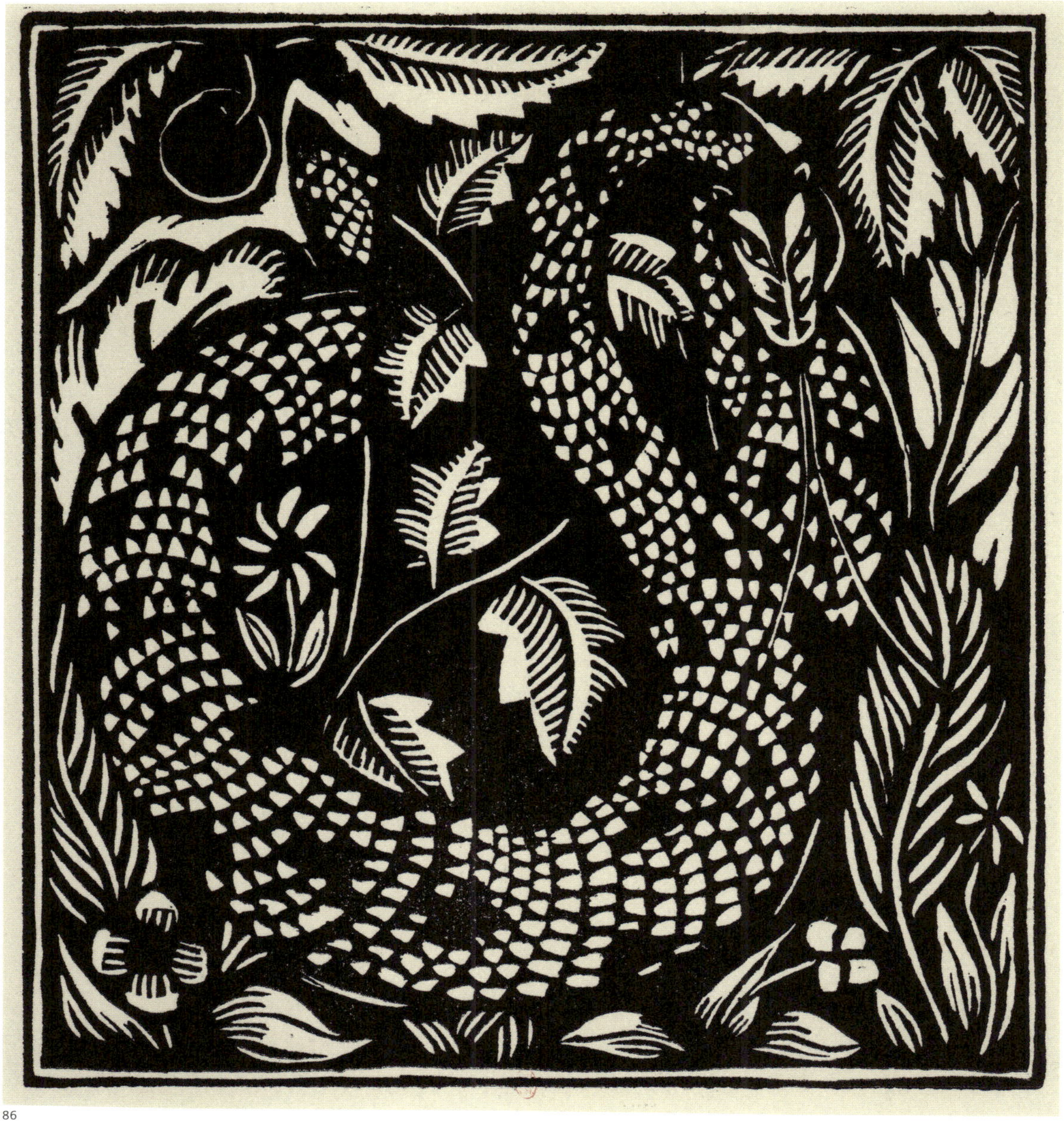

86

86 Raoul Dufy, *The Serpent*, 1910

Written by Guillaume Apollinaire and with illustrations by Raoul Dufy, *Bestiaire ou Cortège d'Orphée* (*Bestiary, or the Parade of Orpheus*) was published in 1911. Apollinaire had initially intended to have his text illustrated by Picasso, but the latter, after a few trial attempts, declined the proposition. Drawing his inspiration from medieval works on heraldry, Dufy conceived twenty-six illustrations for the text, in square format, each depicting the animal described in a quatrain printed beneath the image. He used the woodcut technique, in imitation of 15th century *incunabula*. The images he produced are admirable for the harmonious distribution of their radiant white and velvety black elements. Each print was the result of preparatory drawings and a series of engraved variations. In this plate, which was ultimately rejected, the serpent forms a letter 's' and is placed in the centre of the image to form a balanced composition. It merges into the surrounding luxuriant vegetation, the whole illustration being treated in a decorative manner that leaves no empty space. The apple visible in the upper left-hand corner of the image is an allusion to the serpent in the Book of Genesis. C.C.-C.

Plate rejected for Apollinaire's *Bestiaire* | Woodcut | 20.4 x 19.5 cm (image)

87 Paul Ranson, *Tiger in the Jungle*, 1893

This lithograph, in three colours (black, grey and yellow), appeared in 1893 in the first album of the print portfolio *L'Estampe originale*, published by André Marty. It was inspired by Japanese prints, particularly those of Utamaro, and was intended as a model for a tapestry. It follows the Japanese aesthetic, with its bird's eye view and flattened perspective, and also displays a marked predilection for the decorative line, with its arabesques and undulations. This is associated with art nouveau, as is the style of the plant motifs surrounding the leaping tiger. The contrast between the black outlines and the yellow background recalls Gauguin's famous *Volpini Suite*, a series of ten zincographs in black printed on yellow paper, which was displayed at the Café Volpini during the World Fair of 1889. V.S.-H.

Coloured lithograph | 36.2 x 28.3 cm (image)

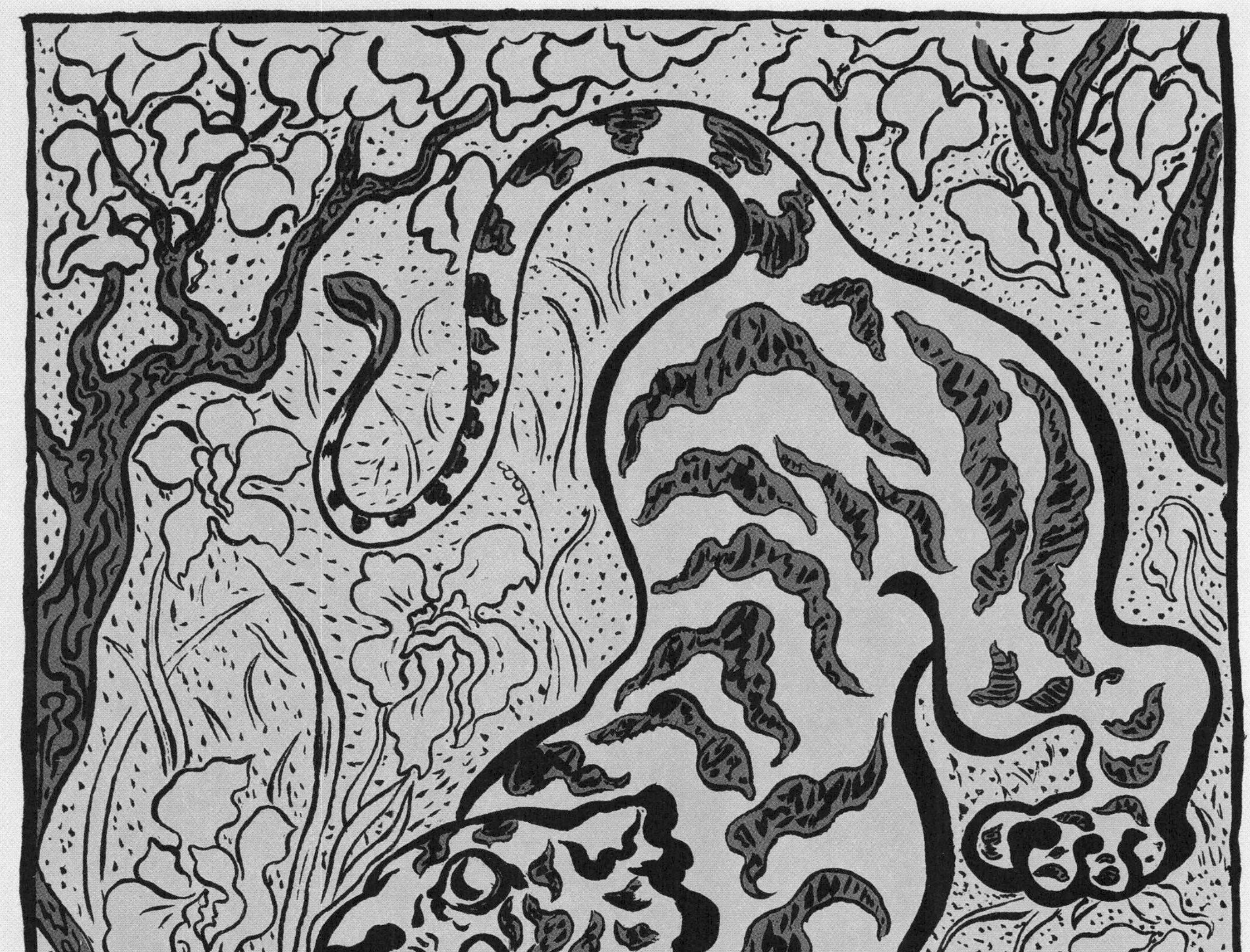

87

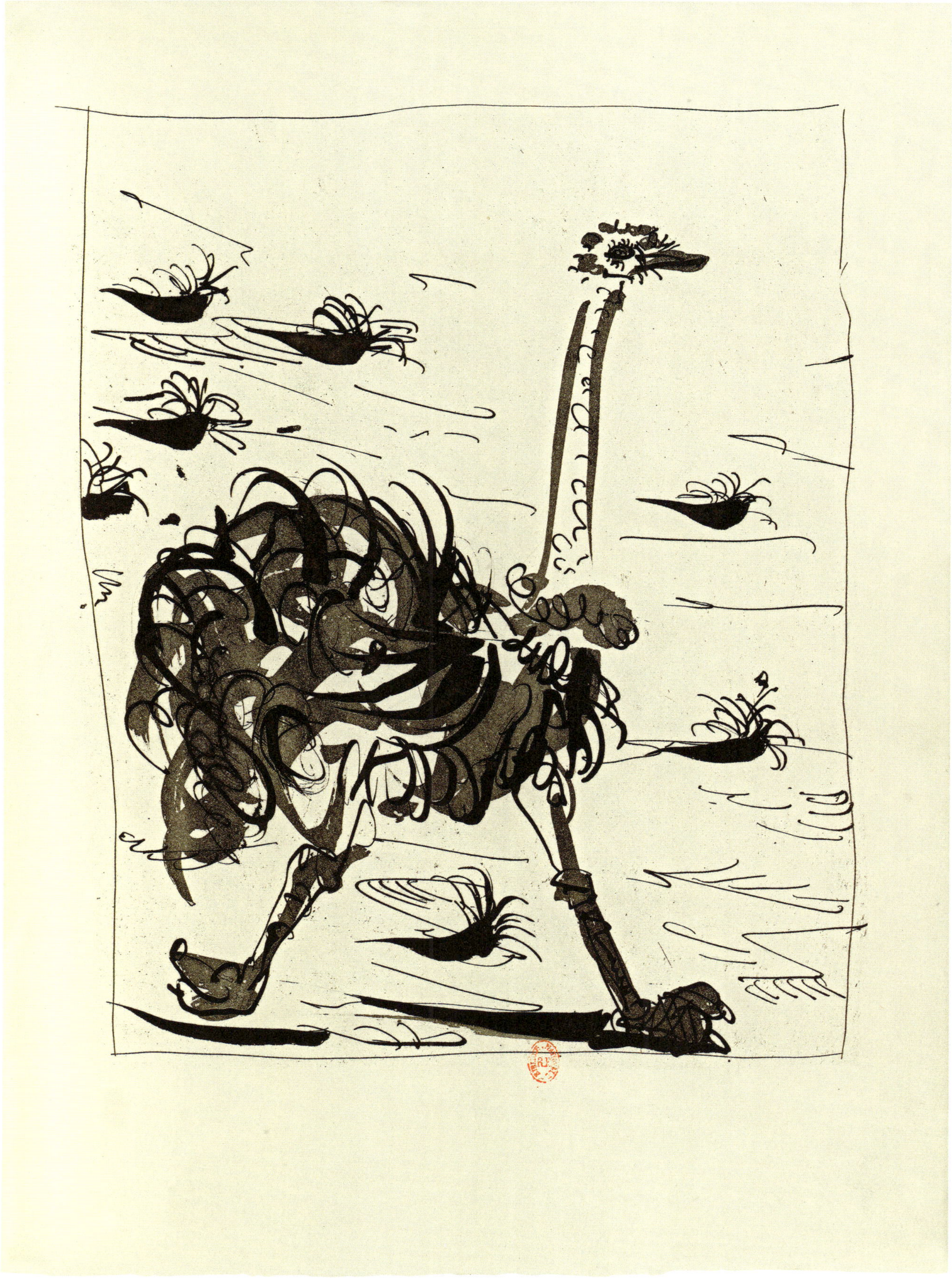

88

88 Pablo Picasso, *The Ostrich*, 1936

→ description on p. 140

89 Henri Matisse, *The Swan*, 1931–1932

→ description on p. 140

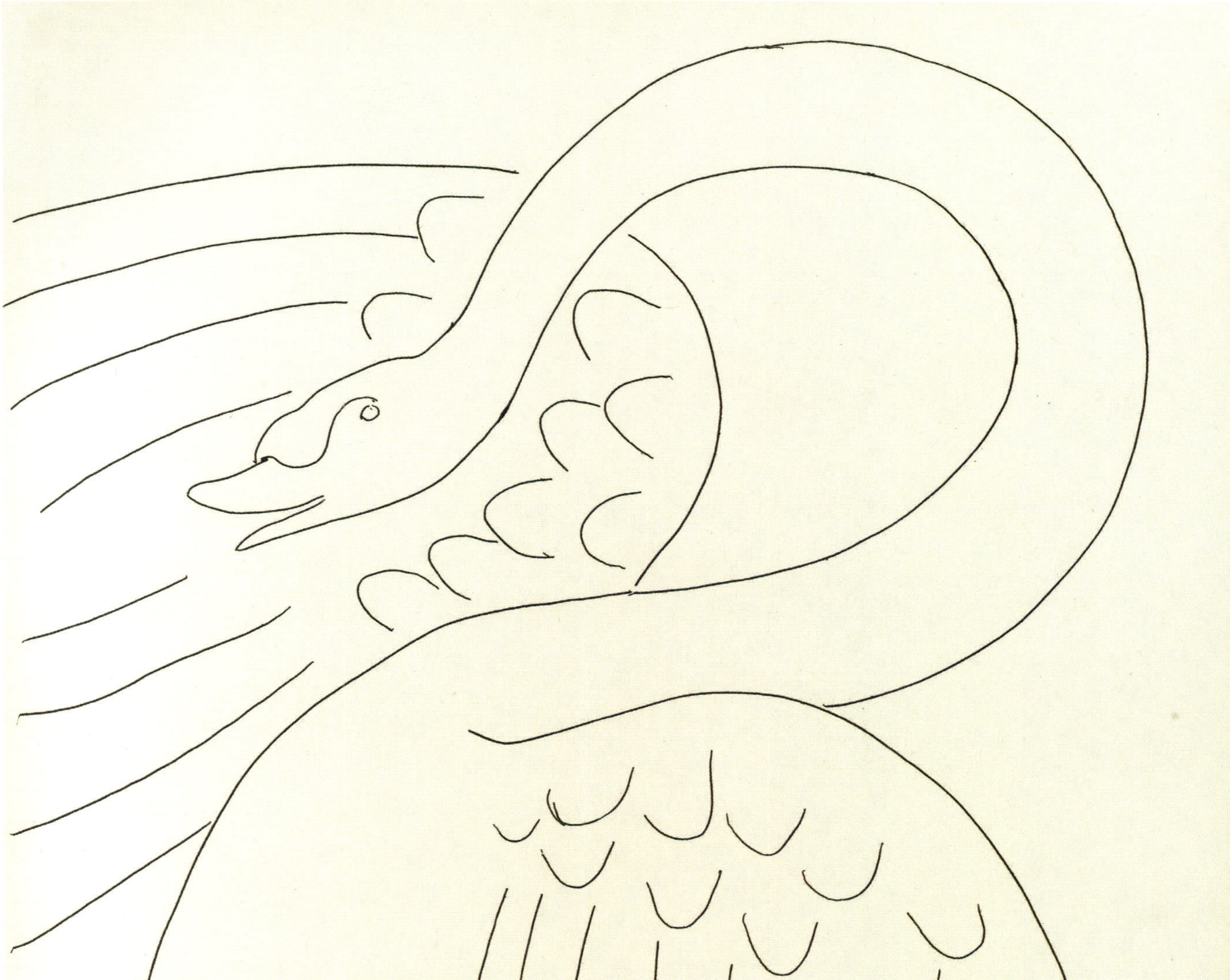

89

88 Pablo Picasso, *The Ostrich*, 1936

→ Image on p. 138

In 1936, after being asked by Ambroise Vollard to illustrate a selection of texts taken from Buffon's *Histoire naturelle*, Picasso created thirty-one engravings of animals at Roger Lacourière's studio. These images, which constitute masterly animal portraiture, demonstrate his ingenious use of the sugar-lift aquatint technique recently introduced to him by Lacourière. This method enabled him to produce an engraved outline similar to that of a painting, together with various grey tones. Whereas the other plates depict the animals in static poses, in this image Picasso has shown the ostrich while it is running, sketching it with a few strokes of the brush and pen dipped into the sugared ink. In this way, he conveyed a sense of movement, the brushstrokes in the background suggesting speed. Following Vollard's death in 1939 the project was resumed and published by his associate and successor Martin Fabiani in 1942. C.C.-C.

Plate from *Histoire naturelle*, by Buffon, Paris, M. Fabiani, 1942| 41.5 x 31.5 cm (print area)

89 Henri Matisse, *The Swan*, 1931–1932

→ Image on p. 139

Stéphane Mallarmé's *Poésies*, published by Albert Skira in 1932, was the first book to be illustrated by Matisse. He worked on this project while he was creating his mural panels *The Dance* for the Barnes Foundation – two simultaneous commissions for the artist, who was obliged to change his format on a permanent basis. The twenty-nine etchings that Matisse created for the publication were markedly linear in style, and formed a harmonious ensemble with the printed text. He made numerous preparatory drawings, sometimes sketched from life, as was the case here, and produced several variations. The model he used for this etching was a swan that had attacked his son, Pierre Matisse, while he was in a small boat on a lake in the Bois de Boulogne. It is this image of the swan, advancing aggressively with outspread wings, which Matisse finally selected. The whiteness of the bird is suggested by the areas left completely blank, the composition being structured around the arabesque formed by the swan's neck. C.C.-C.

Plate from *Poésies*, by Mallarmé, Lausanne, Skira, 1932 | Etching | 33 x 25 cm (sheet)

90 Marc Chagall, *The Dog Who Carries His Master's Supper Around His Neck*, ca. 1930

At the request of Ambroise Vollard, Chagall undertook the illustrations for La Fontaine's *Fables*, and worked on the commission from 1927 to 1931. Unlike the artists who had previously produced illustrations for the *Fables*, he chose a realistic approach, drawing inspiration from the landscapes and animals he had observed during his travels in the South of France and the Auvergne.

From a technical perspective, the *Fables* marked a turning point in Chagall's approach to his engravings. The artist began by painting about a hundred brilliantly hued gouache images, which were exhibited at the Bernheim Gallery in 1930. Vollard would have liked to see these colours reproduced in engravings, but after a few disappointing experiments, Chagall decided to use his paintings as the basis for black and white etchings. He had to exploit all the resources offered by copper-plate engraving in order to find the tones that corresponded to the colours in his gouaches. In this way, he completely modified his approach to engraving, abandoning linear effects in favour of differently toned surfaces, which he obtained by combining techniques and tools in a variety of ways. The *Fables* were not published in Vollard's lifetime, and the project was resumed after the war by Tériade. C.C.-C.

Plate no. 81 from the *Fables* by La Fontaine, Paris, Tériade, 1952 | Etching | 29.2 x 24 cm (print area)

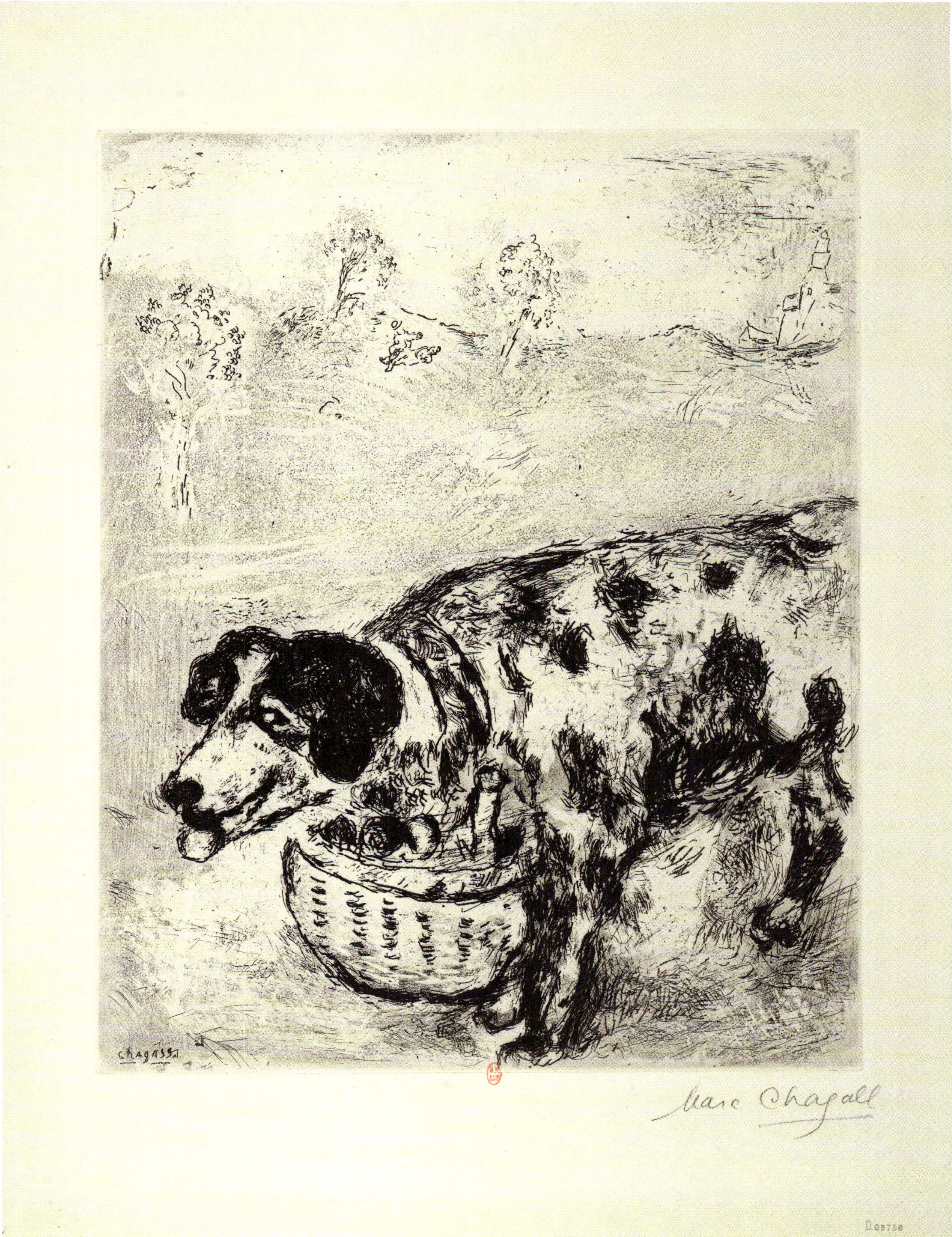
Marc Chagall

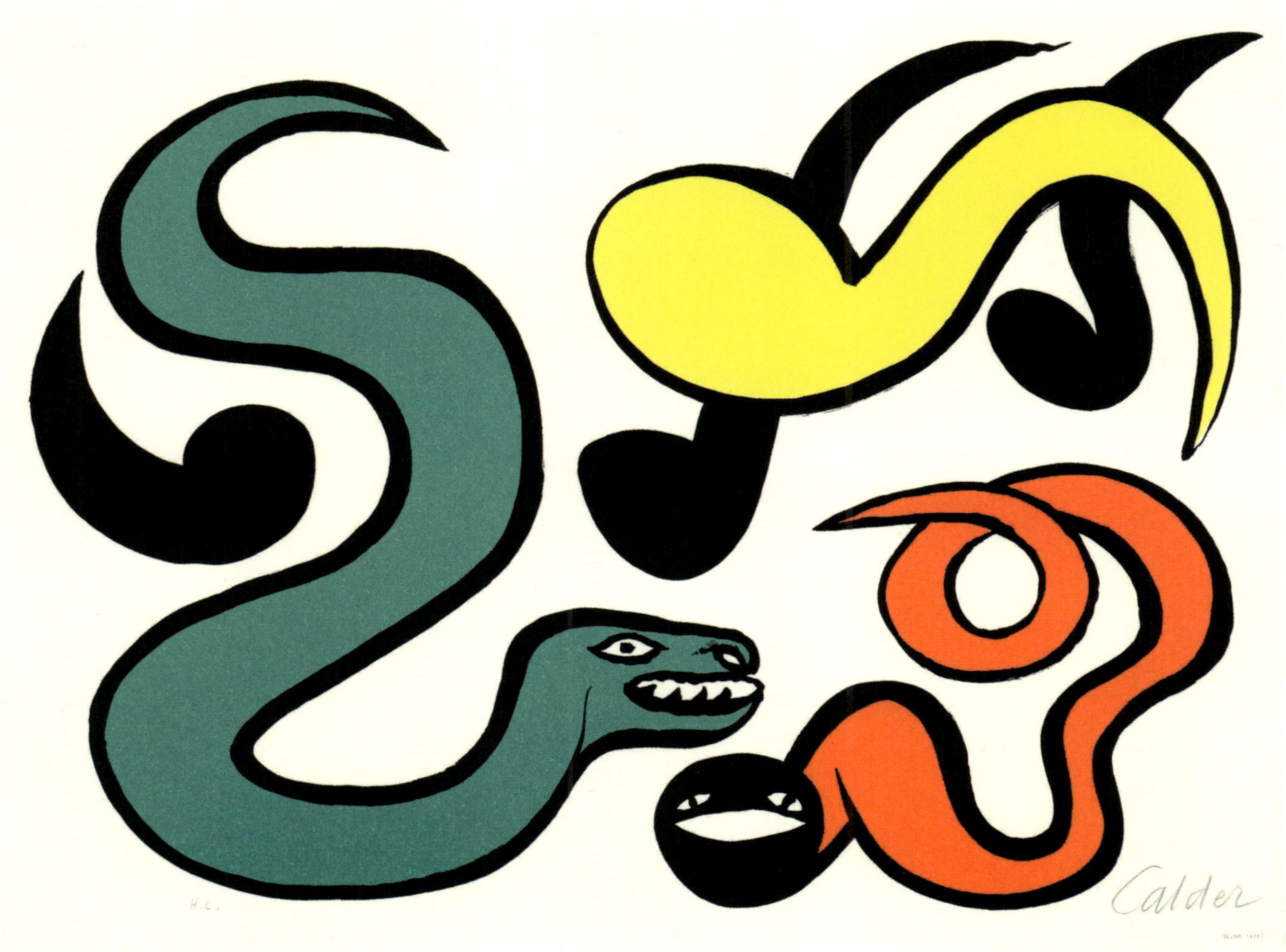

91

91 Alexander Calder, *Choice of Color,* 1975

The American artist Alexander Calder studied engineering and, at the age of thirty-two, he decided to 'paint and work in the abstract' following a visit to Piet Mondrian. In 1931, while in Paris, he joined the Abstraction-Création group and its founder members, Auguste Herbin, Jean Hélion and Georges Vantongerloo. The artist was much better known for his 'poetic mechanics' created from wire, such as *Calder's Circus* (1929), his monumental steel plate sculptures and his coloured mobiles, than for his graphic work. However, he produced prints on a very regular basis from the 1930s, when he engraved a few plates in Stanley William Hayter's Atelier 17. In the late 1950s he created a number of printed lithographs at the Mourlot studio for the Maeght Gallery, illustrating works with wood engravings or etchings: *Fêtes*, a set of seven engravings, accompanies a text by Jacques Prévert printed and published by the Maeght Gallery in 1971. The stylized, laughing snakes shown 'floating' in this print create the illusion of an animated scene, as the vividly coloured reptiles slide across black musical notes, forming a harmonious configuration. L.F.

Coloured lithograph | 58 x 78 cm (sheet)

92 Jean Arp, *Deer,* 1959

Born in Alsace, then German territory, Arp arrived in Paris in 1914 to escape conscription. He later settled in Switzerland, where conscientious objectors had established a home. In the following year he met the artist Sophie Taeuber (1889–1943), who became his wife and collaborator. In Zurich, together with Hugo Ball, Arp embarked on the adventure of Dadaism, a vital period in his career: 'We rejected all mimesis and description, giving free rein to the elementary and spontaneous' (*Abstract Art,* Anna Moszynska, Thames and Hudson, 1990, p. 65). In 1942 Arp joined the Surrealists, seeing this movement as a continuation of Dada, before moving to the Cercle et Carré and Abstraction-Création groups, preferring to devote himself to sculpture. The gallery owner Denise René exhibited his work on several occasions, notably in *Tendances de l'art abstrait* (1948) together with pieces by Sonia and Robert Delaunay, Auguste Herbin, Piet Mondrian and Victor Vasarely. In 1953 the gallery began to publish silkscreen prints, as the multiple images produced from this process enabled these works to be more widely circulated. In 1959 the gallery published a portfolio of eleven silkscreen prints and one drawing, including Arp's *Deer,* fifty copies of which were printed by the Arcay Studio, each bearing the artist's finger print. L.F.

Coloured silkscreen print | 67 x 50.3 cm (sheet)

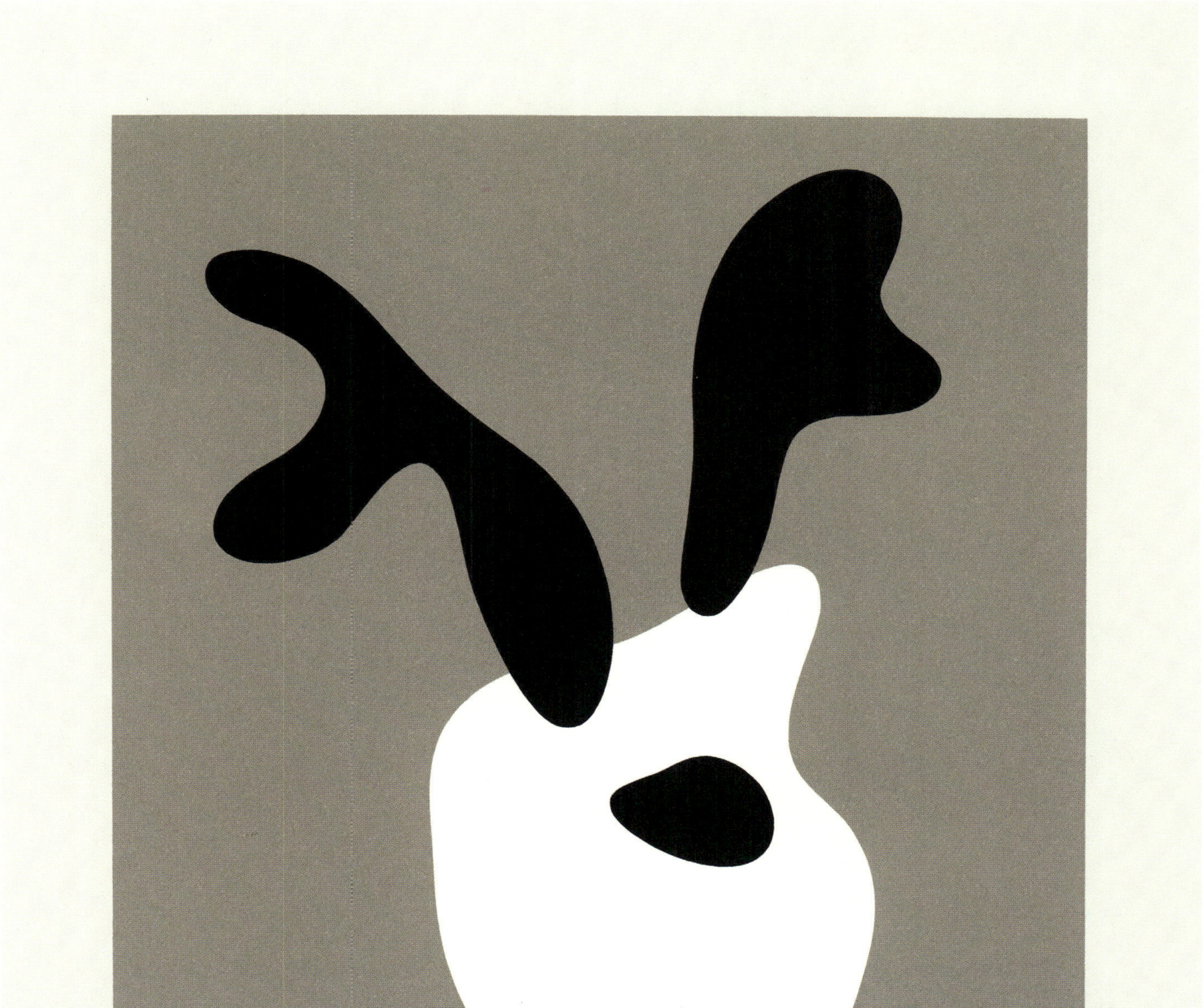

92

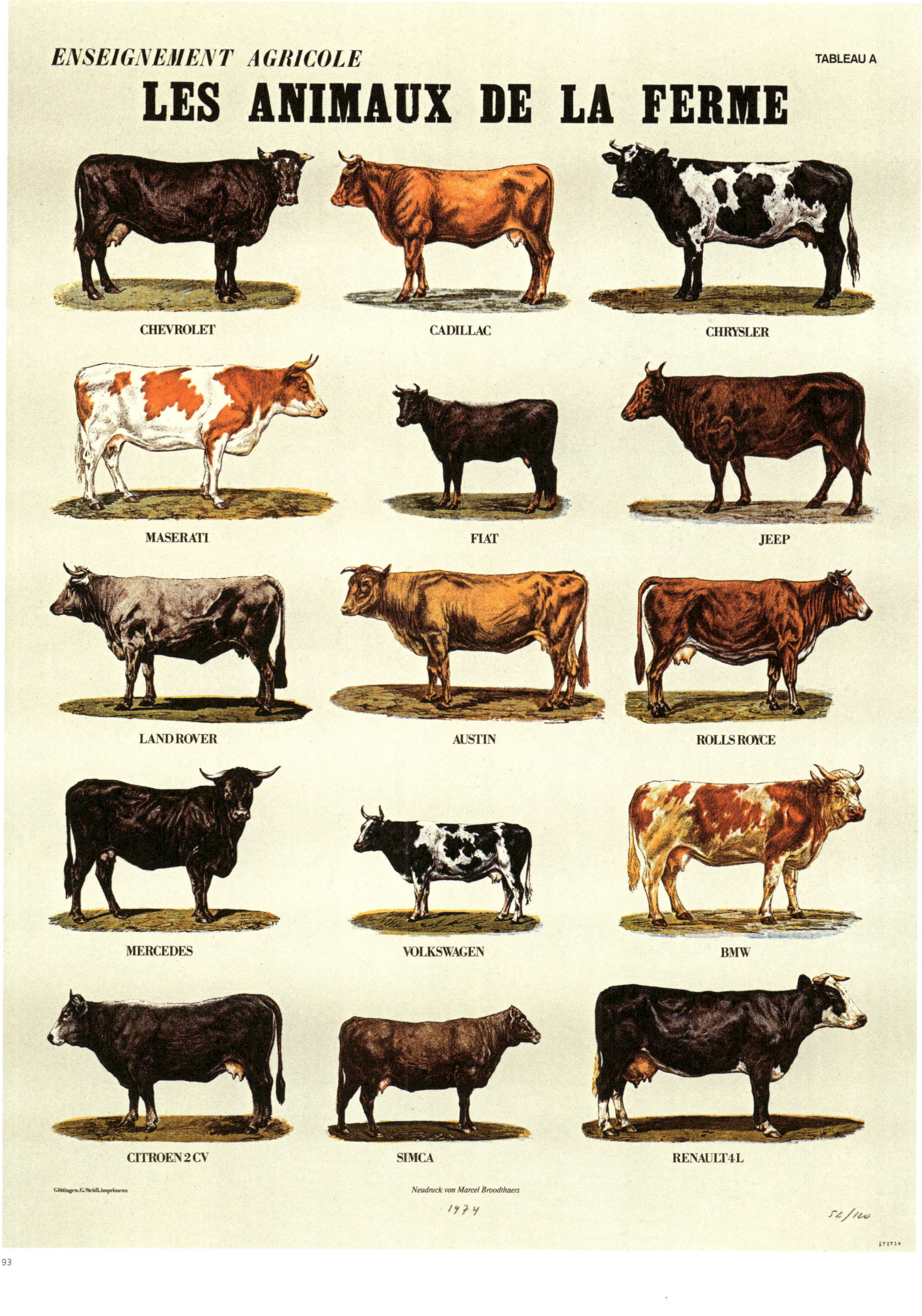
ENSEIGNEMENT AGRICOLE
TABLEAU A
LES ANIMAUX DE LA FERME
CHEVROLET
CADILLAC
CHRYSLER
MASERATI
FIAT
JEEP
LAND ROVER
AUSTIN
ROLLS ROYCE
MERCEDES
VOLKSWAGEN
BMW
CITROEN 2 CV
SIMCA
RENAULT 4 L
Göttingen, G. Steidl, imprimeur
Neudruck von Marcel Broodthaers
1974

93

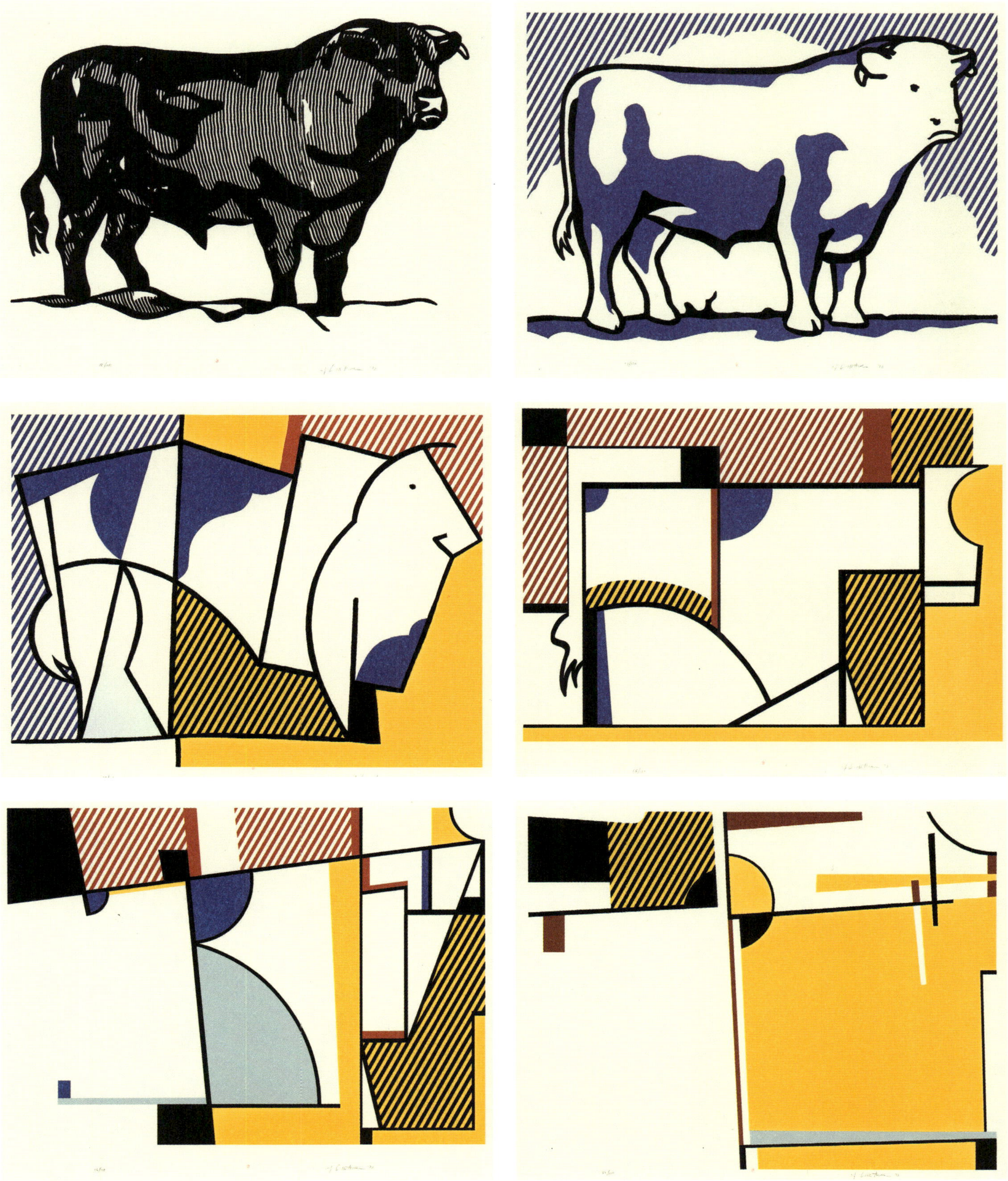

94

93 Marcel Broodthaers, *The Farm Animals A*, 1974
→ description on p. 146

94 Roy Lichtenstein, *Bull Profile Series*, 1973
→ description on p. 146

93 Marcel Broodthaers, *The Farm Animals A*, 1974

→ Image on p. 144

The poet Marcel Broodthaers opened a bookshop in the late 1940s. Associated with the Revolutionary Surrealist Group, he stood opposed to André Breton and struck up a friendship with René Magritte. In 1964, the exhibition *Pense-bête* launched his entry into the domain of the plastic arts. It comprised unsold copies of his collection of poems embedded in plaster, creating a sculpture that combined the written word and the visual form, thereby encapsulating the aesthetic reflection contained within all his forms of expression: painting, assembling, sculpture, film-making and writing. Broodthaers did not use traditional printmaking methods, but instead adopted industrial techniques such as offset printing and typography. In 1975 he wrote: 'What characterizes a work of art? [. . .] in most cases there is no formal difference between something that is a work of art and something that is not.' *Farm Animals* is an educational poster presenting images of cows that the artist subverted by replacing the names underneath the pictures with those of car manufacturers. Is this simply an example of humour, or an indictment against the commercialization of animals, who have been reduced to the status of objects? L.F.

Coloured offset lithograph | 82 x 60.2 cm (sheet)

94 Roy Lichtenstein, *Bull Profile Series*, 1973

→ Image on p. 145

Lichtenstein combined different engraving processes to make the six prints forming the *Bull Profile* series, incorporating the intaglio method, lithography and silkscreen printing with remarkable virtuosity (*Bull III* to *VI*). A major figure in the American pop-art movement, he created engravings from the very beginning of his career, during which he produced about three hundred and fifty prints. From the late 1960s, he regularly collaborated with the prestigious printmaking studio Gemini G.E.L. in Los Angeles, where in 1969 he made two series inspired by Claude Monet – *Cathedrals* and *Haystacks* – which attracted much attention. With his series *Bull Profile*, created in 1973, Lichtenstein explored the development of an image from figurative to abstract depiction. This work was a direct reference to the lithographic series of eleven *Bulls* created by Picasso at the Mourlot studio in late 1945, where a single line is used to suggest the massive silhouette of a bull in the final image. Here the emblematic combination of diagonal lines, black contours and flat, vivid colours so characteristic of Lichtenstein's vocabulary culminates in a simplified, schematized composition in the spirit of Mondrian. C.P.-L.

Gemini G.E.L. Edition of 100 | Coloured lithograph, silkscreen print, line-cut on paper | 68.6 x 88.9 cm (each plate)

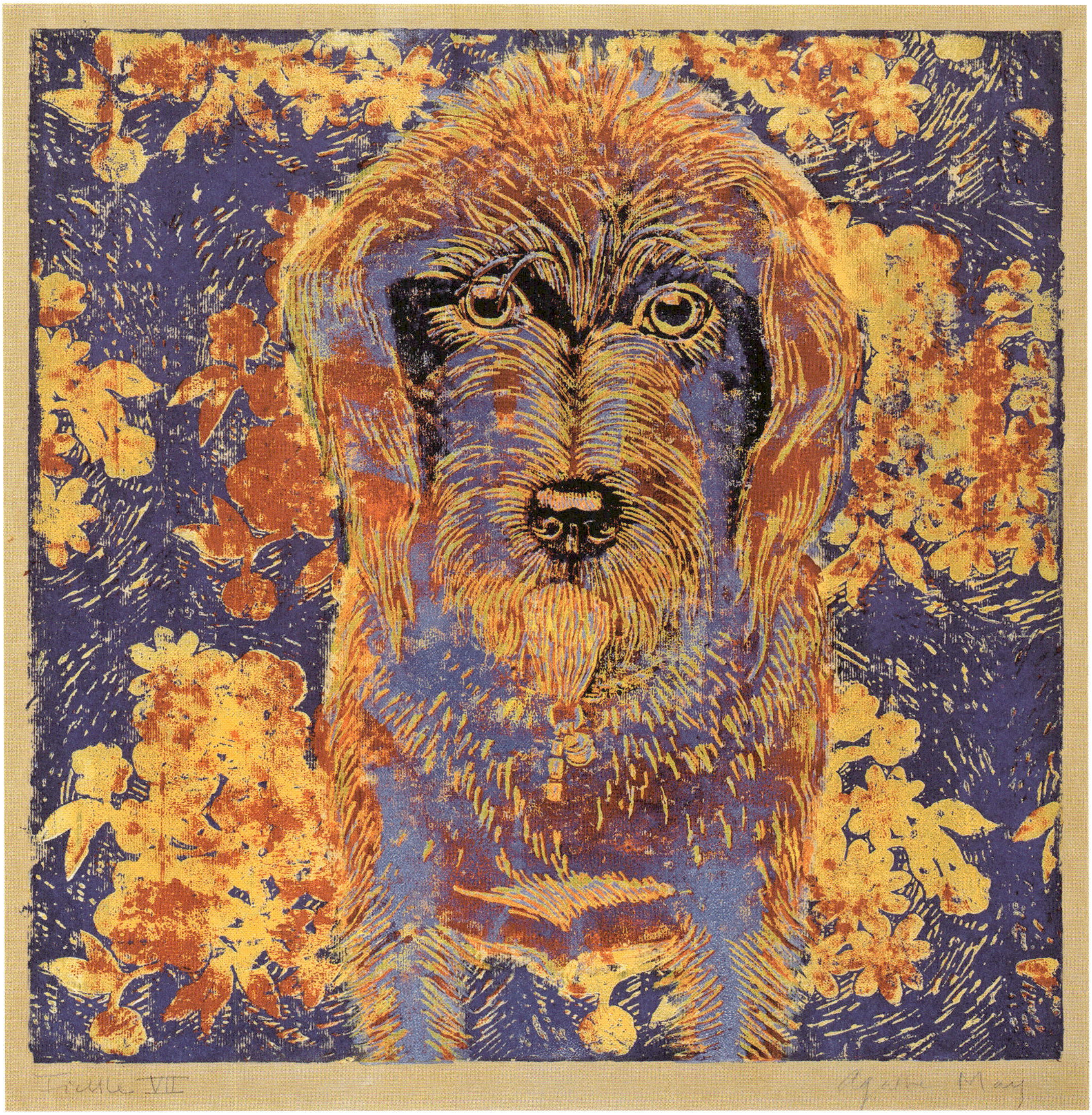

95

95 Agathe May, *'Ficelle' VIII*, 1989

Agathe May studied the intaglio technique at the École nationale supérieure des arts décoratifs, adopting linoleum as a medium in 1985. Her lino-cuts are the culmination of a long creative process, during which the artist makes a large number of preparatory drawings before deciding on her subject and cutting the linoleum surface with a gouge, superimposing lines and enlivening her images with a number of straight and diagonal markings. Agathe May carries out the printing process herself; at this stage she works on the colours, treating them in a highly original manner. Every work is unique, and the artist produces a very limited series of proofs for each image. She chooses her models from those close to her, engraving portraits of her husband, her daughter, her friends and pets. The unusual composition of her works, the discrepancies between subject and setting, the experimentations with colour and the often monumental formats all endow these everyday scenes with a poetic quality that is sometimes unsettling. Ficelle the dog is presented here in close focus against an autumnal background, head forwards and seemingly surrounded by a halo of flames, a figure both familiar and otherworldly. This print forms part of a series of images, eleven of which were printed on paper and two on fabric. C.P.-L.

Coloured linocut | 98 x 98 cm (sheet)

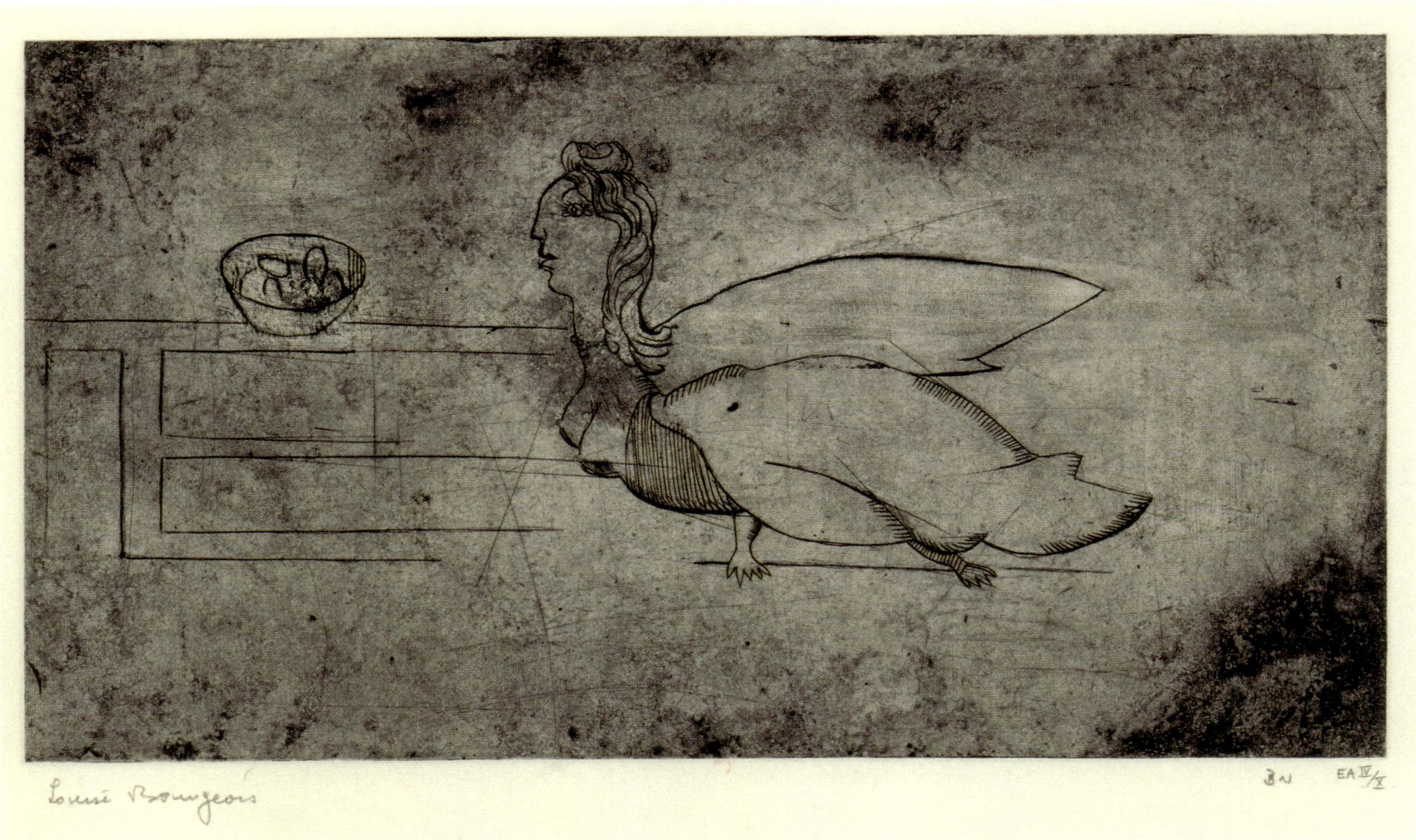

96

96 Louise Bourgeois, *Bosom Lady*, 1990

In 1990 the Galerie Lelong in Paris asked Louise Bourgeois, then at the peak of her career, to undertake a joint print project. The gallery had decided to reprint images engraved by the artist during the 1940s, works that would have been unknown to the public. Her prints, like her sculptures, drawings and installations, are autobiographical in nature, an approach characteristic of her entire creative output: 'All my work is an unconscious self-portrait; it allows me to exorcise my demons.' The *Quarantania* portfolio brings together nine etchings executed between 1942 and 1948. A reflection of the artist's incessant creativity, the plate *Bosom Lady* was reworked in 1990: the small still-life on the left-hand side was reinforced and the horizontal lines on the bird-woman's upper wing were obliterated. Commenting on this representation, Louise Bourgeois declared: 'It is a portrait . . . very intimate and very happy. It is in contrast to the dark self-portraits of low self-esteem. She is very pleased . . . as pleased as can be. She is at ease in her body . . . she is very confident. These are her three eggs . . . her three children . . . her three jewels. The bird will take care of the eggs . . . but the bird can also escape by flight' (*The Prints of Louise Bourgeois,* Deborah and Carole Smith, The Museum of Modern Art, 1994, p. 70). C.P.-L.

Louise Bourgeois, *Quarantania*, portfolio of nine engravings, Paris, Galerie Lelong | Etching and drypoint | 33 x 47.3 cm (sheet)

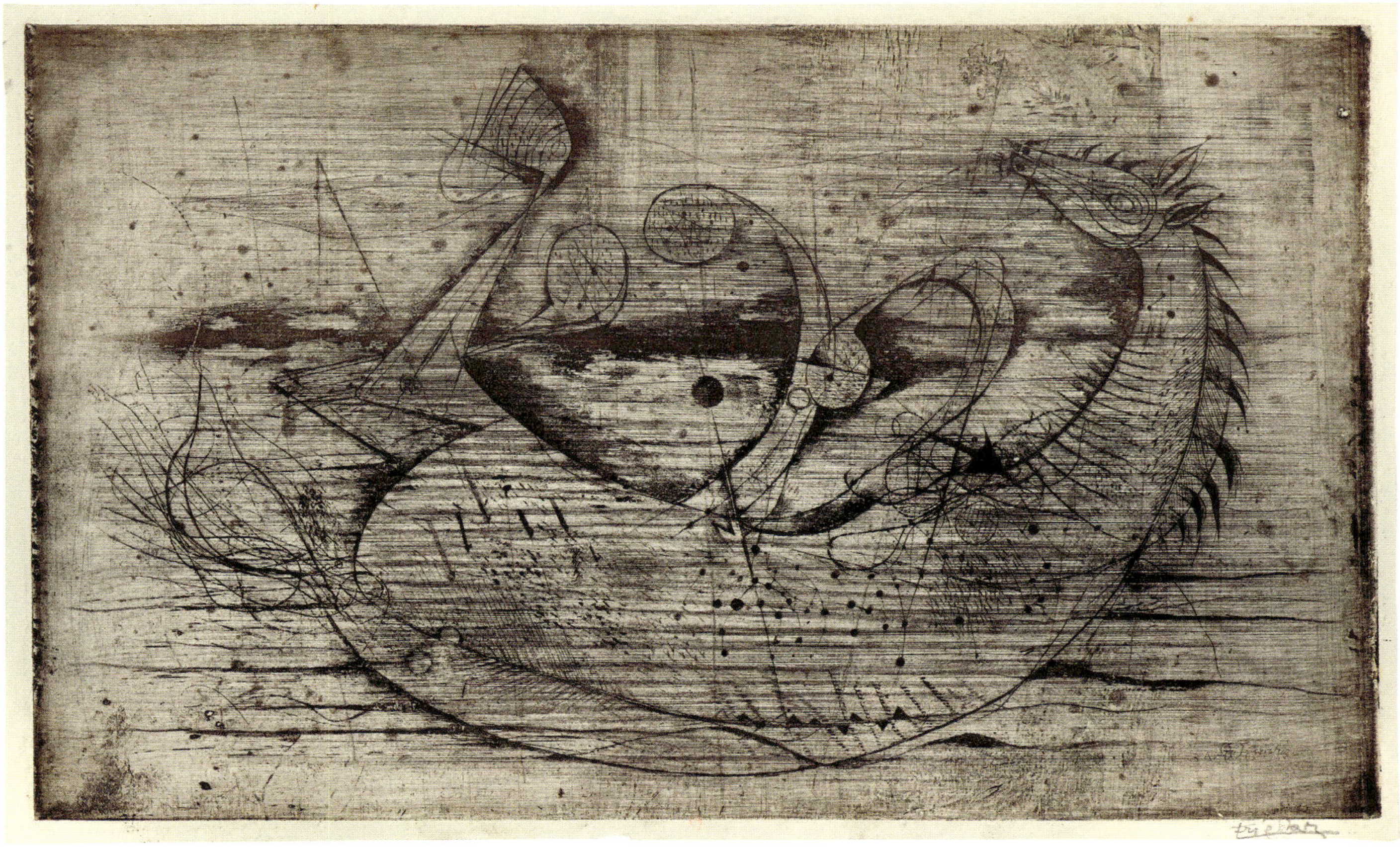

97

97 Johnny Friedlaender, *Horse Lying Down*, 1952

Born in Upper Silesia, Johnny Friedlaender settled in Paris in 1937. Through his friendship with Christian Zervos he met Bernard Gheerbrant, who invited him to present his first exhibition at the Galerie La Hune in 1948. Friedlaender established a printmaking studio with Albert Flocon in 1950, and trained a number of artists in the intaglio technique. In the early 1950s he adopted the theme of animals, although he is not categorized as an animal artist. The animals in his compositions, in this case a horse, are always recognizable, yet he treats them in a stylized manner, leaving their entrails visible in places. Bernard Gheerbrant defined his style in these terms: 'He had a desire to create order, which was perhaps not always fully understood. Instead he was seen in a more analytical manner, with his images of flowers, the female form or animals. Yet what he really did was to integrate the story of these bodies into pure form. He absorbed and ordered these images. That was his motivation. He had a deep need for synthesis.' C.C.-C.

Etching and aquatint | 29.7 x 49.9 cm (print area)

98 Barry Flanagan, *Ganymede*, 1983

After making 'soft' sculptures of cloth and sand in the 1960s, Welsh sculptor Barry Flanagan returned to figurative portrayal in the late 1970s. Working in marble and bronze, he revisited the themes of classical statuary, taking a fanciful and irreverent approach. His sculpted bestiary of elephants, dogs, horses and large, gambolling hares is strikingly dynamic. Flanagan's engravings reflect that same freedom of gesture and thought in a more personal register. Through his images, their energetic lines carved into copper plates or linoleum, the artist uses humour to question his artistic practices and to depict his daily life, his family and friends and the landscapes dear to him. The print *Ganymede* shows the Irish thoroughbred that Flanagan used as a model in a series of preparatory engravings for a bronze horse. The wild beauty and vulnerability of the animal are suggested through a few white lines, cut directly into the supple surface of the linoleum. C.P.-L.

Lino-cut | 36 x 25 cm (print area)

99 Gilles Aillaud, *Camel*, 1988

→ Image on p. 152

The theme of zoology lies at the heart of the unique work of the painter and set decorator Gilles Aillaud. His paintings of animals in zoos question the notions of imprisonment, separation and humanity. They also reflect, as do his drawings, watercolours and prints, his fascination with the diversity in the animal kingdom. In 1987, in collaboration with the lithographer Franck Bordas, the artist conceived a project for an encyclopedia of lithographs that would depict every animal in existence. It was planned to comprise several volumes, each containing fifty-two plates and every one to be accompanied by a previously unpublished article. Four volumes were published in total, featuring 194 black and white plates identical in format but displaying exceptional diversity of execution. Gilles Aillaud's animals are drawn from life; depicted from the front in close-up, or barely indicated by black lines standing out against the white of the paper, they have a powerful presence. The head of the camel is shown in close focus. Viewed from below, it looms over the spectator, who is positioned beneath the impressive nostrils of the somewhat unfriendly animal. The encyclopedia lithographs were printed in Paris or *in situ* in Kenya, with the printing works created by Franck Bordas and set up in the bush. C.P.-L.

Encyclopédie de tous les animaux y compris les minéraux (*The Encyclopedia of All Animals, Including Minerals*), vol. 1, Paris, Studio Franck Bordas | Lithograph | 32.5 x 25.5 cm (sheet)

100 Jean-Jacques Ostier, *The Epistemologist*, 1996

→ Image on p. 153

Jean-Jacques Ostier was born in Vietnam. After studying architecture at the École nationale supérieure des beaux-arts in Paris he embarked on a series of different careers. In 1974 he decided to devote himself entirely to painting, having already practised the art for fifteen years. Inspired by the culture of the Far East – he took over his parents' gallery of ancient Japanese art in 1980 – he sought a technique combining ink, wax and metal. Ostier began printmaking in 1989 and focused particularly on lithography, with its similarity to the technique he used as a painter. The theme of animals recurs very frequently in his art, a fact surely connected with his work at the Muséum national d'histoire naturelle. He always depicts animals with quasi-scientific exactitude and sometimes with a touch of humour, as in this print where the monkey is portrayed as a philosopher. L.F.

Lithograph | 66.5 x 50.5 cm (sheet)

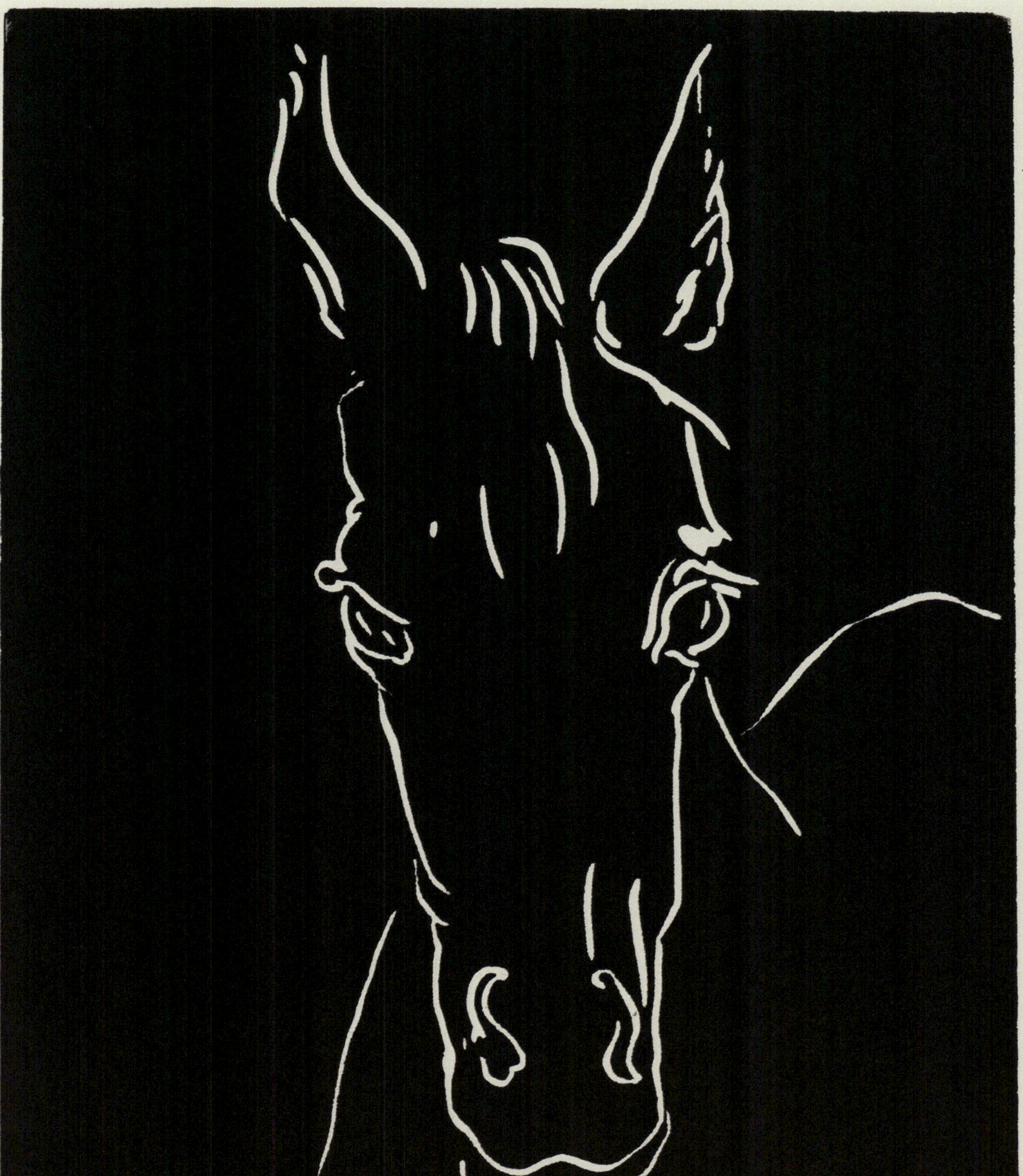

98

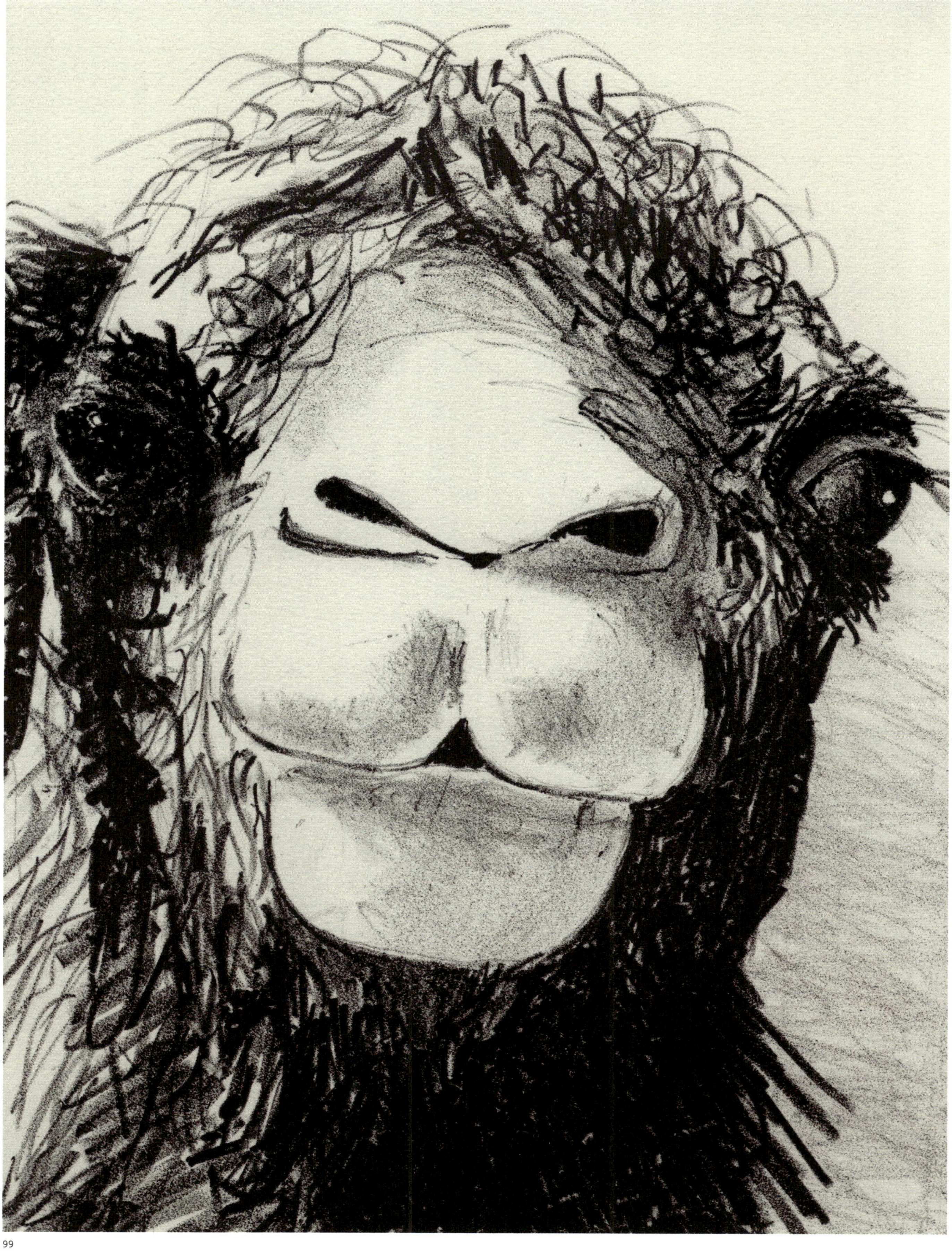

99

99 Gilles Aillaud, *Camel*, 1988
→ description on p. 150

100 Jean-Jacques Ostier, *The Epistemologist*, 1996
→ description on p. 150

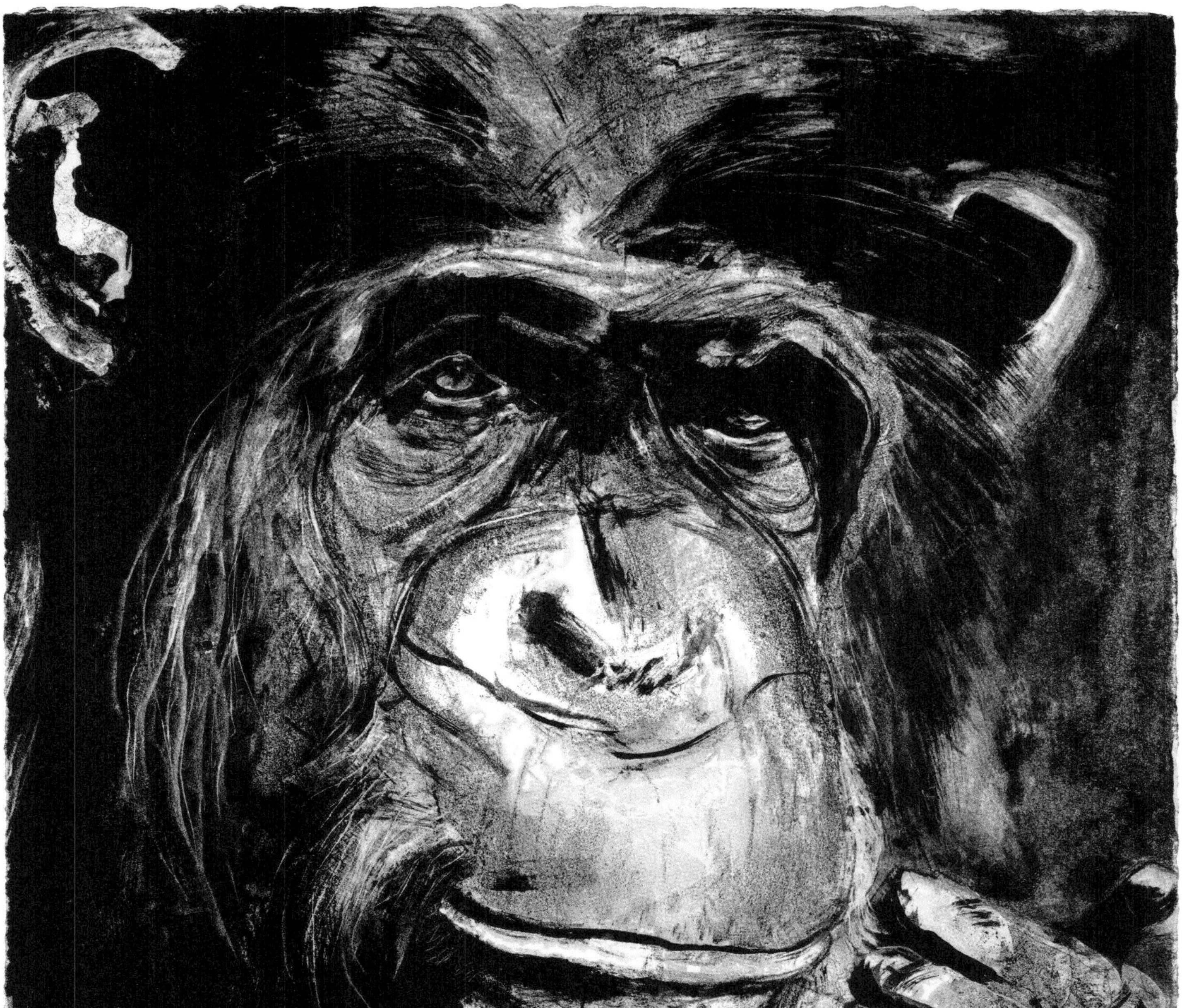

100

101 Miquel Barceló, *Elefandret*, 2007

In the 1980s Miquel Barceló achieved international recognition for his paintings and drawings. Since then he has continually extended his domain of expression, through sculpture and terracotta work, then with large-scale decorative projects and, more recently, with performance art. Inspired by Dubuffet, Tàpies and Fautrier, his work questions the relationship between subject matter and medium. Barceló regularly produces prints, intaglio images and lithographs, which form an important part of his creative output. His engravings often re-interpret recurring themes in his paintings, drawings and ceramics, and are sometimes conceived as preparatory sketches for his sculptures. This is the case with the work entitled *Elefandret* ('straight elephant'), which the artist produced in order to visualize and test the forms and structure of the monumental bronze sculpture bearing the same name that he created in 2004. The plate was first etched and then reworked with aquatint when the print was editioned in 2007; it shows an elephant defying the law of gravity as balances itself on its trunk, which is embedded into a pedestal. C.P.-L.

Etching and aquatint | 83.5 x 66 cm (sheet, each print)

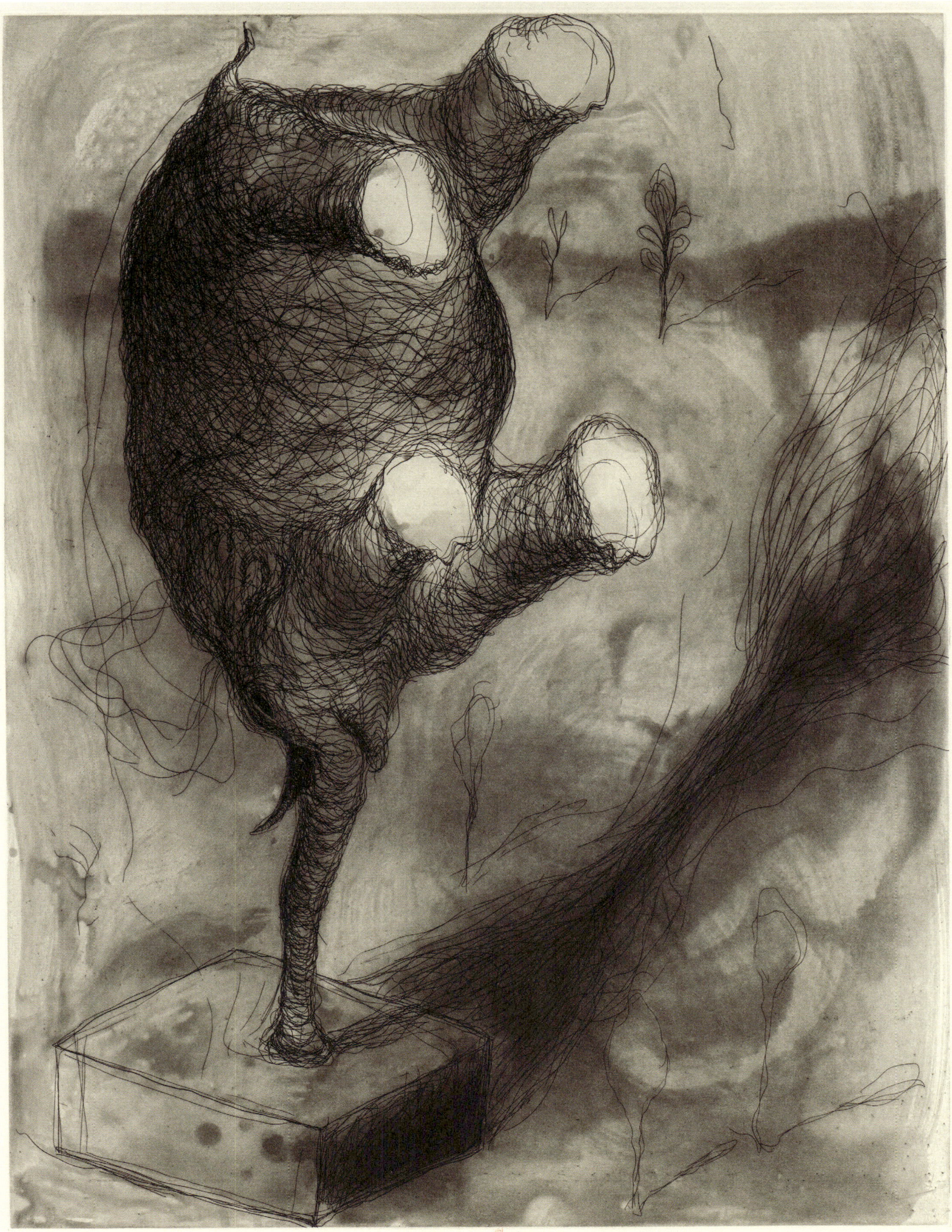

101

GLOSSARY OF PRINTMAKING TECHNIQUES

Certain words or expressions that form part of the vocabulary specifically related to printmaking, but do not require an entry in this glossary, have been *italicized*.

AQUATINT

A variant of etching, the aquatint technique produces hues that differ in their degree of intensity. The plate is coated with a fine layer of resin and is then heated, causing the resin to melt and adhere to its surface. The acid then bites into the exposed areas of the metal, between the grains of resin. A wide range of tonal values may be obtained, with shades of varying intensity, depending on the thickness of the grains of resin and the length of time the plate is exposed to the acid.

BURIN

The engraver creates an image on a metal plate (made of copper or steel), using a tool with a steel shaft ending in a sharply pointed tip, known as a burin. The lines incised into the metal plate by the burin have clean edges with no burrs. By crossing or superimposing these incisions, it is possible to obtain grey hues of varying intensity (or 'value') and shaded effects.

CRAYON MANNER

This intaglio printmaking technique was first used in the 18th century and is intended to produce an effect resembling a crayon drawing. Before it is bitten by the acid, the image is drawn onto the plate with a three-pointed tool, little rollers or 'roulettes', and a type of punch known as a 'mace head'. After the image has been printed, these produce a gently blurred line giving the illusion of a crayon drawing.

DRYPOINT

The engraver works directly on to a copper or zinc plate with the aid of a sharply pointed steel implement. This brings up curls of metal known as 'burrs', which retain the ink during the printing process and produce a deep, velvety appearance.

ETCHING

Using a pointed etching needle, the engraver incises an image onto a plate that has previously been covered with blackened varnish. This is then dipped into a mixture of water and nitric acid – 'aqua fortis', or 'strong water', in alchemy. This fluid is known as a 'mordant', from the French verb 'mordre', meaning to bite. It attacks the metal that has been exposed by the incised lines cut into the plate. This stage varies in length according to the desired intensity of the black sections in the composition. The remaining varnish is then cleaned off the plate, inked, wiped and passed through the printing press.

There are two possible ways of producing *coloured etchings*. In one method, the engraver applies variously coloured inks to one plate as required, just before the printing process. This is the '*à la poupée*' technique, so called after the balls of fabric used to apply the colours, which are known in French as '*poupées*', or dolls. The second method involves preparing as many plates as there are colours in the image and printing them successively on the sheet, a process known as *registration*.

INTAGLIO

Intaglio is the generic term used to describe all the printmaking techniques that involve incising an image into a metal plate. Burin engraving, drypoint, etching, aquatint, soft varnish method, crayon manner and mezzotint all belong to this family of printmaking techniques.

LITHOGRAPHY

Unlike the relief and intaglio techniques, which involve printing from raised and incised surfaces respectively, lithography is a planographic process. Invented by Aloys Senefelder of Germany between 1796 and 1798, it is based on the natural mutual repulsion of water and oil. An image is drawn with pen and lithographic ink or crayon onto a plate, originally made of polished limestone of varying grain size. A chemical preparation consisting of an acidulated solution mixed with gum arabic is then applied to the stone. This 'fixes' the image, surrounding it with a coating that will reject the printing ink. When passed through the press, the oil-based ink sticks to the original image, and is repelled in all other areas, where the lithographic stone has simply been moistened with water.

'*MANIÈRE NOIRE*' OR MEZZOTINT

The metal plate is firstly covered with an even layer of small dots, using a 'rocker' – a tool with a wide, curved and bevelled edge. This long, painstaking work is carried out before the image is made, a process that involves scraping or burnishing the plate's roughened surface, producing white or grey shades on the black background.

MULTICOLOUR LITHOGRAPHY

Multicoloured lithographs require separate lithographic stones to be used for each colour in the image, in addition to a 'key' stone. A variety of different tones may be obtained by juxtaposing or superimposing these colours. Although coloured oil-based inks are by nature somewhat opaque, they may be mixed with varnishes to achieve a more transparent effect.

OFFSET PRINTING

The technique of offset printing derives from lithography, and is an improvement on that process. The lithographic stone is replaced by a flexible printing plate secured to a cylinder, and a rubber offset printing blanket is inserted between the plate cylinder and the paper.

PRINT

An image produced from a composition that has been engraved or drawn onto a surface such as a wooden or metal plate or a lithographic stone. It is possible to pull as many impressions from this print as are required, provided the matrix is still usable. Once the matrix has been inked it is passed through a press, thereby printing the image onto a sheet of paper or another surface. The term 'print' encompasses every technique that is used, and designates wood engravings and woodcuts, intaglio work, lithographs and silkscreen prints. The term 'original print' was first adopted in the 19th century, to indicate that the image on the matrix was created by the artist, as opposed to a 'reproduction print' or an 'interpretative' copy.

PROOF

An example of an engraving, lithograph or silkscreen print, pulled before a particular edition.

SILKSCREEN PRINTING

This technique, which dates from the first half of the 20th century, derives from the much older stencil method of print-making. It is based on the use of fabric (silk or another textile), which is stretched onto a wooden or metal frame known as a screen; ink is then squeezed through the mesh apertures of the material. An image may be produced either by drawing directly onto the screen, by attaching stencils to the mesh, or by coating it with a photo sensitive emulsion, using light to expose an image onto the screen.

SOFT VARNISH METHOD

In this process of engraving using the crayon manner, the plate is covered with varnish and then with a layer of fairly light paper, on which an image is drawn using a hard pencil. Each stroke marks the varnish, which adheres to the back of the paper, leaving the metal exposed. The plate may then be 'bitten' with acid.

STATE

A stage in the condition of a print before any alteration is made to the matrix. Any correction carried out, however minimal, means that the print has passed from one state to another. These are numbered accordingly: 1st state, 2nd state, and so on. The state preceding the definitive state is known the proof state. All written text that appears on a print is known as the letters, or lettering. The term state before letters is used to describe the condition of a proof pulled before the lettering has been added, while state after letters is used when text has been applied.

STIPPLE ENGRAVING

This process, which produces a tonal effect in intaglio prints, involves marking the plate with dots of varying sizes using a finely pointed tool.

TIRAGE

French term designating an impression or a series of impressions taken from a matrix and resulting in engravings, lithographs or silkscreen prints. The number of copies produced varies according to the technique used, ranging from a few dozen in the case of wood engravings and etchings to several hundred in the case of lithographs.

WOOD ENGRAVINGS AND WOODCUTS

The process of wood engraving entails carving into a wooden matrix to produce an image in relief. The protruding surface area is first inked, then passed through a press or printed by hand. A distinction is made between woodcuts, an older technique that involves using gouges, chisels or knives to work on wood that has been cut 'plankwise' to produce side grain blocks, and wood engravings, which are made using endgrain blocks, when the tree has been cut transversely to its length. This technique, which was invented in the early 19th century, involves the use of burins and échoppes (a type of etching needle). In order to create coloured wood engravings, a 'key block' is firstly prepared, followed by as many blocks as there are colours in the composition, with different hues being superimposed to widen the range of effects. The colours are printed sequentially and with great precision to ensure that they are perfectly placed within the image, in a process known as registration.

LIST OF WORKS

The prints reproduced in this publication are listed here under the artists' names in alphabetical order. All the prints shown are held in the Prints and Photographs Department at the Bibliothèque nationale de France (le département des Estampes et de la Photographie) with the exception of nos. 25, 88 and 89, which belong to the collections in the Rare Books Reserve.

Anonymous → 46
Pack of Belgian tarot cards with animal trump scenes
Engraver unknown.
Playing card seller:
François-Arnould Sarton, brothers and sisters, rue de la Madeleine, Brussels, [ca. 1755]
Wood engraving, stencil-coloured
11.3 x 5.9 (card)
Estampes, Rés. Kh-34 (5, 65) – Boîte fol.

Anonymous → 32
Giant Squid, Found Dead in Ireland, 1674
A True Relation of a Strange Monster
Published by Francis Smith, London, 1674
Etching
48.5 x 37.5 cm (print area)
Estampes, Qd-1 (1673) –Fol.

Anonymous → 20
Falsely attributed to Antonio Tempesta
(Florence, 1555 - Rome, 1630)
An Indian Dog
Cane Indicus – Cane d'Inda, 1636
From the *Curiosa Raccolta di diversi animali quadrupedi*, Rome, Giacomo Marucci, 1636
Burin engraving
13.5 x 9.5 cm (boundary line)
Estampes, Jb-26-Fol.

Anonymous → 25
A Pair of Skating Owls
From *Les Plus Illustres Proverbes* (*The Most Important Proverbs*), Paris, Jacques Lagniet, 1663, in-4°
Burin engraving
20 x 14 cm (print area)
Rare Books Reserve,
Réserve Z-1746-4

Anonymous → 21
Satirical Print Showing the Storming of Arras
Published by Jacques Lagniet, ca. 1640
Burin engraving
18 x 12.5 (boundary line)
Estampes, Rés. Hennin, 2851

Anonymous → 2
Gogelu and His Cat,
Latter half of 16th century
Woodcut
35 x 32.4 cm (boundary line)
Estampes, Rés. Hennin, 328

Anonymous → 71
Hippodrome,
"*The War of the Indies*", 1858
Poster, coloured wood engraving
100 x 119 cm (sheet)
Printed by the Rouchon Printing House
Estampes, ENT DN -1 (ROUCHON /18) –ROUL

Anonymous → 45
The Hyena, a Ferocious Animal That Ravaged the Region of Gévaudan from 1764, as Sent to the Court, ca. 1765
Burin engraving
23.5 x 44.5 cm (platemark)
Estampes, Rés. Hennin, 9190

Anonymous → 70
The Giraffe
Épinal, Pellerin Publishing House, 1828
Woodcut, stencil-coloured
41 x 25 cm (sheet)
Estampes, Li-59 (1) –Fol.

Anonymous → 49
The Large Troupe of Curious Animals that Entertained the City and the Court on 11 July 1784, Dedicated to the subscribers
1784
Coloured etching
20 x 18.7 cm (print area)
Estampes, Ib-2-Fol.

Anonymous → 67
The Vanity of the Peacock, or the New Panegyric to 100 Parisian Coquettes,
1821
Coloured lithograph
38.7 x 38.7 cm (sheet)
Estampes, Te mat -1-Boîte fol. n° 1744

Anonymous → 22
The Cats' Singing Master
ca. 1640
Made in Pierre Bertrand's studio (ca. 1600 – ca. 1678)
Burin engraving
30 x 20.5 cm (boundary line)
Estampes, Rés. Hennin, 2933

Anonymous → 73
The World Before the Creation of Man 1885
Coloured lithographic poster
130 x 96 cm (sheet)
Printed by the Émile Lévy Printing House
Estampes, ENT DN-1 (LEVY, Émile /7)- ROUL.

Anonymous → 51
The New "Incroyable", or the Fashionable Goose
1797
Coloured etching
20.5 x 15.2 (boundary line)
Estampes, Tf-19-Fol.

Anonymous → 15
The Peacock, Bad Counsel
ca. 1535-1540
Woodcut, stencil-coloured
40 x 29 cm (boundary line)
Estampes, Rés. Ea-17 (3)-Fol.

Anonymous → 17
The True Portrait of Gunnar's Dog ca. 1690-1700.
Burin engraving
21.3 x 33.3 cm (boundary line)
Estampes, Rés. Hennin 5060

Anonymous → 3
Unicorn Purifying a Fountain
From a series of twelve woodcuts depicting animals, Paris, Philippe Pelletier, ca. 1580
Woodcut
19.5 x 14.5 cm (boundary line)
Estampes, Rés. Ea-79-4, f.87v°

Anonymous → 31
Mice Attached to One Another By Their Tails
Wunder-würdiger und seltzammer Scheusal eines entsetzlich ominösen Ratten-Ungeziefers
Published by J. J. Felsecker, 1683
Mezzotint and typographic content
41.5 x 25 cm (sheet, trimmed)
Estampes, Qb-1 (1683)-Fol.

Anonymous → 72
The Théâtre des Menus-Plaisirs Invisible Creatures
1883
Coloured lithographic Poster
60 x 40 cm (sheet)
Printed by the Émile Lévy Printing House
Estampes, ENT DN-1 (LEVY, Émile/4)- FT 6.

Anonymous → 56
Genuine Portrait of a Live Rhinoceros on Show at the Saint-Germain Fair in Paris
"a Paris chés Charpentier ruë St Jacques au Coq"
1749
Etching and burin work
40.5 x 54.5 cm (print area)
Estampes, Rés. Qb-201 (100)-Fol. / Rés. Hennin, 8630

Anonymous → 19
Zebra fera salvatica
Early 17th century
Etching
20.2 x 29.7 cm (boundary line)
Estampes, Jb-31-Fol.

Aillaud → 99
Gilles Aillaud
(Paris, 1928 – Paris, 2005)

Camel
Gilles Aillaud, *Encyclopédie de tous les animaux y compris les minéraux*
Volume 1; texts by Giorgio Agamben, Gilles Aillaud, Jean-Christophe Bailly, Franck Bordas, Hervé Bordas, Jean-Paul Chambas, Joy Coulentianou, Richard Crevier, Stéphane Deligeorges, Michel Deutsch, Pierre Gaudibert, Jean Jourdheuil, Heiner Müller, Jean-Luc Parant, Jean-François Peyret, Fabio Rieti, Nicky Rieti, Jean-Louis Schefer, Bernhard Weyergraf, Yéfime, Hanns Zischler. Paris, Studio Franck Bordas
1988
Lithograph
32.5 x 25.5 cm (sheet)
Estampes, Dc-3193 (1)-4

Arp → 92
Jean Arp
(Strasbourg, 1886 – Basel, 1966)
Deer
Éditions Denise René, 1959
Printed at the Arcay Studio (Vélizy)
Coloured silkscreen print
50 ex.
67 x 50.3 cm (sheet)
Estampes, Dg-1 (Arp, Hans/ Jean)-Ft 5

Audubon → 63
John James Audubon
(Les Cayes, Saint-Domingue, 1785 – New York, 1851)
Snowy Owl, Strix nyctea. Linn, Male 1. Female 2
ca. 1830
Etching and aquatint, coloured
96.7 x 64.6 cm (print area)
Estampes, Rés. Jb-45-Ft 6

Baldung Grien → 8
Hans Baldung Grien
(Swäbisch Gmünd, ca. 1484 – Strasbourg, 1545)
Fighting Stallions
1534
Woodcut
22.50 x 33 cm (boundary line)
Estampes, Rés. Ca-9 (+) –Fol.

Baquoy → 54
Jean-Charles Baquoy
(Paris, 1721 – Paris, 1777)
After Jacques de Sève († after 1790)
The Wolf
1758
Plate I from vol. VII of *Histoire naturelle, générale et particulière avec la description du Cabinet du roy (Natural History, General and Particular)*, 1749-1788
by Georges-Louis Leclerc, comte de Buffon (1707–1788)
Etching and burin work
19.5 x 15 cm (boundary line)
Estampes, Ja-23 (A)-Fol.

Barceló → 101
Miquel Barceló (Felanitx, 1957
Elefandret
2007
Printed by the René Tazé Studio
Etching and aquatint
83.5 x 66 cm
(sheet, each plate)
Estampes, Cb20-22 (Barceló, Miquel) – Ft 5

Boel → 38
Gérard Scotin
(Antwerp, 1643 – Paris, 1715)
After Pieter Boel
(Antwerp, 1622–1674)
Pelicans
Late 17th century
Etching
25.2 x 35 cm (print area)
Estampes, Jb-37-Ft 4

Boillot → 14
Joseph Boillot (Langres, ca. 1545 – Langres, 1605)
Term representing a Porcupine
From *Nouveaux Pourtraits et figures de termes pour user en architecture (New Portraits and Figures for Terms for Use in Architecture)*, Langres, 1592
Etching
26 x 8.5 cm (boundary line)
Estampes, Ha-4-Fol.

Bonheur → 65
Rosa Bonheur
(Bordeaux, 1822 – Thomery, 1889)
The Durham-Charolais Breed
1845
Lithograph
19.4 x 27.7 cm (image)
Estampes, Dc-285 (a)-Fol.

Bourgeois → 96
Louise Bourgeois
(Paris, 1911 – New York, 2010)
Bosom Lady
Louise Bourgeois, *Quarantania*, portfolio of 9 engravings, Paris, Galerie Lelong
1990
Printed by Piero Crommelynck, Paris
Etching and drypoint
33 x 47.3 cm (sheet)
Estampes, Ce-151-Fol.

Bracquemond → 77
Félix Bracquemond
(Paris, 1833 – Paris, 1914)
The Duck (The Newspaper)
1856
Etching
26 x 21.5 cm (image)
Estampes, Ef-411 (3)-Fol.

Broodthaers → 93
Marcel Broodthaers
(Saint-Gilles-lez-Bruxelles, 1924 – Cologne, 1976)
Les animaux de la ferme (The Farm Animals) A Heidelberg, Edition Staeck (Publisher), 1974
Göttingen, printed by G. Steidl
120 ex.
Coloured offset lithograph
82 x 60.2 cm (sheet)
Nobis, Norbert, 22
Estampes, Cc20-92 (Broodthaers, Marcel) –Ft 5

Bruegel the Elder → 12
Pieter Van der Heyden
(Antwerp? ca. 1530 – Berchem, after 1584?)
After Pieter Bruegel the Elder
(Bruegel? 1525/1530 – Brussels, 1569)
The Big Fish Eat the Little Fish Grandibus exigui sunt pisces piscibus esca, 1557
Burin engraving
23 x 29.5 cm (boundary line)
Estampes, Rés. Cc-5-Fol.

Calder → 91
Alexander Calder
(Philadelphia, 1898 – New York, 1976)
Choice of Color
Éditions Maeght (Publisher), 1975
Printed in the Arte/Maeght Studio
Coloured lithograph
58 x 78 cm (sheet)
Estampes, AA20-5 (Calder, Alexander)

Carlu → 74
Jean Carlu
(Bonnières-sur-Seine, 1900 – Nogent-sur-Marne, 1997)
"*Aquarium de Monaco*"
Oceanographic Museum
1926
Coloured lithographic poster
106 x 76 cm (sheet)
Printed by the Robert Lang Printing House
Estampes, ENT DN -1 (CARLU, Jean) – FT 6

Casanova → 58
Johann Alexander Gottfried Jacobe (Vienna, 1734 – Vienna, 1797)
After Francesco Casanova
(London, 1727 – Brühl, 1802)
Jaguar Killed in America by the Prince of Nassau-Siegen
1787
State before signatures and letters
Mezzotint
64.5 x 79.5 cm (print area)
Estampes, AA-6 (Jacobe, Johann)

Castiglione → 27
Giovanni Benedetto Castiglione (Genoa? ca. 1609 – Mantua, 1664)
Noah and the Animals Entering the Ark
ca. 1650–1655
Etching
20.6 x 40.3 cm (boundary line)
Estampes, Be-9-Fol.

Chagall → 90
Marc Chagall (Vitebsk, 1887 – Saint-Paul-de-Vence, 1985)
The Dog Who Carries his Master's Supper Around his Neck
ca. 1930, issued in 1952
Plate no. 81 from the album containing 100 prints illustrating the *Fables* by Jean de La Fontaine,
published by Tériade, Paris
Etching
29.2 x 24 cm (print area)
Estampes, CA-111 (4) FOL.

Delacroix → 62A
Eugène Delacroix
(Charenton-Saint-Maurice, 1798 – Paris, 1863)

Royal Tiger and Lion of the Atlas
1829–1830
Lithographs
32.7 x 46.7 cm (each image)
Estampes, Rés. Dc-183n (4)-Fol.

Della Bella → 28
Stefano Della Bella
(Florence, 1610 – Florence, 1664)
Female Asian Elephant
ca. 1643–1647
Etching
8.5 x 10.8 cm (print area)
Estampes, Jb-17-Fol.

Demarteau → 60
Gilles-Antoine Demarteau
(Liège, 1750 – Paris, 1802)
After Carle Vernet
(Bordeaux, 1758 – Paris, 1836)
Front view of a Horse's Head
1800
Crayon manner, printed in black
56 x 38.7 cm (print area)
Estampes Rés. Ef-10-Fol.

Desprez → 43
Louis Jean Desprez
(Auxerre, 1743 – Stockholm, 1804)
The Chimera of Monsieur Desprez
1771
Etching
27.5 x 35.5 cm (sheet)
Estampes, Ha-52-Fol.

Doré → 69
Gustave Doré
(Strasbourg, 1832 – Paris, 1883)
The Monkey and the Dolphin
Plate, trial proof for the illustrations for Jean de La Fontaine's Fables
Paris, Louis Hachette, 1868
Wood engraving by A. Ligny from a drawing by Gustave Doré
23.8 x 19 cm (boundary line)
Estampes, Dc-298 (i)-Fol.

Dufy → 86
Raoul Dufy
(Le Havre, 1877 – Forcalquier, 1953)
The Serpent,
1910
Plate rejected for Apollinaire's Bestiaire
Woodcut
20.4 x 19.5 cm (image)
Estampes, DC-485-FOL

Dunstall → 23
François Ertinger
(Weil, Swabia, 1648 – Paris, ca. 1710)
After a print by John Dunstall (? – London, 1693), which was itself after a drawing by Wenceslas Hollar (Prague, 1607 – London, 1677)
Lion and Flowers
Published by François Langlois,
ca. 1665
Etching
27.5 x 17.5 cm (boundary line)
Estampes, Jb-26-Fol.

Dürer → 4
Albrecht Dürer
(Nuremberg, 1471 – Nuremberg, 1528)
The Monstrous Pig of Landser
1496
Burin engraving
12 x 12.7 cm (boundary line)
Estampes, Rés. Ca-4 (+, 5)-Boîte écu

Dürer → 6
Albrecht Dürer
(Nuremberg, 1471 – Nuremberg, 1528)
The Large Horse
1505
Burin engraving
16.5 x 12 cm (boundary line)
Estampes, Rés. Ca-4 (+, 5)-Boîte écu

Dürer → 5
Albrecht Dürer
(Nuremberg, 1471 – Nuremberg, 1528)
The Rhinoceros
1515
Woodcut
Colour tone block added after 1620
21.2 x 30 cm (boundary line)
Estampes , Rés. Ca-4 (b)-Fol.

Dürer → 7
Albrecht Dürer
(Nuremberg, 1471 – Nuremberg, 1528)
Saint Eustace
ca. 1501
Burin engraving
35.6 x 26 cm (boundary line)
Estampes, Rés. Ca-4 (+, 3)-Boîte écu

Duvet → 9
Jean Duvet
(Dijon, 1485 – Langres, 1561)
The Unicorn Purifies the Water with its Horn
ca. 1547–1550
Burin engraving
22.6 x 39.5 (boundary line)
Estampes, Rés. Ed-1 (b)-Fol.

Ertinger → 23
François Ertinger
(Weil, Swabia, 1648 – Paris, ca. 1710)
After a print by John Dunstall (? – London, 1693), which was itself after a drawing by Wenceslas Hollar (Prague, 1607 – London, 1677)
Lion and Flowers
Published by François Langlois,
ca. 1665
Etching
27.5 x 17.5 cm (boundary line)
Estampes, Jb-26-Fol.

Fallours → 40
After Samuel Fallours,
231. *Devil-Fish. Type of Ray*; 232. *Devil-Fish*; 233. *Zeyl-Visch. Swordfish*
ca. 1719
Plate LXIV from vol. 2 of *Fishes, crayfishes and crabs of various extraordinary colours and shapes to be found around the Moluccan Islands and on the shores of lands in the Southern Hemisphere*
by Louis Renard
Coloured etching
28.1 x 20.5 cm (print area)
Estampes, Jb-61-Pet.fol.

Fantuzzi → 11
Antonio Fantuzzi
(Bologna, active from 1537 to 1545)
After Rosso Fiorentino
(Florence, 1494 – Fontainebleau, 1541)
The Elephant Adorned with Fleur-de-Lys
ca. 1542-1543
Etching
29 x 43 cm (boundary line)
Estampes, Eb-14 (d)-Fol.

Flanagan → 98
Barry Flanagan
(Prestatyn, 1941 – Ibiza, 2009)
Ganymede
Published by Waddington Graphics
Printed by Colin Dyer
1983
Linocut
36 x 25 cm (print area)
Estampes, Cd-140 (4)-Fol.

Floris → 10
Joos Gietleughen
(active in Antwerp and Cologne ca. 1550)
After Frans Floris
(Antwerp, 1519/1520 – Antwerp, 1570)
The Bear Hunt
1555
Coloured woodcut, 3 plates
43.1 x 262.5 cm (boundary line)
Estampes, Rés. Aa-6 Floris

Friedlaender → 97
Johnny Friedlaender
(Pless, Upper Silesia, 1912 – Paris, 1992)
Horse Lying Down
1952
Etching and aquatint
29.7 x 49.9 cm (print area)
Estampes, DC-795-FOL

Gautier d'Agoty → 39
Jacques Fabien Gautier d'Agoty
(Marseille, 1716 – Paris, 1785)
Two Butterflies Placed Opposite One Another
ca. 1741
Mezzotint, colours printed using registration method
18.9 x 25.1 cm (print area)
Estampes, Rés. Ad-534 – Boîte fol.

Gietleughen → 10
Joos Gietleughen
(active in Antwerp and Cologne ca. 1550)
After Frans Floris
(Antwerp, 1519/1520 – Antwerp, 1570)
The Bear Hunt
1555
Coloured woodcut, 3 plates

43.1 x 262.5 cm (boundary line)
Estampes, Rés. Aa-6 Floris

Goltzius → 18
Hendrick Goltzius
(Venlo, 1558 – Haarlem, 1617)
Frederick de Vries
1597
Burin engraving
35.7 x 26.4 cm (boundary line)
Estampes, Rés. Cb-101-Fol.

Goya → 61
Francisco de Goya
(Fuentetodos, 1746 – Bordeaux, 1828)
Animal Follies. Other Laws for the People
1819–1824
Etching, aquatint, drypoint
24 x 35 cm (print area)
Estampes, Rés. Bf-4 (j, 45)-Boîte écu

Grandville → 66
Jean Ignace Isidore Gérard, known as Grandville
(Nancy, 1803 – Vanves, 1847)
The Dancing Lesson
Plate n° 25 of *Les Métamorphoses du jour (The Metamorphoses of the Day)*
1828
Coloured lithograph
23.3 x 28.7 cm (sheet)
Estampes, Dc-199 (1,a)-Fol.

Grandville → 68
Jean Ignace Isidore Gérard, known as Grandville
(Nancy, 1803 – Vanves, 1847)
Scenes of the Private and Public Lives of Animals
1840
Poster, lithograph
70 x 53 cm (sheet)
Printed by the Lemercier, Bénard & Cie Printing House
Estampes, ENT DN -1 (GRANDVILLE)- FT 6

Greuter → 24
Matthäus Greuter
(Strasbourg, 1564 – Rome, 1638)
Melissographia
Taken from Apiarium, by Federico Cesi, Rome, 1625 |
Burin engraving
37 x 26.5 cm (print area)
Estampes, Ec-8-Fol.

Guélard → 48
Jean-Baptiste Guélard (active in Paris between 1730 and ca. 1750)
After Christophe Huet
(Pontoise, 1700 – Paris, 1759)
The Hunting Horn
Taken from *Singeries ou Différentes actions de la vie humaine représentées par des singes ("Singeries", or Different Activities in the Lives of Humans Represented by Monkeys)*
ca. 1741
Etching
15 x 19 cm (sheet)
Estampes, Tf-11-4

Guérard → 83
Henri Guérard
(Paris, 1846 – Paris, 1897)
Azor
ca. 1888
Coloured etching
51.3 x 35.3 cm (print area)
Estampes, Ef-477 (8)-Fol.

Hartmann Risler & Cie → 53
Hartmann Risler & Cie
Manufacturing Company
Lintel decoration, Parrot perched on a natural arrangement of fruits and flowers
After a design by Joseph Laurent Malaine (Tournai, 1745 – Paris, 1809),
Lintel. Birds, fruits and flowers in a natural arrangement
1799
Wallpaper, wood engraving on paper, pieced together, colour applied
using block printing method
56.5 x 117.5 cm (sheet)
Estampes, Lz-313 (11) Cadre

Hiroshige → 78
Hiroshige
(Edo, 1797 – Edo, 1858)
Spiny Lobster and Prawns
Plate from the *Large Fish* series
Ca. 1832
Coloured woodblock print
26 x 37 cm (image)
Estampes, De-12- Boîte fol., J.B. 1151

Hiroshige → 79
Hiroshige
(Edo, 1797 – Edo, 1858)
Suidobashi Bridge at Surugadai
Plate from the series *One Hundred Famous Views of Edo*
1857
Coloured woodblock print
33.7 x 22.2 cm (image)
Estampes, Rés. De-10 -Boîte fol., J.B. 1080

Hollar → 30
Wenceslas Hollar
(Prague, 1607 – London, 1677)
Dead Mole
Mid-17th century
Etching
7 x 3.8 cm (print area)
Estampes, Jb-17-Fol.

Hollar → 23
François Ertinger
(Weil, Swabia, 1648 – Paris, ca. 1710)
After a print by John Dunstall (? – London, 1693), which was itself after a drawing by Wenceslas Hollar (Prague, 1607 – London, 1677)
Lion and Flowers
Published by François Langlois,
ca. 1665
Etching
27.5 x 17.5 cm (boundary line)
Estampes, Jb-26-Fol.

Hoüel → 55
Jean-Pierre Louis Laurent Hoüel
(Rouen, 1735 – Paris, 1813)
Elephants Bathing
Plate XIII from *Histoire naturelle des deux éléphans, mâle et femelle, du Muséum de Paris, venus de Hollande en France en l'an VI (The natural history of two elephants, male and female, kept in the Museum of Paris, having come to France from Holland in Year VI)* by Jean-Pierre Louis Laurent Hoüel
Etching
14.7 x 22.8 cm (boundary line)
Estampes, Jb-27-4

Huet (Jean Baptiste) → 64
Jean-Baptiste Huet
(1772 – 1852), designer and draughtsman, and the Lambert brothers, engravers
Merino Ram
1805
Stipple engraving
35 x 42.8 cm (print area)
Estampes, Jb-5 (9)-Fol.

Huet (Christophe) → 48
Jean-Baptiste Guélard
(active in Paris between 1730 and ca. 1750)
After Christophe Huet
(Pontoise, 1700 – Paris, 1759)
The Hunting Horn
Taken from *Singeries ou Différentes actions de la vie humaine représentées par des singes ("Singeries", or Different Activities in the Lives of Humans Represented by Monkeys)*
ca. 1741
Etching
15 x 19 cm (sheet)
Estampes, Tf-11-4

Huquier → 52
Gabriel Huquier
(Orléans, 1695 – Paris, 1772)
Plate Showing Chinese-Inspired Ornamental Motifs
From the *Livre des differentes éspeces d'oiseaux, fleurs. plantes et trophés de la Chine tirés du cabinet du Roy* (*the Book of different species of birds, flowers, plants and trophies from China*, from the King's Cabinet)
ca. 1740
Etching
32.4 x 49.3 cm (print area)
Estampes, Ee-12 (B)-Fol.

Jacobe → 58
Johann Alexander Gottfried Jacobe (Vienna, 1734 – Vienna, 1797)
After Francesco Casanova
(London, 1727 – Brühl, 1802)
Jaguar Killed in America by the Prince of Nassau-Siegen
1787
State before signatures and letters
Mezzotint
64.5 x 79.5 cm (print area)
Estampes, AA-6 (Jacobe, Johann)

Lagniet (printer) → 25
A Pair of Skating Owls
From *Les Plus Illustres Proverbes (The Most Important Proverbs)*, Paris,
Jacques Lagniet, 1663, in-4°
Burin engraving
20 x 14 cm (print area)
Rare Books Reserve
Réserve Z-1746-4

Lagniet (printer) → 21
Satirical Print showing the

Storming of Arras
Published by Jacques Lagniet, ca. 1640
Burin engraving
18 x 12.5 cm (boundary line)
Estampes, Rés. Hennin, 2851

Lambert brothers → 64
Jean-Baptiste Huet (1772 – 1852), designer and draughtsman, and the Lambert brothers, engravers
Merino Ram
1805
Stipple engraving
35 x 42.8 cm (print area)
Estampes, Jb-5 (9)-Fol.

Le Brun → 26
Louis Simonneau (Orléans, 1654 – Paris, 1727)
After Charles Le Brun (Paris, 1619 – Paris, 1690)
Similarities Between the Head of an Ox and a Man
ca. 1683
From *Livre de portraiture pour ceux qui commencent à dessiner (Book of portraiture for those learning to draw),* Paris, Chéreau,
after 1718
Burin engraving
23 x 31.5 cm (boundary line)
Estampes, Da-38-Fol.

Le Roy → 33
Henry Le Roy (?) (Rotterdam, ca. 1579 – Paris, 1651)
Plate showing Birds
Printed by Henry Le Roy
ca. 1630 – 1640
Burin engraving
18.5 x 9.5 cm (print area)
Estampes, Jb mat-3- Boîte fol.

Leclerc → 37
Sébastien Leclerc
(Metz, 1637 – Paris, 1714)
Beaver
1671
From *Mémoires pour servir à l'histoire naturelle des animaux* (translated as Memoir's [sic] *for a natural history of animals)* by Claude Perrault, Paris, Royal Printing House, 1671
Etching
29.5 x 41 cm (platemark)
Estampes, Jb3-Fol.

Lévy (printer) → 73
The World Before the Creation of Man
1885
Coloured lithographic poster
130 x 96 cm (sheet)
Printed by the Émile Lévy Printing House
Estampes, ENT DN-1 (LEVY, Émile/7)- ROUL.

Lévy (printer) → 72
The Théâtre des Menus-Plaisirs Invisible Creatures
1883
Coloured lithographic Poster
60 x 40 cm (sheet)
Printed by the Émile Lévy Printing House
Estampes, ENT DN-1 (LEVY, Émile/4)- FT 6.

Lichtenstein → 94
Roy Lichtenstein (New York, 1923 – New York, 1997)
Bull Profile Series
Gemini G.E.L.
Coloured lithograph, silkscreen print, line-cut on paper
68.6 x 88.9 cm (each plate)
Edition of 100
Estampes, Ce20-1 (Lichtenstein, Roy) –Ft 5

Ligny → 69
Gustave Doré
(Strasbourg, 1832 – Paris, 1883)
The Monkey and the Dolphin
Plate, trial proof for the illustrations for Jean de La Fontaine's *Fables*
Paris, Louis Hachette, 1868
Wood engraving by A. Ligny from a drawing by Gustave Doré
23.8 x 19 cm (boundary line)
Estampes, Dc-298 (i)-Fol.

"The Master of the Playing Cards" → 1
"The Master of the Playing Cards" (Upper Rhine Valley, active ca. 1430 – 1440)
Cards with bear and lion suit symbols
From a pack of cards with 5 suits (bears/ lions, deer/ stags, birds, wild men and women, and flowers)
Upper Rhine Valley, 1435 – 1445
Burin engraving
14 x 9.5 cm (each card)
Estampes, Rés. Kh-25-Boîte écu

Malaine → 53
Hartmann Risler & Cie Manufacturing Company
Lintel decoration, Parrot perched on a natural arrangement of fruits and flowers
After a design by Joseph Laurent Malaine (Tournai, 1745 – Paris, 1809), *Lintel. Birds, fruits and flowers in a natural arrangement*
1799
Wallpaper, wood engraving on paper, pieced together, colour applied
using block printing method
56.5 x 117.5 cm (sheet).
Estampes, Lz-313 (11)-Cadre

Manet → 80
Édouard Manet
(Paris, 1832 – Paris, 1883)
The Cats' Rendez-Vous
1868
Lithograph
43.5 x 33.2 cm (image)
Estampes, Rés. Dc-300 (d,4)-Fol.

Martinet → 42
François-Nicolas Martinet
(1731 – after 1800)
The Canadian Turtle-Dove
ca. 1770
Plate for Georges-Louis Leclerc, comte de Buffon (1707 – 1788) *L'Histoire naturelle des oiseaux (The Natural History of Birds)*
Coloured etching
23 x 18 cm (print area)
Estampes, Jb-34 (A)-4

Matisse → 89
Henri Matisse
(Le Cateau-Cambrésis, 1869 – Nice, 1954)
The Swan
1931-1932
Plate from *Poésies*, by Stéphane Mallarmé, Lausanne, Albert Skira & Cie, 1932 Etching
33 x 25 cm (sheet)
Rare Books Reserve, RES G-YE -88

May → 95
Agathe May
(Neuilly-sur-Seine, 1956)
Ficelle VIII
Printed by the artist
1989
Coloured linocut
98 x 98 cm (sheet)
Estampes, Dh-1 (May, Agathe) –Ft 7

Odet → 16
Léonard Odet
(active in Lyon between 1578 and 1610)
I am a Loyal and Watchful Barbet
Lyon, ca. 1600
Woodcut
49 x 33 cm (print area)
Estampes, Rés. Hennin, 1633

Ostier → 100
Jean-Jacques Ostier
(Saigon, 1945 – Magny-en-Vexin, 2011)
The Epistemologist
1996
Joint edition produced by the artist and the Petit Jaunais Studio, 1996
Nantes, printed by Nancy Sulmont at the Petit Jaunais Studio
10 ex.
Lithograph
66.5 x 50.5 cm (sheet)
Estampes, Dg-1 (Ostier, Jean-Jacques)-Ft 5

Oudry → 57
Jean-Baptiste Oudry
(Paris, 1686 – Beauvais, 1755)
Deer attacked by Dogs
1736
Etching and burin work
36.6 x 26.4 cm (print area)
Estampes, Db-23 (1)-Fol.

Papillon → 44
Jean Papillon
(Saint-Quentin, 1661 – Paris, 1710)
A Bear and Bull Fight to the Death in the Faubourg Saint-Germain
1734
Poster, woodcut
39 x 48 cm (sheet)
Woodcut by Jean I Papillon (? – 1710)
Estampes, Ee-2, t.1-Folio

Pellerin (printer) → 70
The Giraffe
Épinal, the Pellerin Printing House, 1828

Woodcut, stencil-coloured
41 x 25 cm (sheet)
Estampes, Li-59 (1) –Fol.

Picasso → 88
Pablo Picasso
(Malaga, 1881 – Mougins, 1973)
The Ostrich
1936
Plate from *Histoires naturelles*, by G.-L. Leclerc, comte de Buffon, Paris, M. Fabiani, 1942
41.5 x 31.5 cm (print area)
Rare Books Reserve, RES G-S -95

Rabier → 75
Benjamin Rabier
(La Roche-sur-Yon, 1884 – Faverolles, 1939)
The Laughing Cow
1927 (9th edition)
Coloured lithographic poster
160 x 120 cm (sheet)
Estampes, ENT DN-1 (RABIER, Benjamin) –GRAND ROUL.

Rambert → 76
Charles Rambert
(ca. 1820 – ca. 1865)
Usury
1850
Lithograph
42.5 x 30.7 cm (sheet)
Estampes, AA-3 Rambert (Charles)

Ranson → 87
Paul Ranson
(Limoges, 1861 – Paris, 1909)
Tiger in the Jungle
1893
Coloured lithograph
36.2 x 28.3 cm (image)
Estampes, Rés. AA-3 (Ranson, Paul)

Redon → 81
Odilon Redon
(Bordeaux, 1840 – Paris, 1916)
Spider
1887
Lithograph on China paper applied to vellum
26 x 21.5 cm (image)
Estampes, Rés. Dc-354 (5)-Boîte fol.

Rembrandt → 29
Rembrandt
(Leiden, 1606 – Amsterdam, 1669)
The Hog
Signed and dated bottom right:
"Rembrandt 1643"
Etching and drypoint
14.5 x 18.4 cm (print area)
1st state
Estampes, Rés. Cb-13 (a)-Boîte écu

Rhead → 85
Louis-John Rhead
(Etruria, 1858 – Amityville, NY, 1926)
Peacocks
1897
Coloured lithograph
85 x 150 cm (sheet)
Estampes, ENT DO-1 (RHEAD, Louis) – ROUL.

Rösel von Rosenhof → 41
Martin Tyroff
(Nuremberg, 1704 – Nuremberg, 1758)
After August Johann Rösel von Rosenhof (Augustenberg, 1705 – Nuremberg, 1759)
Historia naturalis ranarum nostratium (The Natural History of the Frogs in our Land), Nuremberg, 1758
In-fol., frontispiece
Coloured etching (watercolour, gouache highlights)
38.4 x 6.3 cm (print area)
Estampes, Jb-52-Pet.fol

Rosso Fiorentino → 11
Antonio Fantuzzi
(Bologna, active from 1537 to 1545)
After Rosso Fiorentino
(Florence, 1494 – Fontainebleau, 1541)
The Elephant Adorned with Fleur-de-Lys
ca. 1542-1543
Etching
29 x 43 cm (boundary line)
Estampes, Eb-14 (d)-Fol.

Rouchon → 71
Rouchon (printer)
Hippodrome,
"*The War of the Indies*", 1858
Poster, coloured wood engraving
100 x 119 cm (sheet)
Printed by the Rouchon Printing House
Estampes, ENT DN -1 (ROUCHON /18) –ROUL

Rubens → 35
Pieter Soutman
(Haarlem, 1593/1601 – Haarlem, 1657)
After Pieter Paul Rubens
(Siegen, 1577 – Antwerp, 1640)
The Hunting of the Crocodile and Hippopotamus
Between 1642 and 1657
Etching
46.7 x 63 cm (print area)
Estampes, Cc-34 (i)-Ft 4

Ruotte → 50
Louis-Charles Ruotte
(Paris, ca. 1754 – ca. 1806
After Frans Swagers
(Utrecht, 1756 – Paris, 1836)
The Fashionable Ox
1797
"*À Paris chez Depeüille, Rue des Mathurins St. Jacques, aux deux Pilastres d'Or, et chez tous les Marchands de Nouveautés*"
State before letters and signatures, handwritten title
Stipple engraving
28.1 x 36.7 cm (print area)
Estampes, Tf-18-Fol.

Saenredam → 36
Jan Saenredam
(Zaandam, 1565 – Assendelft, 1607)
Beached Sperm Whale Near Beverwijk in 1601
1602
Burin engraving
40.7 x 59.6 cm (boundary line)
Estampes, Ec-37 (e)-Fol.

Saint-Aubin → 47
Charles-Germain de Saint-Aubin
(Paris, 1721 – Paris, 1786)
Pyrotechnia
ca. 1760
Etching
18.5 x 13.5 cm (print area)
Estampes, Rés. Ef-7-Fol.

Sarton → 46
Pack of Belgian tarot cards with animal trump scenes
Engraver unknown.
Playing card seller:
François-Arnould Sarton, brothers and sisters, rue de la Madeleine, Brussels, [ca. 1755]
Wood engraving, stencil-coloured
11.3 x 5.9 (card)
Estampes, Rés. Kh-34 (5, 65) – Boîte fol.

Scotin → 38
Gérard Scotin
(Antwerp, 1643 – Paris, 1715)
After Pieter Boel
(Antwerp, 1622 – 1674)
Pelicans
Late 17th century
Etching
25.2 x 35 cm (print area)
Estampes, Jb-37-Ft 4

Sève → 54
Jean-Charles Baquoy
(Paris, 1721 – Paris, 1777)
After Jacques de Sève († after 1790)
The Wolf
1758
Plate I from vol. VII of *Histoire naturelle, générale et particulière avec la description du Cabinet du roy (Natural History, General and Particular)*, 1749–1788
by Georges-Louis Leclerc, comte de Buffon (1707–1788)
Etching and burin work
19.5 x 15 cm (boundary line)
Estampes, Ja-23 (A)-Fol.

Simonneau → 26
Louis Simonneau
(Orléans, 1654 – Paris, 1727)
After Charles Le Brun
(Paris, 1619 – Paris, 1690)
Similarities Between the Head of an Ox and a Man
ca. 1683
From *Livre de portraiture pour ceux qui commencent à dessiner (Book of portraiture for those learning to draw)*, Paris, Chéreau, after 1718
Burin engraving
23 x 31.5 cm (boundary line)
Estampes, Da-38-Fol.

Soutman → 35
Pieter Soutman
(Haarlem, 1593/1601 – Haarlem, 1657)
After Pieter Paul Rubens
(Siegen, 1577 – Antwerp, 1640)

The Hunting of the Crocodile and Hippopotamus
Between 1642 and 1657
Etching
46.7 x 63 cm (print area)
Estampes, Cc-34 (i)-Ft 4

Steinlen → 84
Théophile Alexandre Steinlen
(Lausanne, 1859 – Paris, 1923)
The Black Cat Tour
ca. 1896
Coloured lithographic poster
140 x 100 cm (sheet)
Printed by the Verneau Printing House
Estampes, ENT DN-1 (STEINLEN, Alexandre/1)-R

Stubbs → 59
George Townley Stubbs
(Liverpool, 1756 – ca. 1815)
After George Stubbs
(Liverpool, 1724 – London, 1806)
The Horse and the Lion
1770
Mezzotint
46 x 55.8 cm (print area)
Estampes, Cd-24-Ft 4

Swagers → 50
Louis-Charles Ruotte
(Paris, ca. 1754 – ca. 1806
After Frans Swagers
(Utrecht, 1756 – Paris, 1836)
The Fashionable Ox
1797
"*À Paris chez Depeüille, Rue des Mathurins St. Jacques, aux deux Pilastres d'Or, et chez tous les Marchands de Nouveautés*"
State before letters and signatures, handwritten title
Stipple engraving
28.1 x 36.7 cm (print area)
Estampes, Tf-18-Fol.

Telman de Wesel → 13
Telman de Wesel
(active between 1490 and 1510)
Playing cards with rabbit suit symbols
From a pack of cards with 4 suits (carnations, columbine, parrots and hares)
Burin engraving
Lower Rhine region (Wesel?)
early 16th century
6.8 cm (diameter of each card)
Estampes, Rés. Kh-31-Pet. Fol.

Tempesta → 20
Anonymous
Falsely attributed to Antonio Tempesta
(Florence, 1555 – Rome, 1630)
An Indian Dog
Cane Indicus – Cane d'Inda, 1636
From the *Curiosa Raccolta di diversi animali quadrupedi*, Rome, Giacomo Marucci, 1636
Burin engraving
13.5 x 9.5 cm (boundary line)
Estampes, Jb-26-Fol.

Toulouse-Lautrec → 82
Henri de Toulouse-Lautrec
(Albi, 1864 – Malromé, 1901)
The Rabbit Waltz
1895
Lithograph
31.7 x 24 cm (image)
Estampes, Rés. Dc-361 (6)- Fol.

Tyroff → 41
Martin Tyroff
(Nuremberg, 1704 – Nuremberg, 1758)
After August Johann Rösel von Rosenhof (Augustenberg, 1705 – Nuremberg, 1759)
Historia naturalis ranarum nostratium (The Natural History of the Frogs in our Land), Nuremberg, 1758
In-fol., frontispiece
Coloured etching (watercolour, gouache highlights)
38.4 x 6.3 cm (print area)
Estampes, Jb-52-Pet.fol

Van der Heyden → 12
Pieter Van der Heyden
(Antwerp? ca. 1530 – Berchem, after 1584?)
After Pieter Bruegel the Elder
(Bruegel? 1525/1530 – Brussels, 1569)
The Big Fish Eat the Little Fish
Grandibus exigui sunt pisces piscibus esca, 1557
Burin engraving
23 x 29.5 cm (boundary line)
Estampes, Rés. Cc-5-Fol.

Van der Does → 34
Anthony Van Der Does
(Antwerp? ca. 1609 – Antwerp, 1680)
Decoration for the Joyous Entry of Ferdinand of Spain Into Ghent
1635
Burin engraving
30 x 37.5 cm (print area)
Estampes, Qd-6 (1635) –Fol.

Vernet → 60
Gilles-Antoine Demarteau
(Liège, 1750 – Paris, 1802)
After Carle Vernet
(Bordeaux, 1758 – Paris, 1836)
Front view of a Horse's Head
1800
Crayon manner, printed in black
56 x 38.7 cm (print area)
Estampes, Rés. Ef-10-Fol.

Photography Credits

All the works reproduced in this publication belong to the collections held in the Bibliothèque nationale de France. The photographs were taken by staff in the Reproduction Department. Images of the iconographic material from the BNF collections are available for examination and may be found in its image banks <images.bnf.fr>. They can be purchased from the Reproduction Department, reproduction@bnf.fr.

The numbers given here relate to illustration numbers: